Cricket
At The Castle

Duke of Norfolk's XI v Duke of Edinburgh's XI,
Arundel 1953.

Cricket
At The Castle

One Hundred Years of Cricket at Arundel 1895-1995

by
Sir Michael Marshall

Foreword by Sir Colin Cowdrey

Boundary Books

Dedicated to the memory of Bernard,
16th Duke of Norfolk and in appreciation for
all that Lavinia, Duchess of Norfolk has done
to sustain cricket at Arundel.

Boundary Books Ltd
Southlands, Goostrey,
Cheshire, CW4 8NT.

First published 1995

© Sir Michael Marshall, 1995

Designed by Core Graphics, Timperley, Cheshire
Printed and bound by Hartnolls Ltd, Bodmin, Cornwall

Contents

Foreword

SIR COLIN COWDREY

How Duke Bernard loved his cricket! The game came to be one of the major passions of his life and it is good that, in celebrating the centenary of cricket at Arundel, Michael Marshall has drawn so extensively on the matches involving those representing Duke Bernard and those which Duchess Lavinia has sponsored in his memory. Together they cover the period from 1930 until the end of the 1994 season and they include not only the fixtures against International Touring sides which, for many, mark the start of each cricket season but a wide array of Club and representative sides.

It is good, too, that the book also covers a wide range of special fixtures with teams which have been invited to treat Arundel as their home ground and these include - especially in more recent years - teams as varied as Quidnuncs, Harlequins, Sussex Martlets, the Sussex County Cricket Club and even the England Women's International side.

As one who has appeared in so many matches for both the Duke and the Duchess from 1951 until I finally called it a day at the start of the '90's, I wondered how the author would find a theme which could convey the joyous and unique quality of cricket at Arundel Castle. I believe he has found the answer in 'The Laws of Cricket as decreed by Bernard Duke of Norfolk'. He has done so with many examples of matches played at Arundel over the years in a way that shows how the combination of sportsmanship, good manners and playing for the sheer love of the game have influenced so many generations of cricketers both during Duke Bernard's lifetime and beyond. He also shows how those values have been encouraged in Australia and in the West Indies as well as on his own beloved home ground.

The book, too, is a fascinating account of the way in which country house cricket and private patronage have developed, thanks to Duchess Lavinia and her daughters, into one of the most successful cricket clubs in the country with over 2000 members. It also shows how this same club, together with support from the wider Norfolk family, has made such a major contribution to the future of English Cricket through the Arundel Castle Cricket Foundation's construction and development of indoor coaching facilities. These - together with school visits - have already given sporting opportunities to over 80,000 children from the inner cities as well as from the home counties.

In all this, Duchess Lavinia is the first to say that she has been aided by a great army of supporters to whom tribute is paid in this book. They, and their predecessors, are rightly described by the author as "Duke's men" and "Duchess' Men". As one who has been lucky enough to come to know both patrons well, I warmly commend this book both to the general reader and to those who wish to be reminded of the fun that they have had in days in the sun at Arundel.

With good wishes

Colin Cowdrey

Preface

In a centenary history of this kind, it has been necessary to make a selection from the many hundreds of matches played at Arundel Castle. In this process, the author has been greatly assisted by over a hundred of those who took part in these games from the early '30s to the end of the 1994 season. Their contributions speak for themselves and the author is deeply grateful to all those whose personal cricket recollections are recorded here. In some cases, they relate to conversations several years ago, and, sadly, some have died since they were interviewed. However, recognising the lasting appeal for cricket lovers of many of these names, no attempt has been made to differentiate between those who have gone and those who remain.

If the large number of contributors of cricketing memories makes individual recognition inappropriate, the same principle does not apply in respect of the wider aspects of cricket at Arundel. This, in the last twenty years, has been inextricably intertwined with the birth and development of the Friends of Arundel Castle Cricket Club and it was with the Club's first Chairman, Billy Griffith, that the initial plans were made for a centenary publication. His support was maintained by his successor, Ronnie Ford, who provided constructive comments on the draft manuscript. Similarly, Eddie Harrison was helpful in looking at the first outline covering cricket during Duke Bernard's era in which he played so active and so large a part. Thanks are also due to the current Chairman of the Club, Hubert Doggart. Both he and his wife Sue have provided regular hospitality which has greatly facilitated the process of meetings and interviews with cricketers at Arundel.

Despite the wide range of cricketing memories mentioned earlier, special tribute is due to two players whose joint performances cover appearances from 1951 to 1994. The first is Sir Colin Cowdrey who has been exceptionally generous in sharing his recollections and his vision for

cricket at Arundel as well as providing the Foreword to this book. The second is the Club's Director of Cricket, Johnny Barclay, who continues to provide outstanding playing and coaching inspiration.

Beyond the cricketing and Club activities, it is hoped that the book may be seen as a small contribution to the social and family history both of the Arundel community and, above all of the Norfolk family. The pre-eminence of the family in this account is reflected in the dedication to both Duke Bernard and Duchess Lavinia. If Duke Bernard inspired its original concept, Duchess Lavinia has greatly facilitated its production through her no-nonsense approach which was summed up on one occasion when she remarked "You will do much better to get on without interference from me". At the same time she and other members of the family have been particularly helpful in providing much of the information which simply could not be obtained elsewhere.

Thus, for the recollections of Duke Henry and Duchess Gwendy and the early life of Duke Bernard, the author has drawn extensively on the recollections of the Duke's sisters the late Lady Rachel Pepys and, more recently, Lady Winifrede Freeman who were joined on one memorable occasion for a splendid dialogue with the third of Duke Bernard's sisters, Lady Katherine Phillips. Lady Mary Mumford and Lady Sarah Clutton made special personal contributions because of their long interest in organising cricket matches against both their father's and mother's teams, and their memories were supplemented by Duchess Lavinia's other daughters, the Baroness Herries and Lady Jane Ancram. Lady Sarah Clutton also provided invaluable access to family scrap-books and photographs. Similar material was also made available by Lady Rachel Pepys' daughter, Mrs Harriet Sefi. Other members of the family who assisted with research included Dominic Chambers and

Theresa and Frances de Salis.

In the technical production of the book, special thanks are due to those who assisted in the provision of original or re-photographed material including the Friends of Arundel Castle Cricket Club, the Bishop of Arundel and Brighton, Patrick Eagar, Roger Halls, Maurice Joseph, Roger Mann and Chris Monaghan.Other material was provided by the Earl of Arundel, the *West Sussex Gazette*, the *Littlehampton Gazette* and Richard Clark, County Archivist, together with the staff of the County Records Office, West Sussex County Council. Every effort has been made to identify holders of copyright in original material and I apologise if anyone has been overlooked.

In the true spirit of Arundel, the cricket has been more important than the results Scorebook shortfalls and inaccuracies, particularly in earlier matches, mean that not all the scores reproduced, nor all the statistics, can be completely reliable. Nevertheless, every effort has been made to use and confirm original sources.

In the exacting task of typing and preparing material, I have been assisted by a number of secretaries and personal assistants who have worked for me in recent years, including Anne Buckingham, Scott Caroon, Jean Clark, Jo Gardner, Henrietta Shields and above all, my long serving personal assistant Natasha Wall. In the preparation of statistical material, I am grateful for the diligent work of Philip Defriez and for the support of the Arundel Castle Cricket Club Secretaries, Debbie Osborne and Suzanne Weaver. In all aspects of the book's production, I have received much encouragement and enthusiastic support from my Commissioning Editors, Michael Down, Tony Laughton and their colleagues at Boundary Books.

I cannot conclude these acknowledgements without taking the opportunity to thank the readers of this book. Its sale and distribution has been arranged to maximise the return for both the Arundel Castle Cricket Club and the Arundel Castle Cricket Foundation. In this process, we have been given special assistance by Roger Knight and Michael Melluish, the Secretary and Treasurer of M.C.C.; by Patrick Shervington, Director of the Lord's Taverners; and Nigel Bett, Secretary of the Sussex County Cricket Club. The significance of this fund-raising will be evident from Sir Colin Cowdrey's introduction and later contributions. Including the generous initial support from Mr J. Paul Getty Jr., the Foundation has raised £1,200,000 of which £750,000 has been used in building the Cricket School and making essential improvements to the Club's pavilion. Running costs remain a continuing problem and those who feel able to do so are encouraged to consider support through Club Membership and/or sponsorship. Further information can be obtained through The Secretary, The Friends of Arundel Castle Cricket Club, Arundel Park, Arundel.

Finally, I should like to express the gratitude of my wife and my self for the warmth and friendship over so many years of the late Bernard, Duke of Norfolk and his widow, Duchess Lavinia. As for my wife, Caroline, her forbearance and encouragement as a cricket writer's widow has, as ever, been a strength and a comfort.

Michael Marshall
Old Inn House,
Slindon, Arundel.
April 1995

Introduction

Cricket at Arundel Castle will always be associated with Bernard Marmaduke Fitzalan-Howard, 16th Duke of Norfolk. It was he who, in organising matches between the 1930s and the 1970s, created a unique blend between country house cricket and the game at near first-class level. In producing this mixture he used the special ingredients of his own connections with the Sussex County Cricket Club, the Marylebone Cricket Club and, latterly, the Test and County Cricket Board to bring County cricketers and both home and overseas Test Match players to his ground.

What is it that made and makes cricket at Arundel Castle so special? First, there is the undoubted beauty of the setting. With its glimpses of the Castle and the Cathedral, the velvet playing surface and the tree-ringed playing area with the gap created by Duke Bernard to show a great fold of the Downs, the Arun River Valley and Amberley Castle to the north, it is, for many cricketers, the most beautiful ground in the world. Second, many of these same cricketers enthuse about the tradition of the Duke's hospitality. But what perhaps, above all, makes cricket there a special experience is the tradition of manners and sportsmanship coupled with a willingness to accept some of the constraints which, in deference to his host, the good guest imposed upon himself.

The laws of cricket as decreed by Bernard, Duke of Norfolk, were unwritten. Thus, the modest codification which follows would perhaps have been regarded as a grave impertinence. Indeed, the Duke would no doubt have seen this process as unnecessary; he came from a generation in which no gentleman needed a definition of what did or did not constitute proper behaviour. Moreover, so far as cricketers were concerned, his friendships which began in the age of Gentlemen and Players and continued through to the era of overwhelming professionalism were based on a deep admiration for playing skills coupled with a shrewd assessment of

individuals. His invitations to play at Arundel were founded on the precept which he shared with the old Surrey poet Albert Craig that: "All the Gentlemen should be Players and all the Players should be Gentlemen."

He did not, however, let his hero-worship of cricketers blind him to some of their imperfections. Those who, like the author, knew him in the later years of his life were conscious that, in sporting matters such as cricket or racing, it was wise to proceed with care. With the dry sense of humour would come a twinkle in the eye but any departure from the Duke's own high standards would produce a frozen stare. Nevertheless, it is worth risking a posthumous rebuke in listing some of the laws which related to his matches in order to gain an understanding of the atmosphere which makes cricket at the Castle unique.

Law 1 might be defined as: "It shall be the duty of all participants to ensure that matches are played to a finish". To this could be added Law 2: "The side winning the toss shall ensure that His Grace's side has the option of batting last". These laws reflect the Duke's enthusiasm for encouraging his side to undertake a run chase and the possibility of exciting finishes - preferably in the last over.

The informal application of these laws was demonstrated in a match only a year or two before the Duke's death in 1975. Following a declaration from the visiting side, his team were in trouble after the fall of several quick wickets. When the fifth wicket went down, the batsman dismissed was the Duke's playing captain (the distinction is important since, in his later years, the Duke reserved for himself the role of non-playing captain of the team bearing his name). As the playing captain returned to the pavilion, he was met at the top of the steep flight of steps leading from the bank in front of the pavilion on to the playing area by the incoming number seven batsman. This was a young cricketer seeking to establish a place in the Sussex 2nd XI. "I suppose we had better put up the shutters, Skipper?" he enquired. Before there was time for a considered response, a loud booming voice rang out from the large armchair at the top of the steps in which sat their host:

"Not if you hope to play on this ground again, you won't".

In his early playing days, the Duke let it be known that a few runs against his name represented, if not a ducal right, at least part of the guaranteed enjoyment by which visitors could repay their host's hospitality. Accordingly, Law Three may be defined as: "It shall be the duty of the visiting captain to use his best endeavours to ensure that His Grace gets off the mark".

The application of this law was demonstrated in one of the earliest matches in which the Duke played at Arundel when, before he had scored, he hit the ball hard and high towards mid-wicket. Unfortunately, under the shade of the large chestnut tree which still dominates the bank in front of today's pavilion, there stood what one of the participants was later to describe as a wretched youth. This unfortunate ran in at full tilt and made a fine catch. As the Duke left the field he met the young fielder still glowing at his achievement and totally unaware of his gaffe. "Bad luck", he said to the Duke - only to receive the reply: "You don't know the local rules, do you?"

Law Four states simply that "His Grace shall field at mid off". This reflects the custom which was to apply for many years of reserving that position for the Duke. What the Law does not specifically state but which would be recognised in all matches in which the Duke took part was the need for moderation in hitting the ball in his direction. To this was added, as required, the judicious field-placing of a supporting silly mid off backed up by a wide extra-cover and long-off.

Finally, to cover untoward incidents and the general concept of the conduct of matches played under his patronage, Law Five may be summed up in the following terms: "The laws of cricket as decreed from time to time by Bernard Duke of Norfolk shall at all times take precedence over the laws of cricket as promulgated by the M.C.C."

The pre-eminence of impromptu ducal rather than M.C.C. laws was well illustrated by two incidents involving umpiring decisions. The first is probably apocryphal but sums up the spirit which prevailed. It concerns one of Duke Bernard's early matches and his butler.

Normally, the butler's attendance at the match was part of a well ordered routine. The Duke would be chauffeur driven in his Rolls Royce to the cricket ground from the Castle already changed into whites. On arrival, the butler's responsibility was to take Duke Bernard's cricket bag into the marquee which served as the changing room for the teams and to ensure that his master successfully changed into cricket boots.

On this occasion, it is claimed that the butler was called upon, at short notice, to replace a missing umpire. It soon became clear that his knowledge of the game was limited. However, he showed his presence of mind when the Duke, attempting a short single, was run out by half a length of the pitch. When the fielding side appealed, the butler after long and careful consideration is said to have replied:

"His Grace is not in".

The second and fully authenticated example of Norfolk authority in determining the laws of cricket has been well described by George Downs who umpired many matches at Arundel. As he later recalled:

"It must have been one of the earliest games in which I stood for the Duke. I was young and keen and when one of the visiting batsmen failed to ground his bat properly before turning for a second run, I called 'one short'. Before play could resume I was aware of the Duke moving in a slow and stately fashion from deep mid-off towards me. He called me to one side and said: 'Downs, on this ground all those taking part are gentlemen. They do not cheat and there is therefore no question of 'one short.' Do I make myself clear?'. He certainly had and I never called 'one short' again while he was on the field."

These examples may give some flavour of the way in which the Duke exercised his authority as a benevolent despot in matters affecting cricket just as he was reputed to do on State occasions as Earl Marshal. What they cannot fully convey is the kindliness and overwhelming generosity which was extended to all those taking part and the sheer sense of fun he engendered both on and off the field. Duke Bernard had learnt these traditions of hospitality and enjoyment from his father and mother, and they have been sustained to the present day by his widow, Lavinia, Duchess of Norfolk. All of these Norfolks play a critical part in our story but it is to the 15th Duke and his second wife that we must first turn.

CHAPTER ONE

Duke Henry and Duchess Gwendy 1895-1929

The cricket ground at Arundel was literally carved from the side of a slope in the Sussex Downs above Arundel Castle in work which was completed in 1895. This was the inspiration of Henry, 15th Duke of Norfolk, who was born in 1847.

After a short marriage, the Duke had become a widower in 1884. Thereafter he dedicated himself to the well-being of his severely handicapped only son who would die at the age of twenty-two in 1901. Much of the Duke's private life was therefore spent in mourning. Indeed, on the night of the Coronation in 1901, the town of Arundel was ablaze with lights while the Castle was dark following the death of the Duke's heir.

Perhaps to compensate for his private grief, Duke Henry was exceptionally active in public life. In part, this came naturally with his responsibilities as Earl Marshal and from his willingness to serve in Government. In addition, he was known as "Our Little Duke" by English Catholics who recognised him as their principal layman.

At home he followed the trend of other English aristocrats who, in the late nineteenth century, offset the slump in agriculture by providing substantial building work to those employed on their estates. At Arundel this was reflected not only in restoration work on the Castle but in the construction of the nearby Catholic Cathedral - vast in size for a small town. When it came to the construction of a cricket ground, Duke Henry enquired which was the largest ground in England. When told this was the Kennington Oval, he is said to have ordered his own to match it in size. Today, the Oval's playing area of 137 metres by 140 metres compares with the Arundel Castle cricket ground's 152 by 140 metres (although the Oval's total area including buildings is the larger).

For technical advice Duke Henry turned to the President of the Sussex County Cricket Club, the Earl of Sheffield. The Earl, who became the first great English patron of overseas cricket by inviting Test Teams to play at his ground in East Sussex, was quick to offer full support through his groundsmen. He was less supportive, however, when Duke Henry suggested that his ground might prove a suitable venue for County matches.

Work involving up to 200 labourers with a weekly pay-packet of up to sixteen shillings and four pence was carried out in the spring of 1894. The work was completed between 1 April and 27 June 1895 at a total cost over this period of £320.

In the early years after the construction of the ground, it was used by the Castle Works teams and for the Estate XI. The first match of which a record has been kept was on 12 June 1897 when the Castle Works XI met the West Sussex Gazette XI. The County newspaper which, with a staff of over 50, was the largest employer in the town, recorded the scores as follows:

CASTLE WORKS XI		WEST SUSSEX GAZETTE XI	
H. Burt	1	H. Parker	21
A. Lawrence	15	R. Blackman	9
Elbourne	2	G. Glossop	10
F. Barnes	11	F. Blackman	8
Taylor	3	J. Simmons	25
H. Williams	1	H. Smart	0
G. Horrocks	14	J. Sallows	0
G. Isaacs	5	W. Bennett	1
J. Clarke	8	H. Burtonshaw not out	9
Johnson	7	J. Nye	0
W. Twinn not out	7	F. Knowles not out	2
Extras	7	Extras	0
Total	81	Total	85
WEST SUSSEX GAZETTE XI WON BY 1 WICKET			

In its report the newspaper described the match as one which was notable for dramatic incidents and an exciting finish. For example, in the Works XI's total of 81 no less than four members of the team were run out. The report continues:

"The printers started well but at one time the wickets fell quickly and it appeared improbable that a winning total would be obtained. However, Simmons and Nye hit off the necessary runs. The winning hit was too much for Simmons who was overcome with the heat and his exertions and had to be carried off."

Later that year, Duke Henry became President of the Sussex County Cricket Club and returned to the possibility of establishing first class cricket at Arundel. Ambitious plans were drawn up for the construction of a pavilion which would be worthy of County cricket.

These projects were aborted when the Duke, who was serving in Lord Salisbury's Government as Postmaster General, volunteered at the age of 54 to serve in the Boer War. Injured in a riding accident in South Africa, he was invalided home.

Thereafter, he made little effort to extend the range of cricket activities beyond those involving the Estate XI, for his public life at the start of the new century was exceptionally hectic. He was intensively involved with the funeral of Queen Victoria in 1901 and the Coronation of King Edward VII which followed. To these pressures was added the continuing deep sorrow at the death of his only son. There had been little social life at the Castle following the death of the Duke's first wife and it was said that an air of gloom hung about it which was intensified with the loss of his heir.

All this - including the opportunities for country house cricket - changed with Duke Henry's marriage in 1904 to the Scottish heiress, the Hon. Gwendolen Constable-Maxwell, daughter of Lord Herries. At their marriage, the Duke was 56 and his bride 21.

"Gwendy" to her friends, the new Duchess brought a lively disposition and a passion for entertaining to life at the Castle. She also brought with her a large and close-knit family whose connections intertwined with many of the leading Catholic families throughout the United Kingdom.

Her father died in 1908 when she became Lady Herries in her own right and inherited the 14th century family home at Everingham in Yorkshire, which was the traditional gathering place for all the Constable-Maxwells. Although the Duchess had only one sister, the new head of the family, her uncle Bernard, had twelve children after the age of 42 following his marriage to the 20 year old Alice Fraser of the Lovat

clan. Another uncle, Joey Maxwell-Scott, had four sons and three daughters. Through these cousins and their various marriages in Scotland and Yorkshire, Duchess Gwendolen brought a vast army of Nithsdales, Turville-Constable-Maxwells, Maxwell-Scotts, Scotts, Maxwell-Stuarts as well as the Hopes and the Hope-Scotts, to say nothing of the many Norfolk relations, for entertainment at Arundel.

Part of that entertainment was country house cricket. The first fully recorded match illustrates the nature of the gathering. In July 1907, Duchess Gwendolen organised a house party for cricket and racing at Goodwood. The match was arranged with Duke Henry's blessing under the captaincy of his wife's uncle Joey (the Hon. J Maxwell-Scott) against an Arundel Town XI organised by a local cricket patron C. S. Arbery. A glance at the score card shows the Constable-Maxwell influence as well as the M.C.C. blessing in the person of F. E. Lacey (later Sir Francis Lacey) who had been Secretary of the Club since 1898.

HON. J. MAXWELL SCOTT'S XI v ARUNDEL XI
JULY 1907

ARUNDEL XI

E. F. Farrington	c. & b. Maxwell-Scott	35
A. H. Brown	c. Fitzgerald b. Stout	26
E. P. Boxold	c. Lovat b. Stout	12
J. Barnes	c. Stout b. Fitzgerald	34
A. H. Holland	c. Stout b. Maxwell-Scott	0
R. F. Mitchell	c. Lovat b. Johnson	17
C. S. Arbery	c. Fraser b. Fitzgerald	7
R. S. Wix	c. Lacey b. Lord Lovat	64
C. F. Arbery	c. Fitzgerald b. Eyre	42
W. Charman	not out	11
P. Ayling	b. Scott-Murray	7
	Extras	4
		—
	Total	259

HON. J. MAXWELL SCOTT'S XI

Lord Lovat	st. Farrington b. C. S. Arbery	6
A. Scott-Murray	c. Mitchell b. Holland	80
Capt. Fitzgerald	b. C. S. Arbery	2
R. P. Eyre	c. Farrington b. C. S. Arbery	2
E. Dobson	b. Holland	119
Capt. W. Maxwell-Scott	st. Farrington b. C. S. Arbery	0
Maj. Hon.. H. Fraser	c. C. F. Arbery b. C. S. Arbery	0
F. E. Lacey	c. C. F. Arbery b. Lacey	13
P. W. Stout	c. Farrington b. Holland	0
Maj. Bulkiev-Johnson	not out	14
Hon.. J. Maxwell- Scott	b. C. S. Arbery	1
	Extras	4
		—
	Total	241

Bowling

C. S. Arbery 6 for 109
A. H. Holland 3 for 57

ARUNDEL XI WON BY 18 RUNS

To this great clan would soon be added Norfolk reinforcements. Duke Henry and Duchess Gwendolen were especially delighted with the birth of their son and heir, Bernard, in 1908. He already had a sister, Rachel, born in 1905 and she would be followed by Katherine in 1912 and Winifrede in 1914. It was said that these were the happiest days of Duke Henry's life when the great Baron's Hall in the Castle rang with laughter as he played with his young family and their relations in a group known as The Sparrows. This was the name given to the four Norfolks, Bernard and his sisters, together with their four Drummond cousins, David and his sisters Margaret, Bobby and Gillian (who were the children of Duchess Gwendy's sister Angela Constable-Maxwell and her husband Eric Drummond, later the Earl of Perth). Happily, it is from this group that we have been able to draw family memories of the inter-war years of cricket at Arundel.

The collective memory of The Sparrows is of a father and uncle who delighted in his extended family. When it came to the cricket teams invited to play for his wife, he showed continued good humour coupled with an almost schoolboyish relish for the practical joke. On one occasion, the visiting team travelling from London by train on a Friday evening was badly delayed by an accident on the line. When they arrived at the Castle it was after 10 o'clock and they found it in darkness. However they were greeted by Duke Henry who led them in with apparent gruffness saying "You're too late for dinner but I suppose you deserve a quick nightcap." As the group entered the darkened dining room, the lights came on and there was Duchess Gwendy and other guests waiting with an enormous cold supper.

Duke Henry never showed any interest in taking part in cricket matches on his ground. He had no record of ability at the game and age ruled out effective participation. However, he was always keen to involve his cricketing guests and other local friends in a wide variety of other entertainment and sporting activities. His favourite game was croquet and one of his regular opponents, E. R. Harrison, would later recall the competitions which were organised for visiting cricketers. He also remembered how the Duke's enthusiasm for organising charades, fancy dress and other group activities reached its peak when he involved his guests in a form of bridge. This required house guests and other local friends to dress up as playing cards. Dr Harrison as an exceptionally tall man was given the part of the King of Hearts or Spades, while other guests including the cricketers were relegated to the roles of lower value cards. Quite how the complicated exercise of shuffling the pack and dealing was arranged is unclear but the whole process is recalled by the family as one which caused great hilarity and in which the competition was never taken too seriously.

All these carefree activities, including cricket, came to an end with the outbreak of the First World War. However, amid the sparse records which were kept of games at this time, the last recorded match in 1913 is a reminder of the Duke's more serious interests.

DUCHESS OF NORFOLK'S XII V 5TH LONDON INFANTRY BRIGADE
9 AUGUST 1913

DUCHESS OF NORFOLK'S XII

B. Dela Bere	lbw. b. Bantick	17
Hon.. G Scott	b. O'Brien	8
M. Maxwell-Scott	b. Jackson	51
O. C. Riddell	b. O'Brien	1
Hon.. J. F Hope	c. Fitzclarence b. O'Brien	62
Hon.. F. Montgomery	not out	58
A. F. Somerset	b. Fitzjohn	0
A. O. Hope	b. O'Brien	1
Capt. Maxwell-Scott	lbw. b. O'Brien	13
A. Drummond	c&b Jackson	43
Capt. Disney-Roebuck	b. Fitzjohn	0
H. F. Hope	b. Bantick	1
	Extras	19
	Total	274

Bowling (incomplete)

	O	M	R	W
Bantick	7	0	21	2
O'Brien	12	1	64	5
Alexander	4	0	21	0
Dodd	3	0	22	0
Jackson	4	1	19	2
Fitzjohn				2

5th LONDON INFANTRY BRIGADE XII

Lieut. K. R. O'Brien	st. Somerset b. Scott	6
Lieut. A. Wheatley	b. Scott	0
Capt. Sir L. C. Alexander	b. Hope	62
Capt. G. N. Fitzjohn	c. Maxwell-Scott b. Drummond	1
Maj. A. Dodd	b. Scott	1
Capt. J. Cook	c&b. Drummond	2
Capt. F. J. Oxley	c. Montgomerie b. Drummond	0
Capt. W. R. Bubbers	c. Hope b. Drummond	10
Capt. J. de Montmerency	c. Capt. Maxwell-Scott b. Hope	17
Capt. C. J. Bantick	not out	10
Lieut. S. R. Jackson	st. Somerset b. Hope	3
Col. C. Fitzclarence	b. Hope	6
	Extras	14
	Total	122

Bowling (incomplete)

	O	M	R	W
Scott	9	0	28	3
Drummond	5	1	13	4
Montgomerie	5	1	20	0
M. Maxwell-Scott	3	1	16	0
A. Hope	6	0	28	4

DUCHESS OF NORFOLK'S XII WON BY 152 RUNS

As a result of his Boer War experience and a growing concern over German militarism, Duke Henry formed a life-long attachment to the Army. He also became deeply involved in the creation of rifle clubs throughout the United Kingdom as a form of basic national defence training. In addition, each year he offered the use of the Castle Park for military manoeuvres and, as the family picture shows, he took the opportunity of sharing this experience with his young son, Bernard, and his eldest daughter, Rachel.

The match played on 9 August 1913 was between the Duchess of Norfolk's team and the Fifth London Infantry Brigade. Looking at the list of military men involved has a certain poignancy. They would soon be involved in the War against Germany in France; some would return with war wounds and their Captain, Claude Fitzclarence who had won the V.C. in the Boer War, was killed in Flanders in 1914.

The home team was organised and captained on the Duchess' behalf by James Fitzalan-Hope who later became the first Baron Rankeillour. His mother was Lady Victoria Alexandrina Fitzalan-Howard, Duke Henry's sister. Extending the family connection, he included in the side not only his sons Arthur and Henry Hope but also his brother-in-law, the son of 'Squire' Riddell of Northumberland. Most of the other members of the team were related to Duchess Gwendolen including the Scotts, Maxwell-Scotts and the Drummonds. However, the outbreak of war in 1914 and Duke Henry's death in 1917 ended his part in encouraging the great family tradition of cricket at Arundel.

When matches were resumed in 1921, they took the form of a country house rivalry between the Duchess' team from Arundel Castle and one from Goring Castle near Worthing. Once again, James Fitzalan-Hope returned to play for the home team but under the captaincy of his son Captain Arthur Hope who would take over the side from 1922 onwards. The Goring Castle team was led by the son of the house, Arthur Plantagenet Francis Cecil Somerset, who had played for Sussex and toured the West Indies with the M.C.C. before the War. Shown on the score card simply as A. F. Somerset, at the age of 32 he was a very effective middle order right hand batsman and medium pace bowler.

However, his side was consistently outplayed in this series. In 1921 Austin Scott-Murray made a century for Hope's XI and, despite R. D. Tollemache of the great brewing family taking 6 for 54, the home side reached 259. In reply the Goring Castle team made only 83. In the years which followed the pattern was remarkably similar. In 1922 two

CAPT. HOPE'S ARUNDEL CASTLE XII v MR. A. F. SOMERSET'S
GORING CASTLE XII
JULY 29TH 1922

CAPT. HOPE'S XII

Lt. Col. Sir F. S. Jackson	b. Lord	0
A. C. Wilkinson	c. Thomas b. A. C. Somerset	50
D. J. C. Glass	c. Somerset b. Flowers	47
D. S. Cornwallis	b. Bayliss b. A. C. Somerset	12
M. L. Llewellyn	b. A. C. Somerset	7
Capt. A. O. J. Hope	c. & b. A. C. Somerset	16
A. Scott-Murray	c. & b. A. C. Somerset	6
Lord Romilly	not out	56
Major C. L. Gordon	lbw. b. Clanfield	2
Capt. G. Barry	b. A. C. Somerset	48
W. M. Cecil	not out	0
G. Drake	did not bat	
	Extras	10
	Total (for 9 wkts dec)	254

Bowling

	O	M	R	W
Lord	7	1	32	1
Glanfield	13	1	54	1
Donne	8	0	49	0
Flowers	12	1	49	1
A. C. Somerset	15.4	1	60	6

MR. A. F. SOMERSET'S XII

J. Bayliss	b. Glass	0
G. P. Glanfield	b. Barry	0
F. J. Barrett	c. Wilkinson b. Glass	0
W. A. Thomas	c. Cecil b. Barry	1
J. C. Flowers	b. Barry	5
A. C. Somerset	b. Barry	35
A. F. Somerset	b. Barry	8
Capt. E. D. W. Levine	b. Jackson	3
L. V. Donne	c. Lord Romilly b. Scott-Murray	18
W. F. Lord	c. Hope b. Barry	13
F. J. Savill	b. Wilkinson	9
Hon.. R. Frankland	not out	0
	Extras	14
	Total	106

Bowling (incomplete)

	O	M	R	W
Glass	15	2	35	2
Barry	18	7	35	6
Jackson	5	1	10	1
Scott-Murray	1	1	0	1
Gordon	3	0	9	0
Wilkinson	1.3	0	8	1

CAPT. HOPE'S XII WON BY 148 RUNS

one-day matches were played in which the Hope XI scored 254 against 106 and 204 against 59. In 1923 the margin was 227 against 80 and the series came to an end.

A number of notable individuals appeared for the home team. In 1922, the batting was opened by Lt Col. the Rt. Hon. Sir Stanley Jackson of Yorkshire and England. He was known to Duchess Gwendy as her Member of Parliament as his constituency included her family's country home at Everingham. However, he was in his fifty-first year when playing in this match and was taking a break from his duties as Financial Secretary to the War Office. On his first appearance at Arundel, he failed to score being dismissed by W. F. Lord, an Oxford Blue, who played an occasional match for Middlesex. His fellow opener, the Australian born W. A. C. Wilkinson, who made a half century, was a military man who would later tour with M.C.C. in Australia and New Zealand.

A supporter of cricket at Arundel into his nineties, he would later recall that a third match was arranged in 1922 of which no record was kept. The game involved most of the players who had turned out for the Hope and Fitzroy-Somerset teams on previous days. On this occasion, Sir Stanley Jackson scored a century. After he was out, Alex Wilkinson asked him how long it was since he had last played in a cricket match before these games in 1922. "Oh, about ten years," replied the former England Captain.

During this series there were a number of notable bowling performances for the Hope XI. Despite his disappointment with the bat, Sir Stanley Jackson bowled 5 tidy overs to take 1 for 10 in the 1922 match. Throughout the series D. J. C. Glass was a consistent wicket taker. In the second match in 1922, he and R. A. D. Brooks bowled unchanged to take 6 for 21 and 4 for 32 respectively. General Sir Reginald Dallas Brooks as he would later become (and the future Governor of Victoria), was a useful cricketer who played for Hampshire, from 1918 to 1921. His all-round sporting prowess was such that he was an England hockey international and, despite his army career, captained the Royal Navy at golf. To his contribution from the Services was added that of Captain Gerald Barry, who took 6 for 35 (and scored 48) on his only appearance in 1922. Other prominent wicket takers were Dudley Evans, the Hampshire all-rounder and K. O. Hunter, whose two appearances produced the remarkable figures of 11-4-12-2 and 16-2-14-2.

Apart from a match against a Navy XI in 1923, there are no detailed records of further cricket matches at Arundel in the twenties. The start of regular cricket on a planned basis would have to wait until the coming of age of Bernard, Duke of Norfolk, who provides the main theme for our story.

Duke Henry with the future Duke Bernard and his sister Rachel inspecting 5th London Infantry Brigade, 1913.

The future Duke Bernard with bat and ball, 1916.

The future Duke Bernard with his mother, Duchess Gwendy, 1916.

"The Sparrows" in 1917. Duke Bernard (centre) with his sisters Rachel (2nd left), Katherine and Winifrede (last two on right), with their Drummond cousins (the Earl of Perth and his sisters).

CHAPTER TWO

Duke Bernard's XI – Early Years 1930-1932

Born on 30 May 1908, the Duke would later recall that among his earliest memories was the cricket played by the Army during exercises in the Park before the First World War. Thereafter his sister Rachel has described how his passion for the game manifested itself in the war time and post-war years:

"I first became aware of this when I was about twelve and so Bernard would be about nine. He was always trying to get me to bowl to him in the Tilting Yard. I didn't really enjoy it all that much but he could be very persuasive and, even in those early years, he had beautiful manners and made you feel that he really was grateful for your efforts.

"Later when he was about 16 I can vividly recall in our London home, Norfolk House, the anguished occasion when he said 'If only I could go to Lord's. Will they never let me become a member of the M.C.C.?'

"In those days you had to put your name down at birth and I used to pull his leg about this in later years when it seemed that the M.C.C. was constantly pressing him to help as President, Manager of the England Team and so forth. And he would smile and reply ' Yes, I have paid a heavy price for my youthful enthusiasm.'"

In his early years, much of the Duke's cricketing as well as his formal education was undertaken by private tutors. Among them are several who are recalled by the family as preferring to play cricket with the Duke rather than sitting indoors with his schoolbooks. Indeed, Lady Rachel has suggested that this kind of erratic private education was one of the reasons why he failed in his ambition of going up to Oxford. His formal schooling was confined to two years at The Oratory from the age of 17. Here, one of his Headmaster's reports indicated: "This boy has ability but we only see him at his best playing football or cricket". This account reflected more on the young Duke's dedication than his skill. His contemporaries recalled him as an enthusiastic

but undistinguished House cricketer who was willing to keep wicket as well as to bat and bowl.

As Lady Rachel put it:

"He was no great shakes as a player but he simply adored taking part - especially with better cricketers than himself. However, for a time I thought he might give up the game because, when he left school, he and I were quite a team. He was commissioned in 'The Blues' (the Royal Horseguards) and we started doing the rounds together. We both loved hunting and racing and Bernard was a brave and skilful rider at military point-to-points.

"With his military duties and all these riding activities and the parties, he really didn't have much time for cricket. In fact, I can remember how fed up he was when he had to be on duty at Windsor during the time when many people were on holiday and how much he missed the great family reunions at the Castle. So it really wasn't until he came of age and took up his duties as Earl Marshal that cricket came on the agenda."

This happened in 1930. Lady Rachel's scrapbook for that year shows how both she and her brother moved up and down the country in a way which allowed a narrow window of opportunity for cricket. The Norfolk relations all gathered together - as was their regular custom - at Arundel Castle for Christmas and the New Year. Shooting occupied the Duke for large parts of January and early February. Later in February and March, he was hunting in Yorkshire and with the Cottesmore at whose Hunt Ball he and the Earl of Erne were described as Britain's most eligible bachelors. In early April the Duke was riding in the Household Brigade's Hawthorn Hill Point-to-Point races. The Constable-Maxwell relations had their traditional gathering at Everingham at Easter and the Norfolks went abroad to Biarritz in late April returning in time for the Newmarket Spring meeting in May. There followed the round of parties in the London season together with weekend visits to country houses which led to a stay at Longwood from 31 May to 2 June.

Longwood was the Hampshire home of the Earl of Eldon who was a lifelong friend of the Norfolk family. They were related by marriage through the Lovats in Scotland and Lord Eldon was also known to the Duke in his role as Lord-in-Waiting at Buckingham Palace. The Duke's responsibilities as Earl Marshal would increasingly bring them together and they discovered a mutual passion for cricket. Over the following weekend, a match was planned which was to mark the start of the series between the two country houses. In the first game at Arundel on Saturday and Sunday 5 and 6 July 1930, the Duke selected a side which was judiciously balanced between good friends and accomplished cricketers. In batting order it was:

1. Captain A. O. J. Hope.
2. Roger Wethered
3. Robert Laycock
4. H. P. Chaplin
5. Lord George Scott
6. The Duke of Norfolk
7. F. E. V. Smith
8. A. M. Crawley
9. Captain C. G. Lancaster
10. The Earl of Erne
11. Lord Stavordale

This side reflected the Norfolk and Constable-Maxwell family links and other leading Catholic families together with sporting and army friends. Their Captain, Arthur Hope, would be involved with his wife Grizel (another member of the Lovat Clan) in all the matches in the series which continued until 1936. A useful cricketing all-rounder, he served as a member of Parliament and subsequently became Governor of Madras, succeeding to his father's title of Lord Rankeillour.

Roger Wethered, also a regular player in this series, was best known as one of the outstanding British amateur golfers between the wars. At the age of 22, he tied for the Open Championship at St Andrews and he had won the Amateur Championship in 1923. His contemporaries said that the great strength of his wrists which made him an outstanding hitter of long irons was evident when it came to the ferocity of his cutting and driving on the cricket field.

Robert Laycock, Captain Lancaster, the Earl of Erne and Lord Stavordale were all Army or riding friends. General Sir Robert Laycock (as he would become as a war-time hero

directing Combined Operations and later as Governor of Malta) rode in military point-to-point races with the Duke as did Lord Stavordale. "Juby" Lancaster served with the Duke in the Royal Horse Guards. He would become a Conservative Member of Parliament in Lancashire for over 30 years.

The best known cricketers in the side were H. P. Chaplin, Captain of Sussex from 1900-1915 who was still, at the age of 47, a useful attacking batsman, F. E. V. Smith, (one of the Hambledon family) and A. M. Crawley.

Aidan Crawley already had an outstanding record in first-class cricket. Coming down from Oxford only a few days earlier, he was to play for Kent for over 20 years and had already been in the twelve named for the Test Match against South Africa at Lord's in the previous year. While best known as an attacking right-hand batsman, he was also a useful medium pace and offbreak bowler. He was to have the unusual distinction of serving both as a Labour and Conservative Member of Parliament and later as Chairman of London Weekend Television.

Lord George Scott, one of the Duke of Buccleuch's sons, was another family friend from Scotland who would become a regular at Arundel as a talented batsman. As for the Duke, his batting position in the middle order would vary throughout this series, according to his mood and the needs of the occasion.

The game provided a remarkable start to the series. Batting first, the Duke's side were soon in trouble. The young Hampshire medium pace bowler Lewis Harfield proved his worth as the one professional in Lord Eldon's XI when, supported by another useful cricketer, his Lordship's gardener and chauffeur R. Poulter, they reduced the Duke's team to 29 for 6. In Harfield's case this included the supreme *faux pas* of dismissing the Duke for a duck.

At this point, the home side took a no doubt gloomy lunch. However, on resumption, the 22 year old Aidan Crawley went out to bat accompanied by Lord George Scott. Hitting Poulter for 4 from the first ball he received and adding two more boundaries in the next over from Harfield, Crawley went on to complete a whirlwind hundred. When his score stood at 81, he went to his century in the grand manner by hitting the Hampshire professional for 6-6-4-4 and when he was out for 147 he had been at the wicket for only one hour and five minutes.

After this onslaught, the other side were given a solid start by two of their regulars, Captain C. M. Venables-Llewellyn and R. Poulter. They received good support from

DUKE OF NORFOLK'S XI v LOED ELDON'S XI
5TH AND 6TH JULY 1930

DUKE OF NORFOLK'S XI — 1st Innings

Capt. the Hon.. A. O. J. Hope	lbw. b. Poulter	8
R. H. Wethered	b. Harfield	13
R. E. Laycock	b. Poulter	8
H. P. Chaplin	b. Harfield	0
Lord G. Scott	b. Harfield	5
Duke of Norfolk	c. Graham b. Harfield	0
F. E. V. Smith	c. Harfield b Harfield	0
A. M. Crawley	c. Graham b. Harfield	147
Capt. C. G. Lancaster	b. Poulter	32
Earl of Erne	not out	0
Lord Stavordale	did not bat	0
	Extras	1
	Total (for 9 wkts dec)	214

2nd Innings

Earl of Erne	c. Poulter b. Scott	0
Lord Stavordale	b. Scott	0
Capt. A. O. J. Hope	b. Lord Eldon	17
Duke of Norfolk	b. Lord Eldon	5
F. E. V. Smith	b. Lord Eldon	4
A. M. Crawley	c. and b. Harfield	164
R. H. Wethered	run out	48
Lord G. Scott	b. Harfield	4
R. E. Laycock	not out	1
H. P. Chaplin	did not bat	
Capt. A. C. Maxwell		
	Extras	7
	Total (for 8 wkts dec)	250

Bowling

	O	M	R	W
Poulter	17	2	103	3
Harfield	17	5	99	6
Kingdon	2	0	11	0

Bowling

	O	M	R	W
Lord Eldon	12	2	70	2
M. S. Scott	7	0	34	3
Poulter	7	0	76	0
Harfield	8	0	63	2

LORD ELDON'S XI — 1st Innings

Capt. C. M. V. Llewellyn	st. Duke of Norfolk b. Crawley	36
R. Poulter	c. Scott b. Smith	43
M. S. Scott	b. Smith	3
L. Harfield	b. Crawley	0
Lord Eldon	c. Capt. Hope b. Smith	6
Comm. C. Holland	st. Duke of Norfolk b. Smith	32
Wing-Comm. G. C. Maxwell	b. Smith	3
G. Campbell	b. Smith	2
A. Kingdon	hit wicket b. Hope	11
H. Mostyn	b. Crawley	23
J. Graham	not out	3
	Extras	31
	Total	193

2nd Innings

Capt. Llewellyn	b. Smith	75
R. Poulter	lbw. b. Hope	13
Comm. C. Holland	lbw. b. Crawley	25
L. Harfield	run out	58
Lord Eldon	c. and b. Hope	29
M. S. Scott	b. Crawley	9
Wing-Comm. G. C. Maxwell	run out	6
A. Kingdon	not out	5
G. Campbell	b. Crawley	0
E. H. Mostyn	b. Crawley	0
J. Graham	c. Erne b. Crawley	1
	Extras	29
	Total	250

Bowling

	O	M	R	W
Wethered	8	1	28	0
Crawley	18	2	83	3
Smith	14.2	4	41	6
Hope	5	1	10	1

Bowling

	O	M	R	W
Smith	11	0	53	1
Lord Scott	3	0	11	0
Chaplin	3	0	21	0
Hope	15	0	69	2
Crawley	11.2	1	44	5
Wethered	6	0	23	0

DUKE OF NORFOLK'S XI WON BY 21 RUNS

Commander Holland and one of the Duke's own men, his land agent, E. H. Mostyn. Other links in the opposition with the Duke were even closer. Batting briefly at number 7 for the Eldon XI was one of his cousins, Gerald Constable-Maxwell (later Wing Commander Constable-Maxwell M.C. D.F.C. A.F.C.). He was one of the Duke's Uncle Bernard Constable-Maxwell's twelve children. He would contribute directly to the alliance of the two families which continues up to the present day when one of his daughters, Anne, mar-

ried Lord Miles Fitzalan Howard, who was to succeed Duke Bernard as 17th Duke of Norfolk in 1975.

The rest of the details of this match are overshadowed by the contribution of Aidan Crawley. In the Norfolk XI's second innings, Crawley came in with the score at 34-5. He proceeded to put on 214 for the 6th wicket with Roger Wethered, completing his own total of 164 in one and a quarter hours.

Then, when the Eldon XI were making a solid effort to

score 272 runs to win, Aidan Crawley came on as third change bowler with the score at 219 for 4. He proceeded to end the match with a flourish by taking the last four wickets in 3.2 overs. With the Duke's side emerging victorious by 21 runs, Lady Rachel wrote in her scrapbook:

"We retained the Ashes - just".

Over 60 years later, Aidan Crawley recalled his first appearance at Arundel with typical modesty:

"I really don't remember much about the match and I think they may have been kind to a new boy at least in the early stages. I did not know the Duke all that well at the time but he was a close friend of my brother Cosmo and we knew the family through our mutual Yorkshire connections when my father was Chaplain to the Archbishop of York. For me, it was the start of a life-long love affair with cricket at Arundel."

Lady Rachel's recollections of the start of the Eldon series reflect on the range of guests and activities which became a feature of these weekends:

"Apart from the cricket, there was tennis, swimming, croquet and rounders. If it was wet there was a rather vicious form of indoor hockey in The Baron's Hall.

"And then there was golf. Bernard was certainly a better golfer than a cricketer and he and I frequently teamed up to play another couple during our sporting weekends. On several occasions we took on Roger Wethered and his sister Joyce (who was as great a champion in her field as he was in his). We would play at Pulborough or on the course which Bernard had donated to the town of Littlehampton. I think it was about this time that he decided he would like to have facilities even nearer home and began to create a small golf course round the edge of his cricket ground."

But it was cricket which became the main motivation for regular summer gatherings which grew even larger as the Eldon matches became a firm fixture. In the 1931 game, the Duke invited another Army friend, Henry Hunloke, to join his team. He and his family had established local connections when his father was serving on the Royal Yacht at

A typical page from the Norfolk family albums of the period – Duke's XI v Lord Eldon's XI, 1930.

Cowes. He would prove an effective opening batsman for the Duke in the years ahead. As a serious cricketer for his side that year, the Duke also included another of his Yorkshire friends, Colonel Ronnie Stanyforth. Although he would eventually play for his home county, he made his first-class debut as a wicket-keeper and lower order batsman on M.C.C. tours in South America, West Indies and South Africa. These included four games as Captain of England in Test Matches and thus, he led his country before turning out for Yorkshire.

The 1932 match was memorable for the debut of a number of leading players in the series. Opening the batting was the new Crawley partnership of Aidan and his elder brother Cosmo. Their contribution and that of others in the Duke's side would be well summed up by another newcomer, Lord Dunglass.

Known at various stages of his life as Sir Alec Douglas Home or Lord Home of the Hirsel, he was, at this time, Member of Parliament for South Lanark, and he gives an incisive commentary on his first outing at Arundel:

"We knew the Norfolk family from relatively close proximity in Scotland to their place at Kinharvie. After I left Eton and Oxford, my opportunities for playing cricket were restricted because of my duties as a Scottish Member of Parliament and, in any case, I liked to get back to the North. Nevertheless, Arundel was a big draw and looking at the list of the names of the people I played with in 1932 shows what a fascinating cocktail Bernard concocted.

"The secret was that - apart from the occasional professional who would be invited as was the custom of the day to do quite a bit of the bowling - the whole thing was definitely amateur cricket. However, this meant cricket of the highest quality coupled with the enjoyment of balancing the sides with a few enthusiastic duffers.

"Without being unkind, this was true of Bernard. But what we all enjoyed was the enormous pleasure he clearly derived in scoring a few runs and his hospitality was always overwhelming.

"In our side, the Crawleys were a major force. Aidan was a beautiful player possessed of the capacity for enormous straight hitting. I can recall in this match at least two or three sixes which went straight back over the bowler's head into the rhododendron bushes at the Park end. The fielding side had the devil of a job finding the ball. Moreover, when it came to bowling, he could produce a very useful in-swinger with the new ball. In fact, he was really a part of what we later came to know as the leg side attack through Fred Root of Worcestershire and later in Bodyline, but naturally we didn't have any kind of packed leg side field. You have to remember that, in those days, the pitch at Arundel Castle was not exactly fast and true. Indeed, it was often a bit green and would take turn later in the game. This is where Aidan with his ability to open the bowling dipping the ball in quickly was so useful because he could also come on later and bowl respectable off-breaks.

"His brother Cosmo had a beautiful batting style but he suffered from a highly nervous disposition. This made him a bad starter and was perhaps why he never achieved anything like the same first-class ability as Aidan. Nevertheless, they were a formidable pair in opening the batting as I see from their stand of 193 in the 1932 match.

"Others in the Duke's side were pretty useful. Major T. E. G. Nugent (later Lord Nugent) was a professional soldier and a very good batsman. Henry Hunloke was another good Army player. There were one or two other interesting characters in this side. Michael Hornby would be better known for the creation of his great gardens in the West Country and as Chairman of W. H. Smith but in those days he was a handy cricketer. Chichester-Constable was a really fast bowler and I imagine that, in this match, Bernard took him off as too dangerous (his figures at the time were 2 for 3 from 6 overs.)

"I see that Bernard made me bowl quite a lot but Arundel was never a tiring ground on which to operate. It has that marvellous springy turf. All in all, I was delighted to make Arundel my first choice for cricket in England during the Thirties. So, when the matches against the Eldon XI proved so popular and Bernard decided to have an additional series more or less within the family, I was happy to sign up for these as well."

Lord Home's reference to the other family series relates to matches which began against the Hope XI in 1933. We shall look at these games in due course along with the continuing Eldon series but first it is appropriate to consider the other matches which Duke Bernard sponsored in the early Thirties.

Following his father's example, the Duke was quick to offer cricketing opportunities to the Military when they made annual visits for training in his Park. Thus, in 1930, he raised a team to play the Oxford University O.T.C. who were defeated in a low-scoring match by 41 runs.

Among those included in his team was Roger Makins

(later Lord Sherfield). He was at this time serving in the Foreign Office before becoming a distinguished Ambassador in Washington and later an industrialist. At this stage of his life he was a young and enthusiastic bowler who, bowling unchanged in partnership with R. Bathurst, finished with figures of 6 for 21 from 10 overs. Today he recalls:

"I had first been to Arundel Park with the Oxford Cavalry in 1925 when I was playing cricket for two light-hearted teams organised by my college, Christ Church, called the Warrigals and the Coronets. However there was no cricket at Arundel that year and the match in 1930 was one involving Oxford O.T.C. past and present.

"I recall a number of individuals playing in the match, most of whom seemed to have strong aristocratic connections. I was staying with one of the Hursts at nearby Rusper. He was the son of Sir Cecil Hurst, the legal adviser to the Foreign Office in the 20s, and was my contemporary both at prep. school and at Winchester. He went on to New College and the Bar, and married Lady Barbara Lindsay, the daughter of the Earl of Crawford.

"My bowling partner in that match was always known as Bill Bathurst. He was related to the Earl of Bathurst. I can visualise him now - a very amiable, heavy-set fellow who seemed to revel in the exercise. I also recall P. W. Thring, a dark, sallow chap and a very good cricketer who was another Wykehamist contemporary. Then there was Harry Grenfell who is best remembered as Joyce Grenfell's brother-in-law. He never married and spent most of his career in a mining and minerals company in what was then Rhodesia.

"I suppose my real reason for being there was that I was very friendly with Lady Rachel and her cousin Margaret Drummond. As I saw more of the family, I came to realise Bernard Norfolk's rather bucolic exterior belied his efficiency as Earl Marshal and all-round organiser. Certainly, it is fun to be reminded of that 1930 match and what must have been one of the better bowling performances of my rather inglorious cricket career."

One of the victims of that performance was the Oxford O.T.C.'s last man in, Willie Anstruther-Gray. He was then a lieutenant in the Coldstream Guards. He would have a distinguished career as a Scottish Member of Parliament, Government Minister and latterly as Deputy Speaker of the House of Commons. In that capacity, Lord Kilmany (as he became), later told the author:

"I saw something of the Duke of Norfolk in connection with parliamentary business, the State Opening of

DUKE OF NORFOLK'S XII v MAYOR OF ARUNDEL'S XII
19TH SEPTEMBER 1931

DUKE OF NORFOLK'S XII

E. H. Bowley	c. Hearne b. Fowler	34
G. A. K. Collins	st. Williams b. Bailey	20
Capt. P. F. Williams	c. Brown b. Fowler	0
H. L. Wilson	b. Fowler	51
Capt. A. Hardman	c. Hearne b. Sims	7
A. H. H. Gilligan	b. Hearne	4
W. Cornford	c. and b. Harfield	3
V. Humphries	c. Haig b. Hearne	2
G. S. Pearce	st Williams b. Bailey	25
D. M. G. Neligan	c. Lee b. Hearne	0
B. W. Marshall	c. Harfield b. Bailey	5
G. W. Alsford	not out	3
	Extras	10
	Total	164

Bowling

	O	M	R	W
Haig	5	0	23	0
Fowler	18	7	43	3
Bailey	11.3	2	40	3
Sims	11	4	16	1
Hearne	4	1	18	3
Harfield	4	1	14	1

MAYOR OF ARUNDEL'S XII

J. W. Hearne	c. Gilligan b. Wilson	24
L. Harfield	c. Neligan b. Marshall	24
R. Lee	c. Hardman b. Marshall	10
E. Hendren	not out	62
Capt. N. E. Haig	c. and b. Gilligan	33
L. Williams	lbw. Wilson	7
J. M. Sims	not out	9
J. Bailey	did not bat	
A. Brown		
R. G. Blackman		
R. James		
A. Fowler		
	Extras	5
	Total (for 5 wickets dec)	174

Bowling

	O	M	R	W
Pearce	5	1	16	0
Neligan	17.2	6	27	1
Marshall	13	0	40	2
Wilson	18	1	57	2
Bowley	4	0	20	0
Alsford	2	0	14	0
Collins	1	1	0	0

MAYOR OF ARUNDEL'S XII WON BY 5 WICKETS

Parliament and so on and in my work with the National Hunt Committee and the Betting Levy Board. In those days, I did not know him well and we were involved in what was very much a scratch Oxford O.T.C. side including some like myself who had recently come down from the University. I was no great shakes as a cricketer but I do recall that we were almost all required to bowl. What sticks out in my mind is the obvious relief for Duke Bernard that he was no longer involved in day-to-day Army life and yet, at the same time, the passion which he retained in supporting the Military."

It may well be that it was this passion which led to another undated match in 1930 involving the Duke's team and an Army XI whose main star was Lt. Leoline Williams. He showed the batting skills which gave him the opportunity to appear regularly for Sussex as well as for the Army while making the top score of 92 out of a total of 178. This total, however, proved insufficient in responding to a score of 216 by the Duke's team.

Apart from providing cricketing hospitality for his Army guests, the Duke was soon preoccupied in exploring the possibility of arranging more truly representative cricket on his ground. In doing so, he had in mind one of his favourite good causes which was the Arundel Hospital. This project had been made possible as a result of land which the Duke had donated and building work to which he was a major contributor. As part of this fund-raising, the Duke took the opportunity of bringing together on his ground for the first time a large collection of first-class cricketers. He did so by persuading most of the Sussex and Middlesex teams to make themselves available at the end of the season for a match on 19 September 1931 between sides representing both the Duke and the Mayor of Arundel.

The Duke's team consisted mainly of current Sussex players and some of the County's old favourites. The batting was opened by the professional Ted Bowley and one of the County's regular amateur players, G. A. K. Collins. The middle order included two former Sussex captains, H. L. Wilson who, at the age of 50, had only given up first-class cricket in the previous season, and Harold Gilligan who was Captain of the county side in that year. Gilligan was captain of the Duke's team on this occasion thus beginning a family connection which would be maintained through later appearances by his son-in-law, Peter May. Other Sussex stalwarts in the Duke's team were the wicket-keeper W. L. Cornford and the medium pace bowler George Pearce.

For the Mayor's team, the bowling honours went to Archibald Fowler, the Middlesex slow left-arm bowler who would shortly become head coach at Lords. He was supported by James Bailey, then a promising young Hampshire professional who would achieve the double in 1948, and the ever reliable Middlesex and England all-rounder J. W. Hearne.

Hearne continued his good work in a useful opening partnership with the Hampshire professional Lewis Harfield but it was left to his County Captain Nigel Haig and the immensely popular Patsy Hendren to provide the major Middlesex partnership which gave the Mayor's team a victory by five wickets.

The new Arundel Hospital was officially opened on 7 November 1931 by Duchess Gwendy or, as the plaque was

Duke of Norfolk's XII v Mayor of Arundel's XII, 19th September 1931. Charity match in aid of Arundel Hospital.

Duke of Norfolk's XI v Lord Eldon's XI, July 1932. Back row (L to R, players only) – Lord George Scott, D. Drummond, G. Maxwell, C. Holland, P. Scott, R. Laycock, A. Buxton, J. W. Jackson. Front row (L to R) – Lord Dunglass, C. Crawley, A. Hope, T. Nugent, R. Foster, Duke of Norfolk, Lord Eldon, Lord Dalkeith, R. Wethered, A. Crawley.

inscribed, by Gwendolen, Duchess of Norfolk, Baroness Herries. However, funds were still required to equip the hospital and a repeat fund-raising cricket match was arranged in 1932 between the Duke's side and an Arundel Hospital XI with many of the same participants as in the previous year. The match was conducted in a friendly fashion with mainly Sussex cricketers in light-hearted mood and almost everyone had a bowl.

For the Arundel Hospital XI the batting was opened by the Sussex professionals Harry Greenwood and James Langridge. There followed two more Sussex regulars, the professional Harry Parks and the amateur captain, the dashing right-hand batsman R. S. G. Scott. The rest of the batting order was made up of the all-rounder George Pearce, the Goring Castle amateur A. P. F. C. Somerset, V. J. Eaton the current Sussex wicket-keeper, and the first non-Sussex player in the team, Bertie Marshall, who had made a few recent appearances for Nottinghamshire. Little is known about R. Lee's cricketing and possible Sussex connections except that he returned to play briefly again at Arundel after the Second World War. Numbers 10 and 11, however, were two veterans with classic Sussex credentials.

George Cox Senior had played for the County from 1895 to 1928. Now in his 60th year, he was still capable of immaculate slow left-arm bowling. His tail-end companion, A. A. Saunders (later Sir Alan Saunders) had made brief appearances for the County as an all-rounder in the early 1920s. More to the point, as captain of the County's 2nd XI, he had proved tireless in training new Sussex home grown talent which played a vital part in the success which the senior team enjoyed under the captaincy of Arthur Gilligan from 1922 - 1929.

Against this strong Sussex array the Duke produced an almost equally powerful side. Their wickets were shared by Ted Bowley (4-29), J. H. Parks (father of J. M. Parks of Sussex and grandfather of R. J. Parks of Hampshire) and W. L. Cornford, the wicket-keeper who handed over the gloves to Jim Parks in order to enjoy some success with the ball. Two other bowlers for the Duke's side mention special merit. George Cox Junior had made his debut for Sussex in the previous year and this was one of the few occasions on which he and his father appeared together. The other wicket taker, Maurice Tate, then in his prime, was an enormous favourite with the crowd with his wide grin, big heart and big feet.

However, amid all this Sussex talent, the voice of the critic could be heard. The Duke's scorer recorded that the Arundel Hospital XI's batting represented "pretty slow cricket" but added "mainly due to good fielding". The Duke would later enthuse about this early opportunity of taking part in a match with first-class cricketers - an ambition he was able to repeat in later years. On this occasion, however, his team was unable to reach a winning total despite some big hitting by the Sussex professional H. E. Hammond in which he was joined by George Cox Junior. 'Young George', as he would always be known, later told the author:

"This match meant a great deal to me. I had only just made my debut with the County and my father had retired three years earlier. We never played together for Sussex and this was the nearest we came to appearing together in cricket at the highest level. My father was highly critical about my enthusiasm for hitting the ball hard. However, I found that Duke Bernard was more than ready to encourage me and it was from that charity match onwards I formed my great love for cricket at Arundel and the way in which he liked to see the game played. So that is my first great memory of cricket there. The other is of the rocket which my father gave me when I got out hitting. And this despite the fact that I was then - as for so many years afterwards - simply obeying Duke Bernard's instructions to get on with it."

1930
August. Duke of Norfolk's XI 88 (G. D. Popplewell 5-19). Oxford O. T. C. 47 (R. Makins 6-12). Duke of Norfolk's XI won by 41 runs.

1931
July 4th and 5th. Duke of Norfolk's XI 243 (H. P. Hunloke 84, Col. R. T. Stanyforth 56 Capt. R. A. C. Foster 5-39) and 224-7 dec. Lord Eldon's XI 320 (Capt Llewellyn 115, P. Legge 54, Lord Eldon 50) and 104-4. Drawn.

1932
June 11th. Arundel Hospital XI 252 (R. G. S. Scott 55). Duke of Norfolk's XI 216-8 (H. E. Hammond 76*). Drawn

July 2nd and 3rd. Duke of Norfolk's XI 175 (Maj. T. E. G. Nugent 55) and 290-7 dec. (A. M. Crawley 155, C. S. Crawley 74). Lord Eldon's XI 195 (Capt. A. O. J. Hope 6-58) and 140 (Lord Eldon 56, A. M. Crawley 5-12). Duke of Norfolk's XI won by 130 runs.

CHAPTER THREE

The Last Pre-War Years 1933-1939

During the mid-thirties a regular pattern of cricket at Arundel emerged. The first and by now traditional fixture was the game against Lord Eldon's XI which took place at the end of June or the beginning of July. Because of the popularity of these games, Duke Bernard decided to organise a second series against Captain A. O. J. Hope's XI. These matches took place at the end of July or the beginning of August so that they would coincide with Goodwood Race week before the family and many of their friends went up for shooting at the Norfolks' Scottish home at Kinharvie.

Many of the personalities playing in both series of matches were the same but those involved in Lord Eldon's XI still represented the major country house rivalry between Arundel Castle and Longwood. In Lord Eldon's side this was reflected by an increasing determination to create team spirit in establishing his own colours. These manifested themselves in a somewhat garish cap and blazer. For his part, the Duke of Norfolk was content to have a side of many colours - preferably containing at least a few Oxbridge Blues.

The increased cricket activities meant that, with associated events and assorted camp followers, entertainment took place on a large scale. Much of this was directed by the ladies. Duke Bernard's three sisters were now all of an age to act as co-hostesses with their mother. They were also at the time of life when they and their girl friends had many suitors among the cricketing and other guests.

In the event, there were few cricket marriages. However, Lady Rachel would recall moments of drama as on the occasion when she refused a proposal from one of the military cricketers, "who seemed to assume that I should respond as if one were accepting the orders of a superior officer. When I refused, there was a great deal of fuss."

For Lady Winifrede, however, the choice of guests was heavily influenced by the family veto:

"As the youngest, I felt that the others would often gang up against me. I would say to Bernard and Rachel, 'Why don't we invite so and so down for the cricket?' And Rachel would say, 'Oh no, he is much too boring'. Bernard, typically, would add, 'And anyway, his cricket is not good enough.' "

The Duke's cousin, David Drummond (Lord Perth), has described how the activities of the cricketing wives were also not without internal dissension:

"As the cricket got keener and there was greater competition to be chosen, I noticed that quite a verbal battle developed about who was - justifiably or not - selected to play."

One of those who observed this scene with a certain detached amusement was Carrie Constable-Maxwell, the American wife of the Duke's cousin, Gerald Constable-Maxwell.

Extracts from her diaries in 1933 show what a fresh and lively mind and general *joie de vivre* she and others brought to the cricketing weekends. She described how most of the Eldon team would foregather at Longwood for dinner before leaving for Arundel the next morning. On this occasion, their party was made up of the two Scott brothers, the Llewellyns, the Hollands, the Forsters, and two cousins, Tony and Mary Buxton. Others who would be included in the travelling party were the carpenter and chauffeur at Longwood, together with their wives. The party set out reflecting in Carrie's words that "the weekend is always a riot and promises to be even more riotous this year." Despite the promised fun, there was an underlying serious note to the discussion at dinner on the eve of the match which was dominated by the current Depression and President Roosevelt's attempt to obtain international agreement over stabilisation of the dollar. As Carrie noted:

"Roosevelt has so far held out against the whole world. He is a great surprise to people. No one thought when he was elected that he had much conviction."

Dinner the next night after the cricket lived up to the

DUKE OF NORFOLK'S XI v CAPT. HOPE'S XI
29TH AND 30TH JULY 1933

CAPTAIN HOPE'S XI

	1st Innings						2nd Innings		
Major R. T. Stanyforth	b. Cobbold			13	Maj. R. T. Stanyforth		lbw. Rich		40
Major T. E. G. Nugent	b. Eldon			47	Maj. T. E. G. Nugent		b. Crawley		63
K. E. Crawley	b. Rich			5	K. E. Crawley		b. Crawley		17
R. H. Wethered	b. Cobbold			8	R. H. Wethered		c. Crawley b. Cobbold		3
M. Hornby	b. Hunloke			14	M. Hornby		lbw. Crawley		4
Capt. A. O. J. Hope	c. and b. Cobbold			39	Capt. A. O. J. Hope		c. Norfolk b. Cobbold		3
Capt. C. G. Lancaster	st. Home H. b. Poulter			12	Capt. C. G. Lancaster		b. Cobbold		48
Capt. J. Colvin	c. and b. Crawley			22	Capt. J. Colvin		c. Hunloke b. Home W.		16
Capt. C. Holland	not out			0	Capt. C. Holland		not out		14
Capt. W. Forbes	c. and b. Crawley			0	Earl of Hopetoun		c. Home H. b. Eldon		5
Earl of Hopetoun	did not bat				Capt. W. Forbes		b. Eldon		8
	Extras			6			Extras		4
	Total (for 9 wkts dec)			166			Total		225

Bowling

	O	M	R	W
Cobbold	19	2	49	3
Rich	16	4	37	1
Poulter	8	0	26	1
Eldon	3	0	21	1
Hunloke	5	1	21	1
Crawley	3.5	0	6	2

Bowling

	O	M	R	W
Hunloke	7	0	29	1
Rich	13	2	51	0
Cobbold	14	5	40	3
Poulter	5	0	32	0
Eldon	4	0	18	2
Norfolk	4	1	12	0
Crawley	6	1	22	3
Home W.	3	0	17	1

DUKE OF NORFOLK'S XI

	1st Innings						2nd Innings		
C. S. Crawley	b. Hornby			64	C. S. Crawley		c. Stanyforth b. Hornby		34
H. P. Hunloke	c. Hopetoun b. Hornby			22	H. P. Nunloke		b. Hornby		15
R. H. Cobbold	c. Hornby b. Hopetoun			56	R. H. Cobbold		c. Lancaster b. Hopetoun		5
Lord Eldon	c. Hope b. Hornby			18	Lord Eldon		c. Stanyforth b. Forbes		12
Hon.. H. D. Home	b. Hornby			1	Duke of Norfolk		b. Forbes		16
Hon.. W. L. D. Home	b. Hopetoun			12	Hon.. H. D. Home		b. Forbes		0
Sir E. Drummond	b. Hope			2	Hon.. W. L. D. Home		c. Crawley K. b Wethered		6
Duke of Norfolk	b. Hope			2	J. Rich		b. Hopetoun		15
J. Rich	st. Stanyforth b. Hope			2	Sir E. Drummond		b. Hopetoun		1
Capt. E. Mostyn	not out			3	Capt. E. Mostyn		not out		4
R. Poulter	b. Hope			0	R. Poulter		st. Stanyforth b. Forbes		14
	Extras			1			Extras		9
	Total			183			Total		131

Bowling

	O	M	R	W
Forbes	8	0	56	0
Hornby	15	1	59	4
Hopetoun	13	0	53	2
Hope	6	1	14	4

Bowling

	O	M	R	W
Hopetoun	17	2	45	3
Hornby	15	3	39	2
Forbes	6.4	0	19	4
Hope	3	1	5	0
Wethered	4	1	14	1

CAPT. HOPE'S XI WON BY 77 RUNS

promise of hilarity and was followed by "a wild time before going to bed." This apparently took the form of a series of pillow fights in the various guest bedrooms from which Carrie's husband desisted. Indeed, she "went to bed exhausted - only to find that he had gone to sleep an hour before".

Behind all this entertainment lay a great deal of planning. Carrie's diary records that only two weeks later they were back at Arundel for the Norfolks' ball at which there were 1200 guests. The Constable-Maxwells brought with them their American niece, Carol Hewlings, who was staying in England for the summer. Carrie noted that she was "much intrigued by the glitter of jewels and powdered footmen". Along with the other ladies in the party "we danced every dance and stayed until 3.30 a.m. enjoying every moment."

Such events and cricketing weekends required substantial organisation. As Lady Rachel Pepys recalled:

"We would have as many as 24 guest bedrooms occupied in the Castle over those weekends. Of course, there was no shortage of servants in those days and my main impression was the non-stop feeding arrangements. There would be a vast spread at breakfast with great quantities of food in silver chafing dishes to which the guests would help themselves as they drifted in and out and there would be fifty or so sitting down in the dining room at night."

Lady Rachel's youngest sister, Lady Winifrede Freeman, recalls the detailed preparation which went into these catering arrangements:

"Part of the daily routine was for my mother to have her regular meeting with Mrs Wallop. She was a tremendous character who had been a refugee from Belgium during the First World War. She was taken on as a scullery maid and came through the ranks to be head cook. She would arrive with her menu book and there would be a long discussion about meals for the weekend. Usually the fare was quite simple, but my mother knew how to feed young appetites. Even for a straightforward lunch, she would arrange with Mrs Wallop for something like croquettes, roast chicken (and always cold ham on the side), a pudding and a savoury. We were also quite non-denominational and there would be both fish and meat for the non-Catholic guests on a Friday. Then on Monday morning, Mrs Wallop and several of the staff would go off to London in a great big black bus to arrange dinner that night at our place in town, Norfolk House. This would be part of the London Season, and we would all return again to Arundel for those early summer weekends."

Lord Perth has described such weekends from the guests' point of view:

"We would all roll up on a Friday evening, some by car and some by train. Apart from those playing cricket, there would be a great crowd of camp followers. My aunt, Gwendy, was a wonderful person because she did not mind how many games we organised - even of the most violent kind indoors - and never worried about the furniture. On Saturdays, those not playing cricket were free to play golf or go to the sea but we would all forgather for a very large dinner on the Saturday night. My aunt expected you to go to Church on Sunday and no sporting activities were allowed before noon. But she would get very cross if you left that day. You were expected to stay until Monday morning and keep yourself occupied in the various Sunday afternoon sporting activities which were on offer. Sometimes there was cricket, but, in

my case, it was mostly golf, and I particularly enjoyed playing on the nine-hole course which my cousin Bernard created round the edge of the cricket ground.

"You drove off from the big oak tree which was planted in the Park during Queen Victoria's visit in 1845. There was a range of greens organised mostly on top of the bank which runs round the far side of the ground and we hit the ball back and forth across the playing area.

"I know my cousin Rachel has described her game involving her brother and Joyce and Roger Wethered. Well, the Wethereds would also take on Bernard and myself. My cousin was a better golfer than a cricketer but they would play a foursome against our better ball and they always won."

Despite these golfing and other diversions, Lord Perth was expected to play his part when required for cricket.

"I think I played in the 1933 match for Bernard against Jack Eldon's side to make up the number, as I was never much of a cricketer. I am also surprised to see that my father played for the Duke that year in a match against the Hope XI. He was quite an elderly gentleman at this stage and normally much preoccupied as Secretary General of the League of Nations. I think that our joint selection reflects the way in which, in those early days, it was possible to be roped in to make up the side."

Carrie Constable-Maxwell noted in her diary how this policy affected her husband:

"Gerald didn't go in today (he is the worst player on either team and does well to make half a dozen.) He is completely unabashed when he plays. Others, especially the good ones, are quite nervous but he says he has never been able to play cricket so he has no reason to start worrying now." The next day, she added, "Gerald went in to bat soon after the start and made his highest score on the ground. Everyone was amazed and he was loudly cheered." However she went on to reflect that he could not compare with Cosmo Crawley "who was by far the best player we saw on either side."

1933 was a vintage year for Cosmo Crawley. In the match against the Eldon XI he made 144 in just under two hours, of which 96 came in boundaries. He was well supported by his brother Kenneth, who marked his first appearance at Arundel with a half century. Another family link was strengthened when another leading run scorer, Henry Douglas Home, and later the playwright William Douglas Home, both came to play at Arundel with their brother Alec.

With the introduction of the series against the Hope XI,

there was scope for invitations to many old and new friends. Arthur Hope's side included several familiar faces, including Ronnie Stanyforth, Tim Nugent, Kenneth Crawley, Roger Wethered, Juby Lancaster and the Forbes twins, of whom David was a fast bowler and Willie a useful attacking batsman.

Another pair of twins who would feature prominently in matches at Arundel during the Thirties were the sons of the Marquess of Linlithgow, Lord Hopetoun and Lord John Hope. Lord Glendevon (as Lord John Hope subsequently became) provided a detailed picture of matches against the Hope and Eldon XIs when reminiscing at his home in Guernsey in 1993:

"My brother Charlie was a genuine cricketer and could hold his own with anyone in these matches. He had been twelfth man at Eton where the best I could manage was something equivalent to the 4th XI. So, as in that first match against the Hope XI, I was sitting it out on the sidelines. But we were always invited to Arundel together and we had a great deal of fun. It is fascinating looking back at some of the characters whom we then thought of simply as useful cricketers, and who became rather distinguished gentlemen.

"Two of the Duke's best bowlers stick in my mind. There was Ralph Cobbold who had got his Blue at Cambridge only a few years earlier. He only played serious cricket for a few years as his responsibilities at Justerini and Brooks kept him busy which is why he subsequently became their Chairman. The other fast bowler whom I have particular reason to recall was one of the Forbes twins, David. He was fearsomely fast and on my first appearance at Arundel, he clean bowled me first ball. As I came off the field, Henry Hunloke, who enjoyed getting a dig in, said: 'I am sorry I missed your innings. I went into the tent to change my boots as you went out to bat. I made a lightning change only to find you on your way back. I suppose you were out first ball.' Ignoring the implied insult I said - I thought with reasonable *sang-froid* - 'Well I can only say that I didn't notice another one.'

"There were so many interesting characters around. I remember Willy Hill-Wood whose father was the M.P., Sir Samuel Hill-Wood. They each in turn became Chairman of Arsenal Football Club. Another M.P. who was a regular was Aubrey Fletcher. Racing was well represented with Sir Humphrey de Trafford. His father had captained Leicestershire and he would follow in his footsteps as a great horse breeder and a respected figure on the Turf. And then there was another of the connections with the Royal Family in Lord Gage, who was a Lord-in-Waiting and owned the great Sussex pile, Firle Place, near Lewes.

"Two of the other newcomers whom I recall on the Arundel scene have both made their mark in different ways. The first was Ronald Strutt, who later succeeded his father as Lord Belper. He would play a lot of cricket for Bernard.

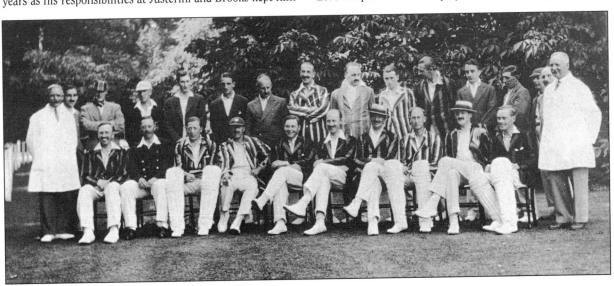

Duke of Norfolk's XI v Lord Eldon's XI, 1935.
Back row (L to R, players only): P. Legge, C. Holland, G. Maxwell, T. Nugent, R. Foster, H. Hunloke, R. Wethered,
A. Maxwell, R. Poulter.
Front row (L to R): Lord Dunglass, M. Llewelyn, M. Scott, R. Chichester-Constable, Duke of Norfolk, Lord Eldon, A. Hope,
K. Homan, C. Crawley, H. Douglass-Home.

DUKE OF NORFOLK'S XI V SUSSEX MARTLETS
1ST JULY 1935

DUKE OF NORFOLK'S XI

H. P. Hunloke	b. E. Harrison	28
R. Cobbold	b. Turner-Inman	1
C. S. Crawley	b. Turner-Inman	18
Lord Dunglass	b. E. Harrison	57
R. H. Wethered	lbw. b. E. Harrison	41
Lord Hopetoun	lbw. b. Atkinson	33
Hon.. W. D. Home	lbw. b. E. Harrison	13
Duke of Norfolk	b. E. Harrison	0
M. Fox	run out	6
J. A. H. Greville	b. Turner-Inman	2
R. Poulter	not out	4
	Extras	6
	Total	209

Bowling

	O	M	R	W
E. Harrison	18	2	95	5
Turner-Inman	18	3	72	3
J. Harrison	5	0	26	0
Somerset	1	0	6	0
Atkinson	1	0	4	1

SUSSEX MARTLETS

J. K. Mathews	st. Home b. Dunglass	11
M. P. Atkinson	b. Cobbold	21
A. Worlock	b. Cobbold	21
R. J. Martin	c. Crawley b. Greville	7
H. S. Mather	c.&b. Cobbold	3
H. E. Bowen	b. Cobbold	2
J. S. Harrison	c. Norfolk b. Dunglass	7
J. Langley	st. Home b. Dunglass	2
E. E. Harrison	not out	3
A. F. Somerset	b. Cobbold	0
P. Turner-Inman	b. Cobbold	4
	Extras	10
	Total	110

Bowling

	O	M	R	W
Dunglass	12	2	26	3
Poulter	6	2	11	0
Hopetoun	4	0	15	0
Cobbold	8.2	0	30	6
Fox	2	0	12	0
Greville	2	0	8	1

DUKE OF NORFOLK'S XI WON BY 99 RUNS

Perhaps even more significantly, he and his sister Lavinia came on to the Norfolk family scene and it wasn't long before she became Duke Bernard's wife.

"In the wider sporting sense, the character who stands out was Sir John Masterman. He was a Don at Oxford where he had been a very fine athlete and had represented England at hockey and lawn tennis. He was a useful all-round cricketer but it was in playing tennis in the Titling Yard that he came into his own.

"I suppose this was all part of what Stephen Potter would later describe as 'gamesmanship'. When a ball landed near the baseline on his side of the court in doubles, Masterman would turn to his partner and shout 'How?' He later explained to me that this was a legitimate enquiry whether the ball was in or out but often his strangulated tones would be taken for a cry of 'out'. As he was one of the more senior figures in the party, this often did the trick when his younger and polite opponents would concede the point."

Apart from the matches against the Eldon and Hope XIs, the most significant development at this time was the start of the series of games against the Sussex Martlets. This club contained many of the leading amateur cricketers in the County. Their sides were run for many years by the Somerset family from Castle Goring and, from the mid-Thirties, by the Matthews family of Worthing.

Their second match against the Duke in 1935 is of special interest since it introduced to Arundel cricket E. E. Harrison. Eddie Harrison is the son of E. R. Harrison, a local industrialist, who had been Duke Henry's King of Spades and regular croquet opponent. The son would become Secretary of the Sussex Martlets for over 30 years and, eventually, take on the organisation of many of the games played under the Duke's name. His recollection of his first appearance on the ground could hardly have been less auspicious:

"I was young and keen at this stage and could bowl reasonably fast. I was very much in awe of our Captain, J. K. Matthews. Although he was then over 50, he had only just given up playing for Sussex and he was a bit of a martinet. Anyway, I see from the records of the match that I bowled a lot of overs and I was very happy when I dismissed some of the Duke's most successful performers. When I got my third wicket, I was particularly delighted as I clean bowled Lord Dunglass who made top score for the Duke and His Grace was next man in. Totally oblivious to what you have described as the laws of cricket as decreed by the Duke, I took an extra long run and bowled him all over the place first ball. I then stood on a hat trick and was feeling very pleased with myself. However, I noticed there wasn't much sign of celebration and I became aware of J. K. bearing down upon me. 'That was the most appalling piece of bad manners I have ever seen', he said. 'You are to take the first opportunity you can to apologise to the Duke and if you ever do that again on his ground you need not expect to be picked to play under my captaincy again.'

Lord Eldon sporting his team colours.

Lord Dunglass and fellow players studying the play.

Henry Hunloke greets the Duke.

Captain Hope with the ladies.

Cosmo Crawley recovering from his exertions.

"The sequel was interesting. The innings ended soon afterwards and I made haste to apologise. The Duke fixed me with his famous icy look and said 'You will never play against me on this ground again.' My heart sank but then, thank God, a twinkle appeared as he added, 'In future, you will always play for me on this ground.' "

The Duke's command (which would be respected for more than forty years) was soon put into effect. Only weeks later Eddie Harrison was required to play for the Duke's side against the Hope XI. His major contribution came first in the unexpected role of batsman. Coming in to bat when the score stood at 65 for 7 - he and the Duke added 82 and together with the Sussex wicket-keeper, John Eaton, he was involved in a ninth wicket stand of 105. When it came to bowling, he was also actively engaged in 18 overs which produced 4 wickets for 65.

The other new face in the Duke's team in this match had been recruited by his sister, Lady Rachel Pepys:

"The game was due to take place at the end of the Goodwood summer meeting and my brother said, 'I am going to be one short. Can you look out for someone for me at the Races?.' Well I was going to the Ladies' Day on Thursday and the match was on the Saturday and I thought that it might be much too short notice. However, when I got to the Races, I saw someone whom I had seen at dances in London and whom I vaguely knew as having something to do with cricket. So I asked him if he might be free to play and he said he would be delighted. When I saw Bernard that evening I told him I had found a cricketer. 'And who might that be?' he asked. I said, 'Its someone called Allen, I think they call him Gubby'. 'Well' my brother replied 'you haven't done badly. He is only the fastest bowler in England and the only problem is that I won't dare use him.'

The records of the match show that Gubby Allen was not called on to bowl but, opening the batting in the second innings for the Duke, he scored a stylish century of which he would later recall:

"Country house cricket like that at Arundel was important for me particularly in batting as my business commitments made it difficult for me to play much County cricket. So far as bowling and generally keeping fit were concerned, I would bowl in the nets and run round the ground at Lords after office work in the summer but I needed to bat in the middle. The general effect of regular club and country house cricket can't have been too bad as I got the captaincy of the England side to go to Australia in the following year."

The other new fixture in 1935 reflected the Duke's local and military commitments. A game was arranged against the Arundel branch of the British Legion which was effectively made up of members from the neighbouring Arundel Cricket Club. Their most dangerous performer was a local coal heaver, Ernie Blackall, who was their regular fast bowler.

In the game played on 4 August, the British Legion's score was kept in check by skilful and unorthodox bowling from J. C. Masterman. The Duke's side were then given a reasonable opportunity of achieving victory thanks to a stand of 116 for the second wicket between Tim Nugent and Cosmo Crawley. Thereafter, wickets fell regularly mainly due to the fast bowling of Ernie Blackall. However, the Duke batting at number 6 had perhaps his finest hour at Arundel in carrying his bat while still pursuing the faint prospect of victory. One of his opponents was Jim Peach, a local reporter, who would later recall:

"I think that this was probably the fastest bowling the Duke had ever faced but he stuck it out and saved his side. For ever afterwards, when the local Arundel team took on his side, he would always ask, 'Have you brought Blackall with you?'

1936 saw a repeat of the by now traditional fixtures against Lord Eldon's XI, the Sussex Martlets and Captain Hope's XI. The Duke's side relied mainly on his regulars but there were some interesting new faces. Chief among them was the emergence of the Ford clan. Neville Ford had made his debut for the Duke's XI in the match against the British Legion in the previous year. In 1936, his brothers Edward and Christopher (who were twins) made their first appearances for, respectively, the Eldon and Hope XIs.

As a trio, the three brothers could virtually match the skill of the Crawley brothers with whom they were closely linked. The Fords were the sons of the Very Rev Lionel Ford, Headmaster of Repton, later of Harrow and then Dean of York. Aidan Crawley takes up the story of the family connection:

"My father was a Canon at York Cathedral when Lionel Ford was the Dean and Neville Ford and I were at Harrow together when his father was the Headmaster. In fact, our sporting lives became almost inextricably linked. We were both in the XI at Harrow together and we were in the same side at Oxford. By the time we met up again at Arundel, he was playing occasional games for Derbyshire and I turned out for Kent.

"He was well over six feet tall, a bit awkward in movement but a fine striker of the ball. The only snag was that he was quite vague about running between the wickets and you had to watch out for his calling which was often non-existent but he was a charming companion and so, although I knew them less well, were his brothers the twins Edward and Christopher who were also useful performers."

Edward Ford was then a student at the Inner Temple. Now in his retirement after long service as Assistant Private Secretary to both King George VI and Queen Elizabeth II, he is modest about his cricketing prowess:

"I was always just below the line in cricketing ability in my family. I was twelfth man for Eton. Then I went up to New College at Oxford and got a Freshman's Trial but I was bowled neck and crop for very few by Ian Peebles. By the time I appeared at Arundel my main cricket was played for the Eton Ramblers whose chief character at the time was Brian Johnston.

"Great things were expected of us as a cricketing family. Three of my uncles had played for Cambridge and Middlesex. F. G. J. was good enough to win Test caps in Australia and W. J. was regarded as one of the biggest hitters of his day. As for my father, he was described as the best bowler in England for one ball because he could bowl off the wrong foot and confuse batsmen with his first delivery.

"Of my brothers, Neville was the star, but my twin, Christopher, was an exceptionally fast bowler who brought the ball down from his full six feet seven inches. He and I had a marvellous introduction to cricket at Arundel in 1936. We were very close to the Crawleys who were already the established stars there and my brother Neville knew the Duke well from the days when they were both studying with an Oxford crammer called Mr Theodopolous. Why Christ Church, in those days of relaxed academic standards, failed to offer the Earl Marshal a place I shall never know, but he was very faithful to his regulars from the Oxbridge sporting scene.

"But he also liked to bring in figures from his other worlds. I remember there was one of the racing Cecils playing in the 1936 matches and, when I played for the Eldon XI that year, I had quite a time keeping out a very steady bowler called Father O'Donnell. He was no doubt in the side as one of the Duke's favourite sporting priests and I see he got me out cheaply in the second innings of the match."

The Eldon XI game to which Sir Edward Ford (as he is today) refers was to prove the last game in the series between Longwood and Arundel Castle. Sir Edward is typically modest about his own performance on that occasion. In fact he made the second highest score in his side's first innings and took six for 42 (of which the first four were all clean bowled) when the Duke's XI were chasing runs in their second innings.

The other star of the match was Lord Dunglass. He not only took eight wickets but scored his first century on the ground. For the two captains, there were also moments to savour at the end of this series. Lord Eldon made top score in his team's second innings while struggling to avoid defeat. On the other hand, the Duke helped to bring his side to victory when he took the ninth wicket, that of his cousin Gerald Constable-Maxwell, who was stumped by another of the brothers playing in the match, William Douglas-Home. With this victory for the home team, by 126 runs, the series came to an end with the balance of matches standing at eight wins for the Duke, two wins for Lord Eldon's XI, and two matches drawn.

The last match of the 1936 season against Arthur Hope's XI achieved special recognition with the emergence of the first Arundel Castle cricketing poet laureate, the Hon. Reggie Winn. One of the sons of Lord Headley and St Oswald, he had been playing occasional matches for the Duke since 1934. On this occasion, he contrived with a fine display of impartiality to incorporate the names of eight of the Hope XI and seven members of the home team in the lines which follow:

> Cricket on the Castle Green,
> Everybody very keen.
> Lovely girls, and charming boys,
> Lots of mirth and lots of noise.
> Stanyforth, with royal mien,
> Bats as if before the Queen.
> Cecil never lets us down,
> In for life, the silly clown.
> Cosmo, keen as mustard still,
> Swallows many a bitter pill.
> The ball is nestling in a thicket,
> Harrow's missed another wicket.
> Arthur Hope, the clumsy lout,
> Receives the ball upon the snout.
> Masterman's a clever bowler,
> But he needs the heavy roller.
> Eldon's like a canny Scot,
> When he bowls, he thinks a lot.

Lord William sports his cricket coat,
His costume wins the Tatler's vote.
Complete with stripes and panama
He's really Wisden's Lochinvar.
Hunloke, by a monstrous fluke,
Obtains a single from the Duke.
Lancaster, as if in fun,
Treats the game as Tip and Run.
This is not quite understood
By poor big boy Peter Wood.
He would never make the grade
But for Cosmo, who has made
Just another cricket bloomer;
Over keen, he has no humour.
A man is missing, I can tell it,
The game's afoot without Flash Kellett.
No batsman ever could feel safe
When face to face with deadly Ralph.
He spins the ball in such a way
That umpires say its not in play.
What would cricket on the lawn be,
If we left out Michael Hornby,
And, now I've mentioned big man Ford,
I'll stop this poem, 'cos I'm bored.

1936 marked the end of the country house rivalry between Longwood and Arundel Castle. It also saw the ending of the partnership between mother and son in receiving guests at their home. The new partnership which replaced it was formed when Duke Bernard and the Hon. Lavinia Strutt married in January 1937 and Duchess Gwendy took her daughters to live at her ancestral home at Everingham in Yorkshire.

Any fears that there might be a change in the pattern of entertainment at Arundel or the warm and welcoming atmosphere which Duchess Gwendy had created were soon dispelled. Duchess Lavinia quickly showed her enormous enthusiasm and drive in all she undertook. Moreover, she was an accomplished sportswoman having competed at Junior Wimbledon. She and Lord John Hope would soon establish a reputation as leading players on the country house circuit. However, it was said that her romance with Duke Bernard had blossomed not while her brother had been playing cricket for him but on the hunting field. She would later recall:

"My main sporting interest was and is in horses. But the thirties were a marvellous time to be alive and I was so lucky to find that I could join in with such a vast crowd of family and friends. I therefore made no attempt to organise any aspect of the cricket. This had been put in place years before and it was Bernard's thing. The staff knew exactly how to carry on with the entertainment of the guests as they had done for many years."

Most of these guests would increasingly be drawn into the Royal activities of 1937. Duke Bernard had been active in his duties as Earl Marshal virtually without a break since the Silver Jubilee of King George V in 1935, the King's funeral arrangements which followed in 1936 together with the uncertainties created by the Abdication Crisis. It seems likely that these events and the massive planning operation which went into the preparation of the aborted Coronation in 1936 and the crowning of King George VI and Queen Elizabeth in 1937 may explain why he and Lord Eldon were unable to organise a return cricket match in 1937.

Certainly, many of their cricketing guests would soon be involved in Royal duties. The Lords Perth, Hopetoun and John Hope were all asked by the Duke to be Ushers at the Coronation. As Lord Perth said :

"I shall always remember that year as one of frantic activity between London and Arundel. Of course it was all much more of an amateur show in the pre-television days but Bernard rounded up many of his friends and relations to help. He had some assistance early on as Earl Marshal from his uncle Lord Edmund Fitzalan-Howard who did the job temporarily until he came of age. However, by the time of the Coronation, Bernard was operating his own show and I can well recall the effective way in which he despatched business at the briefing which he gave at Norfolk House in London. He made a very crisp and short introduction and then invited questions. The Archbishop of Canterbury seemed to be totally pre-occupied in seeking advice on what permutations of religious regalia he should wear to which Bernard simply replied ' I suggest you look to the Almighty'. Then a very senior military man said, 'What do we do in the event of torrential rain?' to which came the reply,' We shall all get very wet.' "

The Coronation took place on 12 May 1937. Many of those who had been directly involved were among the guests when the Duke gathered his cricketing friends and their supporters together on 26 June to resume his traditional series of games against Arthur Hope's XI.

Perhaps the most spectacular guest was the young

Maharajah of Cooch-Behar. He had come to the Coronation as one of the bejewelled representatives of the Indian Princes who swore allegiance to the new Monarch. Despite his official duties, he was widely regarded as one of the most fast moving playboys of those last carefree pre-war days. With his taste for sports cars and attractive actresses, he was also a dashing figure on the polo and cricket fields.

His drinking capacity was also legendary. Indeed, it would be demonstrated to the full when he gave hospitality of such a lavish kind as almost to undermine the playing ability of Lord Tennyson's touring side to India later that year. He would later tell the author that, on his first appearance at Arundel, he was not exactly feeling at his best.

"When I got out for a duck, Bernard didn't say much to me. Moreover, when we had been in the field for some time, it was pretty obvious that I wasn't at my most sprightly, and he said, 'What you need is a good bowl'. Sure enough he put me on with Willy Forbes and together we polished off the tail."

When the Forbes/Cooch-Behar combination also got in the runs in the second innings together with Cosmo Crawley, the Duke was able to declare and to achieve a comfortable victory. Afterwards, he said to the Maharajah:

"Your efforts in this match were a triumph of natural ability over lack of preparation."

Lord John Hope also has good reason to remember this game and the dinner which followed it.

"My brother Charlie and I took some hammer when the Duke's team were chasing runs before making a declaration. However I did have the modest satisfaction of dismissing both Cosmo Crawley and Cooch-Behar.

"But my brother and I were put on the spot at dinner that night. Everyone egged Bernard on to tell a story about the Coronation and the one he chose to tell did not quite show us at our dignified best. We had done our duty in the Abbey as Ushers at the Coronation but afterwards we went out to a series of parties. We finished up in Trafalgar Square which was packed with a massive crowd celebrating the Coronation atmosphere. For some reason, we thought that Bernard ought to get proper recognition for his tremendous work. So we started chanting, 'We want the Earl Marshal.' Quite soon we had gathered a large section of the crowd around us and we marched from Trafalgar Square to the bottom of St James' and lined up in front of Norfolk House. By now we were all shouting in unison, 'We want the Earl Marshal'. Sure enough he came out onto the balcony. I

think he was quite pleased at the time but then he saw my brother and me. 'You bloody fools', he said, and rapidly disappeared inside.

"At dinner that night, he told the story in a tone of mock severity. But somehow, from that time onwards, Charlie and I were expected to be the court jesters at Arundel cricket."

However, the court jesters were unavailable for the return match against the Hope XI in 1938. Useful contributions from the Duke's regulars ensured that his side once again achieved a comfortable victory despite the most successful bowling in the match for the Hope XI by David Stephens.

The tables were turned in 1939 when Dunglass, Stephens, Masterman and Millbank shared the wickets to dismiss the Duke's team for 55. The Hope XI fared little better in making 80 against Harrison, Carver and Winn. Steady batting in the second innings by the Duke's regulars aided by joint top score of 42 from a newcomer, the young trainee lawyer Arthur Collins, allowed the Duke to make a sporting declaration but Captain Hope's XI won the match thanks to a half century from the ever-consistent Major Venables-Llewellyn and an undefeated 34 from Lord Hopetoun batting at number 10.

After the match, there was a final opportunity for the court jesters to resume their comedy routine when Charlie Hopetoun and his brother were called on to entertain after dinner. Lord John Hope recalls:

"By June 1939 we all realised that War was inevitable. We even clubbed together to give Bernard and Lavinia a silver cigarette box inscribed with the signatures of most of those who had taken part in the Eldon and Hope XI games. There was therefore almost a feverish sense of gaiety in what, for many of us, would be the last great country house party of the thirties.

"Charlie and I were persuaded to put on one or two sketches in which we made fun of some of those present. Perhaps our most effective effort was in appearing as two race-goers watching the second race at a Goodwood meeting. In the first race Bernard had an entry which finished last. So we pretended that we were watching the start of the second race. We gave a sort of joint running commentary in which we described how the field was all bunched together and then Charlie said, 'Hang on a minute. There's one horse that's way out in front - he must have got an absolute flyer.' To which my reply was, 'Don't be such a damned fool - that's Norfolk's horse finishing the first race.' I know it all sounds pretty mild now but we all felt the need to cheer ourselves up and that party was the last many of us would really celebrate for a very long time."

Victory for the Hope XI in June 1939 was to prove the last in a series which ended in favour of the Duke's team by five matches to three. After that game, there was time for two more informal matches before the outbreak of war. Each in their own way, was a sign of things to come. The match played on 16 July was against the Michelgrove stable lads and the Duke's side was no doubt a reflection of Duchess Lavinia's priorities. As one of the participants said:

"I think it was the Duchess who gave us the chance to play cricket at that time. She and the Duke were great ones for entertaining us at Christmas parties and so forth. On one of these occasions, she told us that there were three priorities in her life and they were her family, her animals (especially the dogs) and we young stable lads."

The match itself was also remarkable as a Strutt family gathering. The Duchess' brother, Ronald, had now succeeded to the family title of Lord Belper and he and his sons, the Hon. Peter Strutt and Rupert Strutt, took part in the game. They represented the family in the match as Duke Bernard was injured and the rest of his team was made up mainly of those working on the Estate. Details of the match are sketchy but it seems to have been settled as an honourable

draw after several of the stable lads retired voluntarily to give everyone an innings.

A similarly friendly atmosphere prevailed when, following his father's example, Duke Bernard arranged a military match against the Grenadier Guards who were undergoing training in the Park. Again, there are few details but enough is known to tell us that the Guardsmen declared at 125 for 4. In reply, Duke Bernard and Cosmo Crawley put on 71 for the first wicket which, together with an undefeated fourth wicket stand between P. Bisset and W. O'Byrne, saw his team home by seven wickets.

On this happy note, the Duke's pre-war cricketing activities came to an end. It was, as Duchess Lavinia has indicated, a wonderful time in their lives. Perhaps the mood of the period and the lighthearted atmosphere which prevailed was well summed up by the Castle's second poet laureate, the Hon. Peter Wood. The Wood family were known to Duke Bernard through their Yorkshire and government connections. Peter Wood's father, Lord Halifax, was the current Foreign Secretary then grappling with the problems of growing German militarism. Peter Wood had grown up in India while his father was Viceroy and where he became a cricket fanatic. This enthusiasm was sustained when he went to Eton and led to the development of cricket weeks at the Halifax family seat at Garrowby involving Eton masters as

The Duke leads his team off the field for the last time before the Second World War – v Third Battalion, Grenadier Guards, 5 July 1939.

well as school and later Cambridge friends. Exceptionally tall, he is recalled as a handsome young man of strong personality who displayed early talent with the pen.

He played for the Duke as a useful batsman on a number of occasions from 1936 onwards and, in these last pre-war days, added his own irreverent assessment of the atmosphere of cricket at the castle:

Beneath the stately Dukely trees
His Grace's peasants, on their knees,
Were praying that His Grace might not
Be beaten by the first he got.
A scene like this seems strange to you,
But then, the Duke had told them to.
They knelt; they watched; then mighty yells,
And ringing of the Castle bells,
Announced their prayers were not in vain.
He scored a three; they knelt again,
With perspiration on their brow.
They bob and duck, salaam, kow-tow,
As Ladies Katherine, Rachel and
The Duchess, pass them, hand in hand.
Prostrate they lie upon the turf
Until the order: "Rise up serf"
Is given by the Master Butler
(I think it's so - or is it Cutler?)
With smiling condescension they
Pursue their slow and regal way;
But never joining in the prayers
Of those who live "beneath the stairs".
(Now, do not think that I'm a snob,
To tell the truth is but my job).
But I digress, I think that we
Had said His Grace had scored a three.
Now, aided by his peasants' prayers,
His Grace, forgetting all his fears
Of being caught out in the deep,
Indulges in a mighty sweep.
Alas! But prayers are not enough
For second slip has done his stuff.

The peasants rise up to a man
And offer what applause they can.
They clap, they shout, they scream, they cheer
A Bolshy one was heard to jeer.
Two flunkies seized him by the throat
And hurled him in the Castle Moat.
The rest all cried: "A Batsman true!"
But then - the Duke had told them to!

1933

July 1st and 2nd, Duke of Norfolk's XI 317 (C. S. Crawley 144, K. Crawley 54, Capt. R. A. C. Foster 6-126) and 72 (R. Poulter 5-27). Lord Eldon's XI 167 (J. Macrae 5-44) and 153 (Capt. A. O. J. Hope 6-38). Duke of Norfolk's XI won by 69 runs.

1935

August 3rd and 5th. Duke of Norfolk's XI 253 (J. Eaton 92*, J. C. Masterman 6-72) and 217 (G. C. Allen 133). Capt. Hope's XI 269 (G. R. Cox 69, C. S. Crawley 60*) and 202-7 (A. Pearce 50). Capt. Hope's XI won by 3 wickets.

August 4th. British Legion, Arundel Branch 244 (B. Carver 73, J. C. Masterman 6-60). Duke of Norfolk's XI 204-8 (Maj. T. E. G. Nugent 56, C. S. Crawley 56, E. Blackall 5-68). Drawn.

1936

June 27th and 28th. Duke of Norfolk's XI 260 (Lord Dunglass 100, Capt. A. O. J. Hope 56), and 103-7 dec (Sir E. Ford 6-42). Lord Eldon's XI 131 and 109 (Lord Dunglass 6-32). Duke of Norfolk's XI won by 123 runs.

August 1st and 3rd. Capt. Hope's XI 164 and 140 (R. H. Cobbold 7-42). Duke of Norfolk's XI 222 (H. P. Hunloke 76, R. H. Cobbold 70, J. C. Masterman 6-46) and 86-1. Duke of Norfolk's XI won by 9 wickets.

1937

June 26th and 27th. Duke of Norfolk's XI 155 (Hon.. R. Strutt 53, Maj. Erskine 50) and 236-6 dec. (W. E. Forbes 87, C. S. Crawley 57). Capt. Hope's XI 92 and 139. Duke of Norfolk's XI won by 160 runs.

1939

June 24th and 25th. Duke of Norfolk's XI 55 and 198-9 dec. (D. Stephens 5-38). Capt. Hope's XI 80 and 177-8 (Maj. C. M. Llewellyn 59). Capt. Hope's XI won by 2 wickets.

CHAPTER FOUR

Sussex Connections 1951-1952

At the end of the War, it seemed that the Duke's cricketing days were over and with them the resumption of matches at Arundel.

As was the case after the First World War, there was a long gap before cricket was re-started at Arundel. Peter Wood was no longer available to bat for the Duke or to compose his own special brand of poetry. He had been killed in the war as had, among others, the Forbes twins, the dashing Earl of Erne, the unusually tall fast bowler Christopher Ford, and the two Brigadiers, Mike Llewellyn and Charles Trappes-Lomax.

The Duke had major wartime responsibilities. He had commanded a company of the Royal Sussex Regiment in France before being evacuated at Dunkirk. Then, like his father before him, he accepted a post in Government when he became Joint Parliamentary Secretary at the Ministry of Agriculture in Winston Churchill's war time administration. Now, at the age of 43, it seemed that his active cricket days had ended.

The Duke and his entire family were now sharing a passion for horses based, in large part, on the training and breeding at their stables under the direction of the Smyths father and son. The Duke became the King's representative at Ascot in 1945 (and he would assume similar responsibilities on behalf of Queen Elizabeth II.) Duchess Lavinia, while equally keen on horse-racing, had increasing success as one of the best horsewomen in the country in showing her hunters. She was soon joined in the junior classes at horse shows by her four daughters who showed similar enthusiasm and horse riding skills.

Apart from these activities, the Duke was playing a full part in his native county. In 1949 he became Lord Lieutenant, a role which he was to fill for a quarter of a century. A member of West Sussex County Council since 1937, he would soon become its Chairman. In these and in other responsibilities he became famous for his business-like methods and his sense of priorities. When arriving to chair meetings, he would often say: "It may be for the convenience of all present if I advise you that I shall be leaving for Ascot at 12 noon precisely and I propose to organise the agenda accordingly."

With these and his national responsibilities as Earl Marshal and as spokesman for the Catholic laity of England, it seemed that there was little likelihood of his return to an active cricket involvement. However, his links with two organisations were to ensure renewed cricket activities at the Castle.

During his war time service, the Duke had become a great admirer of his commanding officer in the Royal Sussex Regiment who was now General Sir Lashmer Whistler. The General had played a critical role in the D-Day landings in Normandy, when he led the 3rd Infantry Division in the march all the way from France to Northern Germany. He was now living in Sussex and had told Duke Bernard of his concern to maintain links with those who had served in the Regiment during the war. This was a theme close to the Duke's heart. He was quick to send gifts on hearing of the ill health of those who had served under him. Now, when the General raised the possibility of a cricket match involving the Royal Sussex Regiment, the Duke was eager to respond.

So it was that on 1 July 1951, a series of military matches began at the Castle which would last until 1982. One of those who turned out for the Regiment was the newly commissioned Second Lieutenant, J. R. A. Stephenson. Early in 1994, when he had just retired as Secretary of the M.C.C., Colonel John Stephenson recalled the start of the series and some of the military participants:

"Our General who, for some reason, had acquired the nickname of Bolo while he was on secondment in Russia, was always a prime mover. He never went to Staff College

DUKE OF NORFOLK'S XI V ROYAL SUSSEX REGIMENT
1ST JULY 1951

ROYAL SUSSEX REGIMENT

Maj. J. O. Lintott	b. Pelham	13
Maj. R. G. Hunt	lbw. Ford	2
L/C E. G. Lukes	b. Pelham	4
O/C. R. N. Chappell	c. Pelham b. Ford	21
Major J. B. A. Glennie	b. Pelham	16
Cpt. J. Norris	c. Sub. b. Hedley	11
Maj. A. Shields	b. Ford	6
2/Lt. J. R. Stephenson	c. Pelham b. Carr-Gomm	11
Maj. J. A. P. Bartlett	b. Pelham	17
R. Q. M. S. F. Thomas	not out	3
M. Fleming	c. and b. Pelham	12
	Extras	9
	Total	125

Bowling

	O	M	R	W
Pelham	20	2	65	5
Ford	17	4	32	3
Hedley	2	0	8	1
Carr-Gomm	2	0	11	1

DUKE OF NORFOLK'S XI

C. S. Crawley	b. Bartlett	18
C. E. Underdown	b. Fleming	10
Hon. R. Strutt	c. sub. b. Fleming	0
A. M. Hedley	c. Norris b. Hunt	41
Duke of Norfolk	c. Lintott b. Fleming	0
A. Collins	run out	1
Sir E. Ford	c. Stevenson b. Hunt	1
Lord J. Hope	b. Fleming	10
R. Carr-Gomm	not out	10
A. G. Pelham	st. Norris b. Hunt	12
G. R. Smyth	b. Fleming	2
	Extras	3
	Total	108

Bowling

	O	M	R	W
Fleming	17	6	42	5
Bartlett	11	0	33	1
Hunt	7.1	2	18	3
Thomas	2	0	12	0

ROYAL SUSSEX REGIMENT WON BY 17 RUNS

and yet he had gone to the very top in the Army. He was a real man's man and I am not surprised that Duke Bernard wanted to help him in maintaining his links with the Regiment.

"What also impressed me was the Duke's manners and attention to detail. When I arrived as an absolutely new boy, he greeted me with the words: 'How do you do, John.' I had never met him before and it was the same when I came back year after year, he always remembered your name even when - as in my case - there was at least a year's gap between meet-

ings. The other thing I recall is that there were very few supporters in those days and the only facilities were inside a rather scruffy old marquee. But the Duke had specially ordered deck chairs in alternate colours of orange and blue which were the Regimental colours. There was also splendid hospitality and dinner at the Castle and he paid for the lot.

"I had just come out of Sandhurst and I was literally on my way to Egypt to join my battalion. When I came down to Arundel for the first time, I thought - with all the arrogance of youth - that I was in with a lot of old buffers. Looking down the batting list, Major Jack Lintott was a war time officer and Major Robert Hunt was a pre-war Cambridge allrounder who played occasional games for Sussex after the War. Corporal Lukes was an unknown quantity but Officer Cadet Robin Chappell was still at Sandhurst and I suppose they wanted some young blood. He was a good cricketer who had captained the side at Wellington and he, like me, was to play for the Regiment throughout the series. Major Jack Glennie had commanded one of our battalions at the age of 26 in North Africa. Whilst there he captured the German General, Von Arnheim, which was one of the high spots of the campaign. He went on with the Regiment through the Italian campaign and got a D.S.O. Sadly, he is no longer with us, but he was a really good, decent, super chap. After the war, he had been demoted (as was the custom after accelerated wartime promotion) but he went up to command the Regiment and later became a Brigadier. He was a very good club cricketer and a splendid captain for our side for many years. Corporal Norris was a regular soldier who went on to become a Sergeant Major. He was stationed at the Regimental Depot in Chichester, as were R. Q. M. S. Thomas and M. Fleming who was a civilian employee. This leaves Major Shields and Major Bartlett who were both wartime officers."

For his first post-war side, the Duke relied on a number of his pre-war friends in Cosmo Crawley, his brother-in-law Ronald Strutt, Arthur Collins (who was now a leading lawyer in the racing world), Lord John Hope and Sir Edward Ford. Of the rest, Sir Edward recalls:

"I was intrigued to see Edward Underdown play. He was then at the height of his success with the Rank Film Studios and he showed himself a 'dasher' who would score runs if it came off and who would turn out for the Duke on many future occasions. Our top scorer Tony Hedley was also a very useful player who was around for a long time as was - perhaps inevitably - Bernard's assistant trainer, Gordon Smyth.

But my chief recollection of this and a number of the post-war games in which I played was the beautiful bowling action of Tony Pelham, the steadiness of the long serving Sussex committee man, Dr David Rice, and how much work we all had to do as bowlers in our forties!"

As John Stephenson recalled:

"The first match proved a reasonably exciting affair and we were all conscious that it was a great thing to be involved with the start up of cricket at Arundel Castle once again. The only blot on our copy book was getting the Duke out for a duck but we were invited to return the following year. Thereafter, the composition of our side was a sort of minor example of military history as we were serving all over the world. In 1953 for example there was no match because the bulk of the Regiment was in Egypt. But we gradually managed to put together a pretty strong combination based on those who were more or less permanently at our depot in Chichester and our share of often extremely gifted cricketers doing National Service.

"The matches in 1954 and 1955 stick in my mind for these and other reasons. In the 1954 game, our side was strengthened with the addition of Nick Hordern, who was commissioned doing his National Service with the Regiment, and who is the brother of Sir Peter Hordern, the Horsham M.P. Then we had David Mantell - a National Serviceman in the other ranks - who was retained at Depot as he was on the Sussex staff as an excellent wicket-keeper and batsman. Both of them would get hundreds for us later in the series but, on this occasion, there was an early collapse and I found myself going out to bat at number 6 with the score board showing 6 for 4. It wasn't much better when our captain, Jack Glennie, came out to join me with the total at 16 for 5. We had quite a respectable partnership but, I am ashamed to say, very conveniently my captain managed to get in the way of a simple caught and bowled opportunity when I had barely got off the mark. We only managed to make 118 all out but, when it came to their turn, the Duke's side ran into some pretty effective fast bowling by another of our National Service chaps, retained specially for sporting purposes at the Depot, B. W. Hardham. He wanted to play County cricket and he was known as Hard Man. I see he finished up with the figures of 12-4-11-8 and the Duke's side were all out for 42.

"In the following year, our total was restricted to 147 thanks to some very effective bowling by Nigel Broomfield, who later top scored for the Duke when they struggled to reach 91. He is now our Ambassador in Berlin but in those days he had just left school and was on his way to Cambridge with a reputation as a brilliant all-round sportsman. He became a great international squash player and I felt a certain personal pride in his later efforts since I was one of his instructors at Mons Officer Cadet School.

"What was not so much a matter of pride was my own bowling performance. I was operating in harness with 'Hard Man' who, once again, got 8 wickets in the innings. However, as it happened, I was bowling when the Duke came in to bat. Jack Glennie told me that I should give him some runs. I wasn't bowling particularly well at the time and I did not think this would present a problem. The first ball I bowled to him was well wide but swung and cut back only missing the offstump by a fraction. 'Did you hear what I said', said Jack Glennie. Confusing his question with an enquiry as to whether I was trying to bowl the Duke, I replied, 'No Sir, Yes Sir'. The next ball I bowled the Duke snicked for a couple and with the third I clean bowled him only to get another rocket.

"The other major recollection of all concerned in this match was the arrival by helicopter of the Duke of Edinburgh and the presentation of both sides to him. He stayed for quite a long time and this seemed to give a Royal Seal of Approval to our series."

There was another series running in parallel with that of the Regiment which also received Ducal approval. This was one involving the Duke in the dual role of host and President of the Sussex County Cricket Club. He had first accepted this appointment for a year in 1933 but this was a symbolic arrangement while he was still a serving army officer. In 1949 he became President once again for a term which was to last for a quarter of a century.

It was this connection that brought the county cricket team to Arundel on a continuing basis when, in 1951, the Duke agreed to stage a match on behalf of George Cox's benefit. This game also marked the end of civil war in the Sussex camp. In 1950 there had been 'the great walk out' when, during the Club's Annual General Meeting, the Duke had resigned closely followed by the rest of the committee over a dispute involving the apparently enforced resignation of the previous year's captain, Hugh Bartlett. When the committee's decision was challenged by a local priest, supported by the 20 year old Cambridge undergraduate David Sheppard, a vote of no confidence in the committee was carried.

Subsequently, James Langridge was appointed as the County's first full-time professional captain and the Duke resumed his presidency. Although relations improved considerably thereafter, the match at Arundel was part of the peace keeping operation and it also achieved the immediate objective of raising funds for George Cox, whose benefit season reached a new record total for the County of over £6000. The beneficiary would later recall:

"It was typical of the Duke to arrange this match on my behalf. My main benefit game at Hove was spoilt by rain and I really appreciated the fact that we were able to produce a full County team and there was plenty of talent on the other side. However, I didn't fully show my appreciation when I got the Duke out and I didn't improve matters by saying that I hadn't meant to do it!"

Apart from the Duke and the actor Trevor Howard, all the rest of the home team had played first-class cricket. Of these, six had been Test Match players and the credentials of the other three, the former Sussex captain, Hugh Bartlett, Desmond Eagar of Hampshire and the team's wicket-keeper, Dr John Dew who had turned out as an amateur for Sussex, all spoke for themselves.

The match attracted a very large crowd. George Cox's team scored their runs quickly despite a long bowling spell which brought three wickets for the West Indies all-rounder Learie Constantine, then in his sixtieth year. Before the innings ended, there was time for the Duke to take a wicket in which his pleasure was shared when the catch was taken by Trevor Howard.

For the Duke's side the run chase was highly satisfactory with a win in the last over by one wicket. Gubby Allen and Dr Dew saw their side home but the Duke had earlier held up an end batting for a quarter of an hour with his team's century maker, Hubert Doggart, who recalls:

"My chief recollection was how nervous I felt in wanting to do well for the Earl Marshal. You also have to remember that in those days - even in a benefit match - there was an obvious rivalry between the professionals and amateurs in the Sussex team when they found themselves on opposing sides. This was compounded by the fact that - through the activities of certain committee members - I was inadvertently caught up in the captaincy row. My name had been put forward without proper reference to me to share the captaincy of Sussex in 1950 with another amateur, R G Hunt. We had withdrawn when James Langridge became captain but it all added something to the atmosphere when I found myself

playing against my Sussex team mates at Arundel in the following year. As it happened, Alan Oakman grumbled a bit when he thought he had me out before I got my century. But I managed to keep going and I remember that the cover drive seemed to work quite well on that lovely Arundel outfield."

GEORGE COX'S SUSSEX XI V DUKE OF NORFOLK'S XI
8TH JULY 1951

SUSSEX XI

John Langridge	c. Eagar b. Constantine	10
D. V. Smith	st. Dews b. Constantine	86
C. Oakes	c. Howard b. Norfolk	43
G. R. Cox	c. Cowdrey b. Constantine	36
J. M. Parks	c. Constantine b. Doggart	62
D. Bates	b. Eagar	17
J. Oakes	not out	0
A. S. M. Oakman	did not bat	
A. E. James		
R. T. Webb		
James Langridge		
	Extras	12
	Total (for 6 wkts dec.)	266

Bowling

	O	M	R	W
Constantine	15	1	75	3
Shackleton	9	1	26	0
Doggart	10	0	68	1
Cowdrey	3	0	39	0
Eagar	5.1	0	27	1
Norfolk	1	0	2	1
Howard	3	0	17	0

DUKE OF NORFOLK'S XI

E. D. R. Eagar	c. and b. James	14
J. F. Crapp	c. Bates b. James	13
G. H. G. Doggart	c. James b. Langridge Jas.	100
Duke of Norfolk	c. James b. Cox	2
M. C. Cowdrey	lbw. Oakes J.	28
H. T. Bartlett	c. Smith b. Cox	21
Sir L. Constantine	c. Oakman b. Parks	23
G. O. Allen	not out	34
T. Howard	st. Webb b. Langridge Jas.	7
D. Shackleton	c. Oakman b. Langridge Jas.	11
Dr. J. A. Dew	not out	0
	Extras	14
	Total (for 9 wickets)	267

Bowling

	O	M	R	W
Bates	4	0	22	0
James	5	0	19	2
Cox	8	1	42	2
Langridge Jn.	4	1	1	0
Oakes J.	4	0	29	1
Oakman	4	0	19	0
Oakes C.	7	0	42	0
Langridge Jas.	9	1	43	3
Parks	5	0	20	1

DUKE OF NORFOLK'S XI WON BY 1 WICKET

Another of the Duke's team was also under a certain amount of pressure. Colin Cowdrey had been given a year by his father to play cricket after leaving Tonbridge and before going up to Oxford. Over 40 years later, he retains vivid impressions of the occasion.

"I was having a pretty torrid time in making my first-class debut. In looking up the games before the match at Arundel, I see that I scored two against Nottinghamshire and I was easily knocked over by Shackleton when we went to play Hampshire. Then when we went up to Northampton, Freddie Brown who was just back after captaining the England team in Australia, gave me a lot of encouragement and I got some runs, but after that it was pretty disastrous. I went to play in the game against Sussex at Tunbridge Wells and the whole of Tonbridge School were given the day off to come and see me play. They saw me twice in one day as I got 0 and 4. So it went on and I was scheduled for a drop into the Kent Second XI. Before that, I played in a Free Foresters' match and got 100. Hugh Bartlett was playing in that game and he must have said something to the Duke because I got an invitation to play for him against Sussex. This proved the turning point for I went on to get a thousand runs in August and I was on my way.

"However I can't stress too much how important the game was to me. There I was, still a junior cricketer, given the opportunity to appear with all those established players, many of them household names. The only Sussex cricketers I knew well were Jim Parks and Alan Oakman with whom I had played in school cricket but, through this match, I came to know the great Doggart sporting clan. Hubert, who was playing for us was already a great national sporting hero having captained Cambridge in the previous year and making his Test debut against the West Indians. I have happy memories of spending time with him and his family at the big brown house on the coast at Selsey with its squash court in the garden. Of the others on our side, I knew about Trevor Howard who had been a very good cricketer at Clifton against my old school. I also knew Dr John Dew who had been a cracking wicket-keeper while at Tonbridge and who came down to play against us for the Old Boys. He retains his interest in encouraging young cricketers to this day most notably in the coaching scheme which he has introduced that brings 70 boys a year into the Horsham Cricket Club.

"But the chief thing I will always remember about that match was the way in which the Duke handled the public speaking. Over dinner, he had told me that when he had an important speech to make, he would learn it, rehearse it, and speak at a deliberate pace - all things which he had had to learn at a very young age. I can see him now, with a microphone on a long extension lead, which was brought out in front of the marquee when he addressed a very large crowd at the end of the game. He spoke very slowly and you could hear a pin drop as the audience hung on his every word, wondering what he would say next. There was almost total silence and even the ice cream sales stopped.

"He thanked everyone for coming to support Sussex and particularly to help George Cox and he recalled his long association with father and son Cox. Then he came to Learie Constantine and said: 'It is a particular delight for me, and I believe for all of us, that Learie Constantine should find time to grace this occasion'. As I got to know him better in later years, I realised that he had a special affection for the West Indies and an appreciation of their cricketers. He also, incidentally, worked the crowd brilliantly so that George Cox got a very good collection."

The reasons for the return match in 1952 were even more direct. The County's finances were in a poor state with loss-making reported in each of the previous two years. For economy reasons, it had even been necessary to end Patsy Hendren's services as the County Coach. Accordingly, the match played on Sunday 6 July 1952 was organised by the Sussex County Cricket Welfare Association with a collection for the re-establishment of the County's nursery.

The Duke once again put together a strong side. Through his contacts at Lords, he was able to use a gap in Glamorgan's fixture list to include five of their players. He added Hubert Doggart, Billy Griffith and Chris Winn from Sussex together with the veteran Middlesex and England all-rounder R. W. V. Robins and the television personality MacDonald Hobley.

On this occasion, the County gained its revenge with a victory by 22 runs in which they scored consistently and bowled too steadily for the Duke's team. Hubert Doggart has two special recollections of this match concerning the batting of both the Duke and himself:

"I know the Sussex bowlers tried to feed the Duke a bit after his low score in the previous year. This wasn't always easy. If you bowled down the leg side, he would be too late to connect whereas half volleys tended to be too accurate. Nevertheless, we were all delighted when, on this occasion, he got runs. So far as my own innings was concerned, I was especially pleased to get another decent score because Frank

DUKE OF NORFOLK'S XI v C. S. CRAWLEY'S XI
25TH MAY 1952

DUKE OF NORFOLK'S XI

C. E. Underdown	b. Wheeler-Bennett	30
J. F. Priestley	b. Pelham	37
A. M. Hedley	b. Wheeler-Bennett	3
G. R. Smyth	not out	40
Dr. J. A. Dew	b. Wheeler-Bennett	15
Sir E. Ford	c. Crawley b. Wheeler-Bennett	18
E. E. Harrison	c. and b. Pelham	0
Duke of Norfolk	b. Pelham	9
J. A. P. Bartlett	c. Crawley b. Pelham	8
N. S. Collin	b. Wheeler-Bennett	0
P. Evans	not out	4
	Extras	15
	Total (for 9 wkts dec.)	179

Bowling

	O	M	R	W
Pelham	23	6	70	4
A. M. Crawley	4	1	4	0
Wheeler-Bennett	20	2	88	5
Leyland	2	0	10	0
Westmacott	2	0	12	0

C. S. CRAWLEY'S XI

A. M. Crawley	c. Dew b. Harrison	11
P. V. F. Cazalet	b. Collins	27
Hon. L. R. White	b. Priestley	20
C. S. Crawley	b. Priestley	11
R. Wheeler-Bennett	c. Smyth b. Hedley	15
M. Hornby	b. Hedley	15
A. G. Pelham	st. Dew b. Priestley	1
I. Westmacott	b. Priestley	2
Hon. R. Winn	b. Priestley	5
Lord Althorp	not out	0
D. Naylor-Leyland	b. Harrison	1
	Extras	8
	Total	116

Bowling

	O	M	R	W
Priestley	13	6	26	5
Harrison	8	2	38	2
Hedley	4	0	16	2
Collins	6	0	28	1

DUKE OF NORFOLK'S XI WON BY 63 RUNS

Lee (together with Frank Chester) was doing the umpiring. He had stood in my first first-class innings and he was always a great encouragement. Whenever you reached a milestone he would say, 'Take a fresh guard. Keep going. Don't give it away'."

Hubert Doggart continued to take this advice. After scoring 90 for the Duke in 1952, he added another 94 in 1953. As for the series, it settled into a high-scoring relaxed occasion in which the County's challenge in setting a large total was usually just too much for the Duke's side. What was certain, however, was that it would play a crucial part in the bringing together of the County's amateurs and professionals in an era which would soon see the abolition of this distinction.

If the Duke had established himself as a generous host to professional cricketers, he retained all his enthusiasm for the amateur game. 1952 was the year which saw a return to some of the traditional fixtures and the general atmosphere of pre-war country house cricket at Arundel. For this, Cosmo Crawley can claim much of the credit.

"When there was no cricket at the Castle after the war, I was very disappointed. Although I was becoming a rather elderly gent and nothing like the player I had been before the war, I was anxious to see that unique kind of cricket at Arundel once again. I must admit I got a little depressed when, in the early post-war years, I noticed that Duchess Lavinia was exercising her horses on the ground. I was all the more delighted when Duke Bernard allowed the Regiment and the County side to play there in 1951 and we agreed that I would get up a team to appear at the start of the next season.

"By then, he was relying on Eddie Harrison to help him in arranging his side. As he was the Secretary and a regular performer for the Sussex Martlets for many years, this would be his main source of supply. However, he would also be riding to instructions. Bernard liked to have about seven or eight good players so that he could justify three or four moderate performers in which he always included himself. Between us, we managed to put together two teams which, in some ways, were designed to re-create the country house cricket atmosphere of the Duke's games against the Eldon and Hope XIs in pre war days.

"Of the Duke's team only he, Eddie Harrison and Edward Ford, and in our team, my brother Aidan and I, together with Reggie Winn, represented the pre-war Arundel cricketers. On their side, apart from those who had turned out in the previous year against the Regiment, Eddie Harrison had found a useful Sussex Martlet all-rounder in Jack Priestley as an opening batsman and to open the bowling with himself. Otherwise, he had borrowed Major Bartlett from the Regiment and I think the others could fairly be described as Bernard's racing friends, including Nicco Collin who was, as they say, larger than life and kept wicket with some very unusual parts of his anatomy.

"We had some interesting characters in our side. Peter Cazalet who opened the batting with Aidan had been his contemporary in playing both for Oxford and Kent. Like me, they were well into their forties and the Hon Luke White (later Baron Annaly) was our only class young player. As an outstanding schoolboy cricketer at Eton he went straight into the England side for one of the Victory Tests and he played a few games for Middlesex. Otherwise, we included a few keen youngsters some of whom would become Arundel regulars and one of whom, in the person of Lord Althorp, then a serving Officer and Equerry to the Queen, would become better known as Earl Spencer, the father of Princess Diana."

After the game against Cosmo Crawley's XI, the Duke and Eddie Harrison planned a further five matches for the 1952 season. Apart from what were now repeat games against the Sussex County XI and the Royal Sussex Regiment, the remaining three matches were effectively new fixtures. The game against the Eton Ramblers in early June was rained off but the match against the Sussex Martlets at the end of that month marked the renewal of the pre-war series. One of those who played for the Martlets was Keith Jenkin. After leaving school at Hurstpierpoint, and completing his National Service, he was working as a management trainee in the Chichester Dairies and soon found himself playing regularly for the Martlets at Arundel and elsewhere.

"As a 21 year old, I was quickly made aware of the stern, authoritarian ways of our captain, J. K. Mathews. Just as he had given Eddie Harrison a tough time in pre-war days, I felt the same sense of almost serving in the Army when playing for him. By then he was in his late fifties but, as he showed in this match, he was still a forcing batsman. However, he was not averse to a little gamesmanship. 'Don't you bowl short at me, boy' he would tell anyone who was a bit quick and then, when they pitched it up, he would hit them straight back over their head saying, 'That's more like it'. In this game I had a winning partnership with him of 60 odd in which I was scared stiff in case I ran him out. Earlier on, the boot was on the other foot when I had a partnership with Bob Stainton. Although most of his cricket at Oxford and Sussex had been before the war, he could still run like a stag and he made light of the Duke's more than useful opening attack of Tony Pelham and Eddie Harrison.

"So far as the Duke's innings was concerned, I was feeling rather pleased with myself. Coming on as second change, I got two wickets in two overs, the second of which was the Duke's brother-in-law, Ronnie Strutt. This brought the Duke in to bat at number 6. At this point, our wicket-

keeper, Billy Griffith, said to me 'I think perhaps it would be as well if I marked your card. The first thing to remember is to bowl it short so that he has plenty of time to see the ball. The second thing is not to bowl it straight. And the third thing to take into account is that you should on no account appeal. If you should fail in any of these particulars, you should not expect an invitation to play here again.'

"Suitably warned, we saw to it that the Duke got some runs including the odd boundary. Eventually, he hit a skier and I found myself standing almost directly underneath. I speculated on whether or not I should let it drop but eventually thinking, 'What the hell' I caught it. As the Duke went out, purple in the face from his exertions, he said to me 'I am very glad you caught that, my boy. I've had quite enough exercise for one day'."

At the end of the season, another pre-war series was revived when the Duke entertained a side representing the Arundel branch of the British Legion. One of those returning from the war to take part in this local Derby was Lord John Hope:

"I knew that this match was always a keen contest and I had heard of the local demon fast bowler, Ernie Blackall. Sure enough, he got me out and several others, but we all got a few - especially Teddy Underdown who blazed away - and we made a sporting declaration. When they went in to bat we were short of bowlers and after Priestley and Bartlett bowled themselves into the ground, the Duke brought on another Martlet, R. C. Wheeler-Bennett and himself. As luck would have it, his trainer, young Gordon Smyth, was going strong and when he got his fifty off Bernard and virtually won the match, the Duke said to him 'I think you may have to consider your position'."

1952

June 29th. Duke of Norfolk's XI 138 (D. B. T. Lattey 5-42). Sussex Martlets 184-4 (Maj. R. G. Stainton 66, K. R. Jenkin 55*). Sussex Martlets won by 6 wickets.

July 6th. Sussex County XI 222-7 dec. Duke of Norfolk's XI 200 (G. H. G. Doggart 90) Sussex County XI won by 22 runs.

July 20th. Duke of Norfolk's XI 174 - 8 dec (E. Underdown 60). Arundel British Legion 176-4 (G. Smyth 69) . Arundel British Legion won by 6 wickets.

GEORGE COX'S BENEFIT MATCH AT ARUNDEL, 8 JULY 1951

George Cox – c. Cowdrey, b. Constantine 36.

*A famous trio – 'Patsy' Hendren, Learie
Constantine and Trevor Howard.*

*The Duke in conversation with Gubby Allen while
Hubert Doggart studies the play.*

*The Duke's team who played Sussex Martlets, 29 June 1952
Back row (L to R): C. E. Underdown, A. Collins, Duke of Norfolk, C. Crawley, A. Borgnis,
Sir E. Ford, E. E. Harrison.
Front row (L to R): Lord Althorp, P. Hastings, Hon. R. Strutt.*

CHAPTER FIVE

Domestic And International Cricket 1953-1959

Coronation Year was one in which both Duke Bernard and Duchess Lavinia were preoccupied with London commitments. After the Lying in State of Queen Mary earlier in the year, they were both increasingly involved in rehearsals for the Coronation for which the Duchess stood in for the Queen. Following the Coronation Ceremony on 2 June and the obligatory appearance at the Derby on 6 June, Duchess Lavinia recalls that the Duke was "looking forward to his cricket matches at Arundel like a schoolboy who can hardly wait for the holidays."

However, the five matches in the rest of June and early July were notable chiefly for a run of exceptionally low scoring by the Duke's teams. In the match against Cosmo Crawley's XI they were all out for 82 and lost by 94 runs. A week later Dr David Rice was brought into the side to strengthen the bowling against the Eton Ramblers. He would later recall:

"The match in the previous year had been rained off so this was really the start of a new series. Eddie Harrison was unable to turn out for the Duke and suggested my name. After we went on to the field, he said 'I am told you are a bowler. Perhaps you would be good enough to take the Castle end until I tell you to come off. I am afraid it may be rather a long time as we are a bit short of bowling today'. Well, he could have said that again because I see from the record that I bowled 22 and a bit overs unchanged. I was in my late thirties at the time but bowling a lot in club cricket. On this occasion, I was moving the ball about on what I suppose was the quick side of medium. However, when five catches had gone down in the slips, the umpire said to me, 'If I were you, I'd bowl to hit the stumps. They don't often take slip catches down here!'"

The score card shows Dr Rice took this advice by clean bowling six batsmen, getting one l.b.w., another caught and bowled and relying on only one of his fieldsmen for a catch

to finish with 9 for 47 out of a Ramblers total of 152.

However, the sequel was less happy:

"When we went in to bat, I was pretty well knackered and was delighted to be put at number 11 thinking I would have a decent rest and hopefully wouldn't be required. Well, Tony Pelham ran through our side and, in no time at all, I joined the Duke with the score at 22 for 9. 'This won't do at all' he said. 'They will be quite insufferable if we don't improve things'. We managed the largest stand in the innings of precisely 8 of which my share was 0."

Two weeks later, the Doctor was in the firing line once again:

"After the Ramblers match, the Duke asked me to turn out against the Martlets. This time I was bowling in harness with Eddie Harrison and we were greatly encouraged when the Duke included Colin Ingleby-Mackenzie as his wicket-keeper. He took catches and generally smartened things up behind the wicket. Anyway, Eddie and I bowled unchanged to shoot them out for 76, but again I was pretty whacked. When the 50 went up for our side with only one wicket down and Colin Ingleby-Mackenzie and Cosmo Crawley going well, Eddie and I were totally relaxed as we were down to bat at numbers 10 and 11. Blow me down, the next thing we were both out in the middle with the score at 68 for 9. Well we managed to get the runs, and the Duke who was non-playing captain that day, said to us, 'I'll play you for your batting next time'."

Three weeks later, for the match against the Arundel Branch of the British Legion, neither David Rice nor Eddie Harrison was available and much of the bowling depended on Sir Edward Ford.

"I was a veteran by then but was still required to bowl more than my usual ration. Still, things went our way and I remember with what pleasure I saw Billy Griffith take a brilliant catch off my bowling to get rid of their opening batsman, Gordon Smyth. Later, we also got one of their tail-enders through Billy's superlative stumping standing up to my perhaps relatively gentle medium pace.

"I see we got them out for 84 and my 6 for 29 was the best bowling performance I had at Arundel. But I also see that we could only manage 32. Like John Hope, I also recall the fearsomely fast bowling of Ernie Blackall. He took six wickets and even had the effrontery to bowl the Duke first ball."

Despite this general catalogue of batting disasters, there were plenty of runs in both the big games of the year. In the first, the Sussex County side scored consistently to declare at 245 for 6. As recorded earlier, in the run chase which followed the Duke's side fell only 12 short of their target. This was due to the usual major contribution from Hubert Doggart of 94 and strong support from the Middlesex veterans George Mann and Walter Robins.

The match against the County had drawn another large crowd in support of the club's Welfare Association. However, this was dwarfed when, on 2 August 1953, the Duke's side took on one under the captaincy of His Royal Highness the Duke of Edinburgh.

Duke Bernard had seen a good deal of Prince Philip when they served together on the Coronation Organising Committee and he was quick to respond when the challenge came for them to arrange a match as one of a series in support of the National Playing Fields Association. In 1994, The Duke of Edinburgh recalled the background to this match which was to be one of a series and the preparation which went into his first game at Arundel:

"I had enjoyed playing cricket at Gordonstoun and in the odd game in the Navy. But you have to make choices and mine went in favour of polo. Well, with polo you have commitments - polo ponies which need exercise. You can't put them in the corner like an old cricket bat. But Errol Holmes persuaded me to play in these charity games and I agreed if I could get some practice beforehand. I am often asked how it felt to appear before such large crowds. I can only say that it was best to have some practice but also, in those days, people were much more deferential!"

Although he did not take part in the match, Eddie Harrison played a key role in the Duke of Edinburgh's preparation.

"The match was chosen to take place at the end of Goodwood Week. A few days earlier, I got a telephone call from Bernard who said, 'What are you doing next week?' I

DUKE OF NORFOLK'S XI v H. R. H. DUKE OF EDINBURGH'S XII
2ND AUGUST 1953

DUKE OF NORFOLK XI

John Langridge	b. Barnett	18
W. J. Edrich	b. Voce	15
G. H. G. Doggart	b. Robins	25
G. Cox	lbw. Barnett	30
Jas. Langridge	not out	64
Duke of Norfolk	b. Duke of Edinburgh	4
C. Oakes	c. Duke of Edinburgh b. Robins	23
J. Smith	not out	14
R. G. Marlar	did not bat	
J. A. Young		
J. Wood		
	Extras	10
	Total (for 6 wkts. dec.)	203

Bowling

	O	M	R	W
Gover	7	1	13	1
Voce	8	0	13	1
Sims	7	0	42	0
Barnett	10	1	31	2
Duke of Edinburgh	8	0	24	1
Robins	7	0	49	2
Allen	5	0	21	0

H. R. H. DUKE OF EDINBURGH'S XII

L. B. Fishlock	c. and b. Marlar	39
C. J. Barnett	st. Webb b. Young	27
R. E. S. Wyatt	st. Webb b. Young	45
G. O. Allen	c. Marlar b Young	6
Duke of Edinburgh	b. Cox	18
E. R. T. Holmes	c. Marlar b. Cox	0
R. W. V. Robins	c. and b. Langridge	0
S. C. Griffith	c. Marlar b. Langridge	14
Lt. Col. M. Parker	b. Marlar	18
W. Voce	b. Marlar	1
A. R. Gover	lbw. Marlar	3
J. M. Sims	not out	12
	Extras	14
	Total	197

Bowling

	O	M	R	W
Wood	3	0	16	0
Smith	4	0	16	0
Young	16	2	57	3
Marlar	12	0	27	4
Doggart	2	0	10	0
Duke of Norfolk	2	0	11	0
Langridge Ja.	6	0	26	2
Cox	5	2	20	2

DUKE OF NORFOLK'S XI WON BY 6 RUNS

said that I planned my usual round of going to the races in the afternoon and to my office in the morning. 'Oh no you won't' said the Duke, 'You've got to bowl at the Duke of Edinburgh'. Well, I went up to the ground on the next

Monday morning and found that nets had already been set up in the middle of the square on a spare wicket. There were two members of the Estate XI there - one to assist in the bowling and the other to field. I bowled away and the Duke batted. Then he bowled for half an hour over the wicket with off-breaks. He went off to play in the first of the matches in this series at Dean Park in Bournemouth and when he came back to Arundel he told me that he had scored 26. Apparently Billy Griffith who was keeping wicket said, 'You played well, Sir,' to which the Duke had replied that he had been getting practice and coaching from me. 'Good heavens' said Billy Griffith, 'I can't believe it. Eddie's batting is a triumph of determination over skill'. Well, all I can say is that Prince Philip didn't show up too badly in the game at Arundel, although, naturally, I was cheering for a Norfolk victory."

The score-card shows that the victory, when it came, was a close run thing. When the two Dukes went out for the toss, the Duke of Norfolk wore his I Zingari colours, while the Duke of Edinburgh was in the borrowed finery of Errol Holmes' Free Forester blazer. When the Duke of Norfolk won the toss, he decided - contrary to his usual practice - he would give the Duke of Edinburgh's team the chance to chase a winning score.

Despite a steady opening spell by the two veteran England fast bowlers, Alf Gover and Bill Voce, the Sussex and Middlesex batsmen in the Norfolk side scored at over 100 runs an hour enabling a declaration at 203 for 6. Duke Bernard's own contribution to the score had been cut short when, to the huge enjoyment of the crowd as well as the bowler, he was bowled for 4 by the Duke of Edinburgh.

The Duke of Edinburgh's side scored at an equally fast rate. Fishlock and Barnett put on 64 for the first wicket and the score had reached 101 for 3 when the Duke of Edinburgh came out to join R. E. S. Wyatt. They added 31, of which the Duke of Edinburgh got 18, in part from the bowling of his ducal host. At this point, Duke Bernard turned to George Cox and said: "Well he's had a good day. He's got some runs and he's taken a wicket, I think its about time we got him out." George Cox, whose bowling style was best known for its innocuous looking slow swingers, would later recall with a chuckle:

"Of course, he couldn't have asked a better man. I went on and clean bowled him and got a second wicket in the same over when I dismissed his pal Errol Holmes. At this stage, I was in danger of ruining the match and they had to

take me off."

Another Sussex cricketer who, in his case, was making his debut for the Duke of Norfolk at Arundel, was Robin Marlar. He takes up the story of the end of the match:

"I too received the ducal summons. The Duke of Edinburgh's side were going pretty well in the chase for victory and Duke Bernard brought me back for a second spell. He said words to the effect that he liked to finish in the last over but I was to ensure that we won. Well I managed to keep things going but I suddenly bowled the Duke's secretary, Mike Parker, and Bill Voce in the same over and they were 180 for 9. We agreed that they should bat all 12 but Jim Langridge got Billy Griffith out soon afterwards and they were 181 for 10 and still 23 short with the last pair Alf Gover and Jim Sims at the wicket. With what I shall always consider as some skilfully contrived bowling, Jim Langridge and I managed to help the score steadily along and there was great excitement in the crowd as we drew near to the 6.30 finishing time. When we came to the last over, they were 7 runs short of victory and it was obvious that Duke Bernard was keen for me to win the match for him. Perhaps I was lucky but anyway I got an l.b.w. decision against Alf Gover from Tich Cornford who was umpiring with Herbert Strudwick and we had won by 6 runs. The Duke seemed very pleased and said he wanted to see more of me at Arundel. Little did I know that this would turn out to be a long term assignment".

Robin Marlar was appointed Librarian at Arundel Castle in 1954, a post which he would retain until 1959. As he recalls:

"The Duke was incredibly generous to me. He gave me the job partly because his library needed reorganising and I was also able to make myself useful in coaching his daughters with their examinations. Mainly, however, I got the job because he knew that, with my young family, I needed financial support if I was going to go on playing for Sussex as an amateur, particularly when I took over the captaincy in 1955.

"We lived in the town and I gradually came to understand his thinking about cricket. I am convinced that the great match against the Duke of Edinburgh in the previous year had sparked off in his mind the idea of bringing Arundel into the big league of cricket. He had obviously come to the conclusion that there seemed no immediate prospect of vast success as an owner and trainer in the racing world and although he kept up his interest there, I think he saw an opportunity to play a role on the international cricket stage.

The Duke of Edinbugh and Errol Holmes lead out the visitors.

The two Dukes in action - batting.

The two Dukes in action – bowling.

DUKE OF NORFOLK'S XI V DUKE OF EDINBURGH'S XII, ARUNDEL 1953

His great friend, Billy Griffith, had gone from Sussex to be Assistant Secretary of the M.C.C. at Lords and he could count on my own contacts in the County Championship.

"All of this lead to the visit of the first international touring side to Arundel in 1954 which was from Canada.

"They were not to be under-estimated. They were nearly all expatriates from this country and the Caribbean. There were several who had played League or County cricket before leaving for Canada and in the case of F. J. Cameron and Kenneth Trestrail, they had two players good enough to be chosen for the West Indies.

"The majority of our team were Sussex players and it was splendid to see the Parks, father and son, playing together. Jim Parks Senior, who got top score for us, was then in his early fifties and coaching at Trent Bridge. Everyone chipped in and got a few runs and our only disappointment was Denis Compton who failed on one of his rare appearances on the ground.

"However, he made up for this when he dismissed two of their best players, Tommy Brierley who had played for Glamorgan and Lancashire and their best batsman Ken Trestrail, who had been a member of the West Indian Touring side in England in 1950. As the Duke's man, I had to do more bowling than anyone else but the thing which I particularly appreciated was watching the beautiful left-arm bowling action of Bill Voce. He was coaching at Butlins in Bognor Regis in those days and, even as a veteran, he still had a model action."

After this first experiment in international cricket, the Duke was keen to continue the process. However, the South Africans' itinerary in 1955 ruled out a visit to Arundel, but the seed had been sown and the Duke achieved the ultimate prize when, on 28 April 1956, the Australians came to play their first match of the tour on the Castle ground.

With them came for the first time at Arundel a large press contingent. Of these, two reporters caught the spirit of the occasion. Lyle Turnbull, writing for the Melbourne Sun said:

"England gave the Australians a great welcome on Saturday. Even the Duke of Norfolk's deer came up from the forest at Arundel Castle to watch them arrive. Cricket has never been played in a more pleasant atmosphere. Everything of old England was there - an ancient English castle, spreading chestnut trees, rolling downs and a village green atmosphere. It was essentially a picnic match with broadcast announcements about lost dogs, lost children and even one lost wife. They ran a raffle during the afternoon with a list of 135 prize winners read out during the latter part of the Australians' innings. But no one minded. Keith Miller nonchalantly kicked the ball back to the bowler. Ian Johnson swapped reminiscences with umpire Maurice Tate."

For the British press corps, there could have been no more appropriate representative than their present day doyen, E. W. Swanton. As he said in his report, like the

DUKE OF NORFOL'S XII V CANADIAN TOURING TOURING XII
1ST AUGUST 1954

DUKE OF NORFOLK'S XII

J. Parks Sr.	b. Christen	44
D. V. Smith	c. Burns b. Padmore	8
G. H. G. Doggart	c. Padmore b. Christen	29
D. C. S. Compton	c. Trestrail b. Cameron	4
J. Parks Jr.	c. and b. Cameron	10
F. R. Brown	c. Rilstone b. Christen	28
Duke of Norfolk	b. Cameron	2
K. Suttle	c. Bullen b. Christen	23
S. C. Griffith	not out	10
J. J. Warr	not out	1
R. G. Marlar	did not bat	
W. Voce		
	Extras	4
	Total (for 8 wkts. dec.)	163

Bowling

	O	M	R	W
Padmore	8	1	31	1
Stead	5	1	12	0
Cameron	17	2	64	3
Christian	17	1	43	4
Rilstone	4	0	9	0

CANADIAN TOURING XII

E. H. M. Burn	b. Marlar	10
R. N. Quintrell	b. Marlar	44
T. L. Brierley	c. Voce b. Compton	32
K. B. Trestrail	c. Doggart b. Compton	11
F. J. Cameron	c. Smith b. Voce	14
L. Gunn	c. Brown b. Voce	0
W. A. Percival	not out	5
J. M. Rilstone	c. Parks b. Marlar	1
H. G. Bullen	not out	14
	Extras	2
	Total (for 7 wkts)	133

Bowling

	O	M	R	W
Voce	7	1	22	2
Warr	3	0	26	0
Marlar	9	3	27	3
J. Parks Sn.	3	0	4	0
Brown	3	0	13	0
Compton	6	0	30	2
Doggart	4	0	9	0

RAIN STOPPED PLAY - MATCH DRAWN

DUKE OF NORFOLK'S XI V AUSTRALIANS, APRIL 1956

Keith Miller and the Duchess.

Ian Johnson leads his men on to the field.

One of the classic photographs of Keith Miller – a mighty pull during his brief innings at Arundel.

Australians, he was enjoying the delights of Arundel for the first time and his report in the Daily Telegraph continued:

"All things conspired to make both the perfect setting and what for 13,000 odd who came will surely be an unforgettable day.

"The ground has everything. For most of the circumference, a deep broad bank makes a natural amphitheatre. Except for one gap cut to reveal the superb downs and panorama away to the east, the arena is encircled with trees now coming into leaf. The whole scene was a symphony in green with a vivid scarlet splash made by the uniforms of the Grenadier Guards whose band took over the entertainment during the intervals."

The match was played in aid of the National Playing Fields Association and Sussex cricket and, in a foreword to the fund-raising programme, the Duke wrote:

"It is my belief that cricket can be the greatest and therefore should be the strongest link between countries and individuals of all parties, classes and creeds, wherever it is played. Men and women, old and young, and children love it."

Two of those taking part in this match for the Duke had special reason to remember the day.

Colin Cowdrey was particularly pleased with the representation of both old and new faces:

"In the Australian side, it was splendid to see a youngster like Ian Craig playing his first innings in England. He batted as though he was born in Arundel. He showed such certainty on a wicket which was much slower than anything he must have experienced in Australia that we thought to ourselves, 'Surely, here is another Bradman'. Equally, it was a thrill to see some of my early heroes back in action. The Duke had taken the opportunity of paying tribute to some of the England side in the 1950/51 tour of Australia. I think it is often forgotten how well they did. Much of that was due to the tremendous performance of Len Hutton who, in that series, had an average of something over seventy when the next highest was something in the twenties. He had been a wonderful friend and mentor to me and I was delighted to see him coming out of retirement to face the old enemy."

In cricket, as in life, even the best attempts at a happy ending, can go awry. Ian Johnson, the Australian captain, told the author:

"We all realised that this match was very useful practice but that also it was expected that we could enjoy a garden party atmosphere. Ray Lindwall opened the bowling for us

DUKE OF NORFOLK'S XI v AUSTRALIA
28TH APRIL 1956

DUKE OF NORFOLK'S XI

Rev. D. S. Sheppard	b. Johnson	51
Sir L. Hutton	b. Lindwall	0
R. E. Marshall	c. Johnson b. Benaud	48
M. C. Cowdrey	b. Benaud	7
D. J. Insole	st. Langley b. Johnson	24
F. R. Brown	c. Johnson b. Benaud	2
S. C. Griffith	c. and b. Johnson	15
J. J. Warr	c. Rutherford b. Benaud	5
R. G. Marlar	c. Rutherford b. Benaud	18
A. V. Bedser	c. Johnson b. Benaud	7
D. V. P. Wright	not out	2
	Extras	9
	Total	188

Bowling

	O	M	R	W
Lindwall	10	2	36	1
Archer	6	0	28	0
Johnson	7	0	50	3
Mackay	4	0	16	0
Benaud	7.2	0	35	6
Rutherford	5	0	14	0

AUSTRALIA

C. McDonald	st. Griffith b. Wright	19
J. Rutherford	b. Bedser	1
K. Mackay	c. Sheppard b. Warr	1
R. N. Harvey	c. Hutton b. Wright	13
K. R. Miller	b. Marlar	4
I. D. Craig	c. Cowdrey b. Marlar	47
R. G. Archer	b. Marlar	45
R. Benaud	not out	30
R. R. Lindwall	not out	28
I. N. Johnson	did not bat	
G. Langley		
	Extras	1
	Total (for 7 wkts)	189

Bowling

	O	M	R	W
Bedser	6	1	16	1
Warr	12	2	31	1
Brown	8	1	41	0
Insole	4	1	10	0
Wright	3	1	7	2
Marlar	13	0	59	3
Marshall	5	2	25	0

AUSTRALIA WON BY 3 WICKETS

and I told him, 'You'd better give Len one to get off the mark'. Sure enough, he bowled an over which was friendly including several half volleys. But whatever the delivery, Len patted the ball down at his feet or straight back to the bowler. At the end of the over I went up to him and said: 'Len, what on earth is going on? We are trying to be helpful.' And he replied 'I never trust you boogers'. As luck would have it, the first time he attempted an attacking stroke, he dragged the ball onto his wicket. As he left the field with no score, he said to me, 'You see what I mean' and I believe that for years afterwards he would say, 'Don't talk to me about Arundel'.

It was this feature of seeing the new stars from overseas and old favourites in English cricket that has added so much to the attraction of these games and it was from this time on that the tradition of touring teams to England playing the first match of their tour at Arundel became the norm. As if in recognition of this and the Duke's increasing influence on the game, he was nominated by Lord Cobham as his successor for the Presidency of the M.C.C. in 1957. As part of his plans to commemorate this occasion, the Duke did what he was rarely inclined to do which was to spend a substantial period overseas. He decided to take his own particular brand of cricket to the West Indies. His choice fell on the island of Jamaica and his team was drawn principally from those who had been involved in the match against Australia in the previous year and in recent representative games for him against Sussex.

The Touring Party consisted of the following:

E. D. R. Eagar, Captain (Hampshire)

J. J. Warr (Middlesex)

D. E. Blake (Hampshire)

T. W. Graveney (Gloucestershire)

T. Greenhough (Lancashire)

A. C. D. Ingleby-Mackenzie (Hampshire)

R. E. Marshall (Hampshire)

A. E. Moss (Middlesex)

D. V. Smith (Sussex)

G. E. Tribe (Northamptonshire)

W. Watson (Yorkshire)

D. V. P. Wright (Kent)

D. Barrick (Northamptonshire)

Lord Cobham (Worcestershire)

In the opening game of the tour against the parishes of St Mary and St Anne, the Duke showed his willingness to get involved. Batting at number six, his innings of 6 included, thanks to an overthrow, a 5. He also came on to bowl the last over of the match. Tom Graveney recalls the occasion:

"It was marvellous to see his enthusiasm. We tried to help him with his batting and we even managed to get him to make an occasional hit 'on the up'. When it came to bowling, we thought we would give him some direct help. We persuaded one of the locals to give the Duke the charge.

Well, he duly obliged only for Colin Ingleby-Mackenzie to drop the ball and miss the stumping. The Duke just said, 'By the powers vested in me, it may be necessary for you to be incarcerated in the Tower of London on our return'."

Colin Ingleby-Mackenzie, a leading punter, recalls, in racing terms, how he established his position as the Duke's Court Jester:

"It all started out when I found I had picked a loser in the accommodation stakes. We were put up privately while we were in Jamaica and I found myself in a place where I was eaten alive by mosquitoes. I didn't say anything thinking it was just the luck of the draw, but the Duke noticed that I was getting puffed up with bites and said, 'You will come and stay with me at Round Hill'. Well, this was one of the smartest resorts on the island and sharing his accommodation was no strain and we became very friendly.

"Perhaps I was a bit cheeky but this did not stop me pulling his leg in my rather juvenile Old Etonian-Midshipman style. I was always taking the mickey but he seemed to enjoy it even if the threat of incarceration in the Tower came up pretty regularly."

Later in the tour, the Duke was persuaded to turn out for his team on the Test Match Ground at Sabina Park when the opposition was provided by the Jamaica Next XI - the island's second XI. Although, by prior agreement, the Duke, in his 49th year, was allowed to leave the field from time to time, he nevertheless threw himself wholeheartedly into preparation for the match at fielding practice. In the match itself - which was drawn - he was delighted to bat for 20 minutes and his total of 10 included a boundary to which he was known to refer subsequently especially in talking about Test Match grounds.

A few days later his team faced the sterner challenge of a match against the full Jamaica side including the West Indian Test opening batsmen, Allan Rae and Easton McMorris as well as their fast bowler Roy Gilchrist. The match was drawn but the Duke's team went on to win the other two matches in the series. Overall, the team was undefeated - the first visiting side to accomplish this feat since Yorkshire had toured the island in 1936. What was even more significant was the way in which the Duke's brand of attacking cricket - in which everything must be done to achieve a result with defensive cricket rejected - aroused so much enthusiasm. As the Jamaican *Daily Gleaner* said in its editorial when the team left:

"This was memorable in that it resuscitated the goodwill

DUKE OF NORFOLK'S XI v JAMAICA NEXT XI
1ST MARCH 1957

DUKE OF NORFOLK'S XI

D. V. Smith	c. Charvis b. Groves	72
R. E. Marshall	c. Smith b. Mullings	41
D. E. Blake	c. Headlam b. Groves	24
Duke of Norfolk	b. Charvis	10
T. Greenhough	st. Smith b. Maragh	10
T. Graveney	c. Headlam b. Maragh	1
W. Watson	not out	23
J. J. Warr	b. Maragh	0
D. Wright	not out	0
A. C. Ingleby-Mackenzie	did not bat	
D. Barrick		
	Extras	4
	Total (for 7 wkts. dec.)	185

Bowling

	O	M	R	W
Calneck	5	0	21	0
Groves	7	1	28	2
Edwards	9	0	32	0
Mullings	12	1	60	1
Charvis	5	0	20	1
Maragh	9	2	20	3

JAMAICA NEXT XI

G. Smith	c. Watson b. Warr	64
E. Washington	c. Graveney b. Marshall	43
A. Charvis	b. Watson	27
C. Headlam	b. Greenhough	6
D. Edwards	b. Graveney	19
G. Wollaston	not out	9
E. Calneck	not out	8
J. M. Groves	did not bat	
L. Mullings		
R. Maragh		
S. Duncan		
	Extras	9
	Total (for 5 wkts)	185

Bowling

	O	M	R	W
Warr	8	1	21	1
Smith	10	2	21	0
Wright	9	0	36	0
Greenhough	14	3	41	1
Marshall	8	2	23	1
Graveney	8	1	28	1
Watson	1	0	6	1

MATCH DRAWN

tournaments with English teams and local sides which were the rule rather than the exception in the years before World War II." At the farewell dinner for the team, Mr R. K. Nunes, President of the Jamaican Cricket Board of Control said: "This series of matches against Jamaica has provided the type of cricket we have not seen here for generations. Sporting declarations on both sides shows that cricket can still be played by gentlemen."

For several of the participants in these matches there were special memories of the Duke's presence and personality. Allan Rae recalled how he had introduced the Duke into local customs:

"At our various parties, I noticed he felt - as manager - he should be formally dressed in a suit. He came up to me on one occasion and said 'How would you describe your shirt?' Well, I was wearing one of those loose fitting affairs with all the colours of the rainbow. 'We call it a hot shirt, Sir', I replied. 'Well, where do I get one?' he enquired. Naturally, we arranged for a suitable present and he appeared in a much more relaxed fashion from that point onwards. I think he really took to the lifestyle in the West Indies in a big way as a result of this tour."

The Duke confirmed this on his return when, at the M.C.C. Annual General Meeting where he was elected President, he said he had had to take the field more often than he had intended but said, "I have never enjoyed five weeks more in my life".

At the Sussex County Cricket Club Annual Dinner, Arthur Gilligan remarked that the entertaining cricket played by the Duke's side had given cricket a tremendous fillip. In reply, the Duke said his enthusiasm for cricket had - if possible - almost doubled since his visit to Jamaica adding, "I believe the team went about their game as it was meant to be played. They got on with it and if the first or last ball of the day was hittable, they hit it."

The 1957 season at Arundel marked a continuation of touring contacts when, in the match against Sussex, 10 out of the Duke's XI came from his Jamaica side. Given this strength, the Sussex side treated the occasion as one of importance and there was much press comment on the return to fitness of Alan Oakman. He made top score for the county and was joined in some big hitting in a half century by his captain, Robin Marlar.

There was also considerable media interest in the appearance in the Duke's side of Lord Cobham, then on leave as Governor-General in New Zealand. He did not disappoint a crowd of over 4000 when he took a brilliant slip catch and put on 50 in 27 minutes in opening the batting with Roy Marshall. With other swashbuckling contributions from the cricketing parson David Blake and Colin Ingleby-Mackenzie, the Duke's side achieved a comfortable victory. More important were the funds raised for Sussex cricket charities including a special appeal for the Maurice Tate memorial.

The Duke's team in the West Indies 1957

Back row (L to R): G. Tribe, R. Marshall, A. Moss, T. Greenhough, D. V. Smith, A. C. D. Ingleby-Mackenzie, D. E. Blake, D. Barrick.
Front row (L to R): W. Watson, D. Wright, E. D. R. Eagar, Duke of Norfolk, J. J. Warr, T. Graveney.

What was less appealing to the Duke was the media interest in his own injury. He had to leave the field during the Sussex innings when he tore a muscle in his calf. He also damaged a finger and hurt his right ankle and was quoted as saying: "I feel like a race horse that has broken down."

Because of the Jamaican tour, there had been no opportunity to organise a match against the visiting West Indian side. The other big game in 1957 was therefore arranged immediately after Goodwood week. This allowed both the Duke of Edinburgh and the Duke of Norfolk to involve themselves in a return match on behalf of the National Playing Fields Association.

Once again, the Norfolk team brought together most of his Jamaican touring side. Assisted by a top score from the Sussex opener Don Smith, his team acquired runs quickly. However, much of the crowd's interest was directed towards the Duke of Edinburgh who bowled his round the wicket right-arm spinners to take 4 for 60 from 11.5 overs. The big moment of the match came when the Duke of Norfolk arrived at the crease to face his opposing captain. Norfolk got a single off the first ball he received from Edinburgh and added another when facing Jim Langridge at the other end. Between these two scoring shots, there had been time for him to steer a catch off Langridge to Prince Philip in the slips. As the local press write up said:

"There was a lot of juggling and the ball went down. There was a polite little bow between batsman and fieldsman accompanied by broad smiles. But in the next over, Prince Philip's smile was even broader. He completely deceived the Duke of Norfolk and off flew the bails."

The Duke of Edinburgh's side chasing 258 runs to win the match made a good effort with useful scores from almost everyone including the Captain. Naturally, there was much interest in this innings and Robin Marlar takes up the story:

"Duke Bernard had instructed me to make sure that Prince Philip got a six. Now this is not as easy as it sounds. I had had to work very hard in an earlier match to ensure that the Duke of Norfolk could get his own six. The only way to do this was to ensure that you bowled a leg side full toss near enough to the leg stump so that he could be sure to reach it, and slow enough to be certain that he could help it on its way. For the Duke of Edinburgh it was a different proposition. You had to put the ball in the slot just outside offstump so that he could connect with a natural swing of the bat. But I must say he got hold of one of my deliveries in exactly the right way and hit it magnificently over the

boundary at long-off. They couldn't quite get the runs on this occasion but the National Playing Fields Association did very well from the match and I think we were right to stop the series then before the novelty wore off.

"On the other hand, it was fascinating how Prince Philip attracted the public. Soon after this game, I got a letter from C. B. Fry who said, 'You must keep the Duke of Edinburgh playing good class cricket. From what I have seen of him, he seems to have a natural aptitude for the game and he is the most exciting new element we have seen in cricket for a very long time.'"

As to that, the Duke of Edinburgh told the author many years later:

"I think I was right to make representative games like those at Arundel my swan song. Playing at that level you could, for a while, kid yourself that you could keep up with the good players. But once they needed to put on the pressure in a tight finish then the whole thing changed gear and you realised what a vast gap there was between the part-time and the first-class cricketer."

In 1958, the Duke of Norfolk arranged another fixture with the Touring side - in this case New Zealand - at the start of the season. The Duke later described this as the worst day for cricket in his experience and said that the large crowd showed, "the British have a great capacity for displaying their greatest assets in the worst possible circumstances."

Despite the conditions, *The Daily Telegraph* was moved to purple prose:

"Around the supreme ground, the glorious trees were bare and almost sproutless, the grass on the banks was dank and wintry and the odds against rain were no better than evens. Several hundreds braved the elements. At 10.40 the band of the Grenadier Guards played 'It ain't going to rain no more'. Within seconds down came the rain. After a delayed start, Sheppard glanced and Smith drove and having given the side a good start both got out to give others a chance to bat in what was obviously going to be a limited over match. It was Cave, an older and wiser bowler than on his last tour in 1949, who caused a panic in the ducal ranks. Bowling a wet ball from a great height with remarkable accuracy he got one through Graveney's defence and then bowled Compton first ball when he didn't play a stroke at a ball which nipped back and hit the middle stump. After the match was abandoned, the sun mocked momentarily and in the evening the sky was red enough to delight a South Down shepherd."

DUKE OF NORFOLK'S XI v EMERITI C.C.
22ND MAY 1955

EMERITI C. C.

J. Dick	run out	50
H. Hussy	b. Robinson	27
G. P. S. DeLisle	b. Robinson	1
M. Reynolds	not out	51
R. Coleman	b. Bartlett	5
J. Poland	not out	16
Lord Stafford	did not bat	
G. Hemming		
D. C. Smith		
J. Bredin		
L. Toynbee		
	Extras	15
	Total (for 4 wkts. dec.)	165

Bowling

	O	M	R	W
Bartlett	10	0	36	1
Broomfield	15	2	34	0
Robinson	12	2	37	2
Joynson	11	1	43	0

DUKE OF NORFOLK'S XI

E. Underdown	b. Toynbee	7
P. M. H. Robinson	c. Hussy b. Toynbee	0
W. R. N. Joynson	b. Toynbee	6
G. Symthe	lbw. Toynbee	0
Hon. R. Strutt	c. Hussy b. Smith	20
Duke of Norfolk	b. Toynbee	0
A. J. Scratchley	b. Smith	0
J. A. P. Bartlett	b. Poland	7
N. H. Broomfield	not out	3
N. Collin	b. Smith	0
H. M. Rimmer	did not bat	
	Extras	3
	Total (for 9 wkts)	46

Bowling

	O	M	R	W
Toynbee	12	9	7	5
Bredin	7	4	10	0
Smith	7.3	1	25	3
Poland	3	2	1	1

MATCH DRAWN

While the Touring and other major matches at Arundel in the Fifties took much of the limelight (and would soon be followed by visits from overseas clubs like De Flamingos of Holland in 1959) there was still a determined effort to sustain and expand country house cricket.

When the three match series against Cosmo Crawley's XI ended in 1954 (with a two to one advantage to the visitors), it was replaced with a new fixture against Emeriti. This touring team, made up of old boys from leading Catholic public schools, was capable of producing a strong side.

Among those playing at Arundel for the first time in 1954 was the artist Laurence Toynbee. He came from a distinguished academic background. His father was the historian Arnold Toynbee and his mother's father was the Anglo-Australian classical don, Dr Gilbert Murray, with whom he was a near neighbour in his role as an art master at a private school in Oxford.

Laurence Toynbee had already acquired a reputation as a painter of sporting events and several of his pictures of imaginary cricket scenes at Arundel hang in the Pavilion of the Arundel Castle Cricket Club today. Forty years on, married with six daughters, from his home in rural Yorkshire, he recalled his days as a fast bowler and his first encounter with the Duke:

"For some reason, the Duke did not play in the 1954 match and, in the return game in the following year, there was a lot of rain and I found conditions much to my liking. Anyway I got the first four wickets and in came the Duke. Well, I tried to behave like a good guest and he hung around for a while but, eventually, I regret to say that I bowled him for 0. After the game he said to me, 'You had better come back to the Castle and have a bed for the night on your last visit to Arundel!'"

Toynbee's last five overs in this match were maidens and he finished with the figures of 12-9-7-5. Happily, he adds, "The Duke's displeasure was short-lived and I returned to play both for and against him many times."

One of those who made his debut for the Duke's team in this match was Nigel Broomfield. At the age of 18, he was employed as a tutor at a local private school after leaving Haileybury (where he had been a successful all-rounder), and prior to taking up his place at Cambridge:

"I remember that on this occasion we seemed to spend almost more time in the Castle than on the cricket ground. Because of the rain, we had a delayed start which we used to play a fiercesome game of indoor cricket in the Baron's Hall. Then when the match finished early, we had a tour and Laurence Toynbee talked with great expertise about the pictures in the Castle.

"When we got out in the middle I noticed that most of my team-mates were racing friends of the Duke and they seemed to my young eyes a rather elderly bunch apart from Peter Robinson, who did most of the bowling with me. There wasn't a lot of batting in evidence and we just managed to escape with a draw.

"But perhaps the thing which sticks in my mind both

during that game and a number of others in which I played in the same year was the amount of fielding expected of the younger players. I realise why Eddie Harrison was keen to recruit one or two people like myself. Apart from doing most of the bowling, I was the statutory off-side fielder. In these games, my opposite number as the statutory leg side fielder was Peter Robinson. His job was to cover just about everything in the deep from fine leg to long on while I concentrated on a similar arc from third man to long off. Meanwhile, it seemed, the rest of the Duke's racing crowd were happy to let the ball run through to us."

Nigel Broomfield's remarks about Peter Robinson serve to introduce the Duke's second highest run-scorer. Born in Trinidad, he has close ties with cricket in the Caribbean particularly through his cousin, Captain Peter Short, the Chairman of the West Indian Cricket Board of Control. In the W.I.C.B.C. box at Bridgetown, Barbados, during England's historic Test Match victory early in 1994, Peter Robinson, now a successful film and television producer, recalled his long association with cricket for the Duke:

"I took my cricket seriously when I captained the side at Lancing but I had no joy in my pursuit of a Blue at Cambridge where I was up against competition from the likes of Dewes, Doggart, Sheppard and Subba Row among others. I got my compensation in playing squash for Cambridge and England and, afterwards, I was lucky that my early business interests allowed me to play a great deal of cricket for Duke Bernard. At that time, when I was first married, we were lucky enough to rent one of the Duke's houses in Castle Park. So, in a sense, I was captive trade and Nigel Broomfield is right about the amount of fielding expected from the younger players. But, if I'm honest, I must say that I greatly enjoyed it. It is such a joy to field on that perfect turf and one can't escape a certain feeling of satisfaction if you know you can cope better than most of your side and it is appreciated.

"On the other hand, I am not so sure that I entirely appreciated the good fielding on the other side when I played against Emeriti as my debut for the Duke was cut short through a brilliant catch at short leg by a chap called Hussy off the bowling of a very hostile Laurence Toynbee."

Peter Robinson would renew his acquaintance with Toynbee when they returned to play for the Duke in 1956. First, however, the painter demonstrated his liking for the wicket at Arundel when playing for I Zingari against the Duke's side on 2 June 1956. This match marked the start of a new series which has lasted up to the present day and the game provided an exceptionally exciting finish.

After a first wicket partnership of 78 for I Zingari in 45 minutes (of which Aidan Crawley scored 40), Dr David Rice and Robin Marlar bowling unchanged dismissed the visiting side for 116.

The Duke's side were soon in trouble. Jack Fingleton taking a break from reporting the Australian tour of England hit the first ball of the innings from Toynbee for 4 but was dismissed by Aidan Crawley as soon as he got to the other end. Wickets continued to fall regularly to Laurence Toynbee who has described his feelings in bowling George Mann:

"He was a great hero of mine. We all thought he had done a wonderful job captaining M.C.C. in South Africa a few years before and he had been playing regularly for Middlesex up until the end of the previous season. So it was a mixed pleasure when I bowled him first ball and stood on a hat trick".

C. H. Blount kept the innings going almost single handedly until he was joined by Dr David Rice performing another of his tail-end rescue acts. He almost saw the Duke's side home - a task which was completed by the Duke's captain, Robin Marlar.

A week later, the Duke enjoyed another success when Laurence Toynbee made his debut for the home team - against the Eton Ramblers. On this occasion, he shared the main bowling effort with the Oxford Blue, Derek Henderson, and Eddie Harrison. After the Ramblers had declared at 179 for 8, victory came through a partnership of 166 between Peter Robinson and the Chichester Priory Park cricketer, A. G. Avery. Peter Robinson's 95 - which would equal his highest on the ground - led him to reflect on the special needs of playing for the Duke's side:

"I remember we thought the Ramblers had left their declaration a bit late and we lost early wickets in chasing the runs. Then when Avery and I got our partnership going, one faced a special dilemma. You weren't expected to hog it and yet you were strongly encouraged to win. So you had to strike a delicate balance between trying to see your side home and considering whether you should let somebody else have a go. On this occasion, I think I may have got it just about right because I think the Duke regarded a century when his team was batting second as a bit excessive."

Another who made his debut for the Duke in 1956 was Richard Burton. He had recently handed over the captaincy

DUKE OF NORFOLK'S XI v I ZINGARI
2ND JUNE 1956

I ZINGARI

A. M. Crawley	c. Rice b. Marlar	40
J. Foster	c. Collin b. Marlar	35
D. Chetwoode	b. Rice	11
W. R. H. Joynson	b. Marlar	2
D. Henderson	b. Rice	8
Lord Cobham	c. Collin b. Marlar	1
R. A. H. Barnes	b. Marlar	2
R. M. Chaplin	lbw. Rice	4
M. England	not out	3
C. S. Crawley	b. Marlar	4
L. Toynbee	c. Collin b. Rice	0
	Extras	6
	Total	116

Bowling

	O	M	R	W
Rice	17.2	2	58	4
Marlar	16	2	52	6

DUKE OF NORFOLK'S XI

E. Underdown	c. Foster b. Toynbee	0
J. Fingleton	lbw. Crawley	5
E. W. Allen	lbw. Toynbee	11
C. H. Blount	not out	76
F. G. Mann	b. Toynbee	0
D. Hoare	b. Toynbee	0
N. Collin	c. Cobham b. Toynbee	3
R. Harvey	b. Toynbee	4
D. Rice	b. Henderson	13
Lord Belper	b. Toynbee	0
R. Marlar	not out	3
	Extras	7
	Total (for 9 wkts)	122

Bowling

	O	M	R	W
Toynbee	14	1	57	7
Crawley	7	2	24	1
Henderson	8	0	34	1

DUKE OF NORFOLK'S XI WON BY 1 WICKET

of the Lancing Old Boys to Peter Robinson who describes him at this stage of his life as, "a typical public school cricketer whose first movement would be to get the left leg well down the wicket so that he could be very aggressive off the front foot."

Of Richard Burton, another contemporary said: "He always exudes extreme good will with a beaming smile and countenance that is a better looking version of Mr Punch". A former Chairman of Gillette and of the Television Cable Authority, he has vivid recollections of his early matches for the Duke:

"I first played against him for the Martlets. After I got some runs he said to me at the end of the game 'How would you feel about turning out for my side next week?' At the time, I felt rather committed to the Martlets but I thought I would give it a try. It proved to be one of the happiest decisions I have ever made and he kept me busy for almost the next twenty years. Naturally, I have a particularly fond memory of my first appearance for the Duke which was against the local Arundel Cricket Club.

"I appeared in the somewhat unlikely role of opening bowler in partnership with Lord Cobham who was just about to become Governor-General of New Zealand. In fact, we were a rather lordly lot with the debonair Lord Porchester and additional family representation with Lord Belper. I remember we had a good tight match but there is a slight mystery about the end of the game. We played twelve-a-side and most of the bowling was carried out by Peter Robinson and Basil Wood, both bowling spinners. When it came to batting, I see that I was left not out at the end but there is no sign in the score book of Basil Wood who I assume had to leave early. And so it goes down as a loss by 9 runs.

"After that match, I played a few games for the Duke but I was still quite heavily engaged with the Martlets and it was 1959 before I began to give additional time to cricket at Arundel. I remember the year particularly because it was the one in which Tony Thackara burst on the scene."

Commander A. L. S. S. Thackara had just retired from the Navy as an exceptionally fit 42 year old who, in addition to playing Inter-Service cricket, had represented Cornwall and Combined Services. During the next fifteen years, his regular run-getting would make him the highest scorer of all the Duke's men but, as he recalls, his start was somewhat uncertain:

"I don't know about bursting on the scene but I had connections with Arundel through I Zingari. In fact, my first game for the Duke was against I Z. and I arrived with my then girlfriend and a girlfriend of hers. I can only explain the number by suggesting that perhaps my girlfriend at the time didn't trust me. I am glad to report we have been happily married ever since and Arundel has played a great part in our lives."

Peter Robinson gives his impression of these first appearances by Tony Thackara:

"Somehow the image of Tony and pretty girls at that time seems right. He brought an incorrigible sense of humour and a huge enjoyment of life to his cricket. His batting was just the same. As an opener, he would obviously have to look at it for an over or two but he would then proceed in that splendidly bustling style of his to keep the score moving along in the manner of Bill Edrich."

Tony Thackara's first appearance for the Duke will always be recalled as Mordaunt's Match. In opening the batting for I Z, David Mordaunt scored 100 before lunch in just under an hour and his total of 144 included twenty five fours and three sixes. Several of these big hits seemed specifically directed at the oak trees planted by Queen Victoria and Prince Albert. Eventually, Duke Bernard was heard to say: 'Steady on, my boy. Those trees have been in the family for very many years and we'd like to keep them a little while longer.' Perhaps even more alarming, several of Mordaunt's straight drives came perilously close to Duke Bernard fielding at mid off. As Tony Thackara says:

"These were generally hit on the up and passed seemingly within inches of his face. It was only with the greatest difficulty that we finally persuaded him to field at long-off'.

In the match which followed against the Eton Ramblers, Tony Thackara made his first big score on the ground in helping his side to a comfortable victory. His partner in opening the batting was Richard Burton:

"It was hardly an opening partnership. The Ramblers had a very chatty wicket-keeper called Henry Blofeld who would later become known to the world as the cricket commentator 'Blowers'. He took a brilliant catch off Ian Lomax who played for both Somerset and Wiltshire and I departed with my tail between my legs for 0. However, I was out in the middle long enough to see that in Tony Thackara the Duke had found someone special. I also appreciated 'Blowers' wicked sense of humour."

For his part, Henry Blofeld would later tell the author of his relaxed approach in these games:

"I was 19 years of age and I had just got my Blue at Cambridge but I can only say that I found the attitude of several of the members of the Ramblers team to be somewhat subservient to the Duke. Taking a leaf out of Colin Ingleby-Mackenzie's book, I treated him with a hearty irreverence which he seemed to quite enjoy."

For Tony Thackara, this match was a particularly happy occasion made more so by the personalities in the Duke's side:

"Apart from the Duke's regular tail enders, Eddie Harrison, Robin Marlar and David Rice, our middle order had its fair share of characters. William Reginald Hamborough Joynson - always known as Tim - had turned out for Oxford just before the War and was a great figure in Kent with the Band of Brothers. The Hon Mark Tennyson

ETON RAMBLERS C.C. V DUKE OF NORFOLK'S XI
6TH JUNE 1959

ETON RAMBLERS C.C.

H. C. Blofeld	c. and b. Harrison	7
A. M. Wolfe-Murray	b. Toynbee	11
P. Hill-Wood	c. Collins b. Toynbee	6
I. Lomax	b. Henderson	23
C. Gibson	c. Tennyson b. Toynbee	2
A. M. Headley	c. Thackara b. Toynbee	38
R. Napier	c. Tennyson b. Harrison	9
A. J. N. Dawson	c. Buxton b. Shatrushalya Sinhji	40
C. Hodgson	c. Shatrushalya Sinhji b. Rice	1
N. E. W. Baker	c. Thackara b. Shatrushalya Sinhji	0
P. Legge	not out	3
	Extras	6
	Total	146

Bowling

	O	M	R	W
Toynbee	18	8	36	4
Harrison	16	3	41	2
Henderson	6	2	27	1
Shatrushalya Sinhji	6	1	17	2
Rice	2	0	19	1

DUKE OF NORFOLK'S XI

R. Burton	c. Blofeld b. Lomax	0
A. Thackara	not out	81
T. Joynson	c. Wolfe-Murray b. Hill-Wood	17
M. Tennyson	c. Wolfe-Murray b. Hill-Wood	5
A. Henderson	b. Hill-Wood	25
A. Collins	not out	12
P. Shatrushalya Sinhji	did not bat	
Duke of Norfolk		
E. Harrison		
R. Marlar		
Dr. Rice		
	Extras	10
	Total (for 4 wkts.)	150

Bowling

	O	M	R	W
Lomax	12	0	49	1
Hill-Wood	15	3	54	3
Baker	5.2	0	37	0

DUKE OF NORFOLK'S XI WON BY 6 WICKETS

and the impossibly named Prince Shatrushalya Sinhji added a certain aristocratic tone. Mark was a relation of the ex-England captain, Lionel Lord Tennyson, and the Prince was a grandson of the great Ranji. Derek Henderson was still a very useful all-rounder whose family connections with Arundel have been maintained by his son Stephen. And then there was Arthur Collins, a great figure behind the stumps. I think it is fair to say that after an hour or so he was apt to crouch rather than get down but he added gravitas to our proceedings as a distinguished lawyer and he always seemed to do what was needed with the bat."

1953

June 14th. Eton Ramblers 152 (A. M. Hedley 51, Dr D. Rice 9-47). Duke of Norfolk's XI 30 (A. G. Pelham 8-17). Eton Ramblers won by 122 runs.

1955

June 26th. Sussex Martlets 215-7 dec. (M. Tindall 69, J. L. Hope 53). Duke of Norfolk's XI 184 (C. E. Underdown 71, C. Clover-Brown 5-60). Sussex Martlets won by 31 runs.

1957

July 7th. Sussex County C. C. XI 238 (A. S. M. Oakman 65, R. G. Marlar 53*, G. Tribe 5-64). Duke of Norfolk's XI 239-6 (R. E. Marshall 71). Duke of Norfolk's XI won by 4 wickets.

August 4th. Duke of Norfolk's XII 257 (D. Smith 85) H. R. H. Duke of Edinburgh's XII 254-9 (I. Craig 59, G. Tribe 5-45). Drawn.

1958

April 26th, Duke of Norfolk's XI 186-8 dec. (D. V. Smith 83). New Zealand Touring Team. 42-0. Match abandoned.

1959

May 31st. I Zingari 261-5 dec. (D. Mordaunt 144, R. D. L. Lithgow 53). Duke of Norfolk's XI 194 (Hobbs 55, G. D. Massy 6-26). I Zingari won by 67 runs.

1959

August 8th. De Flamingo's XI 269 (G. M. Aim 130, H. A. Wigkhuisen 55). Duke of Norfolk's XI 231. De Flamingo's XI won by 38 runs.

CHAPTER SIX

The Swinging Sixties 1960-1964

The Sixties saw increasing commitments for the Duke and his family in the racing and riding world. Lady Sarah Fitzalan-Howard became first reserve for the British International Show Jumping Team and in July 1962 was the first woman to win the Horse and Hound Cup at the White City. At the same time, apart from their Ascot commitments, the Duke and Duchess were regularly hosting the Queen and Prince Philip at Arundel Park for Goodwood Races and travelling widely to other races.

The sixties also saw the end of a period of uncertainty regarding the future of Arundel Castle. Faced with the ever increasing costs of maintaining a home and effectively an official residence for the Earl Marshal, with a full complement of servants and a large estate staff, the Duke had introduced a Bill in the House of Lords in 1957 in an attempt to hand over the Castle to the Nation as the hereditary home of the Earl Marshal.

Following procedural difficulties in both Houses of Parliament, the Bill was amended to give the Duke freedom to dispose of the Castle as he pleased. At a reception in Arundel Town Hall in November 1959 following his usual practice of laying a wreath on the town's War Memorial, the Duke made a public statement:

"It has been my privilege for 50 years to live in one of the ancient houses of England and I don't intend to give it up. But we are moving to the Dower House which is nearing completion in the Castle Park."

The journalists who were out in force included the *Daily Mail*'s Paul Tanfield:

"The townsfolk up to this point had stood dumbfounded. It seemed that their staple industry, the very heart of the community, was threatened. The cheers that rang out later were of relief. 'Arundel will go on', the Duke said. 'So will the Castle. And so will those who work on my estate.' So too, he might have added, will the cricket."

The Duke's commitment to the game at Arundel seemed to be fully confirmed when the family moved into their new home, Arundel Park. As a result of a casual conversation with Laurence Toynbee after one of his cricket matches, the painter was commissioned to produce a mural in the loggia of the new house. The mural, depicting the four seasons, includes a summer scene of a cricket match in progress in the park.

In fact, the Duke's enthusiasm for promoting cricket at the highest level was, if anything, to accelerate in the Sixties. On the occasion of the first match of the season in 1960, when the visiting side was the South African team, the Duke took the opportunity to stress his feelings about the modern game:

"I wonder", he asked rhetorically, "whether those at home who have the honour to play for their county or their country, appreciate what an honour it really is. I have an idea that too many of the stars have become prima donnas before they have really become stars".

There had also been some concern expressed about the possibility of protests against Apartheid. This had already caused internal dissension when David Sheppard felt obliged to turn down the Duke's usual invitation to captain his side against the Tourists. At the Oval in August 1994, the Bishop of Liverpool recalled the significance of this decision:

"As a priest, it was really the moment of truth for me as far as decisions about 'going public' on political matters were concerned. It's marvellous to see the South Africans back in the fold again but, in 1960, I had just had meetings with Trevor Huddleston and others and we had come to the conclusion that sporting sanctions were one of the strongest weapons we could employ against Apartheid. So I felt I had no option but to turn down the Duke's invitation. He bore no ill will and I was happy to turn out for him in other matches although, as the years went by, it became harder to get the ball off the square without regular practice."

In the 1960 match, there were few signs of political activity at Arundel. Jackie McGlew having won the toss led his side out on to the field, remarking to the massed ranks of news cameramen, 'Come on fellas. Lets have a clear view.' It was noted that there were more police and special constables in evidence than usual but press coverage reflected only small excitements off the field such as a fire in the first aid tent and the disappointment of Keith Miller's admirers when, as captain of the Duke's XI, he was dismissed for a low score. Roy Marshall as ever scored quickly but Tayfield, although expensive, steadily worked his way through the batting order so that the Duke's XI took lunch with their score at 117 for 5. There had been much speculation about the youngest member of the South African side, Geoff Griffin, and his suspect bowling action. However, bowling at half pace, he gave little cause for offence.

During lunch, the band of the First Battalion of the Parachute Regiment entertained the crowd which, on a chilly day, grew steadily to an estimated 3,000.

They were entertained after lunch by some hitting by what was described as a 'slightly more rotund Godfrey Evans' and the top scorer Freddie Titmus who hit Tayfield for two consecutive sixes in his 56 not out.

Miller declared at 220 for 8 made in 175 minutes and although Titmus and Marlar exercised some control, McGlew and McLean in a century partnership ensured victory for the Tourists.

There was no match against the Australians in 1961 but it was business as usual at the start of the 1962 season. On this occasion, the Duke was able to use his friendship with Colin Ingleby-Mackenzie to bring the Hampshire team which had won the county championship in the previous season to face the Pakistan Touring team. The county side which had acquired a reputation for enjoying their cricket (made famous when their captain told a naive reporter he insisted they were always in bed by dawn) were given their usual hard hitting start by Roy Marshall who hit Nasim-ul-Ghani for three sixes in one over including one which hit the *Sunday Times* long focus camera. In reply to the Duke's total of 294 for 6 declared, Pakistan (long before their World Cup success in limited overs cricket) batted cautiously in a style which did not endear them to the Duke and the match was drawn.

It was notable that the ever increasing size of crowds for these touring matches brought with them their own prob-

DUKE OF NORFOLK'S XI v SOUTH AFRICAN TOURING TEAM
30TH APRIL 1960

DUKE OF NORFOLK'S XI

W. Watson	c. Duckworth b. Tayfield	19
R. E. Marshall	c. Pithey b. Tayfield	36
K. R. Miller	lbw. Tayfield	9
K. F. Barrington	c. Tayfield b. Fellows-Smith	13
R. A. Gale	c. Pithey b. Tayfield	29
T. G. Evans	c. Pithey b. Tayfield	25
F. J. Titmus	not out	56
J. R. Gray	b. Griffin	6
D. Shackleton	c. Goddard b. Fellows-Smith	25
J. J. Warr	did not bat	
R. G. Marlar		
	Extras	2
	Total (for 8 wkts. dec.)	220

Bowling

	O	M	R	W
Griffin	5	1	14	1
Goddard	5	1	7	0
Tayfield	24	5	102	5
Fellows-Smith	8.2	1	34	2
McKinnon	12	1	46	0
McGlew	5	1	15	0

SOUTH AFRICAN TOURING TEAM

D. J. McGlew	c. Gale b. Marlar	72
T. L. Goddard	c. Miller b. Titmus	15
A. J. Pithey	run out	19
R. A. McLean	c. Gale b. Titmus	54
C. Wesley	lbw. Marlar	33
C. A. R. Duckworth	not out	20
P. R. Carlstein	not out	10
J. Fellows-Smith	did not bat	
G. M. Griffin		
H. J. Tayfield		
A. H. McKinnon		
	Extras	1
	Total (for 5 wkts.)	224

Bowling

	O	M	R	W
Miller	8	1	41	0
Shackleton	9	2	37	0
Barrington	5.5	1	43	0
Titmus	9	3	39	2
Gale	4.1	1	17	0
Marlar	8	0	46	2

SOUTH AFRICAN TOURING TEAM WON BY 5 WICKETS

lems. On this occasion, the Duke decided to take matters into his own hands in tackling the problem of litter. Using the public address system he told the crowd that he received an adequate supply of daily newspapers and would be grateful if they took their own copies away with them. The appeal proved successful.

Earlier in the day, a small boy had asked him for an autograph when it was patently clear that he had no idea who he

DUKE OF NORFOLK'S XI v PAKISTANIS
28TH MAY 1962

DUKE OF NORFOLK'S XI

R. E Marshall	c. Hanif b. Alam	61
J. R. Gray	b. Farooq	16
H. Horton	b. Farooq	55
D. A. Livingstone	c. Ahmad b. Farooq	36
P. J. Sainsbury	not out	15
H. M. Barnard	b. Farooq	0
A. C. D. Ingleby-Mackenzie	c. Burki b. Alam	14
L. Harrison	not out	2
A. Wassell	did not bat	
D. Shackleton		
M. D. Burdon		
D. W. White		
	Extras	5
	Total (for 6 wkts. dec.)	204

Bowling

	O	M	R	W
Farooq	13	1	42	4
Malik	10	3	27	0
Nasim-ul-Ghani	10	1	48	0
Intikab Alam	18	8	55	2
Saeed Ahmed	6	0	23	0
Mushtaq Mohammad	1	0	4	0

PAKISTAN

H. Mohammad	b. Gray	4
Alimuddin	b. Sainsbury	29
S. Ahmed	b. Wassell	23
J. Burki	c. Livingstone b. Burdon	19
M. Mohammad	not out	37
I. Ahmed	run out	7
I. Alam	c. Sainsbury b. Marshall	45
W. Mathias	not out	3
M. Malik	did not bat	
M. Farooq		
Nasim-Ul-Ghani		
	Extras	6
	Total (for 6 wkts.)	173

Bowling

	O	M	R	W
Shackleton	6	2	9	0
White	2	1	2	0
Gray	4	0	16	1
Sainsbury	15	3	59	1
Wassell	15	8	32	1
Burdon	8	3	24	1
Marshall	4	0	25	1

MATCH DRAWN

was. 'So', said the Duke, 'I simply wrote Bernard Marmaduke Fitzalan-Howard alongside all the sporting heroes and left him with some guess work.'

At the end of 1962, the Duke's commitment to international cricket tours was given special emphasis when he accepted the M.C.C.'s invitation to manage the England tour of Australia.

The Duke's acceptance was by no means a foregone conclusion. He had State commitments which would make it necessary for him to return in the middle of the tour and as these involved rehearsals for the possible funeral of Sir Winston Churchill, he was unable to make any public statement. He was aware that the press would misinterpret his part-time management. When he consulted Duchess Lavinia, she said: "Why don't you go?" He replied, "I can't go away for six months" to which she replied "I'd like you to go. I would be very proud if you went".

There was another practical difficulty to be overcome before the Duke's acceptance was confirmed. Billy Griffith takes up the story:

"As secretary of the Club it was my responsibility in those last touring days of M.C.C. teams to make all the arrangements about travel expenses. I said to the Duke after a meeting at Lord's that we really needed to have a discussion about his expenses and travel arrangements. 'There's no need,' he said, 'but why don't you come and have a drink at the castle this weekend?' As I was at my home in nearby Middleton that weekend, I duly drove over to see him. When I arrived and had been given a drink, the conversation went as follows.

SCG: 'I've got your air tickets here for you.'.

DN: 'There's no need for them. I've already got my tickets.'

SCG: 'But you can't have. It's our responsibility to cover your travel arrangements as well as those of the whole team.'

DN: 'Are you saying I'm inefficient? I've already made my travel arrangements and the tickets are here in the desk in my drawer. If it's the expense, you are not to worry. It is my duty to go as a member of M.C.C. and its former President. I would not dream of letting the club buy my ticket.'

SCG: 'When you get to Australia, you can't pay for your hotels.'

DN: 'You don't know what I might do in Australia.'

SCG: 'Well it's been arranged months ago that the whole team will stay in various hotels and we pick up the bill for all concerned.'

DN: 'Well, I might obey you in that.'

As Colin Cowdrey would later remark, 'The cynic might well say that the Duke could well afford to pay,' but, surely that is not the point."

On hearing the news on the radio on Tuesday 24 July that the Duke was to be manager of the team, an unknown poet sent in his contribution to the B.B.C. making play of the Duke and the names of several of the touring team:

"I hope there's nothing sinister,
Heraldically or otherwise,
About a Duke who manages,
So dextrously to organise,
A funeral here, a crowning there,
Now and again a race or two,
And finally to tour (and Test),
The country of the kangaroo.

A very parfaitt and true man,
Shepherd and knight to all his team,
Anyone else a proper cow,
Drip, square or perfect Tit must seem.

The move to pick the Noble Duke,
Is one that everyone applauds,
And really, truth to tell,
It is not inappropriate for Lords,
To greet with happy smiling faces,
Another Grace to grace the Graces."

The Duke in his Managerial role on the 1962/63 M.C.C. tour to Australia.

Others were more direct in exploring the Duke's relationship with the touring side. Asked about team discipline at his first press conference at Lords, the Duke said: " Most assuredly, I shall be in charge." As to dealing with the press, the Duke said: " I had a gruelling time at the Coronation but I emerged alive."

One of the matters in which the Australian press took an immediate interest was in the Duke's personal affairs. Keith Miller in his role of cricket writer was among the first to see the Duke and put it to him that his most likely nickname would be 'Dookie'. To this, the Duke replied, "Yes, if they decide on that, 'Dookie' it will have to be".

Another Australian journalist was quick to pick up the problem of financing the Castle. "I hear you had a problem", he said. "How did you get round that? Must have had to work a bit of a flanker, I suppose". "Ah yes," replied the Duke. "What did I do about that? Yes, I remember. I sold Littlehampton."

On the more serious cricketing questions in respect of his management, he took the opportunity of outlining his approach to managing the team saying, "I think this is going to be a highly enjoyable tour. I aim to see that the boys who are going with me enjoy it as well. You don't want to lay down hard and fast rules beforehand. For instance, there is the question of when the players should go to bed. I happen not to go to bed early because I don't sleep for very long and if I go to bed too early I don't sleep properly. But others may be different."

Much has been written about that tour and the special relationship between the ducal manager, his assistant manager, Alec Bedser and the captain of the touring side, Ted Dexter. Perhaps comments from the perspective of over thirty years later aptly sum up what proved to be the end of an era.

For Ted Dexter the tour meant the end of amateurism:

"The selection of the Duke as our manager came as a great surprise. I believe that some members of the Selection Committee indicated that there might be difficulty in finding a manager who could handle me. I know that Duke Bernard said, 'Well, I've never had any difficulty with him'. But we did rather wonder how it would all work out particularly as the question of the ending of the amateur status was very much in the air. Only a year or two earlier, the Duke had chaired an M.C.C. Committee which recommended the retention of amateur status. Of course, there was a bit of leg-pulling when this was abolished while we were in the middle of the tour of Australia but the Duke and his deputy, Alec Bedser, were strong believers in the old values and they certainly didn't encourage us to regard the change as one by which we all became equal in seniority overnight. The old Duke was a marvellous man and you knew exactly where you were with him. His standards were plain for all to see - he was never 'one of the boys'. But he had a style that made the team adore him. I remember early in the tour when he was changing with us in our dressing room, the question came up as to how we should address him and he said: ' You should call me Duke or Sir in public, but you may call me Bernard in the bath'."

For Alec Bedser, the division of responsibilities and their respective roles was equally spelt out:

"Early in the tour I went to him with the various accounts and I said, 'I suppose you will want to keep an eye on the books'. 'Good heavens, no', he replied. 'I always have people to do that kind of thing for me and I am sure you are just the man for the job'.

The real significance of the M.C.C. tour of Australia in 1962/63 for the Duke and for cricket at Arundel was the unique link it forged between both the managers and the players in the touring side. While he had collected a group of "Duke's Men" on his private tour in Jamaica in 1957, this was a different challenge. The enthusiasm for attacking cricket had to be tempered by the demands of a Test Match

series in which the Ashes were at stake and the certainty of massive press attention. Yet the ties of friendship were quickly established.

This process was greatly facilitated by the extent of the Norfolk family involvement. On the eve of the Fourth Test at Adelaide, the Duke indicated that he would like to say a few words. There was much speculation among the players as to whether he intended to say something about the slow over rates of both sides (about which he had been critical in the Press) or the general conduct of the match and there was a feeling that these were matters best left to Alec Bedser. However, Peter Parfitt recalls:

"We all appeared in blazers and ties. The Duke wished us well and said what a great honour it was for anyone to represent England and then added 'Now I have an important announcement to make. Tomorrow three of my daughters will be arriving to watch the Test Match. You may wine them, you may dine them, you may dance with them, but that is all you may do with them.'"

The youngest member in the side was the wicket-keeper, Alan Smith, who adds:

"Inevitably, the girls were christened 'the Norfolk Broads' and as one of the few bachelors in the side, I found myself booked by the Duke to do escort duties. It was anything but an onerous task as they were all great fun and the Duke's approach in this as in so many others matters was to make

M.C.C. v Prime Minister's XI at Canberra, February 1963. Sir Donald Bradman's last match – he is seated here between Sir Robert Menzies and The Duke.

us feel part of the family."

The closeness of the relationship which emerged from the tour of Australia was demonstrated soon after the team returned to England in 1963 when Alec Bedser led a side made up from the touring party for the Duke against the West Indies. Despite the recent heavy rain, there was a huge crowd at Arundel as well as an exceptionally large press contingent.

Duke of Norfolk's XI v West Indies Touring XI
27th April 1963

DUKE OF NORFOLK'S XI

K. F. Barrington	b. Sobers	60
B. R. Knight	st. Murray b. Sobers	74
E. R. Dexter	c. sub. b. Solomon	12
M. C. Cowdrey	c. Sobers b. Solomon	2
T. W. Graveney	c. Butcher b. Solomon	11
F. J. Titmus	c. McMorris b. Solomon	21
J. T. Murray	c. Sobers b. Solomon	5
D. A. Allen	c. Worrell b. Solomon	8
A. C. Smith	c. Murray b. Solomon	5
J. D. F. Larter	b. Solomon	1
A. V. Bedser	not out	3
	Extras	1
	Total	203

Bowling

	O	M	R	W
King	8	2	17	0
Worrell	8	2	14	0
Sobers	14	5	29	2
Gibbs	6	0	57	0
Solomom	18	0	65	8
Rodriguez	11	2	20	0

WEST INDIES XI

J. Carew	b. Larter	2
E. McMorris	b. Allen	52
S. Nurse	c. Barrington b. Smith	70
B. Butcher	c. Larter b. Titmus	18
J. Solomon	st. Murray b. Titmus	20
G. Sobers	b. Smith	18
W. Rodriguez	b. Titmus	0
F. J. Worrell	not out	17
D. Murray	not out	1
	Extras	7
	Total (for 7wkts.)	205

Bowling

	O	M	R	W
Larter	12	3	22	1
Bedser	6	3	7	0
Titmus	10	0	36	3
Barrington	4	0	17	0
Allen	14	1	58	1
Dexter	7	1	13	0
Smith	8	0	45	2

WEST INDIES WON BY 3 WICKETS

John Clark wrote: "The mist lifted above the Castle ramparts, cleared the tall trees in the park and, as if the 1963 cricket season had been ceremoniously unveiled, the sun shone from a cloudless sky. Alec Bedser won the toss, the scarlet-coated Grenadier Guards band played a final selection in front of the dressing tents and out came the West Indians to field."

For J. J. Warr: "The visit of the West Indians to Arundel completes a full house for the Duke of Norfolk. All six touring countries have now had the pleasure of playing on the loveliest of grounds. The morning's play was dominated by some sensible hitting from Barrington and Knight who put on 120 for the first wicket. Gibbs, the off spinner, had 57 runs hit off 6 overs. Most of the catching and attempted catching was done by a man in a brown suit in the crowd."

But perhaps the report which gave the Duke the greatest pleasure was that by Robin Marlar, who had now relinquished his role as Librarian at the Castle and Captain of Sussex in favour of work as a cricketing journalist:

"The Press has worked overtime this winter about the mixed successes and failures of the tour in Australia, but really we have much to be thankful for. This has been a day to make life worth living for those who love cricket and happily there was a full house to savour it.

"No one on the ground can have enjoyed it more than the Duke of Norfolk himself. When he managed his own team in Jamaica he met and shared the West Indies approach to cricket.

"As is customary, the guests fielded first and worked their way through the Duke's side after Barrington and Knight had scored 50 in the first hour. This was principally due to the fact that Solomon was providing the bowler's equivalent of dolly mixtures and finding suckers at regular intervals.

"There was no audible creak when Bedser opened the bowling with Larter but when the spinners came on McMorris and Nurse put on over 100 for the second wicket. Butcher and Solomon and Sobers made their contribution and eventually seven were wanted off the last two balls which were to be bowled by wicket-keeper Smith to the elder statesman Frank Worrell who moves like an old and experienced cat. One of the deliveries was finely driven on the off side where Dexter let it through for the sake of theatre. The last ball was a long hop on the leg side which Worrell struck one handed over the deep mid-wicket boundary."

The reference to Alan Smith's contribution as a bowler

DUKE OF NORFOLK'S XI V AUSTRALIAN TOURING XI
25TH APRIL 1964

DUKE OF NORFOLK'S XI

D. S. Sheppard	lbw. Corling	25
R. E. Marshall	c. Potter b. Corling	55
E. R. Dexter	b. Corling	5
M. C. Cowdrey	b. Martin	70
P. H. B. May	run out	2
J. M. Parks	st. Jarman b. Potter	12
F. J. Titmus	b. Martin	10
D. A. Allen	not out	5
D. Shackleton	c. Burge b. Lawry	1
J. S. E. Price	did not bat	
A. V. Bedser		
	Extras	2
	Total (for 8 wkts. dec.)	187

Bowling

	O	M	R	W
McKenzie	6	2	23	0
Connolly	6	0	20	0
Corling	8	0	22	3
Veivers	11	2	44	0
Martin	12	1	35	2
Potter	6	0	26	1
O'Neill	4	0	15	0
Lawry	1	0	0	1

AUSTRALIAN TOURING XI

W. M. Lawry	b. Price	9
R. B. Simpson	st. Parks b. Shackleton	27
N. C. O'Neill	c. Dexter b. Allen	61
P. J. Burge	c. May b. Dexter	18
J. Potter	not out	31
B. N. Jarman	c. Cowdrey b. Titmus	8
J. W. Martin	c. Dexter b. Titmus	27
G. D. McKenzie	not out	6
T. R. Veivers	did not bat	
A. Connolly		
G. E. Corling		
	Extras	6
	Total (for 6 wkts.)	193

Bowling

	O	M	R	W
Price	6	0	13	1
Bedser	4	1	14	0
Shackleton	10	3	20	1
Titmus	12	0	49	2
Allen	9	1	38	1
Dexter	6	0	22	1
Marshall	6	0	31	0

AUSTRALIAN XI WON BY 4 WICKETS

rather than as a wicket-keeper is one which has acquired a certain fame in the re-telling. As J. J. Warr wrote at the time:

"Perhaps the moment of the match was when Alan Smith bowled Garfield Sobers in the last over. This was an incident which will be drilled into generations of Smiths to come and

into any current cricketer who will lend an ear."

In fairness to Alan Smith it seemed only right to seek his version of events which he gave when speaking to a meeting of the Parliamentary Cricket Group in 1994:

"Of course I shall always remember that match. I was given the opportunity for an unusual amount of bowling and although this was supposed to help the West Indies keep up in the run race I managed to get their top scorer Seymour Nurse and of course the great Sir Gary Sobers. I have had my leg pulled about this over the years but I will continue to claim that I totally deceived him!"

The 1964 match against the Australians led by Bobby Simpson brought together a side under the captaincy of Peter May with other old friends from the touring sides to Jamaica and Australia. Once again, there had been heavy rain overnight but the occasion was given special significance with the first Royal visitor attending the Tourists match at Arundel when the Queen Mother was presented to both sides before the start of play.

Her appearance inspired one unnamed visiting Australian reporter to develop a theme suggested by the Queen Mother. He wrote:

"As late as last Wednesday, the ground was three inches under water and the Queen Mother was heard to say 'The going - whatever you call it - will be a bit tricky out there, won't it?'.

"The ground in fact was in remarkably fine trim although, as was to be expected so early and with so little net practice, the going was hard for quite a few. Hawke distinguished himself by becoming the first bowler ever at Arundel - and probably anywhere else - to get the first three wickets of an innings whilst seated in a deck chair. The man on the loudspeaker was in error and it was really Corling, just out of a sickbed, who got the wickets.

"Roy Marshall had some delightful forces to leg and Sheppard enjoyed his outing immensely. Cowdrey baulked at the barrier a few times but once away strode along confidently.

"It was wonderful for the Australians to get their arms over and prance in the field. Lawry and the hook stroke found themselves at variance but Simpson and Burge had some invaluable practice. O'Neill was paramount in the Australian batting. Some, who perhaps would have difficulty in knowing a horse from a giraffe, would not have chosen O'Neill for this tour. Rubbish! They will have their heads in the sand at the finish. He showed us class fit to rate with the

The Duke's team against I Zingari, July 1962.
(L to R): N. Collin, A. O. L. Lithgow, A. Thackara,
L. Toynbee, C. S. Crawley, P. Robinson, Wiseman, W. R. N.
Joynson, Duke of Norfolk, E. E. Harrison. Mr. Wiseman was
the Duke's gardener who helped to prepare the pitch.

best. Martin was jolly although the day was a personal failure as he didn't hit a single six, several times missing by a fraction. Parks won honours from me by standing over the stumps for medium pacers and it warmed the cockles to see Alec Bedser wheeling them down again."

There was a similar anonymous contribution about the batting of the Duke's XI from the British press corps although, in this case, using golfing rather than racing comparisons. The style and humour suggest J. J. Warr:

"Dexter's batting was Wentworth in style, Sunningdale in origin and ended when he was bowled through the gate attempting a long putt. The Rev David Sheppard's batting suggested that a bishopric was imminent and May was run out by some indecisive calling from Cowdrey that brought a

smile of recognition to the face of a watching Denis Compton."

The Tourists won the match in the last half hour in a game that raised £3,000 for the National Playing Fields Association and attracted a crowd of over 10,000. For the two captains, their memories are mainly of activity off the field.

Peter May recalls this as a specially happy family occasion:

"This was one of my, by then, infrequent cricket matches of any significance. What I shall always remember is the way in which the Duke's memory and his courtesy to the guests were demonstrated yet again. He had asked me on a previous occasion whether one of my daughters would like the band of the Grenadier Guards to play anything special. She suggested a selection from 'My Fair Lady' and it was duly played. When I arrived to take part in this game, my daughter was with me once again taking time off from her usual round of horse shows. Within minutes of our arrival, the Grenadier Guards were playing a selection from 'My Fair Lady' and the Duke's wink told me all!".

Bobby Simpson felt that his visit was long overdue:

"I was especially pleased to be at Arundel as I had felt robbed in 1961. Our team that year did not come to Arundel and we were all keen to see the Castle. When the game was interrupted by rain, we had a short tour with the Duke. It was all pretty spectacular stuff but the occasion was made, or marred depending on how you look at it, by Johnny Martin. He was always a bit of a character whether batting or bowling and on this occasion he excelled himself by asking the Duke: 'How many lavatories do you have in a place like this?'. The Duke replied 'I have never counted but I have every confidence that my ancestors ensured that there was never too great a distance to travel'."

Perhaps the final story concerning this particular match is one which may give a clue as to the identity of the Australian journalist quoted earlier. He concluded his piece: "The Duke of

Peter May introducing Queen Elizabeth, the Queen Mother to Rev. David Sheppard
and the rest of the Duke's team.

DUKE OF NORFOLK'S XI v SUSSEX C.C.C.
2ND JULY 1961

DUKE OF NORFOLK'S XI

R. A. Gale	c. Langridge b. Duff	23
D. M. Green	c. James b. Duff	41
J. P. Fellows-Smith	c. Lenham b. Bates	70
C. A. Fry	c. Lenham b. Bates	42
M. Tremlett	c. Pountain b. Oakman	40
R. G. Pollock	c. Pountain b. Oakman	17
G. Cox	c. Dexter b. Oakman	29
D. P. Priddy	c. Suttle b. Langridge	20
P. I. Bedford	not out	5
J. J. Warr	c. Dexter b. Oakman	0
A. E. Moss	did not bat	
	Extras	6
	Total (for 9 wkts. dec.)	293

Bowling

	O	M	R	W
James	7	1	28	0
Pountain	7	0	20	0
Duff	7	1	30	2
Parks	5	0	28	0
Suttle	2	0	8	0
Dexter	5	0	33	0
Bates	7	0	31	2
Oakman	7.2	1	51	4
Langridge	5	0	51	1
Lenham	1	0	7	0

SUSSEX C.C.C. XI

G. C. Cooper	st. Fry b. Warr	107
E. R. Dexter	b. Pollock	20
L. J. Lenham	b. Priddy	23
K. G. Suttle	b. Priddy	25
J. M. Parks	c. Fellows-Smith b. Priddy	10
A. E. James	b. Priddy	0
D. Bates	b. Fellows-Smith	45
F. R. Pountain	b. Fellows-Smith	56
A. S. M. Oakman	not out	3
R. Langridge	not out	4
	Extras	2
	Total (for 8 wkts.)	295

Bowling

	O	M	R	W
Moss	5	1	25	0
Warr	9	1	38	1
Fellows-Smith	8	0	35	2
Green	6	0	43	0
Pollock	3	0	35	1
Cox	2	0	26	0
Bedford	8	1	58	0
Priddy	5	1	15	4
Tremlett	2	0	18	0

SUSSEX C.C.C. WON BY 2 WICKETS
LAST MATCH IN SERIES.

Norfolk has several times been my skipper at Arundel and thus talks directly as a skipper should. 'Tell me,' he said, 'are you still writing for the *Sunday Times* or has it improved?' "

Among the matches referred to by Jack Fingleton (for the clue in the last quotation confirms that it was he), was one against the Eton Ramblers in 1961 in which he took part in an opening stand of 92 with Tony Thackara, who comments:

"Through the early sixties we continued with what you might call our base load of country house cricket against the Regiment, the Eton Ramblers, I Zingari, the Sussex Martlets, the Arundel Cricket Club, and Emeriti. One of the joys of games of this kind was that it allowed some of the great figures of the past to play cricket in a relaxed atmosphere without feeling that too much was expected of them. The partnership that I had with Jack Fingleton was a case in point. He was a charming chap and although very much at the veteran stage he showed after taking a while to get used to things that he was still capable of hitting the ball imperiously all round the field. One thing I noticed batting both with him and David Sheppard was that people like that, who had played at the highest level, had the same technical approach. In the early part of an opening partnership, they would make their first movement by going back on the right foot as the ball was delivered, thus allowing a little extra time to get acclimatised. After a while, sure enough, the strokes would begin to flow off front foot as well as back foot.

"In the nature of things, I found myself opening the batting for the Duke with a wide range of partners. Quite apart from the skill or otherwise of our opponents, we always had a tall order. In these traditional fixtures, the other side - if not dismissed - would be expected to declare by about 3.30 which would leave us with an hours batting before tea. In that time, if we were chasing a big total - as often happened - the Duke expected us to be well on the way to 100."

Apart from posing these challenges, the Duke continued to experiment with invitations for new visitors to Arundel. The needs of Sunday and subsequently limited over cricket meant that Sussex played their last regular match against his side in 1961. This was an all star finale which the County won thanks mainly to a century in 65 minutes by Graham Cooper.

Into the gap came the Kent touring club side, the Bluemantles, who visited the ground as part of their centenary in 1962. Richard Burton takes up the story:

"I don't know whether someone had failed to tell them the form. This seems very unlikely as it was well known that guests were expected to let the Duke's side bat last. Anyway, their captain won the toss and, on rather a green wicket, put

LILLYWHITES CENTENARY XI v THE LORD'S TAVERNERS XII
5TH MAY 1963

LORD'S TAVERNERS XII

M. D. Fenner	b. Bedser	0
R. J. Langridge	b. Martin	50
B. Barnett	c. McIntyre b. Warr	8
E. A. Bedser	st. McIntyre b. Cheesman	57
B. Bresslaw	run out	11
R. Hearne	retired	4
J. Fellows-Smith	c. Clark b. Cheesman	9
R. Subba Row	st. McIntyre b. Lenham	62
W. S. Surridge	c. Benaud b. Pretlove	11
M. Hobley	c. Graveney b. Warr	3
J. Laker	not out	3
P. Haigh	not out	1
	Extras	3
	Total (for 9 wkts. dec.)	222

Bowling

	O	M	R	W
Bedser	6	0	9	1
Warr	9	0	46	2
Martin	8	0	44	1
Benaud	8	2	19	0
Lenham	6	0	33	1
Dexter	6	2	13	0
Cheesman	9	1	24	2
Pretlove	6	0	31	1

LILLYWHITES CENTENARY XI

L. J. Lenham	lbw. Fellows-Smith	27
E. A. Clark	b. Fellows-Smith	3
J. F. Pretlove	c. Fenner b. Bedser	12
H. Masters	st. Barnett b. Laker	30
E. R. Dexter	run out	59
R. Benaud	st. Barnett b. Hearne	53
B. Cheesman	not out	31
T. Graveney	not out	0
A. V. Bedser	did not bat	
J. J. Warr		
J. Martin		
	Extras	8
	Total (for 6 wkts.)	223

Bowling

	O	M	R	W
Fellows-Smith	6	0	21	2
Bresslaw	3	0	20	0
Hobley	2	0	8	0
Bedser	4	0	20	1
Laker	9	1	31	1
Fenner	5	0	58	0
Subba Row	2	0	28	0
Haigh	2	0	20	0
Hearne	2	0	9	1

LILLYWHITES CENTENARY XI WON BY 4 WICKETS

us in to bat. Jonathan Watt who had only recently left Eastbourne College but who had played first-class cricket for Colonel L. C. Steven's XI, played very well and only just

failed to get 100. The rest of us struggled in somewhat difficult conditions of low cloud and chilly weather with the ball swinging about. The weather then improved and they duly knocked off the runs. When we were having drinks afterwards, I said to the Duke, 'Didn't you think they played it a bit tight today?' to which he replied, 'Yes, it has taken them one hundred years to arrange this match and it may well be a similar period before we see them here again.' I can only note that there has so far been no return fixture with the Bluemantles in the third of a century which has followed."

If there was to be no series against the Bluemantles, the continuing local rivalry with Arundel Cricket Club had become a permanent fixture. One of the most exciting matches in that series was in 1962. Pat Coates, then on leave from India, told the author:

"This was a really tight game and I remember how absolutely delighted the Duke was when we managed to get home by one wicket. For much of the match it looked as though we would have no real problem because Eddie Harrison and Tony Gooda got us off to a flying start. In particular, Gooda had a hat trick and he and Eddie Harrison were threatening to ruin the game. So we took them off and a chap called Sugden and I worked our way through the middle order. Then when Tony Gooda came back on again, blow me if he didn't take the last three wickets in 4 balls.

"When it came to our turn to bat, and Ken Shearwood and I had 100 on the board with only two wickets down, we thought we could relax. When we both got out, our wickets tumbled regularly and we only got home by the skin of our teeth."

In 1963 and 1964, the Duke decided to widen his invitation list for visits by overseas clubs. The Staggerers of South Africa were defeated by 24 runs thanks mainly to a not out century from G. D. Massey, but the Australian Old Collegians touring team proved themselves too strong a side for a below strength Duke's team.

However the matches in 1963 and 1964 which were to create the greatest local interest were those arranged to mark Lillywhites' Centenary on 5 May 1963 and the family match between the Duke's XI and that of Lady Mary Fitzalan Howard on 12 July 1964.

The Lillywhite Centenary XI was a strong combination of mainly Test and County cricketers. They were opposed in this charity match by a Lord's Taverners' team with a similar spread of County and international experience.

However, in true Taverner tradition, show business was

represented in the persons of MacDonald Hobley and Peter Haigh from the broadcasting world and acting through Bernard Bresslaw and Richard Hearne.

While much of the cricket was played in a stylish fashion when Eric Bedser and Raman Subba Row were scoring half centuries for the Taverners, which were matched if not out-done in hard hitting efforts by Ted Dexter and Richie Benaud for the Lillywhite XI, Richard Hearne felt that the occasion demanded that he should indulge in some of the tumbling and clowning activities which he had made famous in his role as 'Mr Pastry'. While he was thus engaged at the crease, the Duke who had been appealing from the commentary box for charitable donations made some pungent remarks with-out realising that the loudspeaker system was still switched on. These culminated in the words "get that bloody man off my ground", and, as the record shows, Richard Hearne is marked down as retired for four runs.

However, he compounded his offence by clowning again when he came on to bowl, actually delivering, with the com-plicity of the umpires, consecutive overs from each end. This again aroused the Duke to anger - an anger which was reinforced when Richie Benaud made 'Mr Pastry' a present of his wicket. As the record shows, although the Duke of Norfolk was patron of the Lord's Taverners, it would be a long time before they returned to Arundel.

On the other hand, the fixture which was arranged against Lady Mary Fitzalan-Howard's XI in July 1964 was one which was immediately established as a regular fixture. It's success reflected the following of the four Norfolk daughters. We have noted their impact during the tour of Australia. Back home, as attractive girls in the sporting and social worlds, they had many admirers and they were among the group which brought their own version of the Swinging Sixties to Arundel Castle weekends.

By 1964, Lady Anne Fitzalan-Howard was increasingly involved in her interests in breeding and training horses which led to the establishment of her home at Everingham in Yorkshire. It fell to Mary, therefore, as the next eldest daughter, to respond to her father's suggestion of raising a team which was largely made up of friends of herself and her sisters Sarah and Jane. Mary would bring to this group many friends made through her work as Lady-in-Waiting to Princess Alexandra; Sarah's interests as a leading horse-woman have already been noted and the mixture was varied when Jane became a Sussex Junior tennis champion.

Lady Mary Mumford has described the background to the first game which she and her sisters arranged in 1964:

"My father thought the matches against the Royal Sussex Regiment might be coming to an end and suggested we should get a side together. This was very much a joint effort with my sisters and the great thing about it was that we were able to move into the Castle for our own cricket weekend. With boyfriends and some of the husbands and wives in our crowd, we had as many as 24 staying for the weekend.

"Looking at that first team in 1964, I see many of the regulars who would turn out for us in the years which fol-lowed. Mark Ronaldshay who is now the Marquess of Zetland was a racecourse owner and has become a leading figure in the Jockey Club. Henry Crichton-Stuart was one of our Scottish friends related to the Earl of Bute. I don't know how we managed to get hold of Colin Cowdrey at that time as he was still playing first-class cricket but he made all the difference to the strength of our side and naturally we made him captain. He would be succeeded by Ian Balding who was a Cambridge Blue but for Rugger and Boxing. He was one of our string of trainers. He came from Kingsclere, Adrian Maxwell was from Ireland and Gordon Smyth was in charge of the home team in my father's stables. Edward Cazalet, who is now Sir Edward, the judge, also had racing links because his father Peter was a trainer who had played cricket at Arundel in the Fifties. Simon Fraser, Lord Lovat's heir, was a proper cricketer as was Chips Keswick, now Sir Chips and Chairman of a bank. Michael Burrows was also in for his playing ability as was Johnny Woodcock who became even better known as cricket correspondent of *The Times*.

"Anyway, our side did us proud and rather to my father's surprise, we won the match, so he threatened to make it more difficult for us in the return match the following year."

Lady Sarah Clutton takes up the story of that return match:

"We couldn't call on Colin Cowdrey this time and we brought in quite a lot of other friends, not all of them great cricketers. For example, I don't think our tail-enders Eddie York and James Stamford had played cricket since their prep school days and they brought with them another friend, John Cruikshank. He opened the batting with Robert Newman who was a proper cricketer who had recently got a Blue at Cambridge. There were other new faces who became regulars like Micky Wiggin and John Roberts. Then there was Rodney Forward, whom we knew because his father-in-law was commanding the Household Brigade. That leaves Roger Gibbs who needs a special word."

Sir Roger Gibbs, now Chairman of the Wellcome Foundation, was, at this time, following his father's example as a merchant banker. He describes his special friendship with the Duke:

"I first turned out for the Duke in 1963 when I made a fast 0. He said to me afterwards, 'I assume from your batting that you must be a good fielder.' Well, as it happened, I could usually catch most things and I enjoyed fielding. But I was still staggered at the end of the season to receive a handwritten note from the Duke saying, 'We have all much enjoyed having you with us for the cricket this year and I hope you will be able to join us again next season.'

"As it happened, I played for him against Emeriti at the beginning of 1964. Making his usual entrance just before lunch he found me taking my pads off with the score board showing something like 30 odd for 6. 'This is deplorable' he said. I replied, 'Don't blame me. I got 8, which is equal top score'. 'That remark is quite irrelevant' he replied.

"I had the greatest fun when I became a regular for the girls' team in playing against him. As a matter of fact, I suppose I can claim that I was in line for the captaincy as Mary, being much too nice to make a choice, appointed Ian Balding and myself as co-captains. Well, in that 1965 game, this led to a fair amount of chaos, particularly when the Duke's batsmen were piling on the runs. So at lunch time, I went to Mary and said, 'I hereby resign and suggest you make Ian sole captain'. It was so arranged and he became virtually the permanent captain of the girls' team.

"So far as I was concerned it gave me a lot of opportunities to get to know the Duke better. We would spend hours talking in his study and he was incredibly kind in inviting me to join the family for their holidays abroad when we would regularly play golf.

"As to the cricket, I suppose he liked my idea of having a go at just about everything. In the 1965 match this seemed to come off. The Duke had followed up his Australian tour friendships by inviting the Bedser twins to play for him quite often at Arundel and, on this occasion, Eric was asked to do most of the bowling. I managed to connect with one which sailed away into the big chestnut tree in front of the pavilion. Richard Burton turned to Eric and said, 'My word, he gave that some stick' to which Eric replied, through clenched teeth, 'Yes, he got hold of it nicely, didn't he?' To add insult to injury, when I got out, Chips Keswick carried on by hitting him for several more sixes." Eric Bedser's comment when reminded of these insults today is simply to remark:

"Well, I was bowling to orders you know."

1961

June 4th. Eton Ramblers C. C. 222-7 dec. (J. J. S. Farmer 76). Duke of Norfolk's XI 223-5 (P. Robinson 80, A. W. Thackara 53). Duke of Norfolk's XI won by 5 wickets.

1962

May 13th. Duke of Norfolk's XI 175 (J. Watt 97). Bluemantles C. C. 178-6 (E. McRose 61). Bluemantles C. C. won by 4 wickets.

July 15th. Arundel C. C. 128 (A. Gooda 6-9). Duke of Norfolk's XI 129-9. Duke of Norfolk's XI won by 1 wicket.

1963

June 30th. Duke of Norfolk's XI 187-6 dec. (G. D. Massey 106, B. Thompson 5-45). The Staggerers of Johannesburg 163 (R. Halse 70). Duke of Norfolk's XI won by 24 runs.

1964

June 28th. Australian Old Collegians XI 237-3 dec. (H. Sargent 102, D. Douglas 50*). Duke of Norfolk's XI 184. Australian Old Collegians XI won by 53 runs.

July 12th. Duke of Norfolk's XI 194-8 dec (S. Fraser 5-56). Lady Mary Fitzalan Howard's XI 198-7 (M. C. Cowdrey 84). Lady Mary's XI won by 3 wickets.

Lady Mary and Lady Sarah Fitzalan Howard's XI, 1964.
(L to R): G. Smyth, S. Fraser, H. Crichton-Stuart, C. Keswick,
A. Maxwell, J. Woodcock, M. C. Cowdrey, M. Burrows, E. Cazalet,
M. Ronaldshay, I. Balding.

CHAPTER SEVEN

The Duke's Farewell 1965-1975

Colin Cowdrey's willingness to play for Lady Mary's team was evidence of a growing commitment to the Norfolk family which was further demonstrated when the Duke asked him to captain his side against the visiting New Zealand team in May 1965. Together with Peter May, Ted Dexter, and Tom Graveney, he was one of four England captains in the side who got most of the runs against the visitors.

This match coincided with the opening of the new pavilion. The ceremony was conducted by Billy Griffith in his capacity as Secretary of the M.C.C. On the Duke's instructions, the interior was precisely 22 yards but his daughters were quick to point out some of the missing facilities. "What about showers?", they enquired, to which the Duke replied, "We only play one-day not three-day matches here." The girls were all the more delighted when they heard the New Zealand captain, John Reid, ask the Duke if it would be possible to pop down to the Castle to get a shower and it was not long before these facilities were added to the players' dressing room.

Apart from these internal problems, the match required a certain amount of stage management. As the Duke said on the public address system, "It is a good thing we have faith in Arundel weather despite the unfavourable forecast". In the event, the Tourists batted first in brilliant sunshine but, despite a typically graceful innings by Bert Sutcliffe, were in some trouble before helpful bowling by Peter May and Tom Graveney assisted them to a declaration.

In reply, Ted Dexter made 52 out of 76 scored while he was at the wicket at a run a minute but the Duke's side fell twenty runs short at the end and the match was drawn. It had raised almost a thousand pounds for one of the Duke's more unusual good causes when the proceeds from the collection were donated to M.C.C. funds for encouraging cricket in Ethiopia.

After his successful leadership of the M.C.C. in South Africa in 1965, M. J. K. Smith was invited by the Duke to captain his team against the West Indies at the start of their tour in April 1966. Once again, concern for the weather was very much in evidence but as Robin Marlar wrote at the time:

"Arundel has been a fairy godmother to the West Indians. After April had drenched them by overdoing the showers, the sight of the sun was itself astonishing.

"Sobers' men, then, had the opportunity of playing cricket in the finest setting and on the best turf in the world. As if this was not enough, they were treated most generously by Smith who closed his innings in mid-afternoon and left the West Indians 25 minutes more batting than he had used.

"We do not know whether Smith was trying, in subtle fashion, to draw our attention to the fact that in recent series the West Indians have taken longer to score their runs than England, but the declaration turned the contest into a publican's match."

The Duke with the two captains, John Reid and Colin Cowdrey, at the 1965 tourist match.

DUKE OF NORFOLK'S XII V NEW ZEALAND TOURING TEAM
2ND MAY 1965

NEW ZEALAND TOURING TEAM

B. E. Congdon	b. Gifford	47
A. E. Dick	b. Statham	6
R. W. Morgan	b. Gifford	14
J. R. Reid	b. Gifford	19
B. Sutcliffe	b. Graveney	31
B. W. Youle	c. and b. Hobbs	20
B. R. Taylor	c. and b. Graveney	31
G. E. Vivian	c. Allen b. Gifford	10
R. C. Motz	not out	31
R. O. Collinge	not out	6
F. J. Cameron	did not bat	
J. Ward		
	Extras	2
	Total (for 8 wkts. dec.)	217

Bowling

	O	M	R	W
Statham	10	2	18	1
Palmer	4	1	13	0
Allen	10	1	29	0
Dexter	6	1	16	0
Hobbs	15	3	42	1
May	3	0	32	0
Graveney	4	0	26	2
Gifford	11	3	21	4
Cowdrey	1	0	18	0

DUKE OF NORFOLK'S XII

P. Richardson	c. Motz b. Cameron	2
T. W. Graveney	b. Vivian	35
E. R. Dexter	ct. Youle b. Taylor	52
C. Cowdrey	b. Cameron	44
P. May	b. Cameron	38
J. Parks	not out	12
K. Palmer	b. Motz	3
D. Allen	not out	4
R. Hobbs	did not bat	
N. Gifford		
B. Statham		
D. Foreman		
	Extras	8
	Total (for 6wkts.)	198

Bowling

	O	M	R	W
Motz	7	0	22	1
Cameron	8	0	34	3
Collinge	3	0	17	0
Youle	13	1	63	0
Taylor	4	1	12	1
Vivian	8	1	37	1
Reid	1	0	5	0

MATCH DRAWN

Continuing in this drinking vein, Robin Marlar described Tom Graveney as opening the proceedings with "his own brand of innings of which there is no smoother cocktail. He took 10 off Sobers' first over and managed to look elegant

DUKE OF NORFOLK'S XI V WEST INDIES XI
30TH APRIL 1966

DUKE OF NORFOLK'S XI

M. J. Stewart	c. Kanhai b. Hall	0
N. Hill	c. Hall b. Carew	15
T. W. Graveney	b. Carew	58
K. Barrington	c. Cohen b. Brancker	73
M. J. Smith	c. Carew b. Brancker	25
M. J. Horton	b. Brancker	27
B. Knight	not out	8
G. A. R. Lock	c. Lashley b. Holford	14
D. Allen	did not bat	
A. Long		
L. Coldwell		
	Extras	1
	Total (for 7 wkts. dec.)	221

Bowling

	O	M	R	W
Hall	6	0	24	1
Cohen	5	0	11	0
Sobers	6	1	26	0
Carew	9	1	28	2
Holford	16	0	81	1
Brancker	12	1	50	3

WEST INDIES XI

M. Carew	st. Long b. Horton	54
E. McMorris	c. Long b. Coldwell	0
R. Kanhai	c. Allen b. Lock	21
S. Nurse	b. Knight	61
P. Lashley	not out	61
R. Brancker	c. Smith b. Knight	0
D. Holford	lbw. Lock	0
G. Sobers	not out	21
	Extras	5
	Total (for 6wkts.)	223

Bowling

	O	M	R	W
Coldwell	5	0	23	1
Knight	8	2	24	2
Lock	16	0	85	2
Allen	14	4	41	0
Horton	13	2	45	1

WEST INDIES XI WON BY 4 WICKETS

even when lobbing the slips off the back of the bat. Barrington's top score of the day caught the mood of the occasion which was relaxed but professional and Sobers made a delayed entry as the Castle clock struck opening time in this town of many hostelries and he hit two sixes and two fours off Horton's last five balls."

J. J. Warr was reminded of pantomime and the swinging sixties:

"The visitors were without Charlie Griffith, a little like watching Red Riding Hood without the wolf. In his absence, the bowling of Hall and Cohen was friendly and it must be recorded that their length was nothing like as short as many of the skirts.

"Although the big hitting of Sobers inevitably attracted most press attention, it was Peter Lashley, that much under-estimated Barbadian who, with Carew, set up their victory."

At Bridgetown in 1994, when, apart from England's famous Test victory, the occasion was chiefly memorable for celebrations marking the 40th anniversary of Gary Sobers' debut in Test cricket, Peter Lashley recalled two aspects of this match:

"I had to put up with a lot of leg-pulling from the other members of the team about my so-called winning partnership with our Captain. We put on 29 of which he got 21 and all I had to do was give him the strike. I think he was just about at his best then as what we now regard as probably the greatest all-rounder of them all. That warm-up at Arundel did him no harm and he averaged over 100 in Test matches on the tour as well as taking 20 Test wickets.

"The other thing which I particularly remember was the briefing which our manager Jeffrey Stollmeyer had given us. He warned us to have plenty of sweaters ready because in his first match in Sussex in 1950 (at Eastbourne) they had suffered from heavy snow. He also advised us that, if we wanted to make conversation with the Norfolk family, the best thing to do was to talk about racing. As a result, it turned out afterwards that every single member of the team had asked if they could be given a sure thing. The Norfolk family obviously thought this was hilarious and gave out a massive range of differing tips."

The next touring team to visit Arundel was Australia in 1968. The start of that tour had been marked by the traditional luncheon given for them by the British Sportsmens' Club of which the Duke had just been elected chairman. In his remarks before introducing the Duke of Edinburgh, who was to propose the toast to the guests, Duke Bernard commended to the audience a poem composed specially for this occasion by A. P. Herbert which not only praised Sir Robert Menzies but also had a dig at Harold Wilson's then flirtation with Europe rather than the Commonwealth:

"The British Flag may not be seen so much
But here and there we note the British touch
Wherever cricket still exerts her spell
Democracy is generally well
Australia, greatest island on the earth
Does highest honour to her isle of birth

DUKE OF NORFOLK'S XI v AUSTRALIAN TOURING XI
4TH MAY 1968

DUKE OF NORFOLK'S XI

R. W. Barber	c. Inverarity b. Renneberg	30
P. M. Walker	b. Hawke	4
E. R. Dexter	c. Sheahan b. Walters	14
A. R. Lewis	b. Hawke	8
M. J. K. Smith	lbw. Renneberg	18
J. M. Parks	c. Joslin b. Walters	7
P. B. H. May	c. Inverarity b. Hawke	12
A. W. Greig	not out	33
D. A. Allen	not out	5
A. Buss	did not bat	
I. J. Jones		
	Extras	0
	Total (for 7 wkts. dec.)	131

Bowling

	O	M	R	W
Hawke	13	6	11	3
Renneberg	9	2	27	2
Walters	9	2	25	2
Gleeson	15	7	38	0
Cowper	12	2	30	0

AUSTRALIAN TOURING XI

W. M. Lawry	b. Jones	2
I. R. Redpath	ct. Walker b. Buss	14
R. M. Cowper	not out	19
A. P. Sheahan	b. Grieg	1
K. D. Walters	did not bat	
N. Hawke		
J. W. Gleeson		
D. A. Renneberg		
H. B. Taber		
L. R. Joslin		
R. J. Inverarity		
	Extras	1
	Total (for 3 wkts.)	37

Bowling

	O	M	R	W
Jones	4	0	9	1
Buss	5	0	16	1
Greig	2	0	11	1

RAIN AFFECTED - MATCH DRAWN

You are as solid as we were before
You have some virtues we can boast no more
Our rulers push us into foreign parts
which hold our hopes, perhaps, but not our hearts
We cricketers, at least, would rather run
with lands with which our tongue is number one
How sad we could not borrow for the job
That king of cricket man - whose name is Bob!

74

MATCH AGAINST THE WEST INDIAN TOURISTS, 1966

*The Duke with his two captains – M. J. K. Smith
and Gary Sobers.*

The superb action of Wes Hall.

… and of Gary Sobers.

Hungarians are guiding us to hell
And any alien nonsense rings the bell
But we have still wise friends across the foam
Advance Australia, welcome, Captain Lawry,
You make us feel at home"

Although the Duke's weather failed to the extent that a rain affected match was drawn, Johnny Woodcock added his own lyrical impressions.

"On Saturday it rained in paradise and one could only be grateful that it did so later than the pundits had predicted. This really is a wonderful place for cricket. The outfield is like velvet and the view of Sussex through that window in the trees is something that simply as an Englishman one feels entitled to boast about.

"In the ordinary way, cricket at Arundel is a relaxed affair. This was not. To the connoisseur it was interesting: to the layman it must have seemed unadventurous. To Lawry, the Australian captain, the game was a serious exercise. The pitch was slow and difficult and every run had to be earned so that even Barber was in for 90 minutes for 30 and May an hour for 12. The best of the Duke's batting came from Greig who had the advantage of recent overseas cricket and an enormous reach."

26 April 1969 saw the return of the West Indians to Arundel. Only a few weeks earlier, the Duke had given special recognition to his friends in the Caribbean. At the end of March when a sporting declaration by Gary Sobers enabled England under the captaincy of Colin Cowdrey to win the fourth Test Match and with it the series, he immediately sent a cable to the West Indies captain. In it he said, 'You have done more to bring back attacking cricket than any Test Match captain of modern times. Congratulations.'

In London, a few days later, there was another special Caribbean occasion when, together with the Lord Great Chamberlain, the Duke introduced the new Baron Constantine of Marival of Trinidad and Tobago and Nelson in the county Palatine of Lancaster - better known as the West Indian all-rounder, Learie Constantine. Now, at Arundel, the Duke welcomed the return of another side led by Gary Sobers who, on arrival, said ruefully that, while he had appreciated the Duke's telegram, he would never live it down back home.

So far as the game was concerned, the latest journalist to succumb to the charms of Arundel was Alan Ross who wrote:

"The point about this opening match between the tour-

DUKE OF NORFOLK'S XI v WEST INDIES TOURING TEAM
26TH APRIL 1969

DUKE OF NORFOLK'S XI

J. H. Edrich	c. Foster b. Roberts	61
B. A. Richards	c. Findlay b. Blair	15
R. W. Barber	c. Butcher b. Foster	5
W. E. Russell	c. Findlay b. Davis	2
R. Marshall	b. Foster	31
A. Knott	not out	47
M. G. Griffith	not out	23
D. A. Allen	did not bat	
H. C. Latchman		
R. H. Cottam		
J. S. Price		
	Extras	7
	Total (for 5wkts. dec.)	191

Bowling

	O	M	R	W
Blair	6	1	20	1
Shillingford	8	5	16	0
Davis	9	2	22	1
Roberts	12	1	39	1
Foster	9	3	31	2
Sobers	5	0	31	0
Lloyd	4	0	25	0

WEST INDIES TOURING TEAM

R. C. Fredericks	c. and b. Latchman	27
C. S. Camacho	st. Knott b. Allen	17
M. C. Foster	lbw. Barber	26
C. A. Davis	c. Russell b. Latchman	68
C. H. Lloyd	not out	48
B. F. Butcher	st. Knott b. Allen	1
G. S. Sobers	not out	4
M. P. Blair	did not bat	
M. H. Findlay		
A. Roberts		
G. Shillingford		
	Extras	4
	Total (for 5 wkts.)	195

Bowling

	O	M	R	W
Price	4	0	8	0
Cottam	6	1	8	0
Latchman	17	5	49	2
Allen	16.4	4	78	2
Richards	5	0	27	0
Barber	7	1	21	1

WEST INDIES TOURING TEAM WON BY 5 WICKETS

ing side and the Duke's team is that it is a parade not a competition. Who makes what is immaterial; the purpose of the day is for the visitors to be shown the sights and put on view.

"The circle of trees on what must rank, with the one at St Lucia, as one of the most beautiful grounds in the world, was yesterday about as backward as the Duke's two-year-olds. It was a tribute to the Norfolk covers, helped by a drying wind, that there was any play at all.

"By lunch, with the Duke's XI on 75 for 3, Sobers had given five of his new bowlers an airing. The opening pair, Shillingford and Blair, were kept going for a full hour, perhaps because Sobers had scarcely set eyes on them before. Shillingford operated with leisurely leaping and spectral run, Blair with the soft stepping tentative approach of a man in a quagmire. The hour after lunch, by courtesy of gentle overs from Sobers and Lloyd, produced 120 runs. Marshall let fly in his most generous fashion and the two wicket-keepers Knott and the Duke's captain, Mike Griffith, as similar in shape, size and colouring as a pair of garden gnomes, ran around like lamplighters.

"The West Indies made a predictably sticky start and wanted 75 in the last 40 minutes to win. They meandered comfortably along for a while, but Lloyd with 20 runs from vast heaves in one over, sewed it all up at exactly the right moment."

Apart from the visits by touring Test sides, the late sixties also saw a variety of other visitors. In 1967, the Staggerers of South Africa were on a return tour and in 1968 they were followed by their fellow countrymen in the Grasshoppers team. Their attack and in particular their opening bowler L. Wessels proved too much for the Duke's side. Later in the season, the visitors were the United States Cricket Association. They had been admitted to associate membership of the International Cricket Conference in 1965 and were managed by their representative, the Kent cricket patron, John Gardiner. A closer look at the names of the players in the United States team such as Lashkari, Fernandez, Stollmeyer, and Thackurdhin suggested that their origins were truly international.

However, as Geoff Wills, who was keeping wicket for the Duke in this match, has remembered, the Americans were out in force:

"There was a large American contingent and they all seemed to be festooned with cameras of various shapes and sizes - seemingly with as many as two or three per person. They took a particular delight in what they described as the chance to photograph 'a real live Duke', a delight which clearly was not reciprocated. However, their cricketers proved capable of consistent batting. Then, when we went in, we were perhaps guilty of underestimating the opposition and the Duke was not best pleased when it looked as though we might lose to the United States. Our regular run getters Robinson, Thackara and Co failed and my own long awaited

partnership with David Sheppard lasted exactly one ball. Fortunately, he got runs when we needed them and a rearguard action by Simon Kimmins and our captain, Eddie Harrison, saved the day."

E. E. HARRISON'S XI v S.P.A.R.K.S.
4TH AUGUST 1968

E. E. HARRISON'S XI

C. Bidwell	c. McIntyre b. Cox	14
A. Thackara	c. Russell b. Cox	48
G. Goonesena	c. and b. Welland	10
M. J. K. Smith	c. Priestlove b. Bedser (E. A.)	59
J. Parks	c. Russell b. Bedser (E. A.)	37
P. Ledden	c. Hill b. Bedser (E. A.)	31
A. Lush	c. Wright b. McIntyre	63
A. Duff	c. Russell b. Bedser (E. A.)	42
R. G. Marlar	not out	16
C. Saunders	did not bat	
E. E. Harrison		
	Extras	10
	Total (for 8 wkts. dec.)	320

Bowling

	O	M	R	W
Russell	9	1	52	0
Bedser (A. V.)	9	2	33	0
Cox	6	0	34	2
Welland	7	0	46	1
Priestlove	5	0	35	0
Bedser (E. A.)	10	0	86	4
McIntyre	4	0	34	1

S. P. A. R. K. S.

J. Cook	b. Parks	32
H. Gimblett	b. Parks	48
G. Priestlove	c. Goonesena b. Marlar	44
G. Cox	b. Parks	12
Sir L. Hutton	c. Saunders b. Marlar	7
W. Wright	b. Duff	12
A. C. D. Ingleby-Mackenzie	b. Marlar	71
E. A. Bedser	c. Bidwell b. Duff	6
A. McIntyre	not out	27
A. V. Bedser	not out	2
S. Russell	did not bat	
	Extras	9
	Total (for 8 wkts.)	270

Bowling

	O	M	R	W
Ledden	6	0	29	0
Bidwell	2	0	5	0
Harrison	6	0	33	0
Parks	8	0	56	3
Lush	3	1	3	0
Goonesena	7	0	20	0
Marlar	6	1	31	3
Duff	7	0	45	2
Smith	3	0	17	0
Thackara	2	0	22	0

MATCH DRAWN

Eddie Harrison was also in charge for another special match in 1968 when the Duke invited him to raise an XI to play the SPARKS Charity XI. This was an all star occasion with Gamini Goonesena, M. J. K. Smith, and Jim Parks providing Test match support to Eddie Harrison's Sussex regulars. For the visitors, the pattern was even more varied when a number of SPARKS sporting and theatrical personalities well in excess of the nominated XI were allowed to appear on the field for brief periods. They included the footballers Billy Wright and Jimmy Hill and the actor/playwright, Colin Welland, who recalls that his dismissal of Goonesena caught and bowled "Was a matter of total self-preservation – if I hadn't caught it, I would have been crippled for life." Among the visiting batsmen were the veterans Harold Gimblett and Sir Leonard Hutton, now both in their fifties. The former Somerset opener turned back the clock with 48 runs in the opening partnership of 69. Sir Leonard Hutton batting in the middle order finally, if briefly, got runs at Arundel and was heard to remark afterwards :"I think the time really has come for me to pull up stumps."

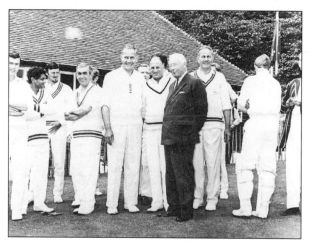

The Duke with the Bedser twins and Sir Leonard Hutton at the SPARKS charity match.

Much the same might be said about the Duke's own decision to end his personal playing involvement in the late sixties. In 1967, he turned out regularly for his team but as he told a reporter: "While I used to enjoy playing with first-class cricketers, I am now too old and too sensible to try that any more." In fact, his final appearances were organised on a typically graceful basis as Tony Thackara describes:

"In the traditional fixtures, we would always have a twelfth man to field when - as was the custom - the visitors took first innings. The Duke would roll up after he had been to church and just before lunch in time for a gin and tonic.

He might then appear briefly on the field after lunch for half an hour or so, but he would usually leave before the end of the innings saying that, 'I must prepare myself for my innings', adding, 'but heaven help you if I am required.'

Michael Cresswell-Wall has described how both he and the Duke were required in the match against the Martlets in 1967:

"I think I can fairly say that Bill Rice and I were the two obvious tail-enders whom the Duke might call on if he was short on the day. On this particular occasion, the Martlets had made a reasonable declaration and thanks to a marvellous innings by Simon Kimmins who only just missed his century, we were in with a chance. However, the Duke and I came together with the score at 208 for 8 needing 17 to win. He kept an end going while I managed a few boundaries. When we got the score up to 222 for 8 and wanted only 3 runs to win, he said, 'We must get them in style'. Whereupon he had an almighty swish for a boundary and was bowled. Alas, we could not add to our total. So we lost by 2 runs but I like to think he went out in style having a go."

Michael Cresswell-Wall's fellow tail-ender, Bill Rice, was a City man and the initiator of a series of matches for boys against the Duke's side which ran from 1967 to 1969. He also provided another local brand of country house cricket at his home in Lyminster.

He describes how, by strange coincidence, he was also involved in a tail-end partnership in what proved to be positively the Duke's last appearance at the crease at Arundel in 1968:

"In our match against the Ramblers, we had managed, thanks to steady bowling by Alec Bedser and Robin Marlar, to keep their score within reasonable proportions. But, once again, we depended on Simon Kimmins to get the runs. This time he got a century and while he was batting with Eric Bedser it looked as though we might well have a chance. However, when Eric got out and later his brother Alec it was left to the tail of Rice, Norfolk and Toynbee to help Simon Kimmins in finding another 60 runs. I managed to stay put while 29 runs were added of which my share was precisely 1. When I got out, the Duke indicated his displeasure as we crossed but I regret to say that he did not last long and, once again, we failed in a near thing."

Another of those playing in the Duke's side on this occasion was Geoff Wills. He had been appearing as a batsman wicket-keeper for the Duke since 1961 as well as turning out regularly for the Sussex Second XI. At his home in Jersey the chartered surveyor recalled his conversation after the match with the Duke:

"He said: 'You know, when I wake up in the morning on a day like today and see the sun shining, I think to myself how lucky you are to have such a marvellous cricket ground and so many wonderful friends in the game. Then I come down here and get out for a duck and I think what a damn silly game and why on earth do I bother?' "

It was entirely appropriate that the Duke's last recorded innings at Arundel in 1968 was his ninety ninth. Having declared his personal innings one short of his century in the interests of his side, his enthusiasm in promoting cricket at the highest levels nevertheless remained as strong as ever. Early in 1970, he mounted one of his most ambitious exercises when he decided to take a team of mainly young England hopefuls to the West Indies. The team with their cricketing credentials at the start of the tour was:

M. C. Cowdrey, Captain (Kent and England)

J. Birkenshaw (Leicestershire)

Earl of Cottenham (M.C.C.)

M. H. Denness (Kent and England)

M. J. Edwards (Surrey)

A. W. Greig (Sussex)

M. G. Griffith (Sussex)

R. N. S. Hobbs (Essex and England)

B. Leadbeater (Yorkshire)

C. M. Old (Yorkshire)

P. J. Sharpe (Yorkshire and England)

D. L. Underwood (Kent and England)

A. Ward (Derbyshire and England)

Colin Cowdrey was then recovering from a snapped achilles tendon which had kept him out of Test cricket. He was thus seen as making a comeback in captaining this side against potentially strong opposition:

"It was a very useful occasion for me to get going again and we had a pretty successful tour. The Duke wanted to go back to the West Indies in a cricketing context before he became too old and it was lovely to see the way in which he involved so many young England hopefuls almost all of whom later played Test cricket.

"There was one aspect of the tour arrangements which was to have a significant effect on my relationship with the Duke. He had asked Jim Swanton to be his Treasurer and effectively, the Team Manager in putting the side together with a simple brief, 'Get me the best twelve young cricketers you can find.'

"Jim approached me and said 'The Duke has asked me to discuss what fee you would like for the tour and for captaining the side.' I said it was a great honour and I did not expect any payment. 'All the others will be getting fees' said Jim. Obviously, I accepted the fact that my air fare and hotel bills would be paid for but I refused to take any additional payment. When the Duke heard of this, there was no doubt it made a difference to our friendship.

"The Duke got into the habit of asking me to lunch with him when he was in London. This was supposed to be an opportunity to discuss the tour arrangements but it developed into something of a game. The Duke would invite me to meet him at the Turf Club at 1.00 p.m. sharp. He would always be early and I would arrive at one minute before the hour. 'I thought you were going to be late' was his usual greeting and then we would get down to talking about everything under the sun even including a little discussion on the forthcoming tour. Lunch was nearly always the same. The Duke loved fish and would like whitebait to start and Dover sole to follow. He never drank red wine but we would do ourselves very well with gin and tonic beforehand and white wine.

"Afterwards, the Duke followed his usual routine. As President of the Automobile Association, a car was always available to take him to Victoria Station and I would quite often accompany him. We would turn into the station by the side exit where an elderly lady had been selling newspapers for many years. She would greet the Duke with some remark such as 'I'm sorry your horses didn't do well yesterday, your Grace. I put money on them.' The Duke would almost always reply in the same way, 'That was a very foolish thing to do. You should stick to selling newspapers,' he would say as he took his newspaper and seemingly never handed over any money. I later learnt that the lady in question would receive a handsome cheque every Christmas.

"One of the nicest moments in our tour came when we actually got the Duke to make one last appearance in top class company. He was very keen to see the pace of Alan Ward at first hand as he was then regarded as the best England fast bowling prospect. In Dominica, the crowd kept calling for the Duke to come onto the field. So, at the start of their innings, I put him at first slip. Rather, I should say, I put him behind Philip Sharpe who was fielding substitute at first slip. Then I told Phil and our keeper, Mike Griffith, 'Your job is to make sure that the ball never gets through to the Duke'. Sure enough, Phil who was probably the best slip catcher in England at the time, and Mike, who was an athletic keeper, ensured that the ball did not reach the Duke except at the end of the over when they threw it to him so that he could return it with relish to the bowler. He was clearly thrilled and honour was satisfied all round when he left the field after a few overs.

"In fact, the highlight of that tour for me was the game in Dominica. It took place in the Botanical Gardens of that wonderful, wild, deeply forested island. After we had scored runs quickly, we had them in trouble when Alan Ward whipped out their openers and, at one point, they were 50 odd for 5. We were used to arranging benefit matches and it was obvious that we had to keep them going. Well we did it so well that we allowed the Shillingford brothers to have a useful stand. However, when Irvine Shillingford got out they were on 9 wickets down still needing over 50 to win. But Grayson Shillingford who was a fast bowler batting at number 10 began hitting our spinners about, the last man kept his end up, and the crowd was going delirious. Knowing the Duke's enjoyment of close finishes, I wasn't too worried but, equally knowing that he was keen that we should win, I did get rather concerned when they were within two boundaries of our score. Fortunately, Tony Greig did the trick for us. Afterwards, the Duke made one of those speeches which were such a success on his overseas tours in which he praised the island, praised their cricket, praised their hospitality and finished by saying: 'It was very close. I thought at one point we might very well lose and I wondered what action I should take if this happened. And I thought to myself that the answer was quite easy - I would merely sack the captain.'"

As Colin Cowdrey has indicated, the Duke's facility with words was always a great asset in expressing his admiration and support for cricket in the Caribbean. This applied to all age groups as it was his usual custom when talking to small boys to enquire "What are you best known for on the cricket field?" Normally, this question would lead to an easy exchange on batting, bowling or fielding and sometimes on all three. However, on one occasion during the tour, the Duke's question was met with a laughing response from a schoolboy cricketer, "Well Sir, I guess I'm best known for dropping catches." The Duke was quick to tell the story against himself on his return in a situation which he said left him "not a little nonplused."

Overall, there was little doubt that the tour was a great

DUKE OF NORFOLK'S XI v SUSSEX COUNTY XI
24TH APRIL 1971

DUKE OF NORFOLK'S XI

R. Marshall	b. Greig	38
W. E. Russell	c. Dexter b. Suttle	77
P. Parfitt	c. Langridge b. Joshi	9
K. Barrington	c. Suttle b. Graves	48
L. Lenham	not out	53
J. T. Murray	not out	19
K. Suttle	did not bat	
A. V. Bedser		
E. A. Bedser		
P. Pocock		
D. Shackleton		
	Extras	10
	Total (for 4 wkts. dec.)	254

Bowling (incomplete)

	O	M	R	W
Snow	7	1	37	0
Greenidge	5	0	16	0
Buss A.	6	1	17	0
Greig	6	1	25	1
Buss M	8	0	38	0
Joshi	8	2	18	1
Suttle	11	2	36	1
Langridge	4	0	15	0
Graves	9	3	26	1
Dexter	3	1	6	0

SUSSEX COUNTY XI

M. Buss	b. Hobbs	33
G. Greenidge	c. Hobbs b. Pocock	37
E. Dexter	run out	83
J. Parks	c. Marshall b. Russell	29
A. Greig	not out	49
P. Graves	c. Murray b. Shackleton	4
K. Suttle	not out	12
J. Snow	did not bat	
U. Joshi		
J. Langridge		
A. Buss		
	Extras	8
	Total (for 5wkts.)	255

Bowling

	O	M	R	W
Shackleton	11	1	41	1
Bedser A. V.	4	0	15	0
Pocock	8	1	35	1
Hobbs	10	0	52	1
Russell	10	1	54	1
Parfitt	8	0	50	0

SUSSEX COUNTY XI WON BY 5 WICKETS

success not only in advancing the cause of some promising young England cricketers but also in identifying new talent in the more remote parts of the Caribbean. As E. W. Swanton said:

"I think the real significance of these matches was the way in which the Duke was able to take a very good side to some of the smallest islands in the Caribbean. I am sure that this had its impact on encouraging the game especially in the Windward and Leeward Islands. This has all been part of the process that has seen the emergence of West Indian Test cricketers from the smaller territories."

Back home, the West Indian connection was sustained in 1970 when the Duke helped finance a visit by West Indies youth clubs. This reflected a growing involvement with Colin Cowdrey in the encouragement of young cricketers in the Caribbean and was exemplified by the time taken out of the annual Norfolk family holiday in Tobago, to which the Kent captain was frequently invited, in arranging coaching sessions for local schoolboys.

The match played at Arundel on 8 and 9 August 1970 showed the value of such encouragement. Among the visitors Larry Gomes and David Murray would both go on to play for the West Indies. In the Duke's side four teenagers, Alan Mansell, Stephen Pheasant, Paul Philipson and John Barclay became Sussex players and another, Nick Pocock, became Captain of Hampshire.

The organisation of the Duke's side in this match was undertaken by Les Lenham who had become the coach for the County side. He would become an Arundel regular in that capacity and in a broader field when he became a national coach. An exceptionally correct batsman, he had been seen at Arundel only a few weeks earlier in the somewhat unaccustomed role of main bowler for the Duke when a special match was arranged to celebrate the Centenary of Brighton Brunswick. The prime mover in arranging this event was Spen Cama, one of the club's longest serving bowlers, who was also a successor to the Duke as President of the Sussex County Cricket Club. Spen Cama would later recall:

"The Duke was very conscious of Sussex cricket history and at Brighton Brunswick we had a very close connection with the County Ground. Indeed, during the 39-45 war when it was taken over by the military, we managed to keep things going on our ground. I played in many matches with our President, Percy Fender, who had been a Sussex cricketer before the First World War and we were able to include Test Match players from all over the world serving in the Forces. The side we brought to Arundel for our Centenary was not in that class but we had a good club side and I recall it took a rear-guard action by George Cox to save the Duke's

side from defeat."

The Sussex connection was strongly in evidence in the following season when a special match was played between the County side and the Duke's XI in the costume of 1870 and under 1870 laws. The match was arranged to launch a book on cricket published for children. Sadly, the weather did not match the occasion. Robin Marlar wrote:

"It was a cold and grey Saturday and the sparse crowd huddled behind their overcoats, their umbrellas shielding them from the wind.

"However, there were a lot of fun things about this match. Among them were the striped coloured shirts, straight from the chorus of 'Oliver'. They proved themselves on a drab day worn over one or two sweaters. The bats, newly and lovingly reproduced from period pieces by Gray Nicholls with splice but no spring were a tribute to the bat-maker's art.

"Some of the players revelled in it. Ken Suttle, longest serving man of Sussex, established his future career as a walk-on actor: in a brown bowler and braces, he was a perfect bookie's runner. As for Ken Barrington, he was a true gallant of yesteryear. With his tall top hat and Mr Punch features, he was a replica of Toulouse-Lautrec's dancer from the Moulin Rouge; chin out, front foot raised, he swung his bat as if he had been coached by Felix.

"Technically, too, the players did what they could. We had underarm bowling and genuine donkey drops, flighted to land on top of the stumps. I fancied I even saw an attempt at the draw, that ancient stroke which helps the ball between body and wicket to the fine leg boundary."

The 1972 season was made memorable by another Royal visit. The Duke had become close to the Prince of Wales when directing the arrangements for his investiture in 1969. The Prince was now serving in the Royal Navy in H.M.S. Norfolk which was at anchor off the Sussex coast. At the request of the Prince, the ship's company was invited to produce a cricket team. This did not include the Prince who preferred to arrive on horseback. At lunch for the team, he made a presentation of a plaque of H.M.S. Norfolk. As to the game itself, Eddie Harrison's collection of local club cricketers proved too strong for the guests. Sadly however one of the home team, Ian Robinson, suffered the ultimate frustration of flying home specially from Texas to take part in this match only to find that, because of travel delays, he did not get a bat or a bowl.

The cricketing highlight of 1972 was undoubtedly the

Prince Charles and his team from H.M.S. Norfolk with the Duke and Duchess, 1972.

DUKE OF NORFOLK'S XI v AUSTRALIAN TOURING TEAM
(50 OVERS MATCH)
22ND APRIL 1972

DUKE OF NORFOLK'S XI

M. H. Denness	c. Francis b. Colley	30
J. A. Jameson	c. Chappell b. Colley	12
M. C. Cowdrey	c. Watson b. Colley	15
E. R. Dexter	lbw. Watson	27
A. W. Grieg	c. Colley b. Chappell	96
R. H. Gilliatt	c. Chappell b. Watson	26
M. G. Griffith	c. Massie b. Chappell	14
D. Wilson	c. Chappell b. Colley	6
R. Hobbs	c. Tabor b. Watson	0
G. Arnold	b. Chappell	2
P. Lever	not out	1
	Extras	12
	Total (49.5 overs)	241

Bowling (incomplete)

	O	M	R	W
Hammond	10	1	62	0
Massie	10	5	18	0
Colley	10	2	44	4
Mallett	8	0	40	0
Watson	10	2	40	3
Chappell G.	1.5	0	5	3

AUSTRALIAN TOURING TEAM

K. Stackpole	b. Greig	18
B. Francis	lbw. Wilson	24
I. Chappell	c. Wilson b. Hobbs	49
G. Chappell	b. Hobbs	20
R. Edwards	c. Jameson b. Arnold	14
G. Watson	lbw. Hobbs	8
D. Colley	run out	8
B. Tabor	lbw. Lever	24
A. Mallett	c. Gilliat b. Greig	1
G. Hammond	not out	11
R. Massie	not out	17
	Extras	19
	Total (for 9 wkts) (50 overs)	213

Bowling

	O	M	R	W
Lever	9	1	22	1
Arnold	10	2	29	1
Wilson	10	1	37	1
Greig	9	2	37	2
Hobbs	10	0	46	3
Cowdrey	2	0	23	0

DUKE OF NORFOLK'S XI WON BY 28 RUNS

return of the Australians to play in the first limited over match between the Duke's team a the Touring side. After steady scoring for the home side, the innings was made memorable by the big hitting of Tony Greig who had twelve 4s and five 6s in his 96. There is little doubt this contributed to his inclusion in the England side later that season for what was to prove a short-lived and highly successful Test career.

While the Chappell brothers were together, Australia appeared to have a chance of keeping up with the required run rate but, when they were dismissed by the leg spinner Robin Hobbs, the task proved beyond them.

It was apt that this match which would prove to be the Duke's last game against a touring side should involve the country which had begun the process in 1956. Colin Cowdrey recalls that the end of this series was a graceful occasion:

"In all these touring matches, we would go to the Castle for dinner afterwards. It became the natural end to the game. We would finish about 6p.m. and when we had changed and got across to the Castle there would be a large drink and a short and highly idiosyncratic tour of the Castle conducted by the Duke in which he would make pungent remarks about the ancestors depicted on the walls. Then there would be a superb dinner with something like poached salmon and strawberries. We would all be spread out at various small tables with the Duke, the Duchess and the girls hosting them. After dinner, the Duke would say just a few words and, as on this occasion, both captains could get up and say that they and their teams had had a wonderful day and the whole party would be over by 9.30 allowing the visit-

ing team to get a reasonably early night.

"It was one of the loveliest things in English cricket, indeed in English life. That touch of leisure was part of a perhaps more gracious age. We miss it desperately today as the players rush by car from game to game."

The Duke's own favourite form of recreation was increasingly centred on the Caribbean. At the beginning of 1973, he was in Tobago with his family and many friends. Ever since his team had toured the West Indies in 1970, he had made it his practice to return to this beautiful and then almost tourist-free island. One of the main attractions was the Mount Irvine Hotel, owned by Pat and Mickey Coghlan. They had become close friends as had their son Tim, who after getting a Blue at Cambridge in 1960 was now a regular performer at Arundel.

The Norfolk family would stay in cottages in the grounds of the hotel inviting friends to join them there. In 1972, the Coghlans had arranged a special party at their house, 'The Reef', when many of the Duke's old cricketing friends including the Linlithgows and the Hopetouns, together with Colin Cowdrey and Roger Gibbs, joined in a surprise celebration when Duke Bernard was given a cardboard crown to mark his fifty five years as Earl Marshal.

The party could swim, play golf, and bring back their catch from deep sea fishing in relative privacy before the island was discovered by the holiday industry and intrusive photographers with long-range cameras. In early 1973, there was a particular need for privacy as the Duke was recovering from a stroke which necessitated bringing his medical adviser, Jack Mickerson, and his secretary, Pat Hay-Will, to the island.

Back at Arundel, cricket was overshadowed by Duke Bernard's increasing ill health. However, he continued his regular attendance at matches where his dry sense of humour and commitment to standards were still much in evidence.

Because of his constant insomnia, the Duke would almost always be up at first light. In the summer months, and especially on match days, it was his custom to walk from the Dower House for a tour of the cricket ground. His groundsman, the former forester, Harry Ireland, was also an early riser and they would meet in the middle for a discussion about the playing surface.

This took the form of a regular game in which the Duke would indicate whether he had found any weeds. "I found a dandelion", he would say, "and that means half a crown off your bonus." As the bonus was given at the end of the season without deductions of any kind, the threat was limited. But it was a matter of pride between the two that there was rarely an opportunity for even a hypothetical deduction.

At the cricket, the Duke's sayings continued to enter Arundel folklore and his influence on the course of the

match remained as strong as ever. He was always concerned with punctuality and would express himself strongly to the two captains if he suspected there was a possibility of a late start. Similarly, if one of his cricketing guests arrived late, the popular excuse about heavy traffic would receive the response, "What you really mean is that you left too late to arrive in time."

His views on the approach of the new generation of serious cricketers could be highly critical. His remarks on defensive batsmanship ("not if you hope to play on this ground again, you won't") have already been noted. Following that instance, later in the same season, he told a cricketing journalist "Nobody seems to play cricket these days unless they are assured of £1,000 for an afternoon's work".

So far as the social arrangements were concerned, the Duke's hospitality continued on a lavish scale. Alan Wadey, the young Sussex fast bowler who had become one of the Duke's regulars in the late sixties, has recalled:

"I was first brought onto the Arundel scene by Eddie Harrison. He was captaining the Martlets side which played us when I was captain of the Seaford College team in a match in 1969. At the end of the day's play, he said, 'The Duke is one short tomorrow. Would you like to play?'.

Naturally, I jumped at the opportunity and as I had - quite illegally - access to my car while still at school, I drove over the next day. I was greeted on the steps in front of the Pavilion by the Duke as though he had known me for years. He always sat in a box-shaped deck chair on wheels near the top of the steps and you would be summoned during the course of the day. I was a good listener and I enjoyed hearing his views on cricket and on life. But when he had had enough, he was most effective in giving you the message with words like 'I mustn't monopolise you' or 'I mustn't keep you from being with your team'.

"The Duke's back-up team introduced me to a whole new world. There was butler service when you arrived, with your own personal towels laid out. And when it came to lunch and tea, the dining area in the Pavilion was laid out with the most tremendous spread. The Duke's caterers, Mitchells of Worthing, would appear in their black vans with the gold lettering and out would come several motherly figures who proceeded to press upon us the first asparagus or the first raspberries of the season. Nothing was too good for the Duke's guests. All in all, the Duke's hospitality was well above the standard I found in County or for that matter any other cricket".

As the host, the Duke was very much in charge and little escaped his notice. Given the popularity of his lunches, it is perhaps not entirely surprising that, of one regular guest, he was heard to remark, "its always a pleasure to see him here, but I don't remember inviting him."

At his table, the Duke liked to keep conversation along familiar lines and, when seated next to ladies whom he was meeting for the first time, he would preface the conversation by saying, "I have two subjects. Cricket and drains. You choose."

It was at this time that the author had the opportunity to join the Duke in regularly watching cricket at the Castle following his adoption as prospective parliamentary candidate for the Arundel constituency. On receiving his first invitation for lunch with the Duke, he was given a short but instructive message on local politics. After lunch, the Duke, having checked there was no one within earshot said: "You must realise that as Earl Marshal, I cannot show any political favours. However, if you would like me to tell you who to avoid round here, I will."

Another local was less fortunate. This particular individual had been employed by the Duke for a long period and decided that the time had come to accept a job overseas. Thinking that the relaxed atmosphere of a cricket match might help in breaking the news, he told the Duke of his intentions. When he found there was no response, he went on in a nervous fashion to outline the various arrangements that he had made for a possible successor, for the sale of housing and for the general redistribution of responsibilities which would follow. As he drew breath, the Duke enquired "Haven't you forgotten anything?" "No, I don't think so", said the retiring employee, only to receive the crushing dismissal, "What about your manners?".

There is a poignancy in reading details of the matches played in 1974 as the last occasions when teams would represent Duke Bernard. Happily, those involved managed their own form of tribute when they went through the season without defeat. Three of his players got centuries and his side gained comfortable victories over the Sussex Martlets and the Eton Ramblers. There was even a double celebration during the Ramblers match when the Duke's horse, Ragstone, which had just won the Ascot Gold Cup, was paraded round the cricket ground prior to a party for many of the Duke's cricketing and racing friends.

Towards the end of the year, the Duke who was now con-

DUKE OF NORFOLK'S XI v LADY MARY FITZALAN HOWARD'S XI 30TH JUNE 1974

LADY MARY FITZALAN HOWARD'S XI

R. Fellowes	c. Saunders b. Mance	11
S. Polk	st. Saunders b. Cox	78
M. Hooper	c. Saunders b. Robinson	59
S. Burn	b. Robinson	14
J. Brennan	not out	30
S. Parker-Bowles	run out	12
T. Coghlan	b. Woods	7
T. Lindsay	not out	5
J. Hastings-Bass	run out	1
I. Balding	st. Saunders b. Woods	4
R. Baker	did not bat	
	Extras	4
	Total (for 8 wkts. dec.)	**225**

Bowling

	O	M	R	W
Kimmins	8	1	48	0
Mance	8	0	47	1
Robinson	8	0	35	2
White	3	0	24	0
Woods	7	0	32	2
Cox	5	0	35	1

DUKE OF NORFOLK'S XI

A. White	b. Hooper	25
D. Walsh	b. Brennan	106
J. Stallibrass	ct. Hastings-Bass b. Balding	64
P. Robinson	not out	15
M. Mance	not out	6
S. Kimmins	did not bat	
G. Cox		
P. Woods		
R. Burton		
E. E. Harrison		
C. Saunders		
	Extras	3
	Total (for 3 wkts.)	**219**

Bowling

	O	M	R	W
Coghlan	5	0	30	0
Hooper	8	1	25	0
Parker-Bowles	8	0	30	0
Hastings-Bass	3	0	20	1
Baker	6	1	31	0
Brennan	7	0	46	1
Balding	3	0	34	1

MATCH DRAWN

fined to bed, began to organise a series of lunches for his cricketing friends. One of his regular visitors was Billy Griffith:

"I have never eaten such delicious meals in a bedroom. However, it was clear that he was concerned about the future of the game on his ground. I couldn't say very much at that time but I tried to give him what reassurance I could - frankly without much to go on. But the Duke maintained his keen interest in the game right to the end of his life and nowhere was this more evident than in the current series in Australia."

Colin Cowdrey was present at another of these lunches when the conversation about this tour and his own involvement became personal.

"Billy and I were with him at the end of that year watching some of the highlights of the First Test at Brisbane when Lillee and Thomson were causing havoc among English batsmen with their short pitched bowling. There had been some injuries and there was speculation that I might be asked to go out and join the side and the Duke with a twinkle said: 'Mr Thomson looks rather fast to me, even for a young 42 year old'.

"As luck would have it, soon afterwards, I got a call from Alec Bedser. They were worried about further injuries to our batsmen which might affect the Second and Third Test matches and so they asked me if I would go out and join them. As soon as the news was announced, I got a telephone call from the Duke. He didn't congratulate me. He just said 'I think its very unfair. They are throwing you into the firing line and you will be on to a hiding to nothing. Do take care of yourself'. Those are the last words he said to me and it was wonderful that, ill as he was, he was still concerned about cricketers' welfare."

Bernard Marmaduke Fitzalan-Howard, 16th Duke of Norfolk, died on 31 January 1975 at the age of 66. Tributes to him poured in from leading figures in the cricket world. E. W. Swanton described him as "Cricket's friend to all and in lineal descent from the noble patrons who have so benefited the game almost throughout its history." Colin Cowdrey following a similar theme paid tribute to "the cricketers' friend" adding, "he had no time for defensive batsmen, maiden overs, ringed fields bent on saving runs and players who nursed averages. Cricket was a game for enjoyment and I had the feeling that good cricket, especially on his own lovely ground, brought him more fun than anything else in the world." Johnny Woodcock, writing as one who had enjoyed the Duke's hospitality in playing as well as reporting cricket at Arundel said "whether on his own lovely ground or on a tour, the atmosphere which he created around him was based not on formality but on friendliness. Cricket could have had no more loyal patron, and a mere cricket writer no stauncher friend."

There were great State occasions to mark the passing of the Earl Marshal. The Prince of Wales and Princess Alexandria accompanied the family at the Requiem Mass which was held in Arundel Cathedral. Similar services took place simultaneously at the Brompton Oratory, St Everilda's, Everingham Park in Yorkshire and at St Andrew's, Dumfries. However, perhaps the memorial which would have found a special place in the late Duke's heart was that organized on 12 July 1975 when the Sussex Martlets arranged a 50 over match in memory of the Duke against the Sussex County Cricket Club.

The game had been arranged before the Duke's death to mark the seventieth anniversary of the Martlets. Now, as a mark of respect for his dedicated service to cricket, it attracted support by the full County side including one of their new recruits, Kepler Wessels, and the Martlets fielded what was probably their strongest ever side. Before the two captains, Mike Griffith for the Martlets and Peter Graves for Sussex, went out for the toss, both teams stood for a moment's silence in memory of the Duke. The Martlets won the toss and batted when Gehan Mendis who, at the age of twenty, came to the side via Sri Lanka, Brighton Grammar School and Durham University, opened the innings with Brian O'Gorman in a stand of 86. Mike Griffith and the former Middlesex player, Bob Gale, lent support with a useful stand before the declaration came at 198 for nine.

Rain came later to reduce the Sussex team's target to 119 from 30 overs. After Johnny Barclay had given them a good start, Nick Wisdom with three for thirty five put the County side under pressure but an undefeated stand by Peter Graves and Austin Parsons brought victory off the penultimate ball of the match.

This was one of seven games arranged by the Martlets through their secretary Eddie Harrison which kept cricket going at Arundel Castle in 1975. The question which was in everyone's mind as the season drew to a close was whether there was any way in which the Norfolk family's interest in cricket could be maintained in the future.

The Memorial Match, 1975.

1967

June 11th. Sussex Martlets 224-5 dec. (J. Lush 89, N. Smith 64*). Duke of Norfolk's XI 222 (S. Kimmins 92). Sussex Martlets won by 2 runs.

1968

June 2nd. Eton Ramblers 231-9 dec. (J. J. Farmer 56). Duke of Norfolk's XI 202 (S. Kimmins 104). Eton Ramblers won by 29 runs.

July 20th. United States Cricket Association 176-8 dec. Duke of Norfolk's XI 117-7. (D. Sheppard 50). Match drawn.

1970

March 2nd. Duke of Norfolk's XI 191. Dominica XI 183, (I. Shillingford 57). Duke of Norfolk's XI won by 8 runs.

July 19th. Brighton Brunswick 213-8 dec (B. Morton 90, J. Baker 57). Duke of Norfolk's XI 132-6. Match drawn.

August 8th and 9th. West Indies Youth Clubs 159 (G. Brasmonie 63) and 193.5 dec (L. Gomes 66, R. Gabriel 58). Dukeof Norfolk's XI 148 (M. Barford 57, B. Sahaded 5-58) and 151-7 (P. Ryan 53*, B. Sahaded 6-55). Match drawn.

1974 June 3rd. Eton Ramblers 214-3 dec. (J. Farmer 100*, J. Leonard 52). Duke of Norfolk's XI 216-4 (A. Parsons 111*). Duke of Norfolk's XI won by 6 wickets.

July 7th. I Zingari 193-8 dec. (M. Wingfield-Digby 52). Duke of Norfolk's XI 185-9 (G. Wills 100). Match drawn.

CHAPTER EIGHT

Duchess Lavinia's Club 1976-1979

The immediate answer to the question regarding the future of cricket at Arundel Castle was provided by Lavinia, Duchess of Norfolk:

"During his last days, my husband often expressed fears about how the game might continue on his ground. He loved having those who were still active in the cricket world like Colin Cowdrey and Billy Griffith for lunch even when he was laid up in bed. They would talk cricket generally but the conversation would always come round to its future at Arundel. After Bernard's death, I was determined to keep cricket going in his memory and so were the girls. Apart from Colin and Billy, the other person I turned to was Ronnie Aird. They were my Three Musketeers."

Colin Cowdrey believes that the role of Ronnie Aird was critical:

"He had spent virtually all his working life as either Assistant Secretary or Secretary of the M.C.C. and so his knowledge of the game and his contacts were tremendous. Moreover, as a widower and a dedicated race goer, he was one of Duchess Lavinia's special friends. He had retired to a cottage in Sussex to be near his daughter and he would often come to Arundel Park for Sunday supper. He was particularly good at after dinner entertainment, both in telling stories which he would deliberately get not quite right and in performing conjuring tricks. Between times, he would often go to the Races with the Duchess and he undoubtedly enjoyed her confidence.

"His advice was to prove crucial. He said that cricket could only continue at Arundel on anything like its former scale if it had proper finance and professional administration. He said he was no longer up to this kind of commitment but, 'The man you want is Billy Griffith'. This is where we were again so lucky because Billy had just completed over 20 years as Ronnie Aird's successor as both Assistant Secretary and then Secretary of the M.C.C. His home was

nearby at Middleton and he readily agreed to take on the administration work in forming a Members' Club. What the Duchess does not mention but which was absolutely critical was the fact that she and the four girls all agreed to chip in £5,000 each so we had a capital fund of £25,000. On top of this, the Duchess also provided an interest free loan of £17,000."

Billy Griffith takes up the story:

"Naturally, I was delighted at the idea of playing a part in the formation of the proposed Friends of Arundel Castle Cricket Club, but it was going to be a great challenge. When Colin and I had had those last lunches with Duke Bernard, we had tried to reassure him, but once one began to see the size of the financial operation, so the degree of the late Duke's patronage became evident. The game was becoming increasingly expensive, particularly in attracting star players who now had agents looking for appearance money. We would have major capital commitments in building an administrative office and a tea hut for the members quite apart from the question of new mowing and other ground equipment. The help from the Duchess and her daughters gave us a breathing space but our initial estimate showed that, working on the most modest basis, we would still need something like £13,000 in the first year. So we had to get down to the business of just what cricket sponsorship and membership we could attract.

"Eddie Harrison had been holding the fort with the Martlets matches and could no doubt continue to help with some of the traditional club games, but for the Tourists and other major matches we clearly needed top level support in producing a strong side for the Duchess. This is where it was such an advantage to have Ronnie Aird as part of our original working party. Quite apart from his contacts and experience at M.C.C., he had recently been made President of Hampshire and the link with our neighbouring county was to be especially valuable. Then again, you might say we were exceptionally lucky with our county contact to the east, because Colin Cowdrey indicated that he was likely to be available in helping us with the cricket when he finished playing for Kent in the following year."

The inaugural meeting of the Friends of the Arundel Castle Cricket Club took place in the Duchess' home on Sunday 26 October 1975 when a management committee was formed led by the Duchess as President and Billy Griffith as Vice- President. As well as the other existing members of the working party, Ronnie Aird and Eddie Harrison, the Duchess invited her friend from Tobago, Pat Coghlan, and Tony Hill as a link with the neighbouring Arundel Cricket Club to be among the first committee members. They would be supported by Colin Cowdrey who sent his apologies for this meeting which was recorded by the new Secretary, Mrs Patricia Sanders.

When she had to relinquish this appointment, Billy Griffith was able to draw further reserves from the M.C.C. and recruited his former secretary, Veronica Lloyd. Equally, when the long serving groundsman Harry Ireland felt that the time had come to retire, the club was fortunate in having

a professional replacement. Typically, Duke Bernard had agreed only shortly before his death to finance the training of a young Arundel groundsman, Colin Dick, who was studying his profession in Australia. When the Duchess telephoned him at the Melville Cricket Club in Perth and asked whether an urgent return would be possible, he responded immediately.

The first major task facing the committee was to build up membership of the club among the many supporters who had attended matches at the Castle over the years. The yearly subscription was set at £5, with life membership at £50, and the search began to attract up to 2000 members.

It was here that the phenomenal energy and dedication of Duchess Lavinia became apparent. She signed all the letters of invitation to join the club and wrote personal letters to thank those who agreed.

By the time the full committee met in the Pavilion at Arundel on 18 March 1976, 102 life members and 684 annual members had been recruited. The committee, whose membership continued to be based on personal invitations from the Duchess, had been strengthened by the addition of Mike Bull as Treasurer, Bill Rice and Michael Cresswell-Wall (the

The spirit of Arundel is captured as the two captains toss before the 1976 tourist match.

LAVINIA, DUCHESS OF NORFOLK'S XI v WEST INDIES XI
8 MAY 1976

DUCHESS OF NORFOLK'S XI

G. W. Johnson	c. Greenidge b. Jumadeen	28
R. A. Woolmer	st. Murray b. Jumadeen	31
D. S. Steele	b. Fredericks	34
R. J. Inverarity	lbw. Fredericks	16
E. R. Dexter	b. Padmore	8
M. C. Cowdrey	c. Murray b. Gomes	40
T. W. Graveney	c. Fredericks b. Jumadeen	15
Asif Iqbal	not out	23
J. T. Murray	did not bat	
R. N. Hobbs		
R. M. Cottam		
	Extras	7
	Total (for 7 wkts dec.)	202

Bowling

	O	M	R	W
Roberts	3	0	6	0
Daniel	6	1	14	0
Julien	8	1	26	0
Jumadeen	15.1	2	61	3
Padmore	14	4	51	1
Fredericks	7	0	20	2
Gomes	4	0	17	1

WEST INDIES XI

R. Fredericks	b. Cottam	6
G. Greenidge	b. Johnson	84
A Kallicharran	st. Murray b. Hobbs	66
L. Gomes	not out	14
C. H. Lloyd	not out	33
D. L. Murray	did not bat	
B. D. Julien		
A. M. Roberts		
R. R. Jumadeen		
A. Padmore		
W. Daniel		
	Extras	2
	Total (for 3 wkts)	205

Bowling

	O	M	R	W
Cottam	5	0	32	1
Woolmer	6	0	34	0
Johnson	11	4	23	1
Hobbs	11	0	61	1
Steele	2	0	27	0
Inverarity	4	1	20	0
Cowdrey	0.3	0	60	

WEST INDIES WON BY 7 WICKETS

Duke's occasional tail-enders) as active committee members together with Major Neil Ormorod because of his contacts with the Royal Sussex Regiment.

The prime task of the committee at this stage was to concentrate on the successful launch of the club through a major match involving the touring team. Billy Griffith

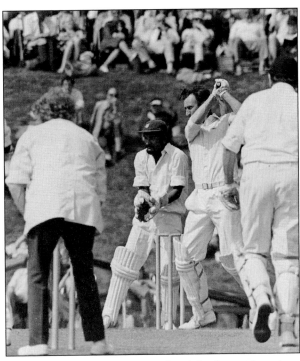

Ted Dexter in punishing mood – wicket-keeper Deryck Murray watches in admiration.

resumes his account:

"Again, we were lucky that the great goodwill Duke Bernard had built up in the Caribbean helped us, coupled with the marvellous continuing support we got from Lords. We were able to re-establish then the tradition, for which Duke Bernard had been responsible, of the touring party taking part in these warm up matches at Arundel - in our case through funding provided by the T.C.C.B. as part of overall tour expenses. Our share was confined to the limited cost - at least in these early days - of the home team. Given the likely boost which we could expect in new membership, all we prayed for on 8 May 1976 was 'Duke's weather' for the match against the West Indies."

The captain of the first side to take the field as Lavinia, Duchess of Norfolk's XI, was Colin Cowdrey:

"When I went out for the toss with Clive Lloyd, I was conscious of the start of a new era and I was also conscious of the tremendous response we had had for this match. Sure enough, we had 'Duke's weather' and a huge crowd. The West Indies paid us the compliment of putting out just about their best side including Andy Roberts and Wayne Daniel to open the bowling. For our side, it was splendid to see the way that several of the 'Duke's Men' like Ted Dexter, Tom Graveney, John Murray, Robin Hobbs and Bob Cottam all rallied round the Duchess' flag. We were also able to include former Test stars like David Steele and John Inverarity who was over from Australia on secondment as a teacher at Tonbridge School. And then there was the Kent contingent of their openers, Graham Johnson and Bob Woolmer, together with the captain-elect Asif Iqbal. I was particularly touched by the response from my old Kent team-mates. We offered them and the other members of our side hotel accommodation but essentially they were digging into their own pockets and it was lovely to see the way that someone like Bob Woolmer had his wife and children with him and made it into a family day.

"As to the cricket, almost all our side did their stuff with the bat but our bowling was swept aside by Gordon Greenidge, Alvin Kallicharran and the captain, Clive Lloyd."

Another great West Indian cricketer who was present on that occasion was the team's manager, Clyde Walcott. Now Sir Clyde Walcott and Chairman of the International Cricket Council, he recalled in 1994:

"This was an invitation which we could not refuse. Of course, it was a very good start to our tour against useful opposition in a marvellous setting. But it was also our tribute to Duke Bernard and to Duchess Lavinia whom we came to know and respect".

This match has a particular memory for the author. Having been invited by the Committee to undertake the ground match commentary with assistance over the public address system by Michael Cresswell-Wall, a working partnership was formed which was to last for many years. It was soon put to the test. At the lunch interval, the author, having completed the usual round of statistics from the score card, handed over to Michael Cresswell-Wall to make the administrative announcements. As part of this process, he waxed eloquent, as was his custom, on the joys of Arundel meat pies and sandwiches and the pleasures of the local brews. So engaged was he in this commercial for the club bar and catering that he became aware, almost too late, that the boys from Christ Hospital whose band had been asked to perform were marching not only on to the field but heading directly across the pitch. Michael Cresswell-Wall with the experience no doubt instilled in him many years before when training for the Brigade of Guards interrupted his commercial to bawl out: "About turn."

This had the desired effect and the Duchess' team was able to resume batting after lunch on an untrampled surface.

Over £3,000 were raised on the day and 170 new members joined.

Several of the other matches arranged for the Duchess' XI during the 1976 season were deliberately designed to maintain the tradition of country house cricket and there was a carry-over from the Duke's long serving men with appearances by Tony Thackara, Eddie Harrison, Robin Marlar, Simon Kimmins, Richard Burton, and George Cox.

Having played their part in what was virtually a handover ceremony, these old faithfuls retired from the Arundel scene. A few others from Duke Bernard's era such as Jonathan Watt, Geoff Wills, John Stephenson, Peter Robinson and above all Colin Cowdrey would continue for a number of years ahead.

There were also some of the younger generation from the same era who now found themselves free to play regular cricket for the Duchess. They included Sussex cricketers like Mike Griffith and Alan Wadey and, from the Martlets, Adrian Ford. Ford and Griffith would become among the highest run-scorers for the Duchess while Alan Wadey still remains top of the list of wicket-takers for her side.

Mike Griffith sums up the attitude of the new generation to the changed style of cricket at Arundel and their role in attracting recruits:

"Around this time a lot of Clubs were finding difficulty in playing friendly cricket on Sundays. This followed the growth of league cricket and what might be seen as a commitment to more serious contests. However, I think my father can take some of the credit for creating an atmosphere in which you can play good cricket and still have fun. He felt that some of the enjoyment was going out of the game and he thought that the people who came to watch were also an essential part of the process. So we ensured that there was no hassle. You could bring your car into the ground with your wife and children and even the dogs. In fact, Duchess Lavinia seemed especially keen to see the dogs given her own constant companions, those splendid labradors.

"Then, again, recruitment was never really a problem at Arundel because so many people wanted to play there. Where the emphasis changed somewhat from Duke Bernard's day was that we had to decide whether to play teams of good cricketers or those who were perhaps of moderate ability but of roughly the same standard. It was difficult to try and mix the two without Duke Bernard's duffers to balance things on each side and so the great majority of cricket at Arundel moved to a much higher standard; thus it was able, from the beginning, to attract a wealth of talent. One of the attractions for them was the involvement of good umpires (like John Langridge and Lloyd Budd for the tourist matches). Current or recent first-class cricketers hate to feel that their performance can be spoilt by poor umpiring.

"You can criticize the wicket as slow but it is almost always true. The other great thing about the ground is its size. It gives slow bowlers a chance. When you play in matches where the boundary is only 50 yds or so away, someone with a big bat can come in and almost score sixes through mis-hits. A six at Arundel has to be a pretty good shot. Moreover, Colin Cowdrey in particular, became an ace in involving the slow bowlers. As a general rule, the relatively slow wicket meant that the opening bowlers would not normally do a lot of damage and you could keep the game moving along with slow bowlers thus allowing both for a declaration and the opportunity to chase a winning total".

The only planned exception to the pattern outlined by Mike Griffith was in the family match played on 3 July 1976. This was a variation of the series which had been played by the girls' team against their father's side to one against their mother's side. The girls' team was now described as Lady Mary's and Lady Sarah's XI since their sister Anne was still in Yorkshire and their youngest sister Jane had married Michael Ancram and was adjusting to the life of a parliamentary wife in Scotland.

Mike Griffith, who captained the Duchess' team recalls the match as the end of an era:

"In our side there were farewell appearances by Tony Thackara, Richard Burton, Eddie Harrison and Robin Marlar. The girls' team had several of their traditional supporters strengthened by Colin Ingleby-Mackenzie and Tony Lewis. Colin would become a regular participant in these matches and Tony Lewis - who had just given up first-class cricket - was persuaded to turn out by the girls' captain, Ian Balding, with whom he had played rugger at Cambridge and from whom he took his racing advice. Both the big names in the girls' side did their stuff but it was one of our Martlets, Jonathan Watt, who got the first century for the Duchess and who, with help at the end from the cricket writer John Thicknesse, virtually saw us to a win in the last over".

Of the other games in that season, perhaps the most exciting was that played against I Zingari. Colin Cowdrey and Robert Green put on 181 in an undefeated stand for the fourth wicket before, typically, Cowdrey declared when his own score was on 96, which was the nearest he would ever come to scoring a century at Arundel. After a superb innings of 142 from M. F. Wright, I Zingari looked to have

matters well in hand when they were within eleven runs of victory with five wickets standing, but three wickets went cheaply and it was left to the tail-enders to see their side home in the last over.

Looking to the future, the most significant match of the year was at the end of the season against a Young England XI captained by Chris Cowdrey. This would be one of the few matches which involved both father and son when Colin Cowdrey put together an opposing side of current county cricketers and former Test stars. They all scored consistently so that he was able to declare at 219 for 6. The young cricketers responded in style with a top score by the brilliant schoolboy cricketer, Matthew Fosh, whose career for Essex in county cricket seemed all too short. He shared a century partnership with Chris Cowdrey and the umpires, Messrs Downs and Billson, showed some flexibility in determining when the last over was bowled. This came, by common consent, when the young cricketers won by 4 wickets.

The match provided a splendid finale to the first season of the Arundel Castle Cricket Club and, with rising membership, its future seemed set fair.

By the start of the 1977 season, there were 1256 members and 141 life members of the club. A twenty year lease had been obtained from the Castle Trust at a peppercorn rent and the Duchess, showing her usual acumen, had invited Major General Ronnie Buckland, the retiring Chief Executive of the Adur District Council, to join the Club committee with a specific remit in seeking rates relief.

During the year, the Duchess' house manager, Bertie Denyer, had also joined the committee when he and his wife took over the Club's catering arrangements. In addition, Sir Alec Durie, who had given great support at the big matches as Director General of the Automobile Association and George Cox, in his role as coach to the Sussex County Team, were invited to give added strength to the committee.

Despite the Club's continuing success, fund-raising was still a key activity in which the Duchess led from the front. Before the first match of the season, she arranged a sponsored walk including, among others, Colin Cowdrey, John Murray, and the locally based entertainer Leslie Crowther.

On this occasion, as so often when supporting her good causes, she showed exceptional fitness in jogging rather than walking a course which ran from the pavilion of the club through the Castle park along the gallops up and down a steep valley before returning to the cricket ground. The effects of this punishing circuit were soon apparent when at

LAVINIA, DUCHESS OF NORFOLK'S XI V ENGLAND YOUNG CRICKETERS
21 JULY 1976

DUCHESS OF NORFOLK'S XI

P. M. Roebuck	c. Fosh b. Still	50
P. A. Slocombe	b. Still	16
V. J. Marks	b. Wilkes	33
M. J. K. Smith	c. Cowdrey b. Munden	31
M. C. Cowdrey	b. Allott	43
J. T. Murray	b. Allott	21
K. S. McEwan	not out	16
G. H. G. Doggart	did not bat	
R. N. S. Hobbs		
J. K. Lever		
D. Shackleton		
	Extras	9
	Total (for 6 wkts)	219

Bowling

	O	M	R	W
Allott	9.4	0	45	2
Kemp	12	1	39	0
Still	7	1	49	2
Patel	3	0	10	0
Wilkes	6	1	23	1
Munden	7	0	44	1

ENGLAND YOUNG CRICKETERS

C. W. J. Athey	c. Cowdrey b. Lever	0
A. L. Jones	c. McEwan b. Shackleton	29
C. S. Cowdrey	b. Marks	65
I. J. Gould	b. Marks	1
M. K. Fosh	c. Roebuck b. Marks	88
N. J. Kemp	c. Roebuck b. McEwan	3
I. J. Wilkes	b. Cowdrey	20
P. R. Downton	not out	4
A. Patel	not out	0
P. J. W. Allott	did not bat	
D. Munden		
S. J. Still		
	Extras	13
	Total (for 7 wkts)	223

Bowling

	O	M	R	W
Shackleton	12	0	35	1
Lever	13	2	28	1
Marks	14	1	38	3
McEwan	4	3	20	1
Hobbs	13	1	63	0
Cowdrey	1.2	0	5	1

ENGLAND YOUNG CRICKETERS WON BY 4 WICKETS

least one civic dignitary had to retire and for some others, like the author, it was only possible to prevent embarrassment by going round the course the wrong way and thus confusing the Duchess as to whether one was in front or behind.

At the A.G.M. in April, it was reported that this event had raised £2,900. Such financial support was necessary as the Club pursued a policy of expanded cricket activities. The chairman, Billy Griffith, reminded the members that the objectives of the club were "the promotion, encouragement, and maintenance of the playing of cricket at all levels at Arundel Castle in memory of Duke Bernard." He added that the committee's additional priorities were "maintaining the right atmosphere, encouraging youth cricket and above all ensuring that everything was done to enhance the enjoyment of members watching cricket on this most beautiful of grounds."

It was decided that the expansion of cricket activities would therefore require the delegation of responsibilities, and match managers would be appointed to arrange the main fixtures. The initial list was made up of Charles Robins, Alan Wadey, Peter Robinson, Mark Faber, Geoff Wills, Tim Coghlan and John Nicholson.

The expansion of cricket that year had a distinctly Australian flavour. Apart from the traditional match against the Touring side in April, Duchess Lavinia in her role as Lord Lieutenant of West Sussex had obtained agreement for their return in August. This was for a match against the Rest of the World as part of her fund-raising efforts for the Queen's Silver Jubilee Appeal. In between these two matches, the Australian Under Nineteen XI, the first team of young Australian cricketers to visit England as a national side, were scheduled to play a Test Match at Arundel against a Young England XI.

A key element in these games was the attraction of major sponsorship. National Westminster Bank, (whose Deputy Chairman, Alec Dibbs, would soon join the Club committee), had signed up for the Tourist match and I.B.M. had agreed to sponsor Australia v The Rest of the World. However, during the season, there were concerns as major financial inducements offered by Kerry Packer raised doubts about the availability of both English and Australian Test cricketers at Arundel.

Happily, these problems did not affect the opening match of the season, when most of the Australian side and six of the Duchess' team had all taken part in the Centenary Test in Melbourne only a few weeks earlier. It produced a match fee of £3,500 for the club with additional bar and catering profits. Much of the success of the occasion was ascribed to Duchess Lavinia's role as hostess. Ray Robinson, writing for the Sydney Morning Herald said:

"The Duchess, slim, sixtyish, is a noble woman of middle

height and more than medium charm. Her Grace's exquisite grooming is always admired by women among onlookers from thousands of deck chairs on the ground's sloping banks. All her Grace knows about cricket - a spill-over from her husband's enthusiasm - would fill few pages in Wisden's Almanac but the women's electoral lobby would be interested to know that Lavinia is in her first year as the only woman steward appointed at Goodwood Racecourse."

For Michael Melford, there was the usual wonder about "a climate which, after the flood and gloom earlier in the week, can bless a days cricket such as that at Arundel when, in unrelenting sunshine, the Australians beat Lavinia Duchess of Norfolk's XI by 20 runs in a 45 over match."

He went on to enthuse about the young Australians:

"Hughes who, in the quick-footed exuberance of strokes to all parts, reminded one of Doug Walters; the tall powerful left handed Hookes with his compelling look of Graeme

Pollock; and the tall upstanding Craig Serjeant all had a useful outing."

When it came to the Duchess' XI' reply, Ray Robinson was equally complimentary:

"Willey played so handsomely, reeling off one magnificently timed stroke after another, and Randall followed him so well, that they put their side in a winning position. But this was very much a friendly affair, as implied by the presence of Colin Cowdrey, Mike Smith and John Murray and it was asking a lot for the retired heroes to come in and engage in what is now a familiar scamper."

Things did not go so well for the Tourists on their return to Arundel in August to play the Rest of the World. The weather was unfriendly with a slow pitch and a soggy outfield following heavy rain. Much of the match was played in gloomy conditions. Against fast and accurate bowling by Bob Willis and Imran Khan, Australia lost their first three

The 1977 Australians match – the two teams with the Duchess.

LAVINIA, DUCHESS OF NORFOLK'S XI v AUSTRALIANS
27TH APRIL 1977

AUSTRALIANS

I. C. Davis	b. Edmonds	7
C. S. Sergeant	c. Old b. Woolmer	65
G. S Chappell	c. Greig b. Woolmer	46
G. J. Cosier	c. Edmonds b. Woolmer	11
K. J. Hughes	c. Lever c. Cowdrey	28
D. W. Hookes	not out	16
R. D. Robinson	not out	1
R. J. Bright	did not bat	
M. F. Malone		
G. Dymock		
L. S. Pascoe		
	Extras	12
	Total (for 5 wkts)	186

Bowling

	O	M	R	W
Old	6	0	27	0
Lever	6	3	9	0
Edmonds	9	2	42	1
Barclay	9	0	41	0
Greig	7	1	29	0
Woolmer	7	2	17	3
Cowdrey	1	0	9	1

LAVINIA, DUCHESS OF NORFOLK'S XI

J. Barclay	c&b. Malone	7
R. A. Woolmer	lbw. Bright	11
P. Willey	c. Robinson b. Dymock	50
D. W. Randall	b. Cosier	41
A. W. Greig	b. Malone	14
M. C. Cowdrey	b. Cosier	1
P. H. Edmonds	b. Cosier	16
M. J. K. Smith	c. Malone b. Pascoe	8
C. M. Old	c. Malone b. Cosier	6
J. T. Murray	lbw. b. Pascoe	0
J. K. Lever	not out	0
	Extras	12
	Total	166

Bowling

	O	M	R	W
Pascoe	8	1	40	2
Malone	9	1	26	2
Dymock	9	2	42	1
Bright	9	0	27	1
Cosier	6.3	0	19	4

AUSTRALIA WON BY 21 RUNS

wickets for four runs and it took a stand between Hookes and Greg Chappell to give their score some respectability. However, the Australian attack proved almost as devastating in difficult conditions and it took dogged efforts by three of the Pakistanis playing in the Rest of the World Team, Sadiq Mohammad, Imran Khan and Zaheer Abbas to achieve a narrow victory.

AUSTRALIA v REST OF THE WORLD XI
18TH AUGUST 1977

AUSTRALIA

I. C. Davis	b. Willis	4
G. J. Cosier	lbw. Imran Khan	5
K. J. Hughes	lbw. Willis	0
C. S. Sergeant	b. Willis	0
D. W. Hookes	b. Proctor	33
R. D. Robinson	b. Imran Khan	0
G. S. Chappell	c&b. b. Underwood	29
K. J. O'Keefe	c. Taylor b. Barlow	13
M. H. N. Walker	b. Barlow	8
M. F. Malone	b. Willis	5
G. Dymock	not out	8
	Extras	1
	Total	106

Bowling

	O	M	R	W
Willis	7.4	3	19	4
Imran Khan	7	1	13	2
Barlow	10	1	23	2
Proctor	10	1	25	1
Underwood	10	3	25	1

REST OF THE WORLD

Sadiq Mohammad	c. Cosier b. Dymock	25
E. J. Barlow	b. Walker	1
K. McEwan	c. Robinson b. Malone	12
A. I.Kallicharran	lbw. Walker	1
M. J. Proctor	lbw. Cosier	11
Mushtaq Mohammad	c. Sub b. O'Keefe	16
Imran Khan	c. Robinson b. O'Keefe	28
Zaheer Abbas	not out	6
R. W. Taylor	not out	3
D. L. Underwood	did not bat	
R. G. D. Willis		
	Extras	7
	Total (for 7 wkts)	110

Bowling

	O	M	R	W
Walker	10	4	13	2
Malone	10	4	20	1
Dymock	10	2	23	1
Cosier	9	0	32	1
O'Keefe	8.2	2	15	2

REST OF THE WORLD WON BY 3 WKTS

So far as cricket's contribution to the Queen's Silver Jubilee Appeal was concerned, thanks to a large crowd, over £8,000 was raised and the Duchess, as Lord Lieutenant of West Sussex, would go on to produce the largest single contribution from any county in the United Kingdom for the Appeal.

As well as the Australian presence, the main feature of the season was the high quality of the youth cricket on display. The limited overs match between the Young England

94

and Australian cricketers was generally regarded as producing the best game of the year. There was a further emphasis on youth in a rain affected but exciting contest between the Duchess' team and the Sussex Second XI.

The firm commitment to traditional as well as representative cricket was maintained in 1977. One of those who took part in both types of match was Alan Wadey:

"As a local, I found myself invited to be the twelfth man for the representative games and I got in quite a lot of fielding in high level company. On one occasion, I even got a bowl to fill in for one of our visiting stars who had been delayed. I was told to keep things going and on no account to take a wicket which would only confuse the scorers.

"This 'on the fringe' activity had its amusing moments. Billy Griffith ran things just like the M.C.C. and there were the same small brown envelopes for those entitled to expenses and match fees.

"On one occasion he handed me just such an envelope. Well I felt that Arundel was virtually my home Club. The idea of being paid was therefore simply not on - especially on Sunday when I was not otherwise engaged so I gave Billy the envelope back and thus became the recipient of a lot of leg pulling by the professionals. I was told that I was the first cricketer to make the grand gesture since Mark Faber had suggested his annual fee for Sussex should be a farthing a year. But most of my cricket was of the traditional club kind and included a lot of friends from the Martlets. My house became a sort of staging post for them and their families on the way to and from Arundel and after the match parties were often late night Sunday affairs.

"I remember three particular matches in that year. The Duchess's side which played against the Royal Sussex Regiment was full of Martlets. There was Colin Oliver - Redgate, a City man whose parents lived in Worthing. We saw a lot of him in those days as I did of my direct contemporary Peter Hall who was one of our best batsmen. Peter Dunn was another useful batsman who is now a leading light in the Hampshire Hogs. When it came to the bowling, I did a fair amount of work but, in the match against the Regiment, we gave the main share to Claude Duval who was better known as racing correspondent of the *Sun* and another of our Martlet regulars Larry O'Callaghan.

"But our most regular Martlet supporter playing for the home side at Arundel was Adrian Ford. In this particular match we saw him at his best. He was always a good sturdy left-hander and the ideal wandering cricketer. He got a

splendid century and he had a big partnership with Stewart Storey who had been such a useful player for Surrey.

"We had a comfortable victory in that match but there is one point of special interest when you look down the list of dismissals. The point is that it was a typical Arundel wicket which was inclined to be slow and keep a bit low. So in these games against the quicker bowlers, you rarely saw anyone mistime the ball and get caught. In the Regiment match, we got five of their batsman bowled and three LBW and that was often the pattern.

"It was a different story when we played the Eton Ramblers that year. This was a good example of Colin Cowdrey's influence when running the Duchess's side. We had a strong team with recent County cricketers like Mark Faber, Dudley Owen-Thomas, Ted Clark and Mike Griffith. The start was delayed because of rain but we managed to score quite quickly thanks to our Captain. He was still a superb batsman and it was a joy to see him in full flow. When they came out to bat, Colin used me to get an early breakthrough and then brought himself on with Dudley Owen-Thomas to bowl spinners. They did the job so well that they teased out several Etonians with stumpings and catches in the deep which enabled us to win a close match.

"The third match which I remember that season was not one in which I took part but I saw part of it. This was the local Derby against the Arundel Cricket Club and they had rather the better of things. Our side was captained by Nicky Wisdom who had just given up playing for Sussex. He opened the bowling and I see from the scorebook he was remarkably inexpensive with figures of 13-7-22-1 but the bowling stars of the day were Jim Stallibrass for us and Neil Chitty for them. Jim with his bald-headed look of the Senator was always a very steady bowler for the Martlets and, on this occasion, he took six for sixty. Then, when we were going well through a good stand by Hole and Wisdom, Neil Chitty had a hat trick and we had to hang on for grim life to escape with a draw."

At the end of the season, both vintage and young cricketers were on display in two special matches which introduced elements of Festival cricket at Arundel. In the first, Michael Creswell-Wall who was currently the County's High Sherrif, produced a young Sussex XI to play against the Duchess' side captained by Colin Cowdrey. With the start of the school holidays, this included schoolmasters like John Inverarity from Tonbridge and Hubert Doggart who was now a housemaster at Winchester. The youngsters showed little

LAVINIA, DUCHESS OF NORFOLK'S XII V SUSSEX FRIENDS OF THE LORD'S TAVERNERS
4 SEPTEMBER 1977

SUSSEX FRIENDS OF THE LORD'S TAVERNERS

A. W. Mansell	c. Tindall b. Morton	23
J. D. Morley	c. Tindall b. Cotton	52
K. Suttle	c. Cotton b. Cowdrey	39
L. J. Lenham	c. Woodbridge b. Tindall	22
E. R. Dexter	not out	42
D. J. Semmence	not out	16
D. V. Smith	did not bat	
M. G. Griffith		
J. Gifford		
T. Gunn		
J. Kemp		
D. L. Bates		
	Extras	21
	Total (for 4 wkts dec.)	215

Bowling

	O	M	R	W
Butler	10	0	31	0
Morton	9	2	26	1
Cotton	11	2	40	1
Stephenson	3	0	7	0
Tindall	7	0	45	1
Cowdrey	6	0	45	1

LAVINIA, DUCHESS OF NORFOLK'S XII

J. D. Nicholson	c&b Smith	9
B. H. Woodridge	b. Dexter	31
J. Watt	c. Morley b. Dexter	45
R. W. Venables	b. Lenham	32
M. J. K . Smith	b. Suttle	1
M. C. Cowdrey	c. Semmence b. Lenham	14
R. M. Tindall	c. Semmence b. Bates	20
G. A. Wills	c. Semmence b. Dexter	24
J. R. Stephenson	st. Gunn b. Dexter	0
J. M. Morton	b. Dexter	7
T. Cotton	not out	10
N. A. Butler	not out	6
	Extras	12
	Total (for 10 wkts)	211

Bowling

	O	M	R	W
Smith	9	3	13	1
Semmence	4	2	3	0
Gifford	3	0	24	19
Bates	8	0	60	1
Dexter	9	1	47	5
Suttle	7	1	28	1
Lenham	7	1	20	2
Griffith	2	0	4	12

MATCH DRAWN

respect for their elders and it was left to an attacking innings by Mike Griffith and dogged defence from Hubert Doggart to give the score respectability. For a while it looked as though it might be sufficient when the Young Sussex XI were reduced to 9 for 3. However, a partnership of 140 between K. Churchward and the 17 year old Colin Wells (who would soon establish himself as a regular player for the County side) gave the youngsters a comfortable victory.

The second Festival match and the last game in the season was one in which the author as Chairman of the newly formed Sussex Friends of the Lord's Taverners was able to bring back a Taverners side to Arundel for the first time since they had incurred the Duke's displeasure fourteen years earlier. This required delicate negotiation. Billy Griffith both as Chairman of the Club and keeper of the Duke's conscience was concerned to ensure that there would be no repetition of the excessive clowning which had so enraged the Duke.

"You will make sure that your people play proper cricket, won't you?" asked the Chairman. Having put the organisation of the side in the hands of Les Lenham to attract an old Sussex squad and obtained agreement from Ted Dexter that he would captain the side, the author felt able to give a satisfactory response.

In the event, the popularity of the proposed fixture proved so great that a warm up and overflow match was arranged with the help of their genial Director Capt. Tony Swainson, who also took part. The venue was at the nearby village of Slindon and included several of those who would be unavailable for the Arundel game. The match was memorable for the performances of two Test veterans. First, Alec Bedser in his sixtieth year showed, for an over or two, a continued ability to move the ball both ways which defeated the village opening batsmen. When he tired, and found himself pulled into the road by a distinctly rustic stroke, he also showed the presence of mind to go down the wicket and say, "You want to learn to play straight, lad."

The other Test star in the warm up game was Richie Benaud. When he arrived at the village ground, it was obvious that he had 'flu but he and his wife Daphne were determined not to disappoint the large crowd. He agreed to play if he could put his feet up for a while. Unfortunately, while he was in this vulnerable condition, one of the Sussex Taverners decided to try and book him for a speaking engagement. When he politely declined because of his imminent return to Australia, the same helper persisted and asked if he would approach X, another well known Test cricketer. To this, Richie Benaud, fighting off the helper's persistence as well as his flu, replied, "I am sorry but I really cannot involve myself in this kind of thing." Again the

Festival match against Sussex Friends of the Lord's Taverners.
Front row (L to R): The Author, Col. J. R. Stephenson, L. J. Lenham, K. G. Suttle, E. R. Dexter, J. D. Nicholson, D. V. Smith,
M. J. K. Smith, G. A. Wills, S. C. Griffith.
Bach row includes the following Arundel stalwarts: Umpire B. Slater (1st left), Josh Gifford (5th left), Jeremy Kemp (7th left),
D. Semmence (8th left), M. G. Griffith (2nd right), Umpire George Downs (far right).

helper persisted saying "Oh, but a word from you would do the trick". When he persisted further, Richie Benaud finally said "X is a shit and there are no circumstances under which I would wish to approach him. Do I make myself clear?" - only to receive the final response, "But surely he is a very loveable shit, isn't he?"

Despite his tormentor, Richie Benaud went on to take five wickets with controlled spin. He followed this with a half century which took the Taverners to victory before retiring to his sick bed.

On the following day, both he and Alec Bedser (because of his duties as a Test match selector) were unavailable for the game at Arundel. Their places in the Taverners' side were taken by the enthusiastic cricketer and local race horse trainer, Josh Gifford, and the equally enthusiastic wicket-keeper and actor Jeremy Kemp. He would share wicket-keeping duties in the usual relaxed on and off the field arrangement of Taverners' matches with the former Sussex keeper, Terry Gunn. The rest of the side were made up of old Sussex regulars, who showed that they had lost little of their batting and bowling skills.

None did so to greater advantage than the Taverners' captain, Ted Dexter. Arriving in front of the pavilion in a Vintage Bentley, accompanied by his glamorous teenaged daughter, he brought a certain dash to the proceedings. Despite the fact that, at this time, he was suffering from muscular problems which required an injection in both fore-

arms before going out to bat, he showed much of his old power and authority in hitting the ball as hard off the back foot as off the front foot in an undefeated innings before making the Taverners' declaration.

Then when the Duchess' side were making good headway through a stand for the second wicket between Woodbridge and Watt, he came on and dismissed them both. In true Taverner fashion, he took himself off and put on the non-regular bowlers to keep the match evenly balanced. However, when the Duchess' team were within 50 runs of victory with three wickets standing, he came on to bowl again and promptly took all three wickets. This apparently gave the Sussex Taverners a victory by twenty five runs but there was some discussion about whether the sides were batting eleven or twelve and the Duchess' opening bowler, N. A. Butler, came out to bat at number 12. The tail-enders hung on and took the Duchess' team to within 5 runs of victory when, well after the appointed hour for the close of play, it ended in an amiable, confused and agreed draw.

The match had proved such a success that a return game was immediately agreed. It was also decided that negotiations should be put in hand to attract sponsorship for future Taverners matches given their obvious potential in raising money for the Club as well as for the charity.

Looking at the financial situation overall, the figures quoted earlier have shown the financial significance of the big matches in attracting both sponsorship and revenue for the club. In 1978 this dependence came into early focus when the Pakistan Cricket Board of Control withdrew from the opening match of the season at very short notice. Fortunately, it was replaced later by a game against the New Zealand touring side which was again sponsored by the National Westminster Bank.

Following the success of the Youth International in the previous year, the first ever three day match at Arundel was arranged as a Test Match between the England and West Indies Under Nineteen sides. Other youth cricket was also supported in a special match which, as part of the ever closer relationship with cricket headquarters, was arranged between Colin Milburn's XI and the M.C.C. Young Cricketers. Finally, by contrast, the club accepted an offer from Watneys for sponsorship of a match involving their Old England XI, and a number of their team would also be made available for the end of term party with the Lord's Taverners Sussex XI.

The cricket in the match against New Zealand in June fully lived up to expectations. Richard Streeton's report was enthusiastic about activities both on and off the field:

"The New Zealanders were beaten off the final ball of the day as their last pair tried to snatch a single that would have brought a tie. It was the perfect finish to the perfect day and Messrs Constant and Budd knew what they were doing when they were willing to give up the rest day from the Lord's Test to stand here.

"From the posse of police and A.A. escorts that greeted us all from the outskirts of the town on arrival, everything was done supremely well. The 92 strong band from Christ's Hospital played and marched at the intervals and even the loudspeaker announcements were undertaken by the local M.P. And if he made some of us smile when he declared that this would be 'a straight cricket match', we knew what he meant."

The New Zealanders played their part nobly in all respects. The pressure was tactfully eased when their new ball attack began too well and the friendliness of the occasion was illustrated when two of their players turned out for the Duchess' side. This was captained by Robin Hobbs, whose leg-spin bought him most wickets in the match. His principal support came from John Emburey and Don Wilson. Both had long bowling spells as well as taking part in an undefeated stand of 62 for the seventh wicket.

Don Wilson returned to Arundel in July in his capacity as Head Coach at Lords when he captained the M.C.C. Young Cricketers in their five wicket victory over Colin Milburn's

LAVINIA, DUCHESS OF NORFOLK'S XI v NEW ZEALAND
18TH JUNE 1978

LAVINIA, DUCHESS OF NORFOLK'S XI

B. W. Luckhurst	b. Hadlee	33
V. J. Marks	b. Hadlee	5
A. P. Sheahan	lbw. Congdon	0
G. D. Barlow	b. Cairns	13
B. A. Edgar	lbw. Howarth	34
D. R. Hadlee	b. Boock	21
J. E. Emburey	not out	51
D. Wilson	not out	28
R. N. S. Hobbs	did not bat	
M. W. W. Selvey		
T. W. Cartwright		
	Extras	3
	Total (for 6 wkts dec.)	188

Bowling

	O	M	R	W
Hadlee	7	2	14	2
Cairns	9	1	38	1
Congdon	8	2	17	1
Boock	9	2	40	1
McIntyre	9	2	22	0
Howarth	7	0	54	1

NEW ZEALAND

J. G. Wright	run out	16
R. W. Anderson	b. Cartwright	13
G. P. Howarth	b. Emburey	32
M. G. Burgess	c. Selvey b. Hobbs	26
B. E. Congdon	c. Luckhurst b. Hobbs	20
J. M. Parker	b. Wilson	3
G. N. Edwards	c. Luckhurst b. Hobbs	41
R. J. Hadlee	run out	0
B. L. Cairns	c&b. Wilson	20
J. McIntyre	not out	9
S. L. Boock	run out	1
	Extras	6
	Total	187

Bowling

	O	M	R	W
Selvey	6	2	12	0
Hadlee	5	2	13	0
Cartwright	6	3	10	1
Emburey	10	3	29	1
Wilson	16	1	64	2
Hobbs	11.4	2	53	3

LAVINIA, DUCHESS OF NORFOLK'S XI WON BY 1 RUN

XI. This was achieved mainly through a century by Jeremy Lloyds who would make his debut for Somerset in the following season. Apart from himself, Colin Milburn's side was made up of young South African cricketers whom he had met while coaching in their country. Although the great hitter (now suffering from impaired eyesight following a car accident) failed to get runs, he showed all his old relish in undertaking a full share of the bowling. His joy was evident when, in a purely reflex action, he made a brilliant caught and bowled dismissal of one of the M.C.C.'s opening batsmen.

A few weeks later both Don Wilson and Colin Milburn were back in action against the Duchess' team playing for the Watneys Invitation XI. The match fully lived up to its billing as an all-star event. The organiser was Adrian Ford:

"I was working for Watneys in their marketing division at Stag Brewery in Victoria and I had recently been best man at Butch White's wedding. We had a conversation about producing an Old England Eleven and I persuaded Billy Griffith that it would be a good match for Arundel. Butch's advice was to involve Fred Trueman and, sure enough, when I approached him he said 'I'll be glad to do it just as long as I am skipper'. He quickly lined up Farokh Engineer, Neil Hawke and Sonny Ramadhin and the others fell into place.

"Half the fun in this match was the non-stop badinage between Fred and Butch. They both did their share of bowling with Fred claiming that he was not only quicker than Butch but also, 'With my faster ball, I'm quicker than anything in the present England squad'. However, the real bowling star for us was Sonny Ramadhin. At the age of 48, he still troubled a lot of the Duchess's experienced batting line-up. Roger Knight for one was honest enough to say, 'I can't work him out. All you see is the hand coming at you with that famous buttoned up sleeve. I'm simply doing what I can to play him off the pitch and playing and missing quite regularly'. However, Peter Willey who had got himself going well against the quicker bowlers earlier on went on to make a splendid 100 and we had a bit of a battle on our hands.

"This became even more of a challenge when Parfitt, Sharpe, Ingleby-Mackenzie and Engineer (our first four) were all out with the score at sixteen. I had the good fortune to take part in stands with Colin Milburn and Don Wilson which gave our score some respectability but their spinners worked their way steadily through our batting order and we lost a very exciting match by 10 runs".

A few days later, the Third Test Match in the series between the England and West Indies Under 19 teams brought a feast of runs. Neil Taylor who would soon make his debut for Kent made top score for England in both innings. However the West Indies generally dominated the match after a big partnership between Lewis and Etwaroo. Lewis went on to make his century and England, already one up in the three match series, played out time for a draw. This was not achieved without some alarm as they were

LAVINIA, DUCHESS OF NORFOLK'S XI v WATNEY'S INVITATION XI
17 AUGUST 1978

LAVINIA, DUCHESS OF NORFOLK'S XI

P Willey	st. Engineer b. Wilson	105
G. Miller	b. Hawke	33
D. W. Randall	c. Parfitt b. Ramadhin	13
C. T. Radley	lbw. Ramadhin	37
G. R. J. Roope	st. Engineer b. Ramadhin	7
M. C. Cowdrey	not out	12
R. D. V. Knight	not out	12
T. E. Jesty	did not bat	
R. W. Taylor		
P. I. Pocock		
M. Hendrick		
	Extras	4
	Total (for 5 wkts dec.)	223

Bowling

	O	M	R	W
White	7	1	26	0
Wadey (sub)	5	1	8	0
Milburn	3	0	7	0
Wilson	14	2	62	1
Hawke	4	0	30	1
Trueman	3	0	21	0
Ramadhin	13	1	65	3

WATNEY'S INVITATION XI

P. H. Parfitt	c. Pocock b Jesty	2
P. J. Sharpe	lbw. Hendrick	2
A. C. D. Ingleby-Mackenzie	b. Miller	7
F. M. Engineer	st. Taylor b. Pocock	1
C. Milburn	b. Knight	35
A. R. Ford	c. Jesty b. Pocock	47
D. Wilson	c. Radley b. Pocock	74
N. J. N. Hawke	b. Miller	0
F. S. Trueman	c. Jesty b. Radley	12
S. Ramadhin	not out	5
D. W. White	b. Radley	0
	Extras	28
	Total	213

Bowling

	O	M	R	W
Hendrick	5	4	1	1
Radley	3.4	0	31	2
Jesty	3	2	3	1
Pocock	8	1	35	3
Miller	6	4	14	2
Taylor	6	3	8	0
Randall	7	1	32	0
Knight	5	0	14	1
Cowdrey	4	0	47	0

LAVINIA, DUCHESS OF NORFOLK'S XI WON BY 10 RUNS

given a testing time by a young Barbadian, Franklyn Stephenson, who would later prove such a valuable all-rounder for Nottinghamshire and Sussex.

The Festival match against the Sussex Taverners was again evenly contested. Mike Griffith got a half century against his old county colleagues which allowed Colin Cowdrey to make a sporting declaration. The Taverners' reply was made memorable by a half century partnership between Jack Robertson and Paul Sheahan. The Middlesex

"I don't know what's going on out there!" – FST, Peter Parfitt and Sonny Ramadhin.

and England opener was almost exactly twice the age of his young Australian partner but he showed much of his old skill and elegance in guiding the ball wide of the fielders and giving his partner the strike. When they were dismissed, there was time for a glimpse of the veteran skills of Ken Suttle and a neat and effective partnership between Derek Semmence and his captain Les Lenham which took the Sussex Lord's Taverners to a four wicket victory.

At the end of the match, Billy Griffith, the guardian of 'proper cricket' at the Club, said to the author:

"We really wouldn't have any objection to seeing one or two showbiz people in the Taverners side next year!"

He was granted his wish in television terms when Ted Moult came in to bat for the Taverners in the following year, supported by the comedian Jasper Carrott.

Because of the success of the earlier Taverners matches at Arundel, it had been agreed that the fixture should be raised to big match status and Lloyds of London provided sponsorship. This was due to the efforts of John Poland, who was one of the club's early benefactors. He not only arranged for its first pension scheme and donated the funds

Skipper Fred leads out his troops.

WATNEY'S INVITATION XI, 1978

for outbuildings to store ground equipment but he also ensured that, in addition to sponsorship for the Taverners by Lloyds, the club received a match fee of £1,000.

The Taverners' collection of funds on the ground - for sporting equipment for the young disabled - was not without its hazards. Apart from a major raffle which included several airline tickets to exotic destinations, the traditional tour of the ground with the blanket was capable of raising over four figures. On this occasion, apart from the cricketers who undertook this task, support came from the Lady Taverners in the persons of Penelope Keith and Anita Harris. Both came quickly under fire from well intentioned supporters throwing, with varying degrees of accuracy, coins in the general direction of the blanket. There was growing concern when enquiries suggested that there might be a gap in the club's insurance policy in respect of damage sustained while collecting funds for charity.

Happily the situation was resolved when the ground match commentators suggested a paper collection together with a relay system for coins passed from hand to hand by large numbers of enthusiastic small boys. These activities - reinforced with the autograph tent and the sponsor's donation - produced a total in excess of £11,000 for the charity and the game immediately established itself as the principal fixture in the Taverners' season.

The Lloyds' team which took the place of the traditional Duchess of Norfolk's XI included Mark Faber and Mike Griffith of Sussex but their top score came from Peter Carroll, an Australian Oxford cricket and rugger Blue who had become an Arundel regular. In the Taverners' reply, the large crowd was vastly entertained when Colin Milburn, seemingly making light of his limited eyesight, scored fifty in thirty five minutes. Shortly before he was out, he hit a huge six onto the bank in front of the pavilion and attempting a repeat performance was caught in the deep by Mark Faber. Thereafter, Colin Cowdrey with a typically cultured innings at better than a run a minute led his side to a three wicket victory.

The rest of the season was notable for a number of new fixtures. In earlier years, E. W. Swanton had brought his Arabs team to play the Martlets at Arundel when they had enjoyed considerable success, "No doubt inspired", as their manager put it, "by the ducal atmosphere and the ducal presence." In 1979 there was no traditional touring match because of the World Cup and the Arabs were happy to step into the breach. However, on this occasion, their six

Lavinia, Duchess of Norfolk's XI v The Arabs
6 May 1979

LAVINIA, DUCHESS OF NORFOLK'S XI

R. A. Gale	run out	21
A. R. Ford	c Prentice b. Stewart	8
K. Tomlin	lbw. Hamblin	21
J. M. M. Hooper	not out	65
A. Patel	lbw. Cattrall	3
N. Cosh	c. Faber b. Fincham	2
C. Goldie	b. Barker	10
N. Wisdom	b. Cattrall	0
T. Rudd	not out	28
S. Dyson	did not bat	
A. N. C. Wadey		
	Extras	4
	Total (for 7wkts dec.)	162

Bowling

	O	M	R	W
Fursdon	5	1	18	0
Stewart	9	3	26	1
Wagstaff	13	4	42	0
Hamblin	3	0	11	1
Cattrall	14	4	30	2
Fincham	5	2	14	1
Barker	6	1	17	1

THE ARABS

M. J. J. Faber	c. Patel b. Wisdom	12
C. B. Hamblin	c. Tomlin b. Dyson	32
C. Prentice	b. Dyson	4
R. Wells	b. Dyson	0
P. R. Carroll	b. Wadey	
A. H. Barker	c Goldie b. Tomlin	34
D. Fursdon	lbw. Patel	0
M. Wagstaffe	c. Goldie b. Gale	3
A. Fincham	b. Dyson	0
P. Cattrall	b. Dyson	8
N. J. W. Stewart	not out	7
	Extras	9
	Total	116

Bowling

	O	M	R	W
Wadey	7	3	16	1
Wisdom	5	2	61	
Dyson	19	3	44	5
Patel	16	5	23	1
Gale	5	1	18	1
Tomlin	2	0	01	

LAVINIA, DUCHESS OF NORFOLK'S XI WON BY 46 RUNS

Oxbridge Blues were outgunned by the seven county caps in the Duchess' side.

The match later in the season designed for maximum sponsorship and a big crowd was that arranged between Australia and New Zealand as a warm up game for the World Cup. However, this proved one-sided when the New Zealanders, weakened by the absence of several of their leading players still involved in county cricket, found the Australian opening attack of Hogg, Hurst and Dymock too much for them.

Revenues from matches of this kind had become increasingly important in meeting the growing overheads for professional management of the club's administration and ground preparation. It was also necessary in providing the extra resources needed to entertain touring club sides from overseas. Two of those able to take advantage of such invitations in 1979 were the Barbados Wanderers and the Canada-UK Forty Club.

The match against the Canada-UK Forty Club provided a comfortable victory for the home side thanks to a century from Geoff Wills and another useful guest appearance from Don Wilson which produced bowling figures of 17-7-31-5.

The match against the Barbados Wanderers was very much a family affair. Their captain, Peter Short, after war time service with the British Army, was now a leading figure in West Indies cricket administration. It was particularly appropriate when the Duchess' team was managed and captained by his cousin Peter Robinson:

"When the idea of this tour came up, I had a quiet word with Billy Griffith. I felt it was important that former colonies like Barbados should be made welcome but club tours of this kind were necessarily arranged on a shoe-string. Billy, who was a great friend of my cousin Peter ever since he had toured the West Indies in 1947/48, immediately said, 'We are here to help' and we agreed a date together and attracted offers of local hospitality.

"In cricketing terms, the Wanderers were by no means a pushover. Looking down their batting order, they produced a good opening partnership between Tony Cozier (who has subsequently made his name as a Test Match commentator) and Arthur Taylor, who turned out for the full Barbados side; so too had several of the others in the team. In addition, Richard Edwards had played for the West Indies and Denis Atkinson had been, for a considerable period, the best all-rounder in the Test side.

"All their batsmen chipped in and they made a reasonable declaration and the runs were going to take some getting against a Test bowler like Richard Edwards and Stephen Farmer who was first change for Barbados after Hall and Griffith.

"I shall never forget the innings which Josh Gifford played. He once told me, 'I would much rather have played at Lord's than won the Derby and he was obviously thrilled

AUSTRALIA v NEW ZEALAND
2 JUNE 1979

AUSTRALIA

A. M. J. Hilditch	run out	77
W. M. Darling	b. Morrison	60
A. R. Border	b. Troup	8
K. J. Hughes	st. Lees b. Stott	32
G. N. Yallop	run out	18
G. J. Cosier	not out	1
T. J. Laughlin	did not bat	
K. J. Wright		
G. Dymock		
R. M. Hogg		
A. G. Hurst		
	Extras	9
	Total (for 5 wkts dec.)	205

Bowling

	O	M	R	W
Chatfield	12	2	28	0
Troup	9	1	21	1
McKechnie	2	0	10	0
Coney	8	1	25	0
Cairns	11	1	41	0
Stott	12	0	50	1
Morrison	6	0	21	1

NEW ZEALAND

J. F. M. Morrison	lbw. Hurst	3
B. A. Edgar	lbw. Hogg	7
J. V. Coney	lbw. Hogg	7
M. G. Burgess	c. Wright b. Hurst	4
J. R. Wiltshire	lbw. Hurst	2
W. K. Lees	c. Wright b. Dymock	7
B. McKechnie	c. Wright b. Dymock	1
B. L. Cairns	lbw. Laughlin	10
W. Stott	not out	3
G. B. Troup	lbw. Laughlin	0
E. J. Chatfield	run out	0
	Extras	8
	Total	52

Bowling

	O	M	R	W
Hogg	6	2	11	2
Hurst	10	1	14	3
Dymock	7	2	9	2
Laughlin	6	1	7	2
Cosier	2	1	1	0
Border	1.5	0	2	0

AUSTRALIA WON BY 153 RUNS

when he got runs against a good opening attack. He hardly hit anything where he intended but he was delighted with his runs. He was followed by Ted Clark of Middlesex and Nigel Paul of Warwickshire. They produced one of the best pieces of batting I have ever seen on this ground. They put on over a hundred and, when Ted got out, there was a nice touch when Peter Short's son Walter came in to help Nigel

Paul in a half century stand that won the match for us."

Alan Wadey who was also playing in the match remembers it as much for the activities off the field as those which took place on it:

"Our visitors really brought a Caribbean atmosphere to the game. They had lots of camp followers and we had the first barbecue which I can remember at the ground and it went on far into the night."

1976

June 27th. Lavinia Duchess of Norfolk's XI 228-3 dec (M. C. Cowdrey 96*, R. Green 84*). I Zingari XI 229-8 (M. F. Wright 142, J. Davies 6-51). I Zingari won by 2 wickets.

July 3rd. Lady Mary's and Lady Sarah's XI 220 (C. Ingleby-McKenzie 81) Lavinia Duchess of Norfolk's XI 221-4 (J. Watt 124). Lavinia Duchess of Norfolk's XI won by 6 wickets.

1977

May 29th. Lavinia Duchess of Norfolk's XI 213-3 dec (A. R. Ford 117, S. J. Storey 52). The Royal Sussex Regiment 101. Lavinia Duchess of Norfolk's XI won by 112 runs.

June 5th. Lavinia Duchess of Norfolk's XI 132 (A. C. F. Pigott 5-31). Sussex C. C. C. 2nd XI 126-7. Match drawn.

June 12th. Lavinia Duchess of Norfolk's XI 140-9 dec. Eton Ramblers 119. Lavinia Duchess of Norfolk's XI won by 21 runs.

July 9th. England Young Cricketers 245-4 (K. Sharp 107, P. Bainbridge 66). Australian Young Cricketers 213-7 (R. Allen 75, A. Handrican 56). 45 overs match. England Young Cricketers won by 32 runs.

July 17th. Arundel C. C. 195-7 (J. McLaughlin 53, J. Stallibrass 6-60) Lavinia Duchess of Norfolk's XI 153-9 (N. Chitty 6-54). Match drawn.

July 24th, Lavinia Duchess of Norfolk's XI 163-5 dec (M. G. Griffith 65). High Sheriff's Young Sussex XI 165-4 (C. Wells 78, H. Churchward 65*). High Sheriff's Young Sussex XI won by 6 wickets.

1978

July 14th. Colin Milburn's XI 180-8 dec M. C. C. Young Cricketers 181-5 (J. Lloyds 103) M. C. C. Young Cricketers won by 5 wickets.

August 20th and 22nd. England under 19 XI 223-9 dec (N. Taylor 68) and 234-9 (N. Taylor 63). West Indies under 19 XI 345-5 dec (L. Lewis 149, T. Etwaroo 51, H. Roach 56). Match drawn.

September 3rd, Lavinia Duchess of Norfolk's XI, 219-9 dec (M. G. Griffith 58). Sussex Lord" Taverners 225-6 (P. Sheehan 77, L. Lenham 60*). Sussex Lord's Taverners won by 4 wickets.

1979

July 4th. Barbados Wanderers 223-8 dec.(A. Taylor 48, D. Atkinson 34). Lavinia Duchess of Norfolk's XI 227-4 (N. A. Paul 116*, E. A. Clark 57). Lavinia Duchess of Norfolk's XI won by by 6 wickets.

July 22nd. Lavinia Duchess of Norfolk's XI 214-5 dec (G. A. Wills 100). Canada/UK "40" 183 (D. Wilson 5.31). Lavinia Duchess of Norfolk's XI won by 31 runs.

September 2nd. Lloyds of London C. C. 209-5 dec. (P. R. Carroll 95). Lord's Taverners 212-7 (M. C. Cowdrey 68, C. Milburn 66). Lord's Taverners won by 3 wickets.

CHAPTER NINE

The Griffith / Ford Partnership 1980-1984

In 1980 there were further serious efforts to put the Arundel Castle Cricket Club's finances on a more secure footing. Although membership stood at over two thousand for the first time, Billy Griffith expressed concern over the club's continuing inability to match income with expenditure.

Sir Alec Durie was prominent in urging that there should be a major appeal to obtain support from banks and city institutions to top up the trust fund which had been established as a result of the initial contribution from Duchess Lavinia and her daughters. Sir Alec, together with Alec Dibbs, Deputy Chairman of the National Westminster Bank and D. Curling of J. Walter Thompson joined the original trustees, Billy Griffith, Colin Cowdrey and Roger Gibbs in efforts which, by the end of the year, took the capital fund up to £50,000.

Income from this trust was urgently needed. The committee of the club acknowledged that they were consistently underpaying their secretary and groundsmen. As a result of the fund-raising efforts, it became possible to provide them with free accommodation on the ground which was in keeping with their involvement in the substantial growth of cricket activity.

In 1980 it was planned to have at least 40 matches made up of 2 or 3 major sponsored games, 9 semi-major matches of which as many as possible would be sponsored and 3 to 4 youth games. The balance would be made up of 12 Martlets matches including the game against the Duchess' XI which would mark their 75th Anniversary and the balance would be offered to the Estate XI.

The overall administration for this substantial fixture list was entrusted to the unflappable Group Captain Ronnie Ford. A former assistant secretary of the M.C.C., he had joined the committee as Deputy Chairman in the previous year when it became clear that Billy Griffith was to assume the Presidency of the M.C.C.

Early in the season, they arranged a special match to commemorate this event. Billy Griffith's team was, with one exception, made up of Test and County players. Five were from Middlesex; two, including his son, were from Sussex and one each from Surrey, Hampshire and Essex. This left the last place for someone of whom the Hampshire captain, Nick Pocock, said in the dressing room, "We won't need to worry about bowling too much today with Malcolm Marshall in the side." He showed considerable charm and diplomacy when it was pointed out that the M. Marshall shown on the score-card did not represent another guest appearance by the West Indian fast bowler but rather a kind invitation by Billy Griffith to include the local Member of Parliament.

For the author, it was a childhood dream come true to take the field with a team of Test and County cricketers when Colin Cowdrey, captaining the Duchess' team, won the toss and decided to bat. However, the hazards of keeping up with the boys in one's fiftieth year soon became apparent when over ambitious attempts in the field resulted in the sound of splitting flannels. As luck would have it, William Hickey of the Express was there to record the parliamentarian's embarrassment, and, with the usual disregard for facts in the interest of local colour, attributed the emergency repairs which were undertaken by his wife to Lady Mary Fitzalan-Howard.

Meanwhile, the proper cricketers in the President's side were giving the home team a good deal of early trouble. A steady opening spell by John Price and Mike Selvey followed by a wicket in his first over from Alan Wadey reduced the Duchess' team to 29 for 3. At this point - as so often in his Arundel career - Colin Cowdrey came in to restore order. Mike Griffith had taken off his quicker bowlers and the attack was entrusted to John Emburey and Robin Hobbs. The captain was content to give most of the strike to Phil Edmonds who showed his liking for the off-spin of his

11TH MAY 1980
LAVINIA, DUCHESS OF NORFOLK'S XI V PRESIDENT OF M.C.C.'S XI

LAVINIA, DUCHESS OF NORFOLKS XI

P. R. Carroll	b. Selvey	19
C. B. Hamblin	lbw. Selvey	4
R. D. Knight	ct. Griffith b. Wadey	1
P. H. Edmonds	ct. Hooper b. Emburey	90
M. C. Cowdrey	b. Hobbs	28
D. R. Owen-Thomas	not out	50
E. A. Clark	b. Emburey	17
P. H. L. E. Wilson	b. Emburey	8
P. I. Pocock	did not bat	
T. Head		
S. Dyson		
	Extras	9
	Total (for 7 wkts. dec.)	226

Bowling

	O	M	R	W
J. S. E. Price	5	1	11	0
M. W. W. Selvey	7	1	14	2
A. N. C. Wadey	6	2	17	1
J. E. Emburey	21	2	88	3
R. N. S. Hobbs	17	2	87	1

PRESIDENT OF M.C.C.'s XI

M. J. Smith	ct. Owen-Thomas b. Pocock	21
J. M. M. Hooper	b. Hamblin	66
N. E. J. Pocock	ct. Wilson b. Hamblin	20
M. Scott	ct. Wilson b. Cowdrey	43
M. G. Griffith	b. Wilson	28
M. Marshall	b. Wilson	0
J. E. Emburey	b. Clark	8
A. N. Wadey	b. Cowdrey	3
M. W. W. Selvey	c. and b. Clark	10
R. N. S. Hobbs	run out	15
J. S. E. Price	not out	0
	Extras	10
	Total	224

Bowling

	O	M	R	W
P. H. L. E. Wilson	8	1	20	2
R. D. V. Knight	4	0	15	0
S. Dyson	13	4	30	0
P. I. Pocock	5	0	38	1
E. A. Clark	12	1	56	2
C. B. Hamblin	5	0	25	2
M. C. Cowdrey	4	0	30	2

LAVINIA, DUCHESS OF NORFOLK'S XI WON BY 2 RUNS

Middlesex team mate and the leg-spin of his former touring companion in racing to a half century which included nine fours and a six. He was particularly severe on John Emburey and added to his discomfort by a stream of light-hearted remarks which suggested amazement at his English selection. When both Cowdrey and Edmonds departed after a century stand, the assault on the bowling was continued by

Dudley Owen-Thomas and, in true Duke of Norfolk style, Colin Cowdrey declared the innings at 3.30.

For a while, the President's team moved easily towards its target of 227 and, thanks to Mike Smith, Mike Hooper and Nick Pocock, the century went up with only one wicket down. When they were dismissed, Mark Scott and Mike Griffith had another good stand and the score reached 181 for 3. At this point, Colin Cowdrey decided to reintroduce Hugh Wilson into the attack. The 22 year old Surrey fast bowler was then striving to establish himself as a young England hopeful. With the first ball of his new spell, he bowled Mike Griffith which brought in the author.

"Push forward" said Colin Cowdrey in his usual helpful way. The score book shows that the innings which followed lasted for 3 balls, the third of which was far too quick for an ageing parliamentarian.

With adroit stage management, Colin Cowdrey took off his fast bowler and brought himself on with Ted Clark. However, both posed their problems for the President's tail-enders and the score was 205 for 8 when Mike Selvey and Robin Hobbs came together. They took the score to within three runs of victory with two balls remaining in the last over of the match. At this point, Robin Hobbs was run out and Mike Selvey, attempting a straight drive to win the game, was caught and bowled by Ted Clark.

"It was", said Billy Griffith afterwards, "exactly the kind of game that the Duke would have loved." Duchess Lavinia, who normally left the cricket in the early afternoon, had stayed to the end and said in her best non-cricketing voice, "Even I enjoyed it."

There were other commemorative matches in 1980. For their 75th anniversary, the Martlets produced a strong side which included six current or former Sussex county players. Among them was Hubert Doggart, now Headmaster of Kings Bruton School, then in his 55th year, who made a special pilgrimage from Somerset to support his old Club side. However, he was not required to bat as Chris Bidwell and Nick Wisdom put on over 150 to allow their side to declare. The Duchess' team, captained by Dudley Owen Thomas, consisted mainly of young cricketers on the M.C.C.'s ground staff at Lords. They showed all the zest of youth in chasing the runs and it required the veteran Doggart to slow them down. Bowling what he would describe in 1994 as "my attempted spinners but more realistically by diddling them" he took two wickets in successive overs. But three fast half centuries for the Duchess' side by Milton, Broad and Scott saw them to the traditional last over victory.

The day was also made memorable by off the field activities. During the lunch interval, Duchess Lavinia presented Eddie Harrison with his portrait painted by the local artist Juliet Pannett. This marked not only his thirty years as Secretary of the Martlets but also his 70th birthday.

The other active participant in the day's proceedings was the film actor Oliver Reed. His brother Simon was playing for the Duchess' team and he was billed as the side's twelfth man. In the equivalent match two years previously, he had caused near apoplexy among some of his hosts when coming in to bat in a suit of armour. After a spectacular and noisy appearance in which he failed to trouble the scorers, he countered subsequent suggestions of restraint by Michael Cresswell-Wall with a series of sword movements which caused the Arundel committee man to make a discreet withdrawal.

On this occasion, Oliver Reed took his twelfth man duties seriously especially when it came to the question of

The Duchess and Billy Griffith join the Sussex Martlets team at the match in 1980. The distinctive twelfth man is actor Oliver Reed.

Lavinia, Duchess of Norfolk with The Royal Sussex Regiment XI, 1980. The President of the Regimental Association and Mrs. G. J. Langridge are seated alongside the Duchess.

LAVINIA, DUCHESS OF NORFOLK'S XI v ROYAL SUSSEX REGIMENT INVITATION XI
1ST JUNE 1980

LAVINIA, DUCHESS OF OF NORFOLK'S XI

A. R. Ford	ct. Nicholson b. Lamb	5
A. Browne	not out	94
J. Davies	lbw. Stanton	24
D. J. Semmence	ct. Pyemont b. Din	34
P. M. Hall	b. Robertson	9
S. Ford	b. Robertson	6
N. Trestrail	not out	4
N. Philpot	did notbat	
T. Stephens		
D. White		
A. N. C. Wadey		
	Extras	17
	Total (for 5 wkts. dec.)	193

Bowling

	O	M	R	W
Robertson	15	2	44	2
Lamb	19	2	58	1
Din	14	1	58	1
Stanton	5	1	16	1

ROYAL SUSSEX REGIMENT INVITATION XI

J. G. Lofting	ct. Semmence b. Davies	39
R. H. Chappell	b. Wadey	0
M. A. Din	ct. Hall b. Stephens	107
P. Pyemont	run out	28
J. Whittaker	b. Stephens	0
J. R. Stephenson	b. White	1
C. J. G. Stanton	not out	0
G. K. R. Robertson	not out	1
S. T. Lamb	b. White	0
J. D. Nicholson	did not bat	
A. M. Armitage-Smith		
	Extras	14
	Total (for 7 wkts.)	190

Bowling

	O	M	R	W
White	10	0	59	2
Wadey	6	0	31	1
Philpot	10	0	47	0
Davies	7	0	31	1
Stephens	3	2	8	2

MATCH DRAWN

providing drinks for his team which seemed to have an unusually strong kick. As the day proceeded, he also offered vocal encouragement of an increasingly direct kind in support of his captain, Dudley Owen-Thomas. His continued calls to the crowd of, 'Lets hear it for Dooders' caused Billy Griffith who was there in his capacity as Martlets President as well as Chairman of the Club, to watch most of the match from the privacy of his motor car.

A week later, the match against the Royal Sussex

Regiment Invitation XI was another special occasion in which Colonel John Stephenson was engaged:

"The match was arranged to mark the 30th year of the first visit of the Regimental side to Arundel. It was an increasing struggle to raise a team which was really representative because of military mergers and the disappearance of a lot of our old stalwarts. I was able to help as Secretary of the M.C.C. by bringing in one or two guests as in this case when we included Asif Din from Uganda who was qualifying for Warwickshire and Gary Robertson who had played for the young New Zealand side. They did most of our bowling, backed up by Sergeant Lamb who played for the Army side and whom we somehow borrowed from the Grenadier Guards. We also had our usual quota of schoolmasters who had served in the Regiment. There was Peter Pyemont, Headmaster at St. Bede's in Eastbourne and one of his masters there, David Nicholson, together with John Whitaker, the Headmaster of Sussex House in London. Otherwise, there were a few old stagers like Robin Chappell and myself and we managed to find a useful batsman from the Army side in J. C. Lofting who was good enough to play for the Combined Services.

"We had a special lunch for Duchess Lavinia when we

Four stalwarts of I Zingari at Arundel for the M.C.C. match in 1980. (L to R) Sir Alec Douglas-Home, Sir William Becher BT., Ronnie Aird, and (seated) Cosmo Crawley.

presented her with a copy of the team photograph which hangs in the pavilion today. So far as the cricket was concerned, it was an exciting affair. A chap called Browne almost got a century for them and Asif Din achieved this for us but, following their declaration, we fell a few runs short. It was certainly a great day's celebration but I think we all had the feeling that the series was inevitably bound to come to an end - as it did a few years later - because we had to go on borrowing more and more players."

The match against I Zingari on 22 June 1980 was another special occasion to celebrate Billy Griffith's presidency of the M.C.C. Alec Home (his predecessor in that role in 1966) was one of Duchess Lavinia's regular house guests for these games. On this occasion, they were joined at lunch by Ronnie Aird (President of the M.C.C. 1968), Cosmo Crawley and Sir William Becher BT.

All of them were listed in the I Zingari's eccentric record book as, 'Candidates for the asylum for aged and decayed Zingari.' It was a toss up for seniority between Lord Home of the Hirsel and Ronnie Aird, although the former Prime Minister as 'Governor fourth wicket down' probably had the edge. Cosmo Crawley had played with his brother Aidan in the first game for IZ. against Duke Bernard's side in 1956 and Billy Becher (who played for Sussex as an amateur before the War) had been the Club's Secretary for many years. All were Zingari freemen to whose select company Duchess Lavinia had recently been admitted as the first lady freeman.

The Duchess' side was captained by Nick Stewart. The old Harrovian, who at some point in his cricketing career had become known as 'the Colonel' was also recognised as the best of cricket auctioneers at charity games. He had assembled an exceptionally strong side. The batting was opened by Conrad Hunte of the West Indies and Jonathan Townsend. They put on 87 for the first wicket as Jonathan Townsend recalled during the South African Test Match at Lord's in 1994:

"It's always been a slight strain coming from a vast family of county and Test cricketers whereas the height of my achievements was a Blue at Oxford and minor county cricket. Still, I was usually lucky enough to get some runs at Arundel and you don't get to open with a Test match partner every day. He couldn't have been more splendidly supportive and when we departed Richard Lewis of Hampshire and Nicky Wisdom of Sussex piled on the runs and we made the expected Arundel declaration.

ENGLAND LORD'S TAVERNERS V AUSTRALIA LORD'S TAVERNERS
31ST AUGUST 1980

AUSTRALIA LORD'S TAVERNERS

T. Vievers	lbw. b. Wilson	12
K. Stackpole	b. Milburn	39
B. Simpson	b. Boyce	39
G. Hole	c. Lever b. Allen	40
A. Turner	st. Livingston b. Durden-Smith	37
G. Gilmour	c. Upton b. Cowdrey	30
D. Colley	not out	8
D. Hoare	b. Lever	5
F. Misson	c. Livingston b. Lever	2
J. Gleeson	did not bat	
A. Connelly		
	Extras	14
	Total (for 8wkts. dec.)	226

Bowling

	O	M	R	W
Price	3	1	6	0
Lever	3.4	0	10	2
Wilson	7	1	32	1
Martin-Jenkins	8	0	36	0
Allen	3	0	25	1
Durden-Smith	7	0	36	1
Boyce	2	0	23	1
Cowdrey	4	0	29	1
Milburn	3	0	9	1
Rumsey	3	1	6	0

ENGLAND LORD'S TAVERNERS

C. Milburn	b. Gleeson	8
R. Prideaux	c. Stackpole b. Colley	4
D. Wilson	c. Vievers b. Simpson	20
D. Ufton	b. Hole	46
W. Rushton	b. Vievers	6
C. Martin-Jenkins	st. Turner b. Misson	58
M. C. Cowdrey	b. Hoare	16
N. Durden-Smith	not out	30
M. Boyce	not out	13
J. Price	did not bat	
P. Lever		
F. Rumsey		
D. Allen		
	Extras	27
	Total (for 7 wkts.)	228

Bowling

	O	M	R	W
Gilmour	7	1	35	0
Colley	3	1	8	1
Gleeson	2	1	2	1
Misson	8	1	31	1
Turner	1	0	5	0
Hole	4	2	9	1
Simpson	6.2	1	26	1
Connelly	3	0	26	0
Vievers	7	0	28	1
Hoare	3	1	12	1
Stackpole	3	0	19	0

ENGLAND LORD'S TAVERNERS WON BY 3 WICKETS

The author, Neil Durden-Smith and the Duchess at the presentation of another New Horizons Minibus for the handicapped at the Gateway-sponsored Lord's Taverners match, 1982.

"But you can never discount the batting strength of an IZ. side and, apart from Alan Wadey, they treated our admittedly rather light bowling resources rather irreverently."

Among the bowlers to suffer on this occasion was Colin Cowdrey whose Arundel credentials were now so firmly established that he was shown in the score book as 'Sussex and England'. He was back in action again in the following week when he led the Duchess' team at the start of a new series against the Combined Services. The match came about because of the friendship between Billy Griffith and Ronnie Ford with Joe Hardstaff. 'Young Joe' as he is inevitably known as the grandson of Joe Hardstaff Senior and the son of Joe Hardstaff Junior had become the third Hardstaff in line to play first-class cricket when he captained the R.A.F.

He managed a Combined Services side of talented cricketers who scored consistently to win the match by five wickets, despite a not-out century for the Duchess by one of the M.C.C. young cricketers, M. O'Neill who would soon follow his father Norman O'Neill in playing for Western Australia.

The only real disappointment for a sizeable crowd in this match was, as the local scorer cruelly noted, the first ball dismissal of Christopher Martin-Jenkins. However, he was back for Billy Griffith's end of term party when the Taverners match on 31 August 1980 was a special event between Australian and English sides. The match marked a further stage in the development of Australia's own Taverners and their side, captained by Bobby Simpson, was, with one exception, made up entirely of Test cricketers.

The England Lord's Taverners included, in addition to Christopher Martin-Jenkins, three other entertainers in Willie Rushton, Neil Durden-Smith and Max Boyce as well as their usual list of former Test and County cricketers. Ten of the side got a bowl as the Australians scored consistently and made a fairly judged declaration.

In turn, Bobby Simpson gave a bowl to all eleven of his players, including the wicket-keeper. This worked so well that half the English side were out for 107. At this point, Christopher Martin-Jenkins and Colin Cowdrey came together and gave the innings some stability. 'C.M.J.' showing all the old facility with the off-drive which had made him good enough to play for Surrey 2nd XI went on to make the highest score in the match. When he was out, his fellow commentator, Neil Durden-Smith and the rugger playing entertainer, Max Boyce, produced the necessary runs for a three wicket victory.

This was a happy ending to Billy Griffith's year as President of the M.C.C. His role as host at the Centenary Test Match at Lords earlier in the year had been spoilt when bad weather had restricted play and there had been arguments involving the umpires and demonstrations by the crowd. As he said:

"I really had a rather difficult year. My health was far from good and, quite apart from the ructions at the Lord's Test, there were a lot of international cricket arguments at the time over which I had to preside. It made Arundel for me what it has always been - a marvellous haven of cricketing peace. This is where I was so lucky to have Ronnie Ford coming in to hold the fort, but I was not unaware of some of the challenges which faced the Club at the start of the Eighties."

The challenges to which Billy Griffith refers had been spelt out by Ronnie Ford in a memorandum on the future of the Club, in June 1980. This covered the familiar list of problems, including proper reimbursement for the secretary and groundsmen, the continued search for finance and sponsorship and the increasing difficulty in raising sides.

Soon after his return as Chairman, Billy Griffith made it clear that he did not feel able to continue as a one-man recruitment team. Colin Cowdrey stepped into the breach and undertook to make time available despite his M.C.C. and business commitments.

His involvement was usually that of Captain of the Duchess's team to which he added a considerable influence in team selection.

Both these attributes were in evidence when he came together with Lady Mary and Lady Sarah Fitzalan-Howard in July 1981 to plan what would be one of the last matches in the family series. As Lady Mary has recalled: "I think we were all conscious that the match was coming towards the end of its allotted span. There was severe competition for more serious cricket and many of our old faithfuls were now getting that much older. However, in 1981 and 1982, we did have a lot of our fiends on parade like Anthony Wates, Robert Fellowes, Mark Faber, Simon Burne, Simon Parker-Bowles, John Brennan, Robin McCall and, of course, our original co-captains, Ian Balding and Roger Gibbs. So far as my mother's team was concerned, this was organised by Colin Cowdrey who had some rather good young cricketers in his side which he balanced by asking some of my father's old friends to be involved."

In 1981, one of these friends was John Poland; soon after he became President of Surrey County Cricket Club in 1994 he told the author:

"At that time, I had problems with my legs following a car injury and I had not played for years. Two things persuaded me to turn out. First, I realised that this was probably the only occasion on which I could play in a proper cricket match with my son Matthew. I also said I would play if the Duchess would run for me. To my amazement, she agreed and I was trapped. In the event - and perhaps just as well - I was put down to play for the girls' team and I did not need to bat when all the regulars got runs and we declared with a record score for the series."

Among the invitations issued by Colin Cowdrey for the older generation were those to the Reverend Michael Weaver, Vicar of St Nicholas' Parish Church in Arundel, and Michael Marshall M.P. They did their share of chasing around in the field but reasonably assumed that they would not be required to bat when Matthew Poland, then in his last year at school, settled down to play a superb innings. He had big partnerships, first with Alan Wadey and then with Colin Cowdrey. However, when the score reached 231 for 4 and only forty odd were needed to win, the captain decided that the time had come to inject some excitement into the proceedings. He also decided to test the alertness of Roger Gibbs who - after what everyone agreed was an exceptionally convivial lunch - appeared to be nodding under the shade of one of the trees in the outfield.

Roger Gibbs duly caught the Cowdrey flier with all his old flair and our captain departed, shaking his fist in mock fury. Ian Balding, to whom the wicket had been credited, now began to spin the ball with renewed confidence with the result that he took a second wicket in the over and the

LAVINIA, DUCHESS OF NORFOLK'S XI V LADY MARY FITZALAN HOWARD'S XI
5TH JULY 1981

LADY MARY FITZALAN HOWARD'S XI

P. Wates	b. Cowdrey	48
R. Fellowes	c. Scott b. Rawlinson	23
M. Faber	c. Cowdrey b. Wadey	33
I. Balding	b. Bacon	8
S. Burne	c. and b. Rawlinson	66
P. Parker-Bowles	b. Bacon	11
J. Brennan	not out	37
R. Gibbs	b. Elkins	1
D. Perrett	run out	24
R. McCall	not out	1
J. Poland	did not bat	
	Extras	19
	Total (for 8 wkts. dec.)	271

Bowling

	O	M	R	W
Rawlinson	9	1	50	2
Scott	11	0	37	0
Wadey	9	1	45	1
Cowdrey	4	0	21	1
Elkins	11	0	63	1
Bacon	9	0	36	2

LAVINIA, DUCHESS OF NORFOLK'S XI

M. Poland	not out	101
N. Bacon	b. McCall	13
A. Rawlinson	b. Balding	18
A. N. C. Wadey	st. Wates b. Brennan	41
M. Weaver	b. Brennan	3
M. C. Cowdrey	c. Gibbs b. Balding	47
R. Scott	st. Wates b. Balding	0
M. Marshall	not out	5
H. Boscawan	did not bat	
D. Elkins		
J. Denver		
	Extras	13
	Total (for 6 wkts.)	241

Bowling

	O	M	R	W
Perrett	8	3	22	0
McCall	11	1	71	1
Balding	13	0	53	3
Parker-Bowles	12	3	35	0
Brennan	10	0	44	2
Gibbs	1	0	3	0

MATCH DRAWN

author was on his way to the wicket.

At this point, three overs remained, 40 runs were required for victory and Matthew Poland was on 99. Despite what might be described as highly encouraging noises from the players' enclosure lead by his captain, he was forced to play out a maiden over from Simon Parker-Bowles. This left the number 8 batsman to face Ian Balding. The trainer ostentatiously rearranged his field, the efficacy of which was soon evident when the batsman's first three shots all went to defensive fieldsmen. However the fourth ball of the over was swept to the fine leg boundary for four and a leg-bye was run off the fifth ball. Matthew Poland, still on 99, was unable to pierce the field off the last ball of the over. At this stage, Ian Balding, realising that the target of 35 off the last over was out of reach (or, as the bowler would later assert, to make absolutely sure that victory was denied us), brought on Roger Gibbs to bowl the last over of the match.

A consultation took place between the two batsmen. The thought of running out the young Poland in front of his father, one of the club's principal benefactors, weighed heavily but it was agreed that a quick single was essential. A push by the parliamentarian to extra cover achieved this and, with a genuine straight drive to long off, Matthew Poland had achieved his maiden century on the ground.

This game seemed, for the author, an appropriate moment to retire, and he watched the final match of the series in the following year from his accustomed place in the commentary box. This proved to be an exercise of the utmost skill on the part of Colin Cowdrey and Roger Gibbs who, in the absence of Ian Balding, finally became captain of the girls' team.

Among the changes in the side was the replacement of Anthony Wates by one of the Norfolk sons-in-law, Roddy Balfour, an Old Etonian whose elegance was such that he was able to field in a panama hat. There were other family links in the two sides. The Robinsons were there in force, led by the evergreen Peter and supported by his two sons, Mark and Jonathan.

For Peter Robinson, the match has especially happy memories:

"First of all, I got to bowl at my son Mark, and it caused me no pain to see him indulging in some big hitting against both myself and Alan Wadey since he was not regarded as the serious cricketer in the family - he just played for the fun of it. Equally, it was marvellous when I found myself batting against his bowling, and not only that, but in partnership with my other son Jonathan who is the serious cricketer of our family. He was only 15 at the time and still at Lancing where he went on to break every school record for batting. During my partnership with him at Arundel, I think I realised for the first time that he had the potential to go on to higher things which he did when he played for Surrey.

"The other happy memory of that match was that Colin

Cowdrey and I had a half century partnership which took us to within a handful of the runs needed for victory. Then perhaps we got a little carried away and I was run out. But the thing I shall never forget was the way in which Colin then took charge of the batting with Alan Wadey. We needed 13 runs to win and it became obvious that he was determined only 12 should be scored. Alan Wadey backed him up but it was Colin who stroked the ball to precisely the right degree including a final push off his legs which he knew would not reach the boundary but which gave him the two runs we needed to draw the match with the scores level. Although it was friendly cricket, it was a masterly performance and a wonderful way to end this series."

Another of those who would increasingly assist Colin Cowdrey, Billy Griffith and Ronnie Ford in producing the Duchess's sides was the Deputy Chairman's son Adrian Ford. After his involvement in the Watney Old England XI's fixtures in 1978 and 1979, his first big match appearance at Arundel had been in 1981 when a new series began against the Minor Counties. He was in impressive company:

"This was the first time I found myself going out to open the batting with a current Australian Test batsman, Martin Kent, knowing that he was to be followed by his Test colleagues Dirk Wellham and Wayne Phillips. Further down the order was the 18 year old Martin Crowe then playing for Auckland and about to play for New Zealand. Naturally, with a side like that, the Minor Counties were keen to do well. The three Australians were playing because they wanted to get some extra practice and it was illustrative of the close co-operation which Billy Griffith had with the Test and County Cricket Board that they chose to come and play at Arundel on a Sunday.

"The Minor Counties put together a pretty useful total before declaring although they said they would have got even more but for the arrival of a young adder on the square. When we batted, Martin Kent went quickly but I had the great experience of a partnership with Dirk Wellham. We put on 79 in just over an hour, of which, it has to be said, he got 52 and I got 23. Then, Wayne Phllips and our captain, Ted Clark of Middlesex, came together. Wayne Phillips played beautifully for a half century and together with our captain, ensured that our scores finished exactly level on runs and wickets when time was called."

More family links were evident when, later in the season, Colin Cowdrey and John Poland asked the Chairman's son Mike Griffith to organise a match against his employer,

OXFORD & CAMBRIDGE PAST XI v COMBINED AUSTRALIAN UNIVERSITIES XI
13TH JUNE 1982

COMBINED AUSTRALIAN UNIVERSITIES XI

A. Courtice	b. Savage	6
L. Robinson	c. Khan b. Northcote-Green	44
D. Gratten-Smith	lbw. Savage	27
C. Tomko	st. Fisher b. Northcote-Green	0
R. Traves	lbw. Khan	2
C. Ross	c. and b. Knight	16
J. Robson	c. Claughton b. Hayes	13
D. Robertson	c. Marie b. Hayes	10
S. Campbell	run out	0
M. O'Sullivan	not out	10
M. Radcliffe	c. Fisher b. Knight	0
	Extras	14
	Total	144

Bowling

	O	M	R	W
Knight	8.2	4	13	2
Hayes	10	1	39	2
Savage	10	3	28	2
Khan	10	2	21	1
Northcote-Green	6	2	29	2

OXFORD & CAMBRIDGE PAST XI

R. Cotgrove	b. O'Sullivan	24
M. J. Khan	c. Traves b. Radcliffe	11
J. A. Claughton	lbw. Radcliffe	2
D. R. Owen-Thomas	b. Ross	21
M. C. Cowdrey	b. Courtice	39
S. R. Northcote-Green	b. Courtice	4
P. J. Hayes	run out	1
G. V. Marie	b. Radcliffe	0
J. M. Knight	c. Robson b. Radcliffe	5
P. B. Fisher	run out	5
R. le Q. Savage	not out	2
	Extras	18
	Total	132

Bowling

	O	M	R	W
Radcliffe	9	1	15	4
Ross	10	1	31	1
O'Sullivan	9	0	20	1
Robinson	7	2	22	0
Courtice	9.3	1	26	2

COMBINED AUSTRALIAN UNIVERSITIES XI WON BY 12 RUNS

Lloyds of London. These games would continue until 1992, by which time it was said that no Lloyds underwriter felt safe in visiting the beleaguered Names in West Sussex. However, Mike Griffith's memories are of a happy start to the series:

"These matches went pretty well and Lloyds made quite a thing of it. A lot of their senior people came down for the day and Alan Dixon who captained our team made sure that it included just about the best available side. Apart from

Mark Faber who was in a class of his own in games like this, he opened the batting with Roger Alwen who is a useful performer perhaps better known as Chairman of Charlton Athletic Football Club. Peter Carroll who made top score for us was already a well known and successful performer at Arundel and the rest of the side were all quite useful.

"Off the field, Bertie Brazier did a lot in putting the side together and, above all, in getting the money which went into the sponsorship. He would shamelessly play one underwriting agent off against another so that people would get a call saying, 'Willis Faber have offered so much, what about you?' The Duchess' side was a strong one with five county caps but more or less everyone got runs for us and we managed to get the better of a draw in a tight finish."

The prize for the most substantial family involvement on behalf of the Duchess at this time must undoubtedly go to Peter Robinson for his efforts against the Eton Ramblers on 6 June 1982:

"I got together as captain and manager of this match with Geoff Wills who agreed to keep wicket and brought along his son, Jonathan, to open the batting. Then I added to this side my sons, Jonathan and Mark, and my cousin, Peter Short, who was over on a visit from Barbados. I even had the cheek to put our family in the batting line up at 4, 5, 6 and 7 but as we and the Wills family constituted the majority of the team, there was not much scope for argument. After two of the Ramblers' regulars had batted for what we thought was rather a long time to put on 150 plus, we were never quite in the hunt. However, we did give it a go. R. I. B. Fisher scored a quick fifty for us and, afterwards, I was proud of the way in which my son Jonathan provided the backbone of the innings. Then Geoff Wills chimed in with some big hitting, but the chase proved beyond us."

The rest of the season had a major Cowdrey involvement. In what was to be his last full season at Arundel, he captained several games and widened the basis of the Club's following.

A typical example of his activities was in collecting together a side of former Oxford and Cambridge Blues to face a Combined Australian Universities touring side in a limited overs match at Arundel on 13 June 1982. All the Oxbridge bowlers had some success and the Australian side made only 144 from their 45 overs.

In reply, the Oxbridge side were given a brisk start by their two overseas players, R. Cotgrove of the University of Tasmania, who had been lent to them by the visiting side and

LORD'S TAVERNERS XII v GATEWAY INVITATION XII
29TH AUGUST 1982

GATEWAY INVITATION XII

K. Bakker	b. Rumsey	18
J. Deri-Bowen	b. Dixon	35
J. Murray	b. White	45
N. Durden-Smith	b. Norman	60
J. Squire	b. White	5
T. Adams	b. White	1
I. Lavender	not out	33
M. C. Cowdrey	st. Long b. Norman	7
D. Waterman	b. Norman	14
K. Prendiville	not out	16
J. Price	did not bat	
C. Worthington		
	Extras	12
	Total (for 8 wkts. dec.)	246

Bowling

	O	M	R	W
Rumsey	8	2	21	1
White	8	0	42	3
Dixon	8	2	16	1
Taylor	6	0	27	0
Clarke	3	0	17	0
Norman	10	0	63	3
Griffith	4	0	22	0
Gifford	3	0	17	0
Dennis	2	0	9	0

LORD'S TAVERNERS XII

M. Griffith	b. Murray	61
R. Kershaw	c. Lavender b. Squire	7
T. Clarke	c. Deri-Bowen b. Waterman	11
A. Long	c. Waterman b. Prendiville	37
A. Dixon	c. Waterman b. Squire	50
J. Taylor	c. Squire b. Murray	8
J. Gifford	c. Murray b. Durden-Smith	17
B. Norman	b. Murray	8
D. White	not out	35
J. Dennis	not out	1
F. Rumsey	did not bat	
B. Ufton		
	Extras	13
	Total (for 8 wkts.)	248

Bowling

	O	M	R	W
Price	4	0	11	0
Squire	6	1	18	2
Waterman	6	0	40	1
Adams	9	0	31	0
Cowdrey	1	0	11	0
Murray	8.3	0	66	3
Prendiville	4	0	24	1
Worthington	3	0	11	0
Durden-Smith	4	0	23	1

LORD'S TAVERNERS XII WON BY 3 WICKETS

the Cambridge Blue Majid Khan who was nearing the end of his career as a Pakistan Test cricketer. However, Majid the magician who had so endeared himself to British crowds when playing for Glamorgan, waved his wand once too often and was caught behind. When Cotgrove and another Australian Claughton followed soon afterwards, it was left to Colin Cowdrey and Dudley Owen-Thomas to mount an effective challenge. They took the score past the century mark with only three wickets down with Cowdrey, in particular, in his old commanding form. However, when they were both dismissed there was an Oxbridge panic with two of their tailenders run out to leave the Australians victorious by twelve runs.

A week later, a further Cowdrey contribution came in an effective bowling partnership with D. Gretton-Smith (another of the Australian University visitors who also top scored for the Duchess). They shared eight wickets between them to end the I Zingari challenge despite an undefeated century by Peter Rudd. The game was given special recognition by the involvement of the Minister of Sport, Neil Macfarlane, who has recalled: "I didn't get many runs but the thing that I will always remember is the joy of playing under the Cowdrey captaincy. He made you feel so welcome and his enthusiasm for sporting cricket was so evident that it was infectious".

Apart from helping with team recruitment, selection and creating the right atmosphere for attractive and enjoyable cricket, Colin Cowdrey was also conscious of the need to give value for money when it came to sponsored matches. In the game against the Combined Services on 27 June 1982, he assembled for the sponsors, London and South of England Building Society, one of his strongest Test, County and First Class Overseas cricketing sides. After an Australian/South African century opening partnership between Veletta and Venter and a Cowdrey declaration, the Combined Services side struggled to escape defeat against effective slow left-arm bowling by the Yorkshire exile Stephen Booth who was about to make his debut for Somerset.

There were more stars on view in the game against the M.C.C. Young Cricketers in the following month. This was a fixture in which Colin Cowdrey had taken a special personal interest ever since he had raised his own side for the game against the Young M.C.C. Cricketers in 1979. On this occasion, the match was sponsored by the local property tycoon Captain Bernard Thorpe. There was much interest in the Duchess' opening partnership of the established Hampshire player Chris Smith and Matthew Poland who was currently having a trial with the County after his maiden century at Arundel in the previous year. However, they were dismissed

cheaply, but a feast of runs followed with a century for Robinson of Western Australia who was well supported by the Kent players Laurie Potter and Derek Aslett.

The Cowdrey declaration was to prove generous, when the M.C.C. stars of the future showed consistent batting form at the top of their order in gaining a four wicket victory.

The last match of the season in 1982 had its own special interest in bringing together the largest ever gathering of cricketing Taverners more or less equally divided between their own side and that representing the sponsors, Gateway Building Society. The Taverners called up many of their regulars while the local and family interests were in the hands of Colin Cowdrey who captained the Gateway side and Mike Griffith who was in charge of the Lord's Taverners. Serious cricket was provided at the start of each innings with the appearance of Fred Rumsey and Butch White bowling for the Taverners and John Price for the home team. This trio would be joined in these matches from the following season onwards by John Snow in a combination which became the Taverners' ex-England resident bowling squad for almost the next decade.

Cultured batting was seen from the professional cricketers: J. T. Murray for the Gateway side; Mike Griffith, Arnold Long and Alan Dixon for the Taverners. But the main feature of the day was undoubtedly the substantial presence of so many Taverners associated with either the entertainment or other sporting worlds.

For the ground match commentator, this presented its problems. Thus, introducing the Gateway's top scorer, Neil Durden-Smith, it was necessary to choose between the unfortunate sounding 'former B.B.C. cricket commentator' or some variation of John Arlott's even unkinder introduction of 'Royal Navy, Combined Services, Lord's Taverners and anyone else who will have him'. Other announcements covering Tom Adams (Enigma Files), Ian Lavender (Dad's Army), Dennis Waterman (Minder) and Kieran Prendiville (Tomorrow's World) also presented their special problems given the dearth of information about their cricketing ability. In the event, some like "the stupid boy", Ian Lavender, demonstrated genuine ability which was recognised when he was named Man of the Match.

Introductions for sportsmen in other fields like Jeff Squire and John Taylor of the British Lions and the racehorse trainer, Josh Gifford, were less demanding. But references to Richard Kershaw (B.B.C.), Barry Norman

LAVINIA, DUCHESS OF NORFOLK'S XI v WEST INDIES
8TH MAY 1980
45 OVER MATCH

WEST INDIES

C. G. Greenidge	c. Mohammad b. Titmus	67
D. Haynes	b. D'Oliveira	19
F. Bacchus	b. Titmus	60
I. V. A. Richards	st. Murray b. Wilson	24
C. King	not out	60
D. Parry	not out	2
C. H. Lloyd	did not bat	
D. A. Murray		
A. M. Roberts		
M. A. Holding		
C. Croft		
	Extras	11
	Total (for 4 wkts.)	243

Bowling

	O	M	R	W
Marshall	7	1	17	0
Higgs	12	1	52	0
D'Oliveira	6	1	44	1
Titmus	8	0	37	2
Wilson	10	1	56	1
Balderstone	2	0	26	0

DUCHESS OF NORFOLK'S XI

M. J. Smith	lbw. b. Holding	7
T. Mohammad	c. Murray b. Roberts	0
J. C. Balderstone	c. Greenidge b. Croft	12
D. I. Gower	st. Murray b. Parry	13
B. F. Davison	b. Parry	0
M. Marshall	c. Haynes b. Croft	10
B. D'Oliveira	not out	55
J. T. Murray	b. King	4
D. Wilson	b. Richards	15
K. Higgs	b. Richards	2
F. Titmus	not out	1
	Extras	3
	Total (for 9 wkts.)	122

Bowling

	O	M	R	W
Roberts	5	1	8	1
Holding	5	1	9	1
Parry	15	1	61	2
Croft	5	1	7	2
King	7	4	10	1
Richards	5	0	11	2
Haynes	3	0	13	0

WEST INDIES WON BY 121 RUNS

(Omnibus), and Johnny Dennis (Players' Theatre) all required some understanding of the performers' world.

In 1983 the Cowdrey appearances were less frequent but he took part in the matches which opened and closed the Club's season. In May, he and another relative veteran in the Duchess' team, Richard Hutton, showed sprightly form in a half century partnership in 28 minutes in the limited overs match against the Minor Counties.

At the end of the season, Colin Cowdrey and his opposite number - John Edrich - displayed skilful stage management to ensure they had a drawn match with the scores level. The game was the now traditional end of season Lord's Taverners fixture with the opposition, on this occasion, provided by the sponsors Kent and Curwen.

Among the team, there was much interest in the cricketing ability of Steve Davis - then at the height of his powers as the World Snooker Champion. The enjoyment of the crowd was facilitated when his manager made it clear that he was especially worried about any possible injuries which his star might sustain. Undaunted, Steve Davis showed that he was not without ability in his undefeated innings.

In chasing 248 to win, the Lord Taverners were given a solid start by Mike Griffith and Richard Kershaw. Thereafter, Leonard Rossiter and Peter Bowles showed an ability to score runs as well as starring in *Rising Damp* and *To The Manor Born* respectively. Nevertheless, wickets fell steadily to the unlikely attack of Barry Norman and Johnny Dennis and it required a tenth-wicket stand of 70 between the Taverners' Cricket Chairman and former Kent player Derek Ufton and the businessman John Fawcett to bring the match to its skilfully pre-conceived draw when the scores were level.

The real significance of the inclusion of so many television and entertainment personalities in these matches was that it brought in crowds which were second in size only to those of the Tourists' matches and this, combined with the Cowdrey commitment, established the series as an ideal family day as well as a money-spinner for both a good cause and for the Club.

The major source of the Club's finances in the early eighties, however, was still international cricket. The Daily Express, reporting on preparations for the West Indies match in May 1980, said that, with fixtures like this and Norfolk family support, the game had been saved from extinction.

"Now cricket is assured for years to come", Ronnie Ford was quoted as saying. What is more, he added, this would allow cricket to continue very much in the tradition of Duke Bernard, "who wouldn't have liked any razzmatazz."

An interview by the same reporter with the owner of the ground, Duke Miles, indicated that he had no intention of interfering in this process:

"I keep very much in the background. It's Lavinia's thing. Last year, I did sneak into the Tourists game, but she was at one end of the ground and I stayed at the other."

As to the 1980 match, Michael Melford wrote in the Daily Telegraph:

"Everything combined to help the West Indies' batting practice - a mild, true pitch, an immaculate outfield, a minimum of fielders near the boundary and bowlers who, with the *savoir faire* of long experience, adapted themselves to the occasion admirably so that the West Indies made 243 for 4 in their 45 overs.

"For the Duchess, many must have hoped to see something of Timur Mohammad, the young Guyanan, who last year averaged 83 for Suffolk and made 179 in the Minor Counties Challenge Match. Sadly, he was out cutting in Roberts' first over.

"Gower played two spectacular strokes, pulling Holding to mid wicket for 4 and driving the offspinner, Parry, through the covers. He then walked forward to play the same bowler and missed. Thereafter, the West Indies were passing through the opposition batting with a speed which discounted the theory that life begins at 40 when they ran up against Basil D'Oliveira, who is 48. He took his side's score to 122 for 9 with valuable help from Don Wilson who is a mere 42 and honour was satisfied with a draw."

In 1981, it was the visitors who were up against it. As Robin Marlar wrote:

"The Australians ran into trouble on God's own acres and were bowled out for 106 in this corner of Sussex that is forever England, slowed down this time by a third of an inch of overnight rain. When Lavinia, Duchess of Norfolk's XI batted, they too made heavy weather of the worsening day and won by only 3 wickets."

Later in his report, Robin Marlar showed his foresight in picking out Allan Border as potentially the most reliable player in the party describing him as "the Maurice Leyland of the troupe and every inch a cricketer." When it came to the Australian captain, Kim Hughes, reference was made to the tremendous challenge he faced in pulling together the previously competing factions of Packer and non-Packer players. However, Robin Marlar continued:

"Hughes was hardly accorded the old Arundel traditional one off the mark. He played back to and missed a ball from Intikhab which was so straight, and kept so low *en route* to middle stump that even the umpire John Langridge's humanity had to lose out to his integrity. A first ball dismissal at Arundel for an Australian captain must be a melancholy record."

LAVINIA, DUCHESS OF NORFOLK'S XI v AUSTRALIANS
16TH MAY 1981

AUSTRALIANS

G. M. Wood	b. Taylor	17
M. F. Kent	c. Tolchard b. Intikhab Alam	9
A. R. Border	c. Imran Khan b. Steele	27
K. J. Hughes	lbw. Intikhab Alam	0
D. Wellham	b. Woolmer	7
T. M. Chappell	c. Steele b. Taylor	11
R. W. Marsh	c. Parker b. Barclay	11
R. J. Bright	b. Wells	4
G. F. Lawson	not out	13
R. M. Hogg	b. Steele	0
T. M. Alderman	b. Steele	0
	Extras	7
	Total	106

Bowling

	O	M	R	W
Imran Khan	4	0	7	0
Taylor	7	2	25	2
Woolmer	6	3	14	1
Intikhab Alam	6	2	11	2
Barclay	9	3	18	1
Steele	9	4	13	3
Wells	2	0	11	1

LAVINIA, DUCHESS OF NORFOLK'S XI

R. A. Woolmer	c. Marsh b. Hogg	11
J. R. T. Barclay	c. Marsh b. Hogg	1
P. W. G. Parker	b. Lawson	6
B. F. Davison	c. Wellham b. Hogg	6
J. F. Steele	c. Border b. Bright	28
C. M. Wells	lbw. Bright	21
Imran Khan	c. Hughes b. Border	8
M. H. Denness	not out	18
R. W. Tolchard	not out	0
Intikhab Alam	did not bat	
L. B. Taylor		
	Extras	8
	Total (for 7 wkts.)	107

Bowling

	O	M	R	W
Hogg	9	3	16	3
Alderman	9	0	36	0
Lawson	9	2	12	1
Bright	9	3	24	2
Chappell	1.1	0	7	0
Border	1	0	4	1

LAVINIA, DUCHESS OF NORFOLK'S XI WON BY 3 WICKETS

Where the Australian captain was accorded the old Arundel greeting was when he came in to bat and this groundmatch commentator extolled his merits at some length, including both his popularity when playing in Scotland, and his outstanding century in batting for Australia in the Centenary Test at Lords in the previous year. All this, and the first ball dismissal, led to an Australian news report which reached Arundel a few days later reading:

LAVINIA, DUCHESS OF NORFOLK'S XI V IRELAND
14TH AUGUST 1981

LAVINIA, DUCHESS OF OF NORFOLK'S XI

B. Richardson	b. Hughes	3
R. A. Smith	not out	115
C. J. C. Rowe	b. Harpur	20
M. H. Denness	c. and b. Halliday	1
D. R. Owen-Thomas	not out	39
M. C. Cowdrey	did not bat	
J. T. Murray		
P. J. Sainsbury		
J. Spencer		
N. J. W. Stewart		
P. Ray		
	Extras	6
	Total (for 3 wkts. dec.)	184

Bowling

	O	M	R	W
Corlett	12	2	46	0
Hughes	15	5	43	1
Halliday	12	5	34	1
Harpur	4	0	18	1
Prior	6	1	13	0
Anderson	5	0	24	0

IRELAND

J. F. Short	c. Ray b. Stewart	24
E. A. McDermott	c. Spencer b. Rowe	60
B. T. Wills	b. Sainsbury	7
I. J. Anderson	c. Murray b. Sainsbury	3
C. C. J. Harte	c. Owen-Thomas b. Sainsbury	3
J. A. Prior	run out	12
T. Harpur	not out	23
P. B. Jackson	lbw. Rowe	3
S. C. Corlett	not out	34
M. Halliday	did not bat	
A. J. Hughes		
	Extras	16
	Total (for 7 wkts.)	185

Bowling

	O	M	R	W
Spencer	5	1	26	0
Stewart	11	2	24	1
Ray	8.2	2	26	0
Sainsbury	15	3	47	3
Rowe	13	3	46	2

IRELAND WON BY 3 WICKETS

"The commentator at Arundel - reputed to be a Member of Parliament - indulged in the most patronising introduction ever accorded an Australian captain. This had it's effect when Hughes was dismissed first ball."

On reading this, Billy Griffith said: "Oh, that it could be so easy to get an Australian wicket!"

Later that season, international cricket at Arundel was given a new perspective with the start of what has become a regular series against Ireland. Mike Denness and Colin Cowdrey put together a team of Arundel regulars and recently retired county cricketers including Peter Sainsbury who was now Hampshire coach and John Spencer who had moved from Sussex to become cricket master at Lancing College. However the star of the side was the 17 year old Robin Smith who had already appeared for Natal and who was about to make his Hampshire debut.

On his first appearance at Arundel he made a dazzling century with fifteen fours and a six which he celebrated by adding two more sixes. The sporting feature about this innings was that it was played despite interruptions from the rain with the Irish team continuing to field in the downpour to ensure that he got his century before the impending declaration.

When Ireland batted, their sheet anchor was the Dublin club cricketer, Anthony McDermott. When he got out, the former Oxford Blue Simon Corlett who, by birth, could claim a Nyasaland qualification, provided the big hitting so that the game ended with an Irish victory in the last over.

The success of the match was such that it was decided to involve both Ireland and Scotland on an alternate basis at Arundel. For the game against Scotland in 1982, there was sponsorship by Barclays Bank International and Green Denman. The match was played twelve a side. For the Duchess, Ted Clark of Middlesex gathered together a strong combination of current and ex-County cricketers. They found themselves facing a stiff target after solidity had been given to the innings by William Donald and Robert Weir, and the big hitting had come from the Scottish rugby international, Andrew Ker.

The Scottish score had been kept in reasonable check by a long spell of tidy off-spin bowling by Nigel Cowley of Hampshire. He showed his versatility in opening the batting and was in such commanding form that, for a time, he seemed likely to win the match almost single-handed. However, the slow left-arm spin of William Morton who would go on to play for Warwickshire combined with the off-spin of George Goddard put the brakes on and gave Scotland the moral victory in a drawn match.

The main international match in 1982 was that against India which marked the start of the season. There was a repeat disappointment for a visiting captain when Sunil Gavaskar, who had not played at Arundel in three previous tours, was out lbw first ball. For the captain of the home team, Tony Lewis, it all went so well that he was able to

LAVINIA, DUCHESS OF NORFOLK'S XII V SCOTLAND
7TH JULY 1982

SCOTLAND

W. Donald	c. Pocock b. Cowley	51
A. Steele	lbw. Hobbs	30
R. G. Swan	b. Cowley	0
R. S. Weir	lbw. Cowley	48
A. B. M. Ker	c. Green b. Bailey	49
R. R. Jones	c. Bailey b. Cowley	18
D. L. Snodgrass	lbw. Bailey	1
W. A. Morton	not out	12
G. F. Goddard	not out	7
J. Clark	did not bat	
P. Rhind		
D. J. Simpson		
	Extras	19
	Total (for 7 wkts.)	235

Bowling

	O	M	R	W
Spencer	12	2	23	0
Jesty	4	2	3	0
Hutton	2	1	4	0
Hobbs	22	4	88	1
Cowley	15	3	30	4
Bailey	12	2	68	2

LAVINIA DUCHESS OF NORFOLK'S XII

N. E. J. Pocock	c. Steele b. Snodgrass	9
N. G. Cowley	run out	61
T. E. Jesty	c. and b. Goddard	17
R. A. Hutton	c. Snodgrass b. Morton	7
D. R. Owen-Thomas	b. Morton	31
N. Venter	c. Snodgrass b. Goddard	17
D. Bailey	c. and b. Morton	5
E. A. Clark	st. Steele b. Goddard	8
D. G. Ufton	not out	8
K. W. Green	not out	
R. N. S. Hobbs	did not bat	
J. Spencer		
	Extras	9
	Total (for 8 wkts.)	172

Bowling

	O	M	R	W
Rhind	4	0	22	0
Snodgrass	5	3	11	1
Donald	3	0	14	0
Morton	18	3	54	3
Goddard	16	3	62	3

MATCH DRAWN

LAVINIA, DUCHESS OF NORFOLK'S XI V INDIA
5TH MAY 1982

INDIA

P. Roy	c. Sadiq Mohammad b. Hutton	17
Ghulam Parkar	lbw. Hobbs	35
A. Malhotra	run out	54
S. R. Patil	c. and b. Hobbs	19
Y. Sharma	not out	66
S. M. Gavaskar	lbw. Thomas	0
S. Nayak	not out	1
R. Shastri	did not bat	
S. Madan Lal		
S. Yadav		
Randhir Singh		
	Extras	9
	Total (for 5 wkts. dec.)	201

Bowling

	O	M	R	W
Thomas	8	1	30	1
Spencer	7	2	18	0
Snow	9	0	28	0
Hutton	9	1	31	1
Hobbs	6	0	47	2
Jameson	6	0	32	0

LAVINIA, DUCHESS OF NORFOLK'S XI

A. W. Stovold	not out	90
Sadiq Mohammad	not out	107
A. J. Hignell	did not bat	
J. A. Jameson		
A. R. Lewis		
J. M. M. Hooper		
R. A. Hutton		
J. A. Snow		
D. Thomas		
R. N. S. Hobbs		
J. Spencer		
	Extras	5
	Total (for 0 wkts.)	202

Bowling

	O	M	R	W
Randhir Sing	9	1	32	0
Madan Lal	8.5	0	27	0
Nayak	9	1	53	0
Shastri	9	1	34	0
Yadav	6	0	30	0
Patil	3	0	21	0

LAVINIA, DUCHESS OF NORFOLK'S XI WON BY 10 WICKETS

engage in some Charles Ryder/Evelyn Waugh nostalgia in a newspaper report headed "Arundel Revisited." In it, he recalled his first invitation to Arundel to play against the Tourists in 1968:

"The notepaper carried the embossed red letters 'Arundel Castle' and said, 'Dear Lewis, the Australian cricketers are playing their first match against my side here on Saturday 4 May and I am writing to ask if you will be good enough to be a member of my side. If you are able to accept, will you let me know whether you need any accommodation and for how many? I would be grateful for an early reply. Yours truly, Norfolk.' My reply was instant and I guess that others were putting pen to paper at the same time. 'Yes, of course I will play Sir'. Nobody refused. It was an honour to be chosen and a delight on the day.

"But times have changed. Cricket at Arundel Castle

AUSTRALIA v NEW ZEALAND
4TH AND 5TH JUNE 1983

AUSTRALIA

G. M. Wood	c. J. Crowe b. Sneddon	7
K. C. Wessels	b. M. Crowe	32
K. J. Hughes	lbw. Cairns	6
D. W. Hookes	b. M. Crowe	13
G. N. Yallop	retired	103
A. R. Border	c. Gray b. Coney	69
R. W. Marsh	c. M. Crowe b. Chatfield	28
T. M. Chappell	b. Bracewell	22
T. Macleay	not out	37
T. Hogan	b. Bracewell	13
G. F. Lawson	not out	12
	Extras	15
	Total (for 9 wkts. dec.)	357

Bowling

	O	M	R	W
Sneddon	14	5	37	1
Chatfield	16	7	30	1
Cairns	19	5	59	1
Bracewell	25	7	76	2
M. Crowe	16	2	62	2
Gray	11	1	36	0
Coney	8	0	35	1
J. Crowe	1	0	7	0

NEW ZEALAND

G. M. Turner	lbw. Lawson	47
B. A. Edgar	not out	50
J. J. Crowe	not out	39
G. P. Howarth		
J. V. Coney		
M. D. Crowe		
J. G. Bracewell		
E. Gray		
W. K. Lees		
I. D. Smith		
E. L. Cairns		
	Extras	4
	Total (for 1 wkt.)	140

Bowling

	O	M	R	W
Lawson	7	2	26	1
Lillee	8	0	52	0
Hogg	6	0	32	0
Macleay	4	1	14	0
Hogan	2	0	7	0
Thompson	2	0	5	0

MATCH ABANDONED

looks the same - but it is not the same. This year, for example, Zaheer Abbas first accepted the invitation and then withdrew. Runs scored for Gloucestershire at Oxford University would be counted as first-class, so this is where he plied his trade. Understandable in the eighties, unthinkable in the sixties."

Tony Lewis went on to make a shrewd assessment of the future of cricket at Arundel, recognising the problems in combining both country house and professional cricket as well as balancing the books. However, he went on to enthuse over the presence of "the present Duke of Norfolk's heir, the Earl of Arundel. His own sport is motor racing but it would be a fine thing for cricket there if his youthful, good-looking and athletic support would be permanent.

"The Duchess herself did well to last out a day which got increasingly cold and said that she felt sorry for the freezing Indians. I did not feel sorry for them. I thought of the English teams in their opening matches on tours with India, white skin peeling, tummies upside down, starving kites swooping inches above their heads and having to trample an outfield as rough as broken egg shells under foot."

As to the match itself, the home side's ten-wicket victory came as a result of a fine partnership by Andy Stovold and Sadiq Mohammad who scored 90 and 107 respectively. The Gloucestershire openers not only made up for the absence of Zaheer Abbas, but no doubt brought particular pleasure to their captain who had led the England team in India a decade earlier.

The Tourist match in 1983 was intended to bring first-class cricket to Arundel when Australia and New Zealand agreed to a three day match. However, heavy rain early in the week meant that the sides had little or no preparation and the match was changed to a two day fixture which would allow the maximum substitution of players.

On the Saturday, Australia made a large one day total thanks to a stand of 147 between Allan Border and Graham Yallop who went on to reach his century. However, when New Zealand came to bat on the Sunday morning, they showed every intention of going after the powerful Australian fast bowling quartet of Lillee, Lawson, Hogg and Thomson. Glenn Turner who had recently transformed himself from a stodgy opening batsman for New Zealand to a free-scoring player for Worcestershire, set the pace with 47 runs in 40 minutes including four successive fours off Lillee.

At this point, the Australian fast bowler left the field with figures showing 0 for 52 off 8 overs. He was replaced on the field by Jeff Thomson but shortly afterwards, with both Bruce Edgar and Jeff Crowe going well, the match came to an abrupt halt. The reason was that a storm which included hailstones the size of golf balls swept over the ground, instantly transforming the Arundel turf into a winter snow scene. In 1994, Geoff Howarth, coach to that year's touring

LAVINIA, DUCHESS OF NORFOLK'S XI V WEST INDIES
1ST JUNE 1984

WEST INDIES

C. G. Greenidge	lbw. Williams	1
D. L. Haynes	c. Russell b. Agnew	1
R. B. Richardson	c. Patel b. Williams	24
H. A. Gomes	b. Ellison	11
A. L. Logie	lbw. Ellison	8
C. H. Lloyd	c. Patel b. Williams	53
T. R. O. Payne	c. Barnett b. Illingworth	5
R. A. Harper	c. Williams b. Illingworth	1
E. A. Baptiste	lbw. Agnew	18
C. A. Walsh	c. Russell b. Ellison	5
M. Small	not out	0
	Extras	13
	Total	140

Bowling

	O	M	R	W
Agnew	9	1	32	2
Williams	8	1	28	3
Ellison	7.1	3	15	3
Illingworth	9	1	34	2
Patel	7	3	13	0
Nicholas	2	0	5	0

LAVINIA, DUCHESS OF NORFOLK'S XI

K. J. Barnett	b. Small	0
C. L. Smith	b. Walsh	1
C. W. J. Athey	lbw. Small	0
D. N. Patel	b. Small	0
M. C. J. Nicholas	b. Walsh	7
M. H. Denness	b. Walsh	4
R. M. Ellison	b. Baptiste	19
R. C. Russell	c. Lloyd b. Baptiste	3
R. K. Illingworth	lbw. Baptiste	0
N. F. Williams	not out	20
J. P. Agnew	b. Gomes	13
	Extras	9
	Total	76

Bowling

	O	M	R	W
Walsh	6	2	13	3
Small	6	2	9	3
Gomes	5.2	1	18	1
Baptiste	5	1	27	3

WEST INDIES WON BY 64 RUNS

side and captain of the team eleven years earlier, said:

"For many of our players it was the first time they had seen hail and it was as well that we managed to get the sides off the field quickly. Some spectators were injured but the Duchess was some kind of big wheel in the Red Cross and their people rapidly appeared despite the weather. Moreover, she entertained two very large squads of overseas cricketers so well that we were reluctant to get away. Mind you, the threat of a further assault from golf balls from above was also quite an inducement to relax over a few beers."

Doug Ibbotson reporting on the match regretted that the weather had ruled out the unique opportunity of seeing first-class cricket at Arundel adding:

"The fixture represents a considerable feat of organisation by Veronica Lloyd, the Arundel cricket secretary, and her two groundsmen whose enthusiasm for the task provided, until the interruption, relaxed and entertaining practice for the two visiting teams.

"Apart from enjoying the grandeur of the Castle, there is always, one suspects, whatever fact or fantasy is to be gleaned from John Dunlop's adjacent racing stable and there was time on Sunday for Arundel's sylvan slopes to echo to the sound of Christ's Hospital band as seventy long-coated musicians counter marched on the outfield."

Perhaps, inevitably, the final word on the game came from the popular press with a heading, "Hail to the New Zealanders."

Two more Test-playing touring sides were involved at Arundel in 1984. June saw the return of the West Indies and in August there was a first visit from Sri Lanka.

For a while, it looked as though the Caribbean cricketers might be in for a real setback as the attack of young England hopefuls, Jonathan Agnew, Neil Williams and Richard Ellison restricted them to 50 for 5. Richard Illingworth chipped in with two more wickets but, meanwhile, the West Indian captain Clive Lloyd remained imperturbable and went on to reach a half century.

Nevertheless, a total of 141 to win looked a possibility for the home team's captain, Mike Denness, and what the press described as his "near Test standard young players." However, the West Indies showed that even in the absence of

Hail stones stop play at the 1983 New Zealand match.

LAVINIA, DUCHESS OF NORFOLK'S XI v SRI LANKA
16TH AUGUST 1984
50 OVER MATCH

LAVINIA, DUCHESS OF OF NORFOLK'S XI

C. Gladwin	c. Dias b. Madugalle	57
C. L. Smith	lbw. S de Silva	33
M. C. J. Nicholas	b. S de Silva	36
P. W. G. Parker	c. and b. S de Silva	10
N. Lenham	b. S de Silva	12
C. M. Wells	run out	0
S. Turner	not out	32
J. R. T. Barclay	not out	15
R. Maru	did not bat	
R. J. Parks		
I. Waring		
	Extras	17
	Total (for 6 wkts. dec.)	212

Bowling

	O	M	R	W
John	9	1	31	0
Ratnayake	10	1	36	0
De Mel	10	0	46	0
Dias	8	0	38	0
S. de Silva	10	1	34	4
Madugalle	3	1	13	1

SRI LANKA

S. Wettimuny	lbw. Wells	6
B. Kuruppu	lbw. Turner	58
R. Madugalle	b. Wells	0
R. Dias	c. Lenham b. Maru	27
D. Mendis	c. Smith b. Barclay	32
A. Ranatunga	lbw. Wells	22
A. de Silva	c. and b. Waring	13
A. de Mel	not out	30
P. Ratnayake	run out	0
S. de Silva	b. Waring	17
V. John	not out	2
	Extras	9
	Total (for 9 wkts.)	216

Bowling

	O	M	R	W
Waring	10	1	44	1
Wells	10	3	21	3
Turner	10	0	37	1
Maru	10	1	32	1
Barclay	9.5	0	73	1

SRI LANKA WON BY 1 WICKET

most of their front line bowlers, they were a force to be reckoned with as Courtney Walsh and Milton Small shared six wickets between them of which five were clean bowled and one l.b.w. Only rearguard actions by Richard Ellison and Neil Williams in the lower order gave the score some semblance of respectability as the West Indies went on to their usual victory.

Interviewed afterwards, Clive Lloyd, who was described as moving steadily on to 40, was asked whether his all-conquering side suffered from complacency, to which he responded (long befor he knew Brian Lara):

"Some of them are young. They can be a bit impetuous and take too much for granted. It is my job to remind them that it isn't so easy and that if you keep winning you can get complacent. I have to impress on everyone the need to concentrate. Yes, I get jaded too. Its important not to lose your enthusiasm by playing too much. So far as I am concerned, at 40 this year, the elastic legs aren't what they were. But I am much more experienced, more mature and my reactions are still pretty good. I would love to make 366 in a Test Match but I don't think my legs will hold up."

For the match against Sri Lanka in August, the Sussex captain Johnny Barclay put together a side drawn, apart from his own county, from the Essex and Hampshire sides. Apart from Colin Wells who was unfortunate to be run out from a deflection off the bowler's foot, everyone played their part in reaching double figures. There was also particular pleasure for the crowd as another family connection was made at Arundel when Neil Lenham did enough to show his talent as an 18 year old who was in the process of following his father into the Sussex team.

In reply, the Sri Lankan captain, Duleep Mendis who had come close to scoring a century in each innings in his country's first Test at Lords only a few weeks earlier, led the way in quick scoring. He was well supported down the list and, with both sides entering into the traditional spirit of these games, it was played on into the gloom of the late summer evening before Johnny Barclay was hit for 4 by De Mel to give the visitors a victory by one wicket.

1980

May 25th. Sussex Martlets 221-4 dec. (N. Wisdom 83, C. J. S. Bidwell 79*). Lavinia Duchess of Norfolk's XI 223-5 (M. Milton 63, R. Scott 62, D. Broad 53*). Lavinia Duchess of Norfolk's XI won by 5 wickets.

June 22nd. Lavinia Duchess of Norfolk's XI 206-5 dec. (J. Townsend 62, R. V. Lewis 56). I Zingari 207-3 (D. Oldridge 65, Commander M. Gretton R. N. 69*). I Zingari won by 7 wickets.

June 29th. Lavinia Duchess of Norfolk's XI 201-6 dec. (M. O'Neill 109*). Combined Services 202-5 (C. Clark 83). Combined Services won by 5 wickets.

1981

June 14th. Minor Counties South 225-5 dec (S. Plum 71, J. Harvey 70). Lavinia Duchess of Norfolk's XI 225-5 (W. Phillips 66*, D. Wellham 52). Match drawn.

July 12th. Lloyds C. C. 216-5 dec (P. R. Carroll 62, C. R. Hayles 50). Lavinia Duchess of Norfolk's XI 214-9 (G. Monkhouse 78, G. Morgan 59). Match drawn.

1982

June 6th. Eton Ramblers 256-5 dec (P. G. Lowndes 113, F. W. Cornwallis 87*). Lavinia Duchess of Norfolk's XI 234-8 (J. D. Robinson 83, R. I. B. Fisher 67). Match drawn.

June 20th. Lavinia Duchess of Norfolk's XI 246-7 dec (D. Gratten-Smith 84, K. Smith 77). I Zingari 210 (P. Rudd 101) Lavinia Duchess of Norfolk's XI won by 36 runs.

June 27th. Lavinia Duchess of Norfolk's XI 181-7 dec (M. Ventnor 59, M. R. Valletta 55). Combined Services 142-7 (S. C. Booth 5-41). Match drawn.

July 4th. Lady Mary Fitzalan Howard's XI 226-9 (J. M. M. Hooper 68). Lavinia Duchess of Norfolk's XI 226-6 (P. Robinson52) 45 over match. Match drawn.

July 18th. Lavinia Duchess of Norfolk's XI 228-4 dec. (L. Robinson 118). M.C.C. Young Cricketers 232-6 (R. N. Berry 68*). M. C. C. Young Cricketers won by 4 wickets.

1983

May 15th. Lavinia Duchess of Norfolk's XI 165-9. Minor Counties XI 169-3 (S. Plumb 65, W. Osman 54). 40 over match. Minor Counties XI won by 7 wickets.

August 28th. Kent and Curwen XII 247-7 dec. (T. Clarke 68, J. Edrich 50). Lord's Taverners XII 247-9 (R. Kershaw 65). Match drawn.

CHAPTER TEN

From Cowdrey To Barclay 1985-1989

The Barclay captaincy of the Duchess's team against Sri Lanka in 1984 was part of a process which saw several new faces in charge of the home team in international matches. Colin Cowdrey had led the way for the Duchess from 1976 onwards but his last game as captain against a touring side was that against Ireland in 1981.

It was no doubt inevitable that Colin Cowdrey should ease off on his cricketing activities as he entered his early fifties. In 1982 and 1983 his appearances were in the country house games when he generally put himself in to bat in the lower order and greatly reduced his bowling. In 1984, he made only occasional appearances and his last games for the Duchess would come in 1985 and 1986. His decision to reduce his playing commitments was also a recognition of his health problems which would lead to a heart by-pass operation. Happily he made a rapid recovery and the Cowdrey involvement in cricket administration at Arundel, at Lord's and abroad was soon as intense as ever.

1985 was a year of exceptional Cowdrey activity. He assumed the role of Master of the Skinners Company in the City of London, and increased his wide range of responsibilities in both the M.C.C. and the International Cricket Council (of which, in the following year, he was nominated respectively as President and Chairman). At the end of the 1985 cricket season, his links with Arundel were given a new and special emphasis when he married Duke Bernard's eldest daughter, Anne Fitzalan-Howard, Baroness Herries, and together they established their home near the Castle.

In 1986, Colin Cowdrey made his last appearance for the Duchess when he captained her side in the end of the season match against the Lord's Taverners. The crowd gave a special round of applause when it became apparent that his role as a Norfolk son-in-law was now nicely matched by his opposing captain, David Frost, who had married Duke Miles' daughter Carina in 1983.

We have noted that the success of these matches had been, in large measure, due to a Cowdrey commitment to the series and his enthusiasm was matched at this time by David Frost as the Taverners' President. Between them they brought together an exceptionally interesting group of sportsmen and entertainment personalities. The involvement of this group was not confined to the field where a positive plethora of talent volunteered to share the ground match commentating. Thus, the slower passages of the game were enlivened by the comedy of Frazer Hines and by Bill Frindall's take off of John Arlott. Other entertainers' perhaps louder contributions were less well received and Ronnie Ford became a regular and tactful filter for both complaints and praise.

The 1986 match was also notable for the firm establishment of sponsorship with I.B.M. - one which was happily sustained without too much contrivance when the company's Chief Executive, Tony Cleaver, made the highest score in the match. He was thus accorded the traditional Man of the Match award of a magnum of champagne. In addition, both sides received handsome engraved glass tankards. For Colin Cowdrey, the final match at Arundel ended on a graceful note as he stroked 31 runs including five fours and bowled the last over of the match in a helpful fashion to ensure the by now traditional Taverners victory.

Despite his many cricketing commitments at Lords and further afield, Colin Cowdrey showed great vision at this time in concerning himself with the Club's future welfare:

"By the mid-eighties, I took the view that we might come to a grinding halt in the early nineties. I felt that the novelty would wear off. We had to face the fact that we were probably the only cricket club in the world which did not have its own regular playing squad and, as tenants on a private estate, we could only make real use of our pavilion for half the year. So, both those who played for us by invitation and our supporters could get only limited use of the Club. We organised lunches in the winter for visiting speakers and these were a great success but the cost of heating and so forth made them only a break-even project. What we lacked was the year round use of the place with bar profits, the fruit machine and all the normal cash flow of most cricket clubs.

"Moreover, our overheads during the season were essentially fixed in maintaining and administering the ground, and our guest players were now seeking more money. I also wondered whether we could continue to count on the support we had enjoyed virtually free first from Billy Griffith and then from Ronnie Ford. There was also a question in my mind about the long-term availability of sponsorship.

"So far as that was concerned, we had approached over one hundred companies when we established our Trust Fund and we found that it was necessary to use almost moral blackmail to achieve any success. Several companies had said that if we could ensure that the club had full charitable status, they and others outside the commercial sector might find it possible to give more solid continuing support.

"At the same time, I had felt over many years a concern at the way in which cricket was disappearing from the State School sector. This seemed to me one of the reasons why we were suffering in terms of our national playing strength and I began to think of the possibility of seeing Arundel not only as a centre of cricket excellence but also as one which could provide coaching over a wide area."

In developing these thoughts, Colin Cowdrey turned first to Roger Gibbs:

Billy Griffith's retirement, 1st September 1985.

"When Colin told me of his ideas, I could see their obvious merits but it was clear that we would need a major input to get the whole thing moving. This is where Colin's role was unique. He went to Paul Getty and found, happily, as so often in the recent history of English cricket, that this marvellous American sponsor was ready to help."

Colin Cowdrey for his part emphasises the value of the Gibbs contribution:

"We could never have gone ahead as we did without Roger's experience. As Chairman of the Wellcome Foundation, he was already well known and experienced in his dealings with the Charity Commissioners. So we were able to make a joint approach to them which went through in record time.

"What was interesting was that we thought the Commissioners might want to see a reduction in the range of our overall cricketing activities at Arundel to favour youth cricket. Obviously, we committed ourselves to increased activities on this front but the Commissioners made it plain that they did not want us to cut back on other matches. Indeed, they took the opposite view. They said it would be marvellous for youngsters to be part of an active cricket scene and they thought that they would benefit from seeing cricket of the highest quality as in the Tourist matches. So we made rapid progress in our negotiations with them and we had to think seriously who could take charge of this coaching and cricket activity on a full-time basis."

Johnny Barclay has described how he first heard of the project some months earlier:

"I was just about to lead Sussex out on to the field at Canterbury when I got a message that Colin Cowdrey was on the telephone. I didn't know him at all well at that time but of course he was one of my heroes. We necessarily had a very brief conversation in which he said that there was a possibility of doing what he described as some kind of cricketing expansion at Arundel to include coaching and asked whether I might be interested to get involved.

"As it happened I had already made up my mind that this would be my last season in county cricket. After ten years on the circuit I was interested in establishing another career but I hoped it could in some way include cricket. So I said that in principle I would certainly be interested.

"I told my wife Marie Lou about this but we heard nothing for several weeks and I had forgotten all about it when I got another telephone call from Colin Cowdrey asking me to come over for tea. When I got to his house I found Roger

Gibbs with him and they began to outline the plans for building a cricket coaching centre behind the Pavilion at Arundel with the suggestion that I might become responsible for both the coaching and the cricket matches."

All these negotiations came to a head when, in October 1986, it was announced that, following the retirement of Sir Alec Durie, Roger Gibbs would become Chairman of the merged Arundel Castle Cricket Trust and Arundel Castle Cricket Foundation. At the same time it was also announced that Mr J Paul Getty had made a gift to the Club of £380,000 and that Johnny Barclay would be appointed Director of Cricket and Coaching with effect from 10 November. A management committee to co-ordinate these activities was established with John Knight as Chairman, charged with the task of directing the cricket school project, liaising with Roger Gibbs as Chairman of the Arundel Castle Cricket Foundation and with Ronnie Ford as Chairman of the Arundel Castle Cricket Club. They were given solid support by the Club committee which had been strengthened by the addition of Peter Robson, the former legal adviser to the Club's Trust.

Another cricketing alliance had been forged earlier in the year when the working partnership between Veronica Lloyd as the Club secretary and Colin Dick as its groundsman led to their marriage. When Veronica Dick retired in the following year after twelve years service, she was replaced by Debbie Osborne who was recruited from Channel Four. All these personalities were soon wholly involved in the twin demands of maintaining a full cricket programme and negotiating a major capital programme for the indoor cricket school.

This negotiation was to prove much longer and more difficult than at first envisaged. It involved detailed discussions between Roger Gibbs and John Knight on behalf of the Arundel Castle Cricket Club Foundation and the Trustees of Arundel Castle who were naturally much influenced by the owners of the cricket ground, Miles, Duke of Norfolk, and his heir, Edward, Earl of Arundel. It was no doubt inevitable that, for the owners, the idea of moving away from the existing lease which allowed cricket matches for half the year to be replaced by a lease which would envisage year-round use of the Pavilion and the new coaching facilities would present challenges. Moreover, the Arundel Castle Trustees had major environmental concerns of which John Knight was made quickly aware:

"When Johnny Barclay and I went to make our first presentation of the coaching school project, we put forward plans for a building which would allow three nets. It would be larger than the Pavilion and, as we saw it, blend into the trees and the slight incline behind. After we had made our presentation, I said to Roger, 'Well, if I say it myself, I think we played a blinder. They seemed most interested and enthusiastic.'

"Soon afterwards, we got their considered response which came as a nasty shock. The environmental representatives of the Trustees were unhappy with the effect on the skyline and there was a general concern over the scale of the operation. We thus began a long negotiation about the size and design of the project which was to take almost two years. Happily, at the end of the 1988 season, I was able to announce to the Club's Executive Committee that we had achieved a series of interlocking twenty year agreements between the Arundel Castle Cricket Club, the Estate, the Arundel Castle Cricket Foundation and the Trustees of Arundel Castle which would give us a revised arrangement both for cricket on the ground and for coaching in a two net school."

The interim period while these negotiations were in hand was not without real financial difficulties. It had been assumed that the income from the Trust Fund following the Getty bequest would substantially underwrite some of the combined overhead costs of both the Club and the Foundation. Such funding had been restricted, however, while negotiations for in-house coaching were in hand. Although Johnny Barclay had thrown himself actively into the process of coaching at schools throughout West Sussex, this attracted little income and this would have to await negotiations when the cricket school construction was complete - a process which was still more than a year away.

Apart from these problems, the Club had its share of natural disasters when the great storm of October 1987 brought down many trees around the ground, one of which fell squarely on to the score box. This caused over £5,000 of damage and there was further destruction to the outbuildings including the storage shed donated by John Poland. Protracted negotiations with the insurance company still left a major gap in replacement and repair expenditures and the Treasurer Mike Bull reported that the Club's accounts were in deficit at the start of the 1988 season.

While these major changes were under negotiation, the Club relied heavily on Ronnie Ford and his support team for the maintenance of the cricket programme. This had now assumed major proportions necessitating the recruitment of

"We need a new scoreboard!" – The storms of 1987.

an additional groundsman, Kevin Snewin.

Ronnie Ford had assumed the chairmanship of the Club on 1 June 1985. This proved an exceptionally difficult year when the club had its wettest season ever. For the Duchess, three matches were won, three lost and three abandoned without bowling a ball and of the other seven games which were drawn all were badly affected by the weather.

Fortunately, at either end of the season, the two traditional opening and closing fixtures did much to safeguard the Club's finances. Although the day was often cold and wet, the Australian match in May was a run feast for Wessels, Ritchie and Border and it required a solid undefeated defensive knock from the former Surrey captain Roger Knight of Sussex and Surrey to save the home team.

He would later recall:

"I had just given up first-class cricket to take up school mastering at Cranleigh and I was delighted to find that I could still do my bit. In fact, I had to do rather a lot of work. Apart from over two hours at the crease, I did most of the bowling and I was rather glad to find that Arundel seemed to suit me. My pace was never quick but you could get the ball to swing a bit and so I was reasonably effective. I picked up three wickets and I remember them quite well. I bowled Kepler Wessels through the gate and I got Ritchie by bowling a couple of away-swingers before bringing one back which he missed and I did much the same to Wayne Phillips. After that, I didn't do quite as well as Allan Border was having a slog before the declaration. At one point, I bowled him quite a decent delivery just outside the off stump which he pulled over the mid-wicket boundary. In rather a nice gesture, he came down the wicket and said, 'Sorry mate, it's Sunday'".

There had been special difficulties producing a suitable team for the Duchess as all the first class counties were cur-

LAVINIA, DUCHESS OF NORFOLK'S XI v AUSTRALIA
5TH MAY 1985

AUSTRALIA

G. M. Wood	run out	28
K. C. Wessels	b. Knight	44
D. M. Wellham	b. Sivaramakrishnan	29
G. M. Ritchie	lbw. Knight	72
W. B. Phillips	lbw. Knight	5
A. R. Border	c. Willis b. Ratnayeke	65
G. R. J. Matthews	not out	4
G. F. Lawson	did not bat	
M. J. Bennett		
R. B. Phillips		
J. R. Thomson		
	Extras	14
	Total (for 6 wkts. dec.)	261

Bowling

	O	M	R	W
Willis	14	2	28	0
Ratnayeke	6.5	0	39	1
Sivaramakrishnan	11	1	86	1
Knight	14	3	47	3
Selvey	9	0	51	0

LAVINIA, DUCHESS OF NORFOLK'S XI

D. C. Boon	c. Bennett b. Lawson	33
N. J. Lenham	b. Thomson	5
B. Hassan	c. Phillips b. Thomson	4
J. H. Hampshire	c. Wellham b. Bennett	8
R. D. V. Knight	not out	63
D. K. Standing	b. Bennett	16
R. Ratnayeke	not out	1
S. N. V. Waterton	did not bat	
L. Sivaramakrishnan		
M. W. W. Selvey		
R. G. D. Willis		
	Extras	15
	Total (for 5 wkts.)	145

Bowling

	O	M	R	W
Lawson	14	4	20	1
Thomson	9	1	36	2
Matthews	16	5	31	0
Bennett	14	4	47	2
Wessels	2	1	5	0

MATCH DRAWN

rently engaged in championship matches. As a result, her side was made up of mostly recently retired or overseas players. On the other hand, the Australians had been written off by some critics after a lean spell but as Allan Border said on arrival at Arundel, "You keep on underestimating us which suits us fine."

The Times in its report carried the headline, 'Thomson returns to lord it over Duchess' men', Marcus Williams adding in his column, "Thomson with the new ball embarked successfully on his campaign to prove that, even at the age of 34, he can unnerve English batsmen."

For Simon Barnes:

"This is an eccentric fixture, the mixture of village green, festival cricket and serious practice. Murray Bennett (of Australia) bowled 14 overs of mean-spirited slow left-arm as he acclimatised. He looked like a benign but rather sedentary G.P. 'I got used to English conditions last year', he said. 'I played in the Lancashire League for Ramsbottom. No one at home could believe that was the real name of the place.'

"Jeff Thomson doesn't look like a G.P. and doesn't look sedentary either. Reports that he is in his dotage are somewhat exaggerated. He bowled five overs quickly and sent down the occasional cheery throat-ball to keep everyone amused. His partner Lawson was not hanging about either: this is a side that can bowl a bit.

"It is also one that can bat a bit. We all know about Border, the captain, and he has not lost touch. He is one of those stocky, aggressive, moustached Australians (as opposed to the other type - the rangy, aggressive, moustached Australian). Ritchie also looks more than handy and yet we learn that he was lucky to make the tour. It would not do to underestimate this bunch."

The end of the season match saw a century made in just over an hour by Austin Parsons for the Duchess and equally quick scoring for the Taverners by John Snow and Bill Frindall. Among those making his first appearance for the Taverners at Arundel was the future President of the Charity, Tim Rice, who recalled during the equivalent match in 1994:

"I had actually played for the Kent and Curwen side in the previous year but 1985 was my first opportunity to play under David Frost's captaincy. I recall again with particular pleasure that my undemanding left-arm spin was rewarded when I got Austin Parsons out (although he had got a lot of runs and probably helped me). I also had the pleasure of taking part in a hilarious partnership with Willie Rushton which took us to the traditional last-over victory.

"My overall impression was that this was the fun match for the Taverners. Indeed, I became a regular in the game at Arundel and it did a lot in encouraging me to take on the Taverners' Presidency".

The Club began the 1986 season with the unusual expectation of a substantial profit in the year ahead. This was somewhat gratuitous since the largest contribution came from a tax refund but it also reflected the enormous success of the Australian match in the previous season. More controversially, it also included a special payment of £5,000 for

allowing the Silk Cut Single Wicket Challenge matches to take place at Arundel after the end of the normal season.

This departure from the usual cricket played at Arundel had been opposed by Ronnie Aird when it was first put to the club committee. Although there was considerable sympathy with his argument that individual cricket of this kind was against the spirit of Duke Bernard's team games, the fact that the club faced special financial pressures while the negotiations for the future of coaching and cricket at the ground were underway was the decisive factor.

In the event, a crowd of 3000 saw a battle over two days between the Hares and the Tortoises which ended, as the local press put it, when, 'Play Safe Rice is King of the Castle.' In batting and bowling against each other, over two days, seven of the world's leading all-rounders sought to score as many runs as possible and to take their maximum quota of wickets while reducing to the minimum their own dismissals and the runs conceded while bowling. Although Ian Botham far outstripped the other competitors in run-getting (hitting the winner of the competition for four huge sixes over long-on), it was Clive Rice's consistency which prevailed in a winner's table which read as follows:

Name	Runs Scored	Times Out	Wickets Taken	Runs Conceded
Clive Rice (£7,000)	128	0	6	135
Imran Khan (£5,000)	118	0	5	121
Richard Hadlee (£4,000)	107	1	4	134
Vivian Richards (£3,000)	169	7	6	152
Ian Botham (£2,500)	224	6	3	211
Simon O'Donnell (£2,000)	164	7	2	144
Graham Gooch (£1,500)	168	12	6	181

The start of the 1986 season saw another rain affected Tourist match against India when the Duchess's team passed their reduced target of 178 from 41 overs with 2 overs to spare thanks mainly to their top scorer, Trevor Jesty, who had recently moved to Surrey after his long service with Hampshire. They also found inspiration from their captain, Roger Knight, who was becoming a regular in the Tourist matches and whose economical bowling helped to keep the Indians in check:

"Although I was now out of first-class cricket, I found the atmosphere in these games was extremely pleasant and, as in the previous year against Australia, I found that conditions suited me quite well. I got Patil l.b.w. because I was swinging the ball but my dismissal of Roger Binny was

LAVINIA, DUCHESS OF NORFOLK'S XI v INDIA
4TH MAY 1986
50 OVER MATCH

INDIA

K. Srikkanth	b. Monkhouse	37
R. Lamba	b. Monkhouse	14
M. Azharuddin	lbw. Igglesden	1
M. B. Amarnath	b. Monkhouse	6
S. M. Patil	lbw. Knight	31
R. N. Kapil Dev	b. Jesty	16
C. S. Pandit	st. Taylor b. Butcher	34
R. M. H. Binny	st. Taylor b. Knight	0
C. Sharma	not out	49
N. S. Yadav	b. Igglesden	11
Maninder Singh	not out	1
	Extras	17
	Total (for 9 wkts.)	217

Bowling

	O	M	R	W
Igglesden	10	0	39	2
Jesty	10	4	37	1
Monkhouse	10	2	57	3
Knight	10	3	26	2
Butcher	8	1	22	1
Sykes	2	0	22	0

LAVINIA, DUCHESS OF NORFOLK'S XI

A. R. Butcher	c. Azharuddin b. Singh	25
M. A. Lynch	b. Azharuddin	24
M. A. Roseberry	c. Srikkanth b. Singh	3
T. E. Jesty	b. Binny	74
D. G. Aslett	c. Pandit b. Dev	45
R. D. V. Knight	not out	4
G. Monkhouse	not out	0
J. F. Sykes		
R. W. Taylor		
D. Wilson		
A. Igglesden		
	Extras	6
	Total (for 5 wkts.)	181

Bowling

	O	M	R	W
Kapil Dev	10	1	44	1
Binny	10	1	46	1
Azharuddin	9	1	36	1
Singh	6	1	21	2
Sharma	4	0	28	0

LAVINIA, DUCHESS OF NORFOLK'S XI WON BY 5 WICKETS
MATCH WAS REDUCED TO 41 OVERS DUE TO RAIN

LAVINIA, DUCHESS OF NORFOLK'S XI v NEW ZEALAND
22ND JUNE 1986

NEW ZEALAND

T. J. Franklin	b. Kelleher	74
J. G. Wright	b. Kelleher	5
K. R. Rutherford	b. Kelleher	3
M. D. Crowe	c. Goldsmith b. Bracewell	70
J. J. Crowe	st. Blain b. Bracewell	35
J. V. Coney	c. Scott b. Clarke	44
E. J. Gray	not out	1
I. D. S. Smith	not out	10
D. A. Stirling	did not bat	
W. Watson		
E. J. Chatfield		
	Extras	13
	Total (for 6 wkts. dec.)	255

Bowling

	O	M	R	W
Clarke	14	2	45	1
Kelleher	16	3	44	3
Knight	7	0	27	0
Bracewell	17	3	64	2
Dale	12	0	64	0

LAVINIA, DUCHESS OF NORFOLK'S XI

S. Goldsmith	c. Smith b. Chatfield	28
B. Edgar	c. Rutherford b. Watson	7
A. Stewart	c. J. Crowe b. M. Crowe	24
A. Blain	c. J. Crowe b. Chatfield	0
T. Jesty	not out	68
R. Scott	b. Coney	10
J. Bracewell	b. Gray	15
R. Knight	not out	20
D. Kelleher	did not bat	
C. Dale		
S. Clarke		
	Extras	12
	Total (for 6 wkts.)	184

Bowling

	O	M	R	W
Stirling	9	1	36	0
Watson	8	0	51	1
Gray	7	1	37	1
M. D. Crowe	4	1	10	1
Chatfield	6	4	7	2
Coney	5	1	22	1
Rutherford	2	0	18	0

MATCH DRAWN

almost entirely due to Bob Taylor. I bowled an out-swinger which was almost doing too much because it went well down the leg side but Bob gathered it in and made one of the most brilliant stumpings I have ever seen."

Richard Streeton, writing in the Times, was another who was impressed by Taylor's wicket-keeping but whose report

coupled him with another veteran:

"Two senior citizens, in cricket terms, caught the eye. Gavaskar did not play, but brought much pleasure by patiently signing autographs for small boys as if he was starting his first tour rather than his umpteenth. Then too, there was the wicket keeping of Bob Taylor, now aged 44, whose figure was as trim, and whose work as polished, as at any time in his career."

The New Zealand Bank sponsored a second Tourist match at Arundel in 1986 against their national team which was organised on a friendly basis to give the visitors as much practice as possible at the start of their tour. As a result, three of their side, Bruce Edgar, Tony Blain and John Bracewell, played for the Duchess' team. However, they did little to influence the course of events after New Zealand had scored quickly, mainly through a century partnership between Trevor Franklin and Martin Crowe. Once again, it was left to Trevor Jesty to provide the main run-scoring for the Duchess' side. He was well supported by his captain Roger Knight in a successful rearguard action when the visitors were pressing for victory.

There were three other matches of special interest in 1986. The game against the M.C.C. was restricted to 55 overs a side. The visiting captain, Mike Brearley, led from the front with his solid and neat century and then showed his captaincy skills in leading a side of mainly County cricketers in an effective containment exercise. On paper, the Duchess' side led by Dudley Owen-Thomas should have had the edge with three caps from New Zealand, two from Pakistan and one from Australia. In the event, only Mushtaq Mohammad could produce a big innings and the M.C.C. bowling - mainly entrusted to the Test veterans Norman Gifford and David Steele-quickly ran through the tail.

The match on 17 August 1986 against the Sussex Martlets had a particular poignancy. Ronnie Aird, a key founder member of the Friends of Arundel Castle Cricket Club and the defender of Duke Bernard's standards, had died on the previous day. A minute's silence was observed by both teams before the start of play. Thereafter, they produced sparkling cricket of which the highlight was 98 by Philip Davy for the Martlets which was not quite enough to win the season's most exciting match.

Earlier in the season, there was a special tribute to an active Sussex cricketer when Wang sponsored the game against the Combined Services as a benefit match for Johnny Barclay.

As a result, the Duchess' team was made up largely of Sussex county cricketers of whom Dermot Reeve (in the days before he was released to Warwickshire's great advantage) and Paul Phillipson showed good form with the bat. Despite the presence of Imran Khan to open the bowling for the home side, the Combined Services put up strong resistance. Their principal star was Matthew Fleming who had Arundel

LAVINIA, DUCHESS OF NORFOLK'S XI v M.C.C.
27TH JULY 1986

M. C. C.

N. Maclaurin	c. and b. Reed	50
D. S. Steele	b. Stirling	2
J. M. Brearley	c. Blain b. Barrett	110
S. J. G. Doggart	st. Blain b. Ward	32
N. J. Kemp	b. Stirling	22
T. J. Yardley	not out	6
C. Trembath	not out	0
C. W. Chilton-Taylor	did not bat	
N. Gifford		
W. G. Merry		
J. Lumley		
	Extras	13
	Total (for 5 wkts. dec.)	235

Bowling

	O	M	R	W
Stirling	11	2	40	2
Barrett	10	1	57	1
Reed	11	1	49	1
Pringle	11	3	40	0
Mustaq Mohammed	9	0	29	0
D. M. Ward	3	0	13	1

LAVINIA, DUCHESS OF NORFOLK'S XI

Shoaib Mohammed	c. Chilton-Taylor b. Kemp	12
M. Waugh	b. Trembath	1
D. M. Ward	b. Trembath	8
Mushtaq Mohammed	b. Gifford	68
T. E. Blain	c. Yardley b. Merry	2
D. R. Owen-Thomas	c. Yardley b. Merry	4
N. Pringle	c. Chiltern-Taylor b. Gifford	7
R. Briance	c. Lumley b. Steele	16
D. A. Stirling	st. Chilton-Taylor b. Gifford	29
B. J. Barrett	c. Maclaurin b. Steele	6
S. Reed	not out	0
	Extras	11
	Total	164

Bowling

	O	M	R	W
Merry	9	2	16	2
Trembath	7	0	47	2
Kemp	7	0	25	1
Gifford	9.4	4	26	3
Steele	10	1	30	2
Lumley	5	1	17	0

M. C. C. WON BY 71 RUNS

connections as a nephew of Roger Gibbs and who would go on to further success for Kent after he left the Army.

For the beneficiary, Johnny Barclay, the match was not without embarrassment:

"I very much appreciated the thought on the part of the Arundel Castle Cricket Club and of the sponsors. It was my last season with Sussex and my benefit year, but it was still some time before I knew that my future would lie with the Club. In any event, I formed the view that matches of this kind were not really appropriate at Arundel. It is such a family atmosphere that I felt I was passing the plate round among my chums. I thought then that, if I had any say in the matter, we should avoid over-commercialisation at Arundel."

Johnny Barclay was given his say in the Club's affairs when, only a few weeks later, he was appointed as its first Director of Cricket. He also added immediate playing strength to the Duchess's team in the 1987 season. Both as a coach and resident cricketer, he was able to maintain his form and use his captaincy experience for the benefit of the home team. So far as the selection of individual sides was concerned, he saw no need for dramatic changes:

"The system had worked very well when Billy and Colin were actively involved and it had been maintained by Ronnie Ford with detailed back up through Veronica Dick and later Debbie Osborne.

"I was happy to carry on with the process by which we would select match managers in October or November each year and largely give them responsibility for putting together their sides. Naturally, they would have their regulars and so we tried to vary the composition of the match managers to bring in differing support. We would always check if they needed some help and we felt free to suggest a few names. For example, we would soon establish the principle of having our own resident cricket scholar, and we naturally wanted to give him as much cricket as possible. Then there would be one or two overseas cricketers who were keen to have a game at Arundel and, of course, match managers were always very grateful for suggestions about bowlers.

"It is never a problem getting eleven people but I sometimes worried about the question of balance. It is not really my problem if we delegated the main selection to a match manager and I probably worried unnecessarily on occasion as it usually seemed to work out pretty well."

One of the ways in which Johnny Barclay was able to give added strength to the home side was through his extensive range of contacts in first-class cricket. Increasingly, the opportunities of drawing on players from current county sides was limited by the overcrowded fixture list so that in the 1986 season, only Surrey had players available to come to Arundel for the two touring matches against India and New Zealand. On the other hand, Barclay had access to sev-

eral others who had retired early from county cricket:

"There are so many good players about who for one reason or another had left the county cricket scene early. Two in particular come to mind. John Rice who was with Hampshire has become the first person to score over 1000 runs at Arundel. He gave up first-class cricket when he was well established to become Director of coaching at Eton. In fact, we laugh in anticipation when we see he has agreed to play as he almost always gets 100 as he did in my first season as Director of cricket.

"Then there is Charles Rowe, who looks as if he is well on his way to getting 1000 runs here. He was the major school boy star when I was beginning. Like David Gower, he came from King's School, Canterbury. He was an extremely talented batsman and if not quite in the Gower class was certainly a better all-rounder. I came in touch with him playing for Public Schools against the English Schools Cricket Association and for the M.C.C. Schools against the Combined Services. I got to know him even better when we toured India together with the English Schools side. There is nothing like sharing a sleeping berth with someone all the way from Bombay to Calcutta to get to know them really well and I watched his career with interest.

"As I say, he was one of the most talented players of our generation but he found it a bit of a struggle when he went to Kent. They had a very strong side and it was hard to break in. He succeeded by establishing a place as an opening batsman and got his cap but he told me that he always felt threatened. 'Every time I go in to bat, I think it will be my last innings for the county', he used to say. I would encourage him to play as he had done in his schoolboy days with such enormous success and enjoyment but I think he was really quite glad when he got out of county cricket. He married Suzie Morgan, who had been the leading Junior Wimbledon tennis player of her time; they have a boy and a girl and tell them that if breeding counts for anything they should produce champions! Charles went into the City where he has been highly successful and it has been a joy to find him such a regular player at Arundel where, soon after my arrival, he got centuries against both the Martlets and the Eton Ramblers."

Both John Rice and Charles Rowe were involved in Johnny Barclay's first match at Arundel as Director of Cricket although on this occasion Charles turned out, as was his custom, for the Arabs. This was the game which has become known as "Roope's Match". After Bristowe, Knight and Barclay had given the Arabs' score some substance, Graham Roope, who was now playing for Berkshire after his Surrey and England career, came on as third change bowler for the Duchess. His first two overs were maidens; he conceded one run from the third and then took the wicket of Roger Knight. With the last ball of his next over he dismissed Johnny Barclay caught behind. Suitably encouraged, he took three wickets with the first three balls of his sixth over which made four wickets in four balls and gave him a final analysis of 5.3-2-8-5. He was not required to bat when John Rice showed his usual Arundel form in scoring 71 not out in a victory for the Duchess' team by 7 wickets.

Barclay's first match as the Duchess's resident captain was a week later against the Minor Counties. He found it a testing experience:

"They won the toss and decided to bat. We got an early wicket and then we were engulfed in a whirlwind. Reuben Herbert who came from South Africa and played for Middlesex, was joined by Paul Todd who was a former Nottinghamshire player. They are typical of some of those who leave first-class cricket and become exceptionally successful in playing for Minor Counties. On this occasion, I see they put on a little matter of 188 runs in 86 minutes of which Paul Todd got 153 before he got out, giving me the charge.

"However, when the ever reliable John Rice and John Claughton, who had played for Warwickshire as well as captaining Oxford, put on 167 for us at better than a run a minute, I thought we would get the 253 we needed. But once they were out, wickets fell with alarming regularity and we only just escaped by the skin of our teeth."

The game between Quidnuncs and Harlequins on 17 May 1987 marked the start of a new series at Arundel between Oxford and Cambridge graduates. The first match was notable for a century by David Holliday who played for Cambridgeshire as well as Cambridge University. The top score for the former Oxford University cricketers was made by Roger Moulding who made a single appearance for Middlesex but who had the unique distinction of appearing in the University match in six successive seasons.

In reviewing his first season as Director of Cricket, Johnny Barclay saw the Oxbridge input as of special value:

"It was fun to see the old Varsity matches re-created and the series soon became firmly established. What was particularly useful for us was that it introduced a whole range of people who were almost all former Blues and who could help

QUIDNUNCS V HARLEQUINS
17TH MAY 1987

QUIDNUNCS

A. J. Murley	c. Luddington b. Toogood	4
D. C. Holliday	not out	112
S. P. Henderson	b. Toogood	5
P. J. C. Mills	b. Curtis	30
R. D. V. Knight	c. Carr b. Curtis	11
S. J. G. Doggart	c. Toogood b. Curtis	2
K. I. Hodgson	st. Luddington b. Curtis	38
M. A. Cotterell	not out	2
A. G. Davies	did not bat	
P. J. Hayes		
J. Spencer		
	Extras	10
	Total (for 6 wkts. dec.)	214

Bowling

	O	M	R	W
Toogood	20	6	52	2
Hamblin	4	1	14	0
Varey	11	3	36	0
Curtis	19	1	82	4
Carr	9	3	21	0

HARLEQUINS

A. J. T. Miller	st. Davies b. Spencer	26
J. D. Carr	st. Davies b. Hayes	10
J. O. D. Orders	b. Knight	13
G. Toogood	b. Knight	4
T. Elliott	b. Cotterell	24
R. P. Moulding	b. Hodgson	74
J. G. Varey	c. Mills b. Knight	30
R. Luddington	not out	4
R. Topham	b. Hodgson	0
C. B. Hamblin	not out	2
I. Curtis	did not bat	
	Extras	6
	Total (for 8 wkts.)	193

Bowling

	O	M	R	W
Hayes	9	1	29	1
Hodgson	11	0	51	2
Knight	14	5	44	3
Spencer	9	2	36	1
Cotterell	5	0	30	1

MATCH DRAWN

us as potential match managers and in raising good sides.

"So far as the rest of the season was concerned, we had a particular set back in the early part of the year when the wet weather interfered with several of our games, most notably in preventing any play in our big money spinner which was the scheduled match at the start of the season against Pakistan.

"The match against the Royal Sussex Regiment in May was the end of an era. This fixture had marked the start of post-war cricket at Arundel and they had done remarkably well to keep the game going for so long. They produced most of their old faithfuls and it was good to see the Pyemont and Stephenson fathers and sons in the field together. They all did their stuff and it took a determined knock from one of our old Sussex regulars, Derek Semmence, to ensure that the match was drawn.

"In the game against the Eton Ramblers, I rather unusually turned out for them. Normally the only time I played for the Ramblers was in the Cricketers Cup. However, I remember the game with a certain pleasure and managed to get some runs and wickets which was perhaps just as well since they had been in short supply up to then and I thought they might be getting worried about their new Director of Cricket. The Ramblers match was a good one. Adrian Ford and Patrick Allen of Wisden Cricket Monthly magazine put on 50 for the first wicket for the Duchess and they were well supported by Mike Griffith and John Spencer. When it came to our turn to bat, John Spencer showed he was still a very useful bowler and he, together with Sandy Ross, made us work for the runs which mainly came from some big hitting by Jonathan Deedes.

"The game against the M.C.C. Young Cricketers was now a well established fixture and they always brought a side which was mustard keen. This year, we managed to get Alan Wadey's family building company to sponsor the match. So far as the cricket was concerned, Charlie Rowe and I did a lot of bowling and he, in partnership with our captain, Bob Woolmer, had to work hard to save us from defeat.

"However, we won a low scoring match against the full M.C.C. side led by Mike Brearley, thanks mainly to the bowling of our Australian imports, Wilkinson and McNamara, who got six wickets between them.

"The last Club match played that year was against the Martlets. Apart from the usual marathon bowling spell by Sandy Ross which included my wicket, the feature of their victory was a real display of youthful exuberance when Jonathan Wills and Martin Speight put on 150 for the Martlets with Martin's 100 coming up in 87 minutes.

"There were two big matches that year. The first was the game against the Rest of the World side which was part of their warm up for the match at Lords as part of the M.C.C. Bicentenary. Wadham Stringer's sponsorship and a good crowd helped us to restore what would otherwise have been a rather disastrous season. Moreover, it was a real joy to see the opening partnership of Gavaskar and Haynes with good

LAVINIA, DUCHESS OF NORFOLK'S XI v REST OF THE WORLD
9TH AUGUST 1987
55 OVER MATCH

REST OF THE WORLD

S. M. Gavaskar	c. Neale b. Pocock	26
D. L. Haynes	lbw. Merry	19
D. M. Jones	not out	143
A. R. Border	b. Pocock	29
Kapil Dev	b. Woolmer	11
P. J. L. Dujon	not out	22
J. G. Bracewell	did not bat	
Maninder Singh		
J. R. Ratnayeke		
B. A. Reid		
K. W. McLeod		
	Extras	12
	Total (for 4 wkts.)	262

Bowling

	O	M	R	W
Newport	8	1	37	0
P Van Der Bijl	10	1	39	0
Merry	10	1	55	1
Pocock	13	1	51	2
Hick	6	0	37	0
Woolmer	8	0	33	1

LAVINIA, DUCHESS OF NORFOLK'S XI

T. S. Curtis	c. Bracewell b. Reid	22
R. A. Woolmer	lbw. Kapil Dev	1
G. A. Hick	not out	85
D. B. D'Oliveria	c. Dujon b. McLeod	7
P. A. Neale	b. Kapil Dev	20
P. J. Newport	b. Kapil Dev	0
J. M. Brearley	not out	21
C. F. E. Goldie	did not bat	
P. I. Pocock		
V. A. P. Van Der Bijl		
W. G. Merry		
	Extras	13
	Total (for 5 wkts.)	169

Bowling

	O	M	R	W
Kapil Dev	9	2	38	3
Reid	8.5	0	38	1
McLeod	10	0	47	1
Maninder Singh	5	1	37	0

LAVINIA, DUCHESS OF NORFOLK'S XI WON BY 5 WICKETS
MATCH REDUCED TO 35 OVERS – RAIN

contributions from Border, Kapil Dev and Dujon. The feature of the day, however, was a ferocious innings by Dean Jones who got his hundred in better than even time".

The second match which drew a big crowd in 1987 was the end of season game against the Lord Taverners. Their President elect, Sir Tim Rice, takes up the story:

"I have good reason to remember that match. After the usual tidy opening spell from our three England Taverners' fast bowlers, Butch White, John Snow and John Price, the Duchess's team, which included our sponsor Tony Cleaver of I.B.M., scored runs quickly in their 40 overs.

"When it came to our turn to bat, we had arrived with a squad of no less than 17. Celebrities were thick on the ground. Apart from our England bowlers, we had Jim Yardley of Worcestershire and Notts keeping wicket for us and he, together with the actor Christopher Blake, got the early runs. The Rugger player John Taylor and Richard Kershaw chipped in but two of our regulars, Richard Stilgoe and Willie Rushton stayed all too briefly and at about 140 for 6 it looked as if we might be in a spot of bother.

"At this point, I came to the wicket with Bill Wiggins. We are both left handers and, happily, we managed to get the runs with 30 odd a piece. The real point of the story is that, when we came off the field, I was feeling pretty pleased as this was the best innings I had played at Arundel. But it was Bill Wiggins whom the crowd mobbed. Indeed, he is not known as Bungalow Bill for nothing. His was the signature which was in demand in the autograph tent and the reason was that he was, as they say, walking out with Joan Collins. All day long, there was speculation whether or not she would come to support him and, meanwhile, he was the star of the day and this game became known as Bungalow Bill's match".

In 1988, the major challenge for the Barclay selection process was for the first match of the season against the West Indies. The only county without a first-class fixture on 8 May was Sussex. The county captain Paul Parker was persuaded to bring four of his team mates to represent the Duchess and, out of respect for his predecessor as county captain, he asked Imran Khan to take charge of the side. The rest of the team was made up of recently retired first-class cricketers.

The West Indies deployed virtually their full strength side. Quick half-centuries from Haynes, Hooper, Logie, and fast scoring from Arthurton allowed Vivian Richards to make an unusually early declaration. This came after he had dismissed the second ball delivered to him by Andy Babington for a huge six over long-on.

By contrast, the batting for the Duchess's team was seen at its most cautious. Paul Parker's first seventeen scoring shots were singles and it took half an hour for the team to reach double figures. Parker settled down to keep one end intact while, at the other, wickets fell on a regular basis. This was hardly surprising given the West Indies attack of Ambrose, Bishop, Walsh and Marshall all of whom showed

LAVINIA, DUCHESS OF NORFOLK'S XI v WEST INDIES
8TH MAY 1988
40 OVER MATCH

WEST INDIES

D. L. Haynes	c. Lenham b. Pocock	50
P. V. Simmons	lbw. Rice	0
C. L. Hooper	c. Lenham b. Babington	52
A. L. Logie	run out	53
K. L. T. Arthurton	not out	35
I. V. A. Richards	c. Rice b. Babington	7
M. D. Marshall	did not bat	
D. Williams		
C. A. Walsh		
I. Bishop		
C. Ambrose		
	Extras	4
	Total (for 5 wkts.)	201

Bowling

	O	M	R	W
Imran Khan	5	3	2	0
Rice	8	1	34	1
Turner	4	0	23	0
Pocock	7	0	47	1
Underwood	8	1	49	0
Babington	8	1	42	2

LAVINIA, DUCHESS OF NORFOLK'S XI

P. W. G. Parker	b. Hooper	39
N. Lenham	b. Ambrose	4
D. L. Amiss	b. Marshall	5
C. T. Radley	lbw. Marshall	1
C. E. B. Rice	b. Marshall	0
Imran Khan	not out	56
I. J. Gould	not out	20
S. Turner	did not bat	
D. L. Underwood		
P. I. Pocock		
A. Babbington		
	Extras	10
	Total (for 5 wkts.)	135

Bowling

	O	M	R	W
Ambrose	7	0	17	1
Bishop	8	0	32	0
Walsh	5	0	9	0
Marshall	6	2	7	3
Hooper	8	2	19	1
Richards	4	0	17	0
Haynes	1	0	16	0
Arthurton	1	0	11	0

WEST INDIES WON BY 66 RUNS

every sign of taking the opportunity for serious practice. It was only with the introduction of Hooper and the non-regular bowlers that runs began to flow but, despite a half century partnership between Paul Parker and Imran Khan, there was never any chance of overtaking the West Indies total in

LAVINIA, DUCHESS OF NORFOLK'S XI V SUSSEX XI
17TH JULY 1988

A SUSSEX XI

R. Alikhan	c. Speight b. Gilbert	4
A. Green	b. Gilbert	12
N. Lenham	b. Cairns	6
A. Wells	c. Cairns b. Wilson	56
P. Parker	st. Speight b. Allbrook	52
Imran Khan	st. Speight b. Allbrook	11
C. Wells	c. and b. Wilson	21
P. Moores	b. Allbrook	5
S. Kimber	c. Pringle b. Wilson	0
T. Pigott	not out	0
A. Babington	c. Barclay b. Allbrook	0
	Extras	4
	Total	171

Bowling

	O	M	R	W
Gilbert	7	2	21	2
Cairns	7	1	20	1
Callaghan	6	1	21	0
Wilson	17	2	73	3
Allbrook	12	4	32	4

LAVINIA, DUCHESS OF NORFOLK'S XI

D. Callaghan	st. Moores b. Green	57
M. Speight	c. Moores b. Babington	39
R. Knight	not out	34
J. Orders	b. Green	9
M. Pringle	c. Wells b. Green	24
S. Gatting	not out	0
C. Cairns	did not bat	
J. Barclay		
D. Gilbert		
M. Allbrook		
D. Wilson		
	Extras	9
	Total (for 4 wkts.)	172

Bowling

	O	M	R	W
Imran Khan	8	1	28	0
Pigott	5	0	23	0
Wells	6	0	23	0
Green	16	3	52	3
Babington	6	1	10	1
Kimber	5	0	26	0
Parker	1.3	0	2	0

LAVINIA, DUCHESS OF NORFOLK'S XI WON BY 6 WICKETS

this limited overs match.

Apart from his responsibility in organising teams in 1988, Johnny Barclay was increasingly engaged in coaching and lecturing at schools throughout West Sussex and the neighbouring counties as preparation for the opening of the new cricket school in the following year. Thus, his appearances for the home team were limited. However, he was

LAVINIA, DUCHESS OF NORFOLK'S XI V SRI LANKA
29TH JULY 1988

LAVINIA, DUCHESS OF NORFOLK'S XI

G. S. Clinton	c. Rajadurai b. Samarasekera	107
J. F. Sykes	st. Kuruppu b. Rajadurai	41
P. W. G. Parker	b. Ramanayake	50
A. J. Stewart	not out	4
R. Knight	did not bat	
I. A. Greig		
R. J. Parks		
J. R. T. Barclay		
A. Clarke		
S. P. Hughes		
M. P. Bicknell		
	Extras	12
	Total (for 3 wkts. dec.)	214

Bowling

	O	M	R	W
Labrooy	8	0	25	0
Ramanayake	12	0	52	1
Rajadurai	16	3	58	1
Samarasekera	9.2	2	29	1
Anurasiri	10	1	47	0

SRI LANKA

R. Mahanama	not out	12
B. Kuruppu	not out	9
R. Madugalle		
A. Ranatunge		
D. Mendis		
A. Samarasekera		
G. Labrooy		
C. Ramanayake		
A de Silva		
D. Anurasiri		
B. Rajadurai		
	Extras	2
	Total (for 0 wkts.)	23

Bowling

	O	M	R	W
Bicknell	6	3	15	0
Hughes	5	2	6	0

MATCH ABANDONED

involved in two matches which were special Sussex occasions.

On 17 July, Paul Parker brought most of the regular County side to Arundel to play a match against the Duchess. The Sussex captain and Alan Wells (who would succeed him in that post) scored half centuries but a total of 171 proved inadequate when the young South African David Callaghan and the Sussex hopeful Martin Speight had a century opening partnership for the Duchess. The match was seen as a rehearsal for the planned Sussex presence in 1989 as part of the County Cricket Club's 150th Anniversary. Alan Wadey as

Spin bowling has always been well to the fore in Arundel matches. Here De Silva of Sri Lanka is carefully watched by Umpire John Langridge and Hampshire's Chris Smith.

a committee member of both the County and the Castle clubs acted as the link in talks involving both parties.

The match against Sri Lanka at the end of the month was a Surrey/Sussex occasion when the two counties provided seven of the team and, in the case of Roger Knight, the captain of the team, the eighth place could have been shown as Sussex or Surrey because of his dual qualification. Graham Clinton with a century and Paul Parker with a half century made the top scores for the Duchess but the match had to be abandoned due to rain soon after the Sri Lankan side began their innings.

For Johnny Barclay, the outcome of the match was disappointing:

"I always enjoyed taking part in these matches against Sri Lanka. They played the game in such a splendidly uninhibited way and their school coaching is in so many ways reminiscent of the old English tradition. They all play very straight and bring such a lot of enjoyment to the game as well as to the spectators. I was particularly sorry that we were unable to play out a game to which we had attracted an especially good side of contemporary English county cricketers."

1985

August 25th. Lavinia Duchess of Norfolk's XII 210-7 (A. Parsons 104). Lord's Taverners XII 211-7 (J. Snow 71, W. Frindall 53). Lord's Taverners won by 4 wickets.

1986

June 15th. Lavinia Duchess of Norfolk's XI 201-6 dec. (D. Reeve 82, P. Phillipson 51). Combined Services 190. Lavinia Duchess of Norfolk's XI won by 11 runs.

August 17th. Lavinia Duchess of Norfolk's XI 222-4 dec. (C. Worlidge 65, I. Hodgson 62*). Sussex Martlets 219-5 (P. Davy 98). Match drawn.

August 24th. Lavinia Duchess of Norfolk's XIV 175-7 dec (A. B. Cleaver 53). Lord's Taverners XVI 177-8. Lord's Taverners XVI won by 7 wickets.

1987

May 3rd. Arabs 150-9 dec. (R. D. V. Knight 59, G. R. J. Roope 5-8). Lavinia Duchess of Norfolk's XI 151-3 (J. M. Rice 71*, M. Newton 50). Lavinia Duchess of Norfolk's XI won by 7 wickets.

May 10th. Minor Counties 252-4 (P. A. Todd 153, R. Herbert 53). Lavinia Duchess of Norfolk's XI 243-9 (J. M. Rice 106, J. Claughton 56). Match drawn.

May 31st. Royal Sussex Regiment Invitation XI 186 (G. Longfield 5-77). Lavinia Duchess of Norfolk's XI 161-6 (D. Semmence 84). Match drawn.

June 7th. Lavinia Duchess of Norfolk's XI 198. Eton Ramblers 200-6 (J. W. Deedes 62). Eton Ramblers won by 4 wickets.

July 5th. M. C. C. Young Cricketers 231-7 dec. (J. Lumley 60, I. Kidd 53). Lavinia Duchess of Norfolk's XI 182-9 (C. J. C. Rowe 82, R. A. Woolmer 50). Match drawn.

July 26th. M. C. C. 125. Lavinia Duchess of Norfolk's XI 126-6. Lavinia Duchess of Norfolk's XI won by 4 wickets.

August 16th. Lavinia Duchess of Norfolk's XI 205-8 dec. (J. Kilbee 59) Sussex Martlets 200-6 (M. Speight 103, J. G. Wills 60*). Match drawn.

August 30th. Lavinia Duchess of Norfolk's XI 206-7 dec. (J. M. Wooley 63, M. Denness 56). Lord's Taverners XI 208-6 (C. Blake 50). Lord's Taverners XI won by 4 wickets.

David Gower at Arundel – the "perfect setting" for his talents.

CHAPTER ELEVEN

The Ford/Doggart Succession 1989-1993

With cricket activities in safe hands, Ronnie Ford was able to direct his energies towards improved organisation of the Club's affairs. At a meeting of the Executive Committee in 1988, he had pointed out that committee members were becoming older and moving further away from the district which created problems in providing cover on match days. He had also stressed that, as the club was becoming more commercial, there was a need for more guaranteed assistance.

As a result of the Chairman's initiative, a re-shaped Executive Committee was formed consisting of himself, the Vice Chairman, Colin Cowdrey, the Treasurer, Mike Bull, the Chairman of the Cricket Coaching Working Party, John Knight and the Director of Cricket, John Barclay. They were supported by three locals, Major General Ronnie Buckland, Michael Cresswell-Wall, and Tony Hill. Sadly, the ever cheerful Tony Hill who had been one of the club's most active helpers in covering tasks all round the ground on big match days died in 1990. In 1991, Michael Cresswell-Wall also died after a long illness and was commemorated by a specially engraved wooden bench which recognised his services as a founding member of the club and as the enthusiastic voice over the loudspeaker of the ground administration.

Following these losses, Ronnie Ford devoted much effort to expanding the committee with special concern for local support. By the time of the club's A.G.M. in April 1991, he was able to report that the full Advisory Committee was now made up of the previously quoted members of the Executive Committee together with:- The Earl of Arundel; R. Balfour; Wing Commander R. A. G. Ellen; B. G. Denyer; A. R. Ford; R. F. Gray; C. G. Greaves; Lt. Col. D. A. Lloyd; Major N. H. Ormorod; E. J. Rice; P. Robson; A. N. C. Wadey.

The involvement of the Earl of Arundel and his brother-in-law, Roddy Balfour, was indicative of the local and family links which had evolved with the coming together of the joint interest in both the Club and the Cricket Foundation. Cameron Greaves, a chartered accountant, had joined the committee to provide cover for the Treasurer, Mike Bull, who would soon feel obliged to retire because of ill health.

The need for this strengthened committee was increasingly apparent as the club had steadily built up to a programme of over forty days cricket in a four and a half month season. Typically, these would include one (and sometimes two) matches against Touring sides, up to fourteen other sponsored matches, seven days for Sussex youth cricket matches, seven days for Martlets games and a similar period for the Estate XI including the match against the Earl of Arundel's XI. There was also an increasing need to relate all these activities to the agreed policy of moving towards the provision of first-class cricket facilities at Arundel which would involve Sussex County Cricket Club both in Championship and One Day Matches.

Looking back on these major commitments, Ronnie Ford would later tell the author in 1995:

"There are two aspects of the growth and development of the Arundel Castle Cricket Club which are worth stressing. The first is the fact that the Club is a benevolent autocracy; no Officers or Members of the Committee are ever elected. Should a vacancy occur it has been the process since the inception of the Club in 1975 for the Chairman to lobby amongst senior members possible names for filling the vacancy which has arisen. When the Chairman is reasonably satisfied as to the name he then approaches the President who, if all is well, agrees to invite that name to take up the vacancy. This particular aspect Club was written into the rules of the Club when they were revised and brought up to date with the advice of Peter Robson in March 1989. But, essentially, the practice continues of co-option and confirmation at the subsequent A.G.M.

"When Billy decided, in view of the state of his health, his

Presidency of the M.C.C. and his acceptance of an invitation by the M.C.C. Committee to bring the laws of cricket up-to-date, that he had too much work on his plate, he asked me in 1985 whether I would be prepared to take his place as Chairman. I said I would and he raised the matter with the President who agreed to invite me to take Billy's place.

"As regards the responsibility of the Club, the recently approved lease of the ground for a further 20 years from the Castle Trustees which was the result of considerable negotiation between the Club and Lord Arundel now means that the Club is responsible for all cricket on the ground. This is organised within the framework of the present existing organisation of the Club which is the Chairman working very successfully with the President and certain key members of the Committee. This explains the supporting roles played by Colin Cowdrey, John Barclay, Mike Bull et al in this development.

"In financial matters, greater emphasis given to sponsorship was the key to our success. The annual deficit which at the Club's formation amounted to some £6,000 was eliminated entirely. The loan by the President was repaid and over the last 4 or 5 years it has been possible to run the Club without resorting to any overdraft or further loan. But with success came major challenges to our limited manpower consisting almost entirely of volunteers. This first became really evident in 1989.

"One of the biggest problems was put on our plate right at the start of the season. Of course, the Tourist match was very important for us and could literally make or break the club's finances, but there was a real difficulty in trying to cater for what were increasingly large crowds. My thinking on this matter was brought sharply into focus that year when we had the Australian Tourists at Arundel. We obviously had to satisfy several groups of people. First, there were the sponsors and members. I felt reasonably confident that we could make proper provision for them with our pavilion and marquees. Second, there were the players for whom we wanted to make this a special occasion, especially given the fact that they made themselves available to us at modest cost. Finally, there was the wider public - many of them regular supporters - for whom we had to make decent provision even though it was effectively a 'one-off' occasion".

In illustrating some of these needs, Ronnie Ford referred the author to two written contributions. The first was an article by David Gower, writing in the Leicestershire Mercury under the heading, 'Beautiful Arundel is a perfect setting' in

LAVINIA, DUCHESS OF NORFOLK'S XI v AUSTRALIA
7TH MAY 1989

AUSTRALIA

D. C. Boon	retired hurt	114
M. A. Taylor	lbw. b. Agnew	3
T. M. Moody	st. Whitticase b. Waller	72
A. R. Border	c. Boon b. Needham	66
M. Veletta	c. Whitticase b. Parsons	8
S. R. Waugh	not out	44
T. J. Zoehrer	c. Willey b. Taylor	1
M. G. Hughes	c. Agnew b. Taylor	1
G. F. Lawson	not out	2
T. B. A. May	did not bat	
T. M. Alderman		
	Extras	3
	Total (for 6 wkts.)	314

Bowling

	O	M	R	W
Agnew	8	0	38	1
Taylor	9	0	42	2
Parsons	7	0	49	1
Willey	7	0	56	0
Waller	10	0	66	1
Needham	9	0	61	1

LAVINIA, DUCHESS OF NORFOLK'S XI

P. Willey	c. Boon b. May	39
M. P. Speight	b. Hughes	55
D. I. Gower	lbw. b. Hughes	9
T. J. Boon	c. Moody b. Waugh	37
A. Needham	c. Hughes b. Waugh	8
P. Whitticase	not out	26
C. T. Radley	not out	13
G. J. Parsons	did not bat	
L. B. Taylor		
J. P. Agnew		
C. E. Waller		
	Extras	7
	Total (for 5 wkts.)	194

Bowling

	O	M	R	W
Alderman	6	1	17	0
Lawson	9	0	23	0
Waugh	9	1	52	2
Hughes	10	2	23	2
May	10	2	43	1
Border	4	0	26	0
Veletta	2	0	5	0

AUSTRALIA WON BY 120 RUNS – 50 OVER MATCH

which he said:

"There are many attractions about the life of an English cricketer lucky enough to be able to play the game for a living, and the other day proved the point to me again. I travelled down to Arundel to captain the Duchess of Norfolk's XI against the Australian Tourists and it would be difficult to imagine a more sublime cricketing experience. Peter Willey and I drove to Sussex from Northampton on the Saturday evening after our exciting County championship game and the disappointment of a narrow defeat soon retreated into the background.

"The charming town of Arundel, overshadowed by the famous castle, matched the summery, friendly ambience. An unspoilt English setting on a perfect summer's evening remains an aesthetic delight even to the most blasé traveller and the Norfolk Arms Hotel right beneath the castle battlements proved the perfect resting place.

"We ate hare and saddle of venison, accompanied by a bottle of Barolo, a splendid robust Italian wine, and this relaxing meal was the ideal prelude to the following day.

"We started play at a sensible time - 11.30 - and proceeded to watch the ball disappear out of the ground with some frequency as the Australian batsmen enjoyed themselves. Then it was our turn to try to make some sort of game of it, and we came a comfortable second at that.

"But it was the atmosphere of the day that was so special rather than the undemanding exercise out in the middle. The scene was twentieth century English with picnics going on all round the ground, the popping of corks, the spreading of rugs, the warm reception for the tourists, the appreciative ripple of applause for a good shot. A gorgeous day brought out a crowd of around 10,000. The Duchess strolled around with her daughters. Colin Cowdrey was beaming benevolently at all and sundry and that civilised man John Barclay - now Cricket Manager of the Arundel ground - provided amusing company.

"Arundel has to be the prettiest cricket ground in England. No wonder the top photographers never tire of trying to capture its unique character; no wonder the Tourists always love playing there at the start of each Summer."

Ronnie Ford's second collector's item was a piece submitted by someone who described himself as a regular at these matches. In it the unknown author outlined some of the high and low spots of the days activities.

The athleticism and professionalism of the visiting Australian team with their strenuous exercise session before the start of play was contrasted with the more relaxed approach of the home team whose leader was described as "the boy David". There was some light-hearted reference to the work of the ground match commentator with the author accused of "using his best welcoming host's voice" to mark the entry of the Australian openers Messrs. Boon and Taylor while "secretly nurturing hopes of an early wicket." For

Michael Cresswell-Wall it was suggested that "he could be guaranteed to provide one of the regular features of the day in announcing that 'another dog is in distress in a green Range Rover and will the owner please return to it at once'".

Ronnie Ford's unknown correspondent went on to describe the more unusual incidents at the match as when a swarm of bees held up play for some minutes. "Not surprisingly", he added "a beekeeper is always readily at hand at Arundel. Additional professional attention was needed when one of Allan Border's vast sixes hit a woman spectator. Visibly upset, the Australian captain lost his wicket soon afterwards but the lady's day was made for her when she received a get-well card signed by the entire Australian team."

Meanwhile, the problems of the day were described as "too much sun and not enough entertainment or comfort facility". These last criticisms referred to the vast queues which a sell-out match of this kind caused of those endeavouring to get a cup of tea or to visit the limited toilet facilities.

They also referred to problems in the car parks when "overheated bodies and overheated company cars ended the day in shared discomfort".

Ronnie Ford and his strengthened committee used feedback of this kind to tackle a wide range of improvements. In the months which followed, the Club minutes were full of plans for improved sanitation, traffic control, car parking and gate control, renewed seating and the need for an improved public address system.

There were other notable written contributions submitted to the club in the 1989 season including two from regular players. In the first, Mike Brearley described the M.C.C. match which took place on Sunday 23 July:

"M.C.C. lost the toss and fielded. We took an early wicket, which brought to the crease the left-handed J. A. Orders, who has played for Oxford University. For an hour, Orders played like a novice. He did give a single mark of his talent, a sumptuous, lazy off-drive. But, apart from that, his footwork was minimal and tending to retreat; he played and missed at two balls out of six. He simply wasn't good enough to get a touch.

"At last, at the end of the hour, he did edge one. It came low and straight to me at first slip. My dreamy hands did little towards grasping the nice red ball; the plain fact is, I dropped it.

"From that moment Orders, on 12, awoke from his mesmeric state and batted like a man possessed. He smote us hip and thigh, like Samson smote the Philistines, or indeed like a not-so-poor man's Graeme Pollock murdered anyone, Philistine or not. We couldn't bowl to him. Outside the off-stump the ball flashed through the covers; straighter, it disappeared, thumped, dragged, hoiked, to all parts of the leg-side boundary. The occasional mis-hit dropped, tantalising to us, in empty spaces. His innings was a *tour-de-force*, a rare combination of ineptitude and plenitude.

"Unsurprisingly, the rest of the day's players, though in many cases competent, charming and effective, were inevitably mundane and human in comparison with (taking Holy) Orders. J. Hall played very well, especially through the sticky patch; N. Lenham and R. Knight showed elegance and style in the later overs.

"The M.C.C. attack, already a bit thin had been depleted by the absence of W. G. Merry, who had fallen ill the night before, so there was little support for the excellent A. D. Towse, of the M.C.C. groundstaff, who bowled superbly. His first spell was nine overs, one wicket for 11 runs; it might have been five for 11.

"234-3 seemed likely to be too tall an order for a team whose batting also lacked class against Duchess Lavinia's interestingly varied attack. As it turned out, M. Pringle, from South Africa, was a bit too good with the new ball and a debacle loomed at 14-3. However A. J. Goldsmith and M. E. Gear, with sensibly mounting aggression, took us to 101-3, against good spin bowling from leg-spinner I. D. K. Salisbury and D. Wilson look-alike, W. G. Lovell. At this point a target of seven an over proved too high and a collapse followed. The match sauntered to a peaceful conclusion."

The second written contribution came from nearer home when the Director of Cricket, Johnny Barclay, said in his 1989 Cricket Report to the Club how things did not always go his way, when he described the conclusion of the match against the Combined Services on 11 June:

"Chris Worlidge, captain of the Duchess' Team, carefully set the field and with an encouraging 'good luck' tossed me the ball. Combined Services were facing a tough ordeal: 79 runs required, plenty of wickets in hand but only eight of the final twenty overs remaining. M. Turner of the R.A.F. had just come in, nervously taken guard and was ready to face some gently flighted off-breaks. The first two balls were strongly defended. "Perhaps they are playing for a draw", I thought as I prepared to bowl the next ball. Not for long was I left in doubt for his next stroke was a scything on-drive

which sent the ball skimming over mid-on for six. It took some time to find the ball and while the search was on I caught the eye of our groundsman Colin Dick, on the boundary's edge. He was laughingly cupping his hands to his mouth pretending to shout a warning to people peacefully boating on the river Arun two miles away that Barclay was bowling from the Castle End.

"I hope they took cover because my next three overs were cruelly savaged by Turner who made 63 runs in as splendid a display of hitting as you could wish to see (unless you were bowling). Combined Services won the match in the final over to conclude a lovely day and one which epitomised the healthy spirit of Arundel Castle's cricket. It was indeed just one of many enthralling encounters in a summer of endless warm sunshine."

Meanwhile Ronnie Ford's passion for improvements to the Club facilities was given added impetus when he decided to limit his term of office as Chairman:

"I realised that I should think in terms of retirement within a year or two but I told our Executive Committee that I would carry on until my successor was identified. Nevertheless, I was determined to do all I could to get our facilities up to the highest possible standard.

"By the time of our A.G.M. in 1989, I was able to assure members that, despite the hurricane and the building work both for the indoor cricket school and improvements to the pavilion, we could soon look forward to the full restoration of our ground. We could also look forward to the special accolade of first-class cricket once we could reach agreement with the Sussex County Cricket Club.

"All of this required a great deal of negotiation. In this we were much assisted by Alan Wadey since he served on the committees of both clubs. Nevertheless, we had to overcome a number of obstacles such as agreement to the temporary provision of advertising hoardings around our ground which was far from popular with the Castle Trustees. Then there was the general question of demarcation of responsibility between the County Club and ourselves. In the event, they took the lead with our support".

The value of all this preparation was evident when Sussex won the toss on Wednesday 25 July 1990 and went out to bat against Hampshire. After early shocks, the quality of the pitch proved so good that Sussex recovered to make 383 for 9 wickets declared. For this they were chiefly indebted to Colin Wells who made the first championship 100 at Arundel. He was followed by Chris Smith with a century for

LAVINIA, DUCHESS OF NORFOLK'S XI v NEW ZEALAND
6TH MAY 1990

LAVINIA, DUCHESS OF NORFOLK'S XI

I. J. F. Hutchinson	b. Priest	19
A. I. C. Dodemaide	c. Sub b. Snedden	131
P. W. G. Parker	c. Priest b. Millmow	90
A. P. Wells	c. Crowe b. Millmow	16
M. P. Speight	lbw. b. Snedden	0
C. M. Wells	run out	2
I. J. Gould	not out	1
V. J. Marks	did not bat	
A. R. Hansford		
J. Boiling		
J. K. Lever		
	Extras	18
	Total (for 6 wkts.)	277

Bowling

	O	M	R	W
Millmow	10	2	55	2
Thomson	10	2	58	0
Priest	10	1	42	1
Snedden	10	1	42	2
Bracewell	9	0	57	0
Rutherford	1	0	7	0

NEW ZEALAND

T. J. Franklin	b. Lever	82
J. J. Crowe	b. Hansford	43
M. J. Greatbatch	c. Hansford b. Boiling	20
M. D. Crowe	not out	89
K. R. Rutherford	not out	32
S. A. Thomson	did not bat	
M. W. Priest		
J. G. Bracewell		
M. C. Snedden		
A. C. Parore		
J. P. Millmow		
	Extras	12
	Total (for 3 wkts.)	278

Bowling

	O	M	R	W
Lever	9	1	48	1
Wells	10	1	39	0
Marks	10	0	63	0
Boiling	9	0	57	1
Hansford	9	0	58	1
Parker	0.2	0	1	0

NEW ZEALAND WON BY 7 WICKETS – 50 OVER MATCH

Hampshire and the match fizzled out into a draw.

However, the game had been blessed with fine weather and the crowd on the first day of over 3000 was larger than that which the county could normally expect for a mid-week game at Hove. As a result, over £11,000 was taken in gate money and the Club received a match fee of £1,500. This, together with the take-up of hospitality tents, all encouraged Sussex to confirm their commitment to return in the follow-

ing season. Their view was endorsed when both teams voted the catering some of the best they had experienced on the county circuit. Subsequently, a three year agreement was signed for County Cricket at Arundel which was a fitting tribute to the work of the Chairman and his team.

1990 was to be Ronnie Ford's penultimate year in the chair. From the vantage point of 1995, he recalls:

"Obviously, the introduction of first-class cricket was the highlight for us that year but there were a number of other high spots. The match against the New Zealand tourists was particularly pleasant. They are always such a splendid bunch and somehow the match almost seems a family occasion. Paul Parker brought down seven of the Sussex side for us and put on a little matter of 180 runs for the second wicket with Tony Dodemaide. This produced the highest-ever total by the home side against the tourists but the New Zealanders made light of the challenge when they all got runs against what one journalist rather unkindly described as an attack of 'has beens' and 'not quites'.

"Later in the month, we faced a real challenge. We had agreed to stage a match between Miles, Duke of Norfolk's XI and the Bishop of Arundel and Brighton. This was in itself an historic occasion as it would be the first time that the 17th Duke (and for that matter the Bishop) had put out teams on our ground. We naturally wanted to accommodate our benefactor, the owner of the ground, in every possible way, but our committee was somewhat alarmed when we were told that they might wish to have several thousand worshippers taking part in a service before the match to mark the twenty fifth anniversary of the Diocese. We managed to reach an agreement whereby the crowd kept off the playing area and the entire boundary was surrounded by priests from every part of West and East Sussex. It was a moving sight as they joined in prayer and it was a splendid way to recognise our links with the Cathedral and the Bishop as well as with the Duke and the principal Catholic layman.

"As far as the cricket was concerned, it was good to see Lord Arundel captaining his father's side. He brought with him many of his regulars who played in the match against the Estate eleven including David Frost and we managed to provide some serious cricket support through the Director of Cricket and Colin Cowdrey who came out of his Arundel retirement especially for this match. Both he and Johnny Barclay got runs for the Duke and the Bishop had a successful bowling spell including the wicket of Lord Arundel's brother-in-law, the actor, Patrick Rycart."

Miles, Duke of Norfolk's XI v Bishop of Arundel and Brighton's XI, 26th May 1990. The Bishop
tosses the coin with the Duke and later takes charge in the field.

To the author, this match also presented problems in the commentary box where, despite the assistance of Father Tony Lovegrove from the diocese, there were special difficulties in identifying the (unknown in cricketing terms) members of the Bishop's side. Of them, only Bishop Cormack's predecessor, Archbishop Michael Bowen of Southwark had any known cricketing form. In his address to those attending Mass at the match, he recalled his meetings with the Duke at the cricket and his tendency to ask awkward questions such as, "Is there any evidence of a Bishop bowling a maiden over?" He went on to express the hope that he and his Episcopal colleagues might prove able to respond to the challenge of this great occasion.

However, when he and Bishop Cormack came together in a batting partnership, the *Arundel and Brighton Diocesan News* rather irreverently reported "the Archbishop was bowled for a single and Bishop Cormack, after spending many minutes at the crease, also fell after scoring one run."

There was also considerable confusion as to the playing conditions of the match. Originally scheduled as a 25 overs a side game, this was varied by what was later described as episcopal rules. Thanks to a brisk top score by Johnny Barclay and a graceful 20 odd from Colin Cowdrey in what

was to be his last innings at Arundel, the Duke's XI finished their 25 overs with a score of 150 for 8. When the Bishop's XI completed their 25 overs some runs short of this total, it seemed that the seventeenth Duke of Norfolk had been victorious through the first team appearing for him at Arundel under the captaincy of his son. However, after a short pause, play was continued for several more overs allowing the Bishop's eleven to reach 151 for 7 which meant, as the Diocesan newspaper said, that "the Bishop's team had won as well".

If this result created a record of its own kind, there was another of a much more potent kind in cricketing terms when the Minor Counties team came to play at Arundel a few weeks later. Ronnie Ford has recalled:

"This was the tenth year of I.B.M. South East's sponsorship and they were rewarded when Blake and Gilbert put on 302 for the first wicket for the Minor Counties. Then, to add insult to injury, they had somehow managed to persuade us to make Johnny Barclay available as a substitute for one of their players. He proceeded to dismiss Peter Graves of Sussex but fortunately most of our batsmen did their stuff and we got away with a respectable draw."

Ronnie Ford's last season as Chairman was in 1991. It

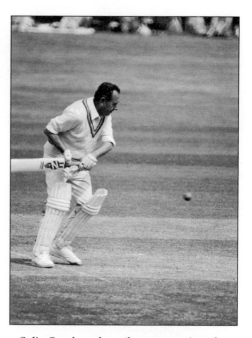

Colin Cowdrey chose the game against the Bishop's team for his farewell appearance at Arundel. In his 58th year he could still show the younger generation how to keep their eye on the ball.

The Earl of Arundel in full cry, 26th May 1990.

The first County Match at Arundel – Sussex v Hampshire, July 1990. (photo Daily Telegraph)

SUSSEX V HAMPSHIRE
25TH, 26TH AND 27TH JULY 1990

SUSSEX — First Innings

				Second Innings		
N. J. Lenham	c. Maru b. Ayling	15		N. J. Lenham	b. Connor	15
J. W. Hall	lbw. b. Marshall	4		J. W. Hall	run out	36
P. W. G. Parker	b. Marshall	0		P. W. G. Parker	b. Ayling	18
A. P. Wells	c. Scott b. Udal	53		A. P. Wells	b. Maru	32
M. P. Speight	c. and b. Udal	37		M. P. Speight	run out	24
C. M. Wells	c. Ayling b. Udal	107		C. M. Wells	c. Cox b. Udal	6
A. I. C. Dodemaide	lbw. b. Marshall	2		A. I. C. Dodemaide	not out	2
P. Moores	c. Smith b. Udal	61		A. C. S. Pigott	b. Udal	5
A. C. S. Pigott	not out	64		Extras		6
I. D. K. Salisbury	run out	0				
B. T. P. Donelan	not out	11		Total (for 7 wkts. dec.)		144
Extras		29				
Total (for 9 wkts. dec.)		383				

Bowling

	O	M	R	W			O	M	R	W
Connor	12	4	20	0		Connor	8	1	23	1
Marshall	16	4	35	3		Marshall	9	4	18	0
Ayling	15.4	8	36	1		Maru	6	0	51	1
Maru	32.2	5	105	0		Ayling	6.2	0	36	1
Udal	43	7	144	4		Udal	2	0	12	2
Scott	4	1	21	0						

HAMPSHIRE — First Innings

				Second Innings		
T. C. Middleton	b. Pigott	50		T. C. Middleton	b. Donelan	28
C. L. Smith	not out	132		C. L. Smith	st. Moores b. Donelan	61
R. J. Scott	c. Dodemaide b. Salisbury	13		R. J. Scott	st. Moores b. Donelan	16
M. C. J. Nicholas	run out	0		M. C. J. Nicholas	c. Moores b. Pigott	1
M. D. Marshall	c. Dodemaide b. Salisbury	11		M. D. Marshall	c. Donelan b. Salisbury	34
R. M. F. Cox	c. Moores b. Dodemaide	9		R. M. F. Cox	not out	35
J. R. Ayling	not out	28		J. R. Ayling	c. Hall b. Salisbury	22
R. J. Parks	did not bat			R. J. Parks	not out	15
R. J. Maru				Extras		8
S. D. Udal						
C. A. Connor				Total (for 6 wkts.)		220
Extras		11				
Total (for 5 wkts.)		254				

Bowling

	O	M	R	W			O	M	R	W
Dodemaide	20	9	31	1		Dodemaide	10	2	23	0
Pigott	18	7	43	1		Pigott	1	3	12	1
Wells	5	0	18	0		Wells	11	1	31	0
Donelan	19	5	44	0		Salisbury	16	1	69	2
Salisbury	36	5	108	2		Donelan	19.4	4	79	3

MATCH DRAWN

was given special distinction when Colin Cowdrey spoke at the Club's Spring Luncheon. At this time, he was about to complete the second of his four year term of appointment as Chairman of the International Cricket Council. Taking Club members into his confidence, he spoke of the major problems facing the game through the harassment of umpires, short-pitched bowling, verbal abuse and slow over rates. Expanding on his theme and the role of the I.C.C. in tackling this problem, he said that the players were unhappy with many of these things but were caught up in a vicious circle when substantial amounts of money were at stake. This could lead to abuses and retaliation.

Colin Cowdrey went on to outline the I.C.C.'s plans for the future. First, they must defend umpires and he saw the appointment of a match referee as valuable for both this purpose and in instilling greater discipline in the game. He commended the idea of using old players who were knowledgeable about "all the tricks of the trade" and who would deal with the Captain of each side rather than with individuals in the teams who might be guilty of infringement. The plan would be to ensure that there was an immediate hearing at the end of the day's play leading to decisions over fines and possible suspension. This would follow the practice of other sports bodies such as the Professional Golf Association where matters were determined rapidly without leaving all concerned in suspense.

Colin Cowdrey concluded his speech by looking ahead to the forthcoming visit of the West Indian Touring side at the start of the season. Drawing on the inspiration of the spirit of cricket at Arundel, he recalled how he had personally experienced the same spirit even when playing Test cricket against the West Indies in tense situations. He described how, at the end of the 1967-8 Tour in which his opposing captain was Gary Sobers, England came to Guyana for the final Test one up in the series. On the last day he was batting with Alan Knott when a further wicket would mean that the West Indian bowlers would have an opportunity of running through the England tail. He went on:

"After we had been batting half an hour or so together, Alan Knott turned Gibbs off his hips a little bit uppishly. Gary Sobers fielding at short leg dived far to his right and my heart almost stopped as he appeared to make a brilliant catch. He threw the ball up in the air and the crowd went wild. When the ball came down Gary tossed it back to the bowler saying "no catch". Meanwhile, many in the crowd became angry and he was actually booed for quite a long time. At the end of the over I went up to him and said: 'That was one of the finest sporting gestures I have ever seen. I am most grateful'. Gary replied 'No need to thank me. I love to get you out with good bowling or fielding, but cheating, man, that's no way to enjoy the game'. The Club's Vice-Chairman concluded his speech by saying: "It's people like that, that I must defend and support".

It was with this background, that Ronnie Ford would recall the two major events of his last season as Chairman:

"First, we beat the West Indians in the opening match of the season. Then, in August, the Prince of Wales came down to perform the official opening ceremony of our Indoor Cricket School." Christopher Martin-Jenkins was to write elegantly of both events. His report on the West Indies match read:

"The atmosphere of this happy annual event is a cross between a point-to-point and a charity match. Well behaved labradors stroll with their owners behind the elegant white

LAVINIA, DUCHESS OF NORFOLK'S XI v WEST INDIES
12TH MAY 1991

WEST INDIES

C. G. Greenidge	c. Azharuddin b. Donelan	22
P. V. Simmons	c. Azharuddin b. Donelan	40
R. B. Richardson	b. Bainbridge	5
B. C. Lara	b. Donelan	15
C. L. Hooper	c. Krikken b. Bainbridge	1
A. L. Logie	c. and b. Bainbridge	61
I. V. A. Richards	c Azharuddin b. Barnett	17
P. J. L. Dujon	not out	21
H. A. G. Anthony	c. Butcher b. Mortensen	4
I. B. A. Allen	not out	2
B. P. Patterson	did not bat	
	Extras	23
	Total (for 8 wkts.)	211

Bowling

	O	M	R	W
Mortensen	10	1	32	1
Lever	10	3	33	0
Bainbridge	10	1	36	3
Donelan	10	1	41	3
Barnett	6	0	32	1
Azharuddin	4	0	24	0

LAVINIA, DUCHESS OF NORFOLK'S XI

K. J. Barnett	c. Dujon b. Patterson	12
B. R. Hardie	b. Anthony	18
J. E. Morris	c. Logie b. Anthony	98
M. Azharuddin	c. Logie b. Hooper	21
R. O. Butcher	b. Hooper	0
T. J. G. O'Gorman	b. Allen	13
P. Bainbridge	c. Hooper b. Richards	8
K. Krikken	not out	7
B. Donelan	c. Dujon b. Patterson	1
O. H. Mortensen	not out	1
J. K. Lever	did not bat	
	Extras	33
	Total (for 8 wkts.)	212

Bowling

	O	M	R	W
Patterson	8	2	23	2
Allen	10	1	41	1
Anthony	10	1	56	2
Simmons	10	0	52	0
Hooper	6	1	13	2
Richardson	1	0	4	0
Richards	2.4	0	5	1

LAVINIA, DUCHESS OF NORFOLK'S XI WON BY 2 WICKETS
50 OVER MATCH

marquees with the air of knowing the scene inside out but there are visitors from further afield. There was even a distinctly antipodean shout of 'Have a go' as Greenidge and Simmons played with great care and occasional discomfort for the first ten of the fifty overs. These produced only fifteen runs as Lever and Mortensen found some early swing and even a bit of bounce in a normally comfortable pitch.

"The traditional opening match of the cricket tour to England is much more about the occasion than the result. Nevertheless, it was not wholly without significance that the West Indies, carelessly conceding 32 extras, should have been beaten yesterday by two wickets nor that one of the most handsome stroke players in England, John Morris, should have helped to achieve this result. Morris scored 98 driving and square cutting with immense relish for a 6 and 13 fours.

"His innings along with some tidy off-spin bowling by Brad Donelan, presently only a reserve for Sussex, were the main ingredients in the victory which enabled the Duchess's side to beat a touring team for the first time since 1986.

"The Duchess was in attendance despite recent ill health and will have been pleased that £24,000 was taken to underpin the Club's finances. The occasion will also have delighted Ronnie Ford, the retiring chairman of A.C.C.C. and the Director of Cricket, John Barclay."

Apart from the importance of a rare success against the West Indies, there was a deeper significance in the way in which this particular match was played. This related to some of the excesses of which Colin Cowdrey had spoken in his address at the Club's Spring Luncheon and, in particular, to some of the events in the series between England and the West Indies in the Caribbean in the previous winter. Apart from events on the field, they had suffered from a situation in which Vivian Richards had virtually declared war on the British Press and yet, as Alan Lee in 'The Times' said:

"True to the word of their captain, the West Indians encountered that rare impostor, defeat, in a nice and gentlemanly way.

"Losing by two wickets to a patchwork side comprising six of Derbyshire, a Sussex reserve and four men brought out of retirement might seem an alarming start for the undisputed world champions but no one here was fooled.

"Richards was spreading goodwill, posing smilingly for amateur photographers and patiently signing autographs through the Pavilion window. However, he made only fifteen after being warmly applauded when he came to the wicket. The West Indies were sustained, as so often, in the middle order, by Gus Logie and his formidable shovel strokes through the on side."

As to Ronnie Ford's second major event in his last year as Chairman - the visit by the Prince of Wales for the opening of the indoor cricket school, in August - Christopher Martin-Jenkins wrote:

"The significance of the occasion was that, before his visit, 48 primary school children from Greenwich, Islington, Tower Hamlets and Hackney had enjoyed two days of coaching with matches on this gloriously smooth outfield."

On his arrival, the Prince was persuaded to play Kwik Cricket with a plastic ball in a game involving several of the youngsters. Without removing his immaculately tailored jacket, the Prince went out to bat with Sam Stephenson, aged 11, against the bowling of another 11 year old, Luke Macdonald. The local press reported the bowler as saying, 'I thought I was going to bowl him out quickly but he showed he could bat a bit.' His partner's worry was 'in case I ran him out'. This almost happened when he lapped the Prince as they ran for two.

All this provided an entertaining prelude before the Prince unveiled the usual commemorative plaque. In her speech of welcome, Duchess Lavinia recalled that the opening ceremony was taking place a year later than planned because of an injury which the Prince had sustained while playing polo. She invited him to play more cricket at Arundel, "as it is obviously much safer".

In response, the Prince said that he hoped a great deal of talent was being identified for the future of English cricket, adding, "and a great deal is needed." As he left, the Prince was presented with two children's cricket bats for Prince William and Prince Harry and remarked, "I know you are looking for new talent but I'm not sure you can rely on us".

Looking back on the event, Ronnie Ford said:

"This was certainly a highlight for me as Chairman and, by the end of that season, I had followed the procedure which had applied for my own appointment by consulting senior members of the Club before recommending to the Duchess that she invite Hubert Doggart to take my place. All this had been agreed and it was a good time to make my exit"

The hand-over ceremony for Hubert Doggart came at the end of the Annual General Meeting of the Club on 8 April 1992 and was in good time for the start of the season which was marked with a visit by Pakistan.

As in the previous year's Tourist match, it seemed that this was another occasion when the visitors were keen to mend fences. Alan Lee in *The Times* wrote:

"Pakistan showed a desire to polish their reputation after much of the criticism which had been thrown at them when they won the world championship but made few friends by their behaviour on the field. One of the most genial visitors

LAVINIA, DUCHESS OF NORFOLK'S XI V PAKISTAN
3RD MAY 1992

PAKISTAN

Aamir Sohail	retired	104
Rameez Jaja	b. Jean-Jaques	23
Salim Malik	b. Base	84
Javed Miandad	not out	31
Asif Mujtaba	not out	2
Zahid Fazal	did not bat	
Wasim Akram		
Moin Khan		
Naved Anjum		
Salim Jaffer		
Aqib Javed		
	Extras	9
	Total (for 2 wkts.)	253

Bowling

	O	M	R	W
Base	10	0	51	1
Robson	10	0	44	0
Jean-Jaques	10	0	60	1
Kendrick	10	0	44	0
Donelan	10	0	50	0

LAVINIA, DUCHESS OF NORFOLK'S XI

P. D. Bowler	b. Mujtaba	82
N. J. Lenham	b. Mujtaba	36
T. J. G. O'Gorman	b. Aqib	69
A. P. Wells	b. Anjum	30
R. O. Butcher	not out	5
P. Moores	not out	1
A. Robson	did not bat	
B. T. P. Donelan		
N. Kendrick		
M.Jean-Jaques		
S. J. Base		
	Extras	17
	Total (for 4 wkts.)	240

Bowling

	O	M	R	W
Wasim Akram	10	0	45	0
Aqib Javed	10	0	50	1
Salim Jaffer	10	0	49	0
Naved Anjum	10	0	47	1
Asif Mujtaba	10	2	37	2

PAKISTAN WON BY 13 RUNS – 50 OVER MATCH

on the day was the Pakistan High Commissioner and, among the other visitors, Brian Johnston and the M.C.C. President, Michael Melluish, were at their most entertaining at the lunch. The Duchess, too, was there to greet the visitors together with the Club's new Chairman.

"As to the match, Aamir Sohail appeared another threat to England with a dazzling century ending with a massive six before retiring.

"Peter Bowler of Derbyshire and Tim O'Gorman of the same county looked as though they might take the home side to victory but Wasim Akram and Aqib Javed defended their total superbly at the end."

For the new Chairman the opening match had gone well. After losing this closely contested match, it seemed that the Duchess' team could do little wrong. Victories came against the Eton Ramblers by 120 runs and against the Minor Counties by 9 wickets. The feature of both games was the seemingly inevitable century from John Rice. Between times, Lloyds was beaten by 3 wickets in the last match in the series and the home side had much the best of the drawn match with Combined Services thanks to a spell of 4 for 34 by Johnny Barclay.

When the Duchess's team declared at 220 for 5 against the M.C.C. on 12 July following an undefeated century by the former Warwickshire player Geoffrey Tedstone, they must have felt that they had presented the visiting side with a good challenge. However C. K. Bullen and D. C. Elston, in a record stand of 224, gave Roger Knight's visiting M.C.C. side a ten wicket victory.

There was another run feast in the match against I Zingari on 26 July but the rivalry in this match had been sharpened by events in the previous year. Nigel Draffan, a Cambridge Blue , who also organised annual fixtures for his company, the local estate agents, Clutton's, had been match manager and captain of the Duchess' side against IZ since 1986. He takes up the story of the 1991 game:

"I should perhaps explain that in getting together my side against IZ, I have always drawn heavily on my collection of 'Grannies'. This is a cricket club' which started when three of us who were great friends turned out for my college 3rd XI at Cambridge and, for some reason, the University captain was playing in this match. After we had let several hits go astray he said: 'You three field like a bunch of old grannies'. Well we decided afterwards that, when we came down from Cambridge, we would form a 'Grannies' Cricket Club. Today, it has over 250 members and includes one England player, John Stephenson. We originally started the Club as an antithesis to the sometimes excessive keenness of league cricket. Our approach was to play hard but we didn't regard a dropped catch as the end of the world.

"In 1991, we contained IZ. to a reasonable score despite a big innings by D. Fischel and the usual effective contribution from Bill Holland. When our openers Wills and Sykes began hitting the ball all round the ground, as Captain, I was feeling very relaxed. However, when they were just short of a

LAVINIA, DUCHESS OF NORFOLK'S XI V AUSTRALIA
2ND MAY 1993

AUSTRALIA

M. J. Slater	b. Graveney	13
D. C. Boon	c. Parks b. Headley	14
M. E. Waugh	b. Headley	6
D. R. Martyn	c. Garner b. Botham	5
A. R. Border	b. Botham	18
S. R. Waugh	b. Garner	59
I. A. Healy	not out	47
B. P. Julian	c. Cowdrey b. Headley	20
P. R. Reiffel	b. Headley	9
S. K. Warne	b. Headley	0
W. J. Holdsworth	did not bat	
	Extras	12
	Total (for 9 wkts.)	203

Bowling

	O	M	R	W
Garner	10	2	32	1
Headley	10	1	51	5
Graveney	10	2	32	1
Botham	10	1	29	2
Fleming	7	0	32	0
Greig	3	0	22	0

LAVINIA, DUCHESS OF NORFOLK'S XI

T. R. Ward	run out	33
G. Fowler	c. Healy b. Julian	11
P. W. G. Parker	lbw. Holdsworth	77
G. R. Cowdrey	c. Waugh S. b. Waugh M.	0
M. V. Fleming	c. Healy b. Waugh M.	0
I. T. Botham	b. Waugh M.	13
I. A. Greig	c. Healy b. Waugh M.	6
R. J. Parks	c. Healy b. Waugh M.	1
D. Headley	c. Waugh M. b. Julian	16
J. Garner	b. Julian	8
D. Graveney	not out	5
	Extras	26
	Total	196

Bowling

	O	M	R	W
Holdsworth	9.5	1	42	1
Julian	10	0	49	3
Reiffel	10	0	35	0
Warne	10	1	26	0
Waugh	10	2	32	5

AUSTRALIA WON BY 7 RUNS – 50 OVER MATCH

half-century partnership, Sykes - who was one of our 'Grannies' - played a ball dead at his feet and tossed it back to the bowler. Someone appealed and the Umpire had no option but to give him out. Well, you can imagine, that this caused strong feelings and there were some not too subtle references to, 'What the Duke would have said if he had been alive today'.

"So, when I won the toss in the 1992 match, you can imagine I was keen for our batsmen to pile on the runs. We lost Mike Barford, an accountant, who was a friend from Cambridge days early on. But Neil Trestrail who has scored many runs for us in these games had brought one of his friends with whom he had played for Hampshire II, Derek Pepperell, and the two of them put on 275 before, barely concealing my smirk, I declared. Unfortunately, I have to admit that there was no happy ending for us when Bill Holland and Dickie Doggart proceeded to put on 241 for the first IZ wicket and we lost by 9 wickets. Still, I think we can fairly claim that we were the sensation of the 1992 Season".

1993 was a year of exceptional international activity at Arundel. Inevitably, the visit of the Australian touring team attracted most of the limelight but there was a mixture of new and old fixtures involving three countries in all.

In July, the Australian Crusaders on their bi-annual visit scored 250 runs in 193 minutes before declaring. When the home team reached 180 for three, they appeared to be cruising towards a comfortable victory, but C. Howard with 5 wickets in 4 consecutive overs caused a collapse and it was left to the Director of Cricket and Michael Durden-Smith (the former cricket commentator's son making his debut at Arundel) to undertake a rearguard action to prevent defeat.

In August the Australians once again had the edge when, in a new fixture, their Combined Services side ran up the biggest score of the year thanks to undefeated centuries by Jones and Bloom. Following an opening partnership of 153 by Skinner and Macleay the Duchess' team, led by Charles Rowe, made a good effort in chasing the runs, but the task proved beyond them.

The visit by club sides from Australia always ensured an enthusiastic if small crowd of members of the Arundel Castle Cricket Club. However, the two big matches in 1993 brought in a much more widely based audience together with the media.

On 28 July, England met the West Indies. The unique feature about this match so far as Arundel was concerned was that it brought, for the first time, women's international sides to the ground in what proved a vital game in ensuring that the English women would become World Cup champions.

Their victory at Arundel was not achieved without some alarm. After the England bowlers had performed steadily and had been backed up by splendid fielding - none more so than that of wicket keeper Barbara Daniels - the West Indies score of 120 from 59.4 overs seemed inadequate.

When England reached 63 for 1 thanks to Jan Brittin, the prolific England opener, 4 wickets fell for 13 runs in 5 overs following the introduction of West Indian spinners after tea. The large crowd of Caribbean exiles who were there to cheer their team on did so with a will and, as Stuart Jones wrote in *The Times*, "At 76 for 5, England tottered momentarily on the edge of defeat. They were rescued by Jo Chamberlain, a fast bowler, who struck 34 in a little over an hour. The female version of the village blacksmith, she claimed a decisive boundary and the Player of the Match award".

Other members of the Press concentrated their attention on the partial sponsorship of the series by Dame Barbara Cartland and the willingness of some members of the England team to pose for fashion photographs for a certain weekend tabloid.

The Press had been out in even greater force at the start of the season when the match against the Australian touring side drew a crowd of over 15,000. They were attracted, according to several Press reports, by the presence of Ian Botham and the Prime Minister.

While this was certainly true of the former England all-rounder in what was likely to be one of his last major appearances, the reports regarding the Prime Minister's attendance went strictly against the whole planning process which had led up to this match.

Indeed, behind the first visit by a Prime Minister to the cricket at Arundel lay many weeks of planning. When he had first responded positively to an invitation, it had been necessary to work closely with Hubert Doggart over several months in making the necessary preparations which, for security reasons, were in strict confidence.

On the day, the Prime Minister drove from his Huntingdon constituency to West Sussex and, after a brief stop in a nearby village, arrived at the Arundel Castle Cricket ground just after the start of play. Meanwhile, a massive crowd - already attracted by the combination of Ian Botham and the Australians - had been filling the ground. When word of the Prime Ministerial visit spread, the crowd grew until - for the first time ever - it was necessary to close all the entrances to the ground.

Meanwhile, the Press described the cricket as "a surprisingly serious match." The Australians won the toss and batted and within the hour were reduced to 68 for 5. The main damage was done by Dean Headley, son of Ron and grandson of George, who was well supported by Ian Botham. The former England all-rounder showed his old flair for the big occasion when he bowled the Australian captain Allan Border. When he came off he had figures of 10-1-29-2. It was at this stage that Ted Dexter, interviewed by the B.B.C. cricket commentary team, said presumably the Australians were trying to play Botham into the Test side. He later made it clear that this was intended as a light-hearted remark and sent his apologies to Ian Botham. Meanwhile, so far as the Australians were concerned, it was left to Steve Waugh and

"Have you heard this one?" Brian Johnston entertains Michael Melluish, the Treasurer of M.C.C.

Success brings a spring to the stride of Ian Botham.

THE AUSTRALIAN TOURISTS MATCH, 1993

WOMEN'S WORLD CUP
ENGLAND V WEST INDIES
28TH JULY 1993

WEST INDIES

E. Caesar	run out	10
A. Browne	c. Brittin b. Smithies	11
J. Sterling	c. Taylor b. Smithies	15
C. James	c. Daniels b. Smith	4
E. Gregg	lbw. Smith	3
S. Power-Wilson	c. Daniels b. Taylor	23
C. Singh	c. Daniels b. Hodges	19
E. Cunningham	b. Taylor	2
D. Luke	c. Smith b. Hodges	15
P. Felicien	not out	5
J. Robinson	run out	3
	Extras	10
	Total (59.4 overs)	120

Bowling

	O	M	R	W
Chamberlain	12	5	12	0
Taylor	12	3	15	2
Hodges	12	5	27	2
Smithies	12	3	24	2
Smith	6.4	0	18	2
Stock	5	0	22	0

ENGLAND

J. Brittin	c. Caesar b. Singh	46
W. Watson	lbw. Luke	4
C. Hodges	b. Luke	11
B. Daniels	b. Luke	7
K. Smithies	c. Caesar b. Singh	0
J. Chamberlain	not out	34
D. Maybury	lbw. Sterling	7
D. Stock	not out	7
G. Smith	did not bat	
C. Taylor		
J. Smit		
	Extras	7
	Total (46.1 overs, 6wkts.)	123

Bowling

	O	M	R	W
Robinson	8	0	29	0
Cunningham	6	0	22	0
Luke	12	2	27	3
Singh	12	3	20	2
Sterling	7	1	16	1
James	1.1	0	9	0

ENGLAND WON BY 4 WICKETS – 60 OVER MATCH

Ian Healy to rescue their side in a partnership of 82. This ended when Joel Garner,(who had emerged from his retirement to bowl in this match), showed he was still capable of producing the unplayable delivery to bowl Waugh.

Seeking 204 runs to win the match, the Duchess' side was making reasonable progress at 66 for 1 with Paul Parker playing his traditional role of holding the side together against the Tourists. However, three wickets went down without adding to the total before Parker and Headley had a useful stand for the eighth wicket. The tail wagged but when Holdsworth began the last over to Paul Parker, 22 runs were required for victory. Amid growing excitement from the vast crowd, he took 14 from the first four balls of the over and, seemingly, four leg-byes came from the fifth ball. Amid the general excitement, most of the crowd failed to notice that Parker had been given out lbw and there was some confusion on the part of those who had miscounted the over as to whether the match had ended in a draw.

When all became plain, it was agreed that this was one of the most exciting matches involving the Tourists at Arundel. Apart from the cricket, there was special appreciation for the involvement of two visitors.

Ian Botham had shown touches of his old ability with both bat and ball in what proved to be the great all-rounder's last season in first-class cricket. As he himself later told the author: "I'm glad that one of my last outings against the Australians should have been at Arundel. It was a marvellous place for a swan-song and I really appreciated the Prime Minister's friendliness towards me."

As to Ian Botham's contribution, he left nothing but good memories at Arundel for, as the Chairman's wife, Sue Doggart, said: "Many critical things have been said about Ian Botham but I shall always remember him signing autographs for over an hour through the window of the players' dressing room for a huge crowd of small boys."

The Prime Minister had been equally generous , ignoring security in signing autographs and in posing for pictures with the players. However, his visit had not been without its complications. Such had been the need for secrecy that the Earl of Arundel (Lord A) was unaware of the Prime Minister's visit. Thus, when he arrived at the ground just before the start of play, he had a somewhat confused conversation with one of the Local Government Organisers (L.G.O.) as follows:

L.G.O. (Referring to the Prime Minister's impending arrival): "Aren't we lucky to have such a special visitor here today".

Lord A (Assuming that the question related to Ian Botham): "Oh yes, I've always hoped we would see him play on this ground".

L.G.O.: "But surely you didn't expect to see him turn out against the Australians".

Lord A.: "I don't see why not. I think that he has still got a lot of good cricket left in him".

The match against the 1993 Australian tourists. Prime Minister John Major with the two captains, Paul Parker and Allan Border – flanked by the author, Hubert Doggart and John Barclay.

L.G.O.: "But isn't he a bit old to play at this level?".

Lord A.: "You had better not let him hear you say that. He might give you a punch on the nose".

It was apparently at this stage that both parties realised the reason for this mutual confusion. As for the Prime Minister who, not for the first and no doubt not for the last time during his administration, faced exceptional personal and political pressure, he uttered perhaps the perfect farewell line when, on leaving the ground, he said: "A day like this makes you realise there are other things in life than politics".

The day had been a considerable success for the committee and its Chairman who would comment later: "A visit of this kind by the Prime Minister leaves one with mixed feelings. One part of me is delighted to have such a genuine cricket lover as John Major with us. The other part has to reflect on all the complexities of organisation involving the Club with the police and the local authorities while recognising that our resources are strictly limited. Nevertheless, I think we can report that it all went off very well".

The time for that report came in the following March at the Club's Annual General Meeting, Since this marked the start of the 99th year, the author determined to keep a jour-

The Prime Minister signs the bat of two very polite young spectators.

nal of events in 1994 and the entries which follow from this point and on through the final chapter reflect his impressions at the time.

30 March. The Club's Annual General Meeting took place on one of those indeterminate grey, late Winter, early Spring evenings in the pavilion with 30 members arrayed in front of a top table at which sit the Chairman, Treasurer and Secretary. For the second year in succession, Duchess

Lavinia was unable to take the Chair because of ill health. We are reminded of her brisk method of conducting the business of the meeting and her impatience with attempted flattery. One's thoughts also go back to her constant involvement - despite her stated position as a non-cricket lover - not only at meetings but on match days where her charm and steely determination have worked to the Club's advantage in obtaining both volunteer help and sponsorship. The fish, once landed, would be greeted with the words, "Oh you are so kind. Here is a list of things I have put down for you to do".

There is a special interest in the Chair this year when Hubert Doggart (who was unable to preside because of ill health in the previous year) makes his debut. Not surprisingly, he brings to the task all the expertise gained in his long years as a schoolmaster. He is supported, as ever, by that paragon of cricketing and schoolmaster's wives, Sue Doggart, who sits in the front row with the look of one keeping a sharp eye open for any difficult parent while her husband reports on the boys' activities.

Our Chairman, after inviting the meeting to agree the minutes of the previous A.G.M. which are unavailable now but "which have been available for perusal in the office during the year", obtains its silent consent. He then introduces the Treasurer in the style of one giving a new Second Master the chance to perform. This the bespectacled Cameron Greaves does with professional flair as he tells a slightly bemused audience that his report has been changed because of technical amendments laid down by the Institute of Chartered Accountants in England and Wales. However, his listeners are quick to appreciate his summary which shows that the success of the Australian match in 1993 has turned the Club's deficit into a positive balance.

He is followed by the Chairman who has clearly decided to play his schoolmaster role to the hilt. Telling the audience of a teacher's positive relish in the process of annual reports, he confesses that this can sometimes present a particular challenge. He instances two examples of mixed parental reaction when he said of one boy (of whom he could find little positive to say), "He will no doubt, in due course, become an excellent parent" and, of another of whose idle tendencies he said, "This boy is a self-confessed criminal".

However, our Chairman has no need for faint praise as he proceeds to list those to whom appreciation is due. He carries the audience with him in wholeheartedly expressing the gratitude of members for their President's inspiration and their wish for her speedy return to better health. He goes on to thank the staff for their skill and service to the Club. The strengthening relations in the post Cricket Foundation era are recognized with his thanks to the Earl of Arundel and the Arundel Estate staff. To this, the Chairman adds his thanks to John Barclay who is applauded not only for his work as Cricket Director but also as the new Chairman of the M.C.C Indoor School Sub-Committee. He adds congratulations to Sir Roger Gibbs, Chairman of the Foundation, who has been awarded a Knighthood in the New Years Honours List.

The Chairman continues with the traditional thanks to the two groundsmen, Colin Dick and Lee Farquher, and to the two secretaries, Debbie Osborne and Suzanne Weaver. Others in his batting order to whom the Club is greatly indebted, "include Fran Smith and her catering staff, Ray and Julie Madison-Metcalfe behind the bar, Pat Lockyer in the tea hut, and all those who do the scoring and operate the score board". He concludes his list of thanks with appreciation to "our panel of umpires and the devoted team of helpers who go on duty Sunday after Sunday, as well as on the big match days".

The Chairman has clearly struck a warm family note in thanking those involved in the past year. He couples this with an outline of future plans for the Centenary Year in 1995 which will include a Young Cricketer Appeal, a Membership Drive, a possible dinner in the Indoor School and a Members' Draw. Finally, he mentions the proposed history of the Club and asks for a short preview.

The author judged that it might be appropriate to outline the career records of at least three of those present. Referring to the book's statistical section, John Barclay's position as the leading all-rounder for the Duchess (364 runs and 42 wickets) was mentioned as was Alan Wadey's role as her leading strike bowler with 62 wickets. As for the Chairman, his seniority and consistency with the bat was recognised with the report of his average of 47.63 for Duke Bernard's team and a score of 22 not out in his only innings for the Duchess.

Appropriately, the vote of thanks to the Chair follows and we retire to the bar for a discussion on the prospects for the new season.

1989

June 11th. Lavinia Duchess of Norfolk's XI 203 (N. Kemp 67, R. Vyvyen 50, J. P. Barrett 6-25). Combined Services 206-6 (M. Turner 62, J. P. Barrett 61). Combined Services won by 4 wickets.

July 23rd. Lavinia Duchess of Norfolk's XI 234-3 (J. Orders 106*, J. Hall 50). MCC 159 (A. J. Goldsmith 60). 50 over match. Lavinia Duchess of Norfolk's XI won by 75 runs.

1990

June 17th. A Minor Counties XI 302-1 dec (N. W. Gilbert 172, R. Blare 109*). Lavinia Duchess of Norfolk's XI 264-5 (D. Ferreira 85*, M. W. Pringle 60). Match drawn.

1992

July 5th. Lavinia Duchess of Norfolk's XI 220-5 dec (G. A. Tedstone 106). MCC 224-0 (C. K. Bullen 132*, D. C. Elston 84*). MCC won by 10 wickets.

July 26th. Lavinia Duchess of Norfolk's XI 276-1 dec (D. Pepperell 130*, N. Trestrail 116*). I Zingari 281-1 (W. E. J. Holland 123*, R. C. Doggart 111). I Zingari won by 9 wickets.

CHAPTER TWELVE

The Ninety Ninth Year And Beyond

As indicated earlier, it seemed appropriate to give as full an account as possible of the 1994 matches at Arundel Castle Cricket Club. In this process, the author's journal entries were supplemented by the Director of Cricket, Johnny Barclay, whose additional comments are shown after the initials J.R.T.B..

Sunday 24 April v The Arabs: This match has now established itself as our regular opening fixture. One of the main features of the day is the arrival of the Founder of the Arabs, Jim Swanton. This always brings a touch of style to the proceedings as he appears on the ground with his customary blend of geniality and gravitas wearing his Band of Brothers panama hat. As ever, he is accompanied by his charming and unassuming wife Ann who perhaps few members of the growing crowd appreciate has been a championship golfer and who is a pianist able to bring joy to those who like music in the Caroll Gibbons manner.

The Swanton party makes a regal entrance from the lower car park, receiving tributes all along the way to the Club office where the reception committee of the Chairman, the Director of Cricket and the Secretary are waiting. They are joined on this occasion by the author who is greeted by the Swanton opening, "How is the book coming along". This is no idle question as Jim Swanton has always shown great generosity to fellow writers and has already recorded some of his recollections of Duke Bernard for the centenary history. Jim, supported by his teams, will play a special part in that history by producing the sides for both the opening and closing matches of our season.

When the author congratulates the Founder on his ability to raise an exceptionally strong side with not only his usual complement of Oxbridge Blues but also several County players and, in the person of Chris Cowdrey, a Test Cap, he receives a typical deadpan response of, "Oh, its just another average Arab side you know".

J.R.T.B.: "I have been in the habit of turning out for Jim in these matches. He is an exceptionally kind person who has done a great many good turns for young cricketers. Of course, he has had to take in his stride both those who make fun of him as Brian Johnston did over the years in talking about the Pope arriving on the ground and so forth but he can laugh at himself and he is always quick to take part in the leg-pulling which goes on in the Arabs matches.

E. W. Swanton's Arabs at Arundel. (L to R): Steve Henderson, Bryan Hamblin, David Foster, Archie Cotterell, E. W. Swanton and John Barclay.

"Something which always makes his team laugh is the relationship which he has with his Captain, Archie Cotterell. To hear Archie talk, you would think that he had never played cricket for Cambridge. In fact, you would not think of him as a leading figure in the City either. He is always talking about writing a novel which never seems to get finished but this all seems more credible than his real life occupation as a leading stockbroker. But the real joy of the day is the nervousness both actual and contrived which appears when it comes to his negotiations with Jim who is always referred to as the Founder. The Founder takes a keen interest and loves to see the game played in the way in which he thinks it should be played. In that sense, he is very much in line with the tradition of Duke Bernard.

"The first part of the day's drama is always about the toss. 'Oh God I hope the Founder is not here', says Archie already obsessed with the difficulty in deciding whether to bat or not. Well, this year we won the toss and batted and the next worry was naturally when to make the declaration. Archie would often try to have a discussion on the subject with the Founder over lunch only to receive the reply: 'Its up to you Captain, you are in charge of the side'.

"All this is really part of the fun and games in these matches. On this occasion it really didn't present too much of a problem. Bill Holland who always gets on with it and Charlie Rowe about whom I have enthused earlier, had a century opening partnership and Stephen Henderson who is a very good player piled on the runs. It was nice to see a little cameo innings from Chris Cowdrey. He has a marvellously dry sense of humour as have all the Cowdreys for that matter. I greatly admire Chris for the way in which he has based his entire after dinner speaking material on his short-lived England Test career. He was treated very badly by the Selectors and it must have hurt at the time, but sensibly he thought the best way ahead was to make fun of the whole thing.

"When it came to our turn to take the field, I was asked to do most of the bowling and I managed to do a bit of damage in the middle order but I see I was rather expensive which is probably why the home team got the necessary runs after a few shocks".

Sunday 1 May. v The New Zealand Touring Team; a fine spring day brought in a crowd of over 7,000. This was much better than many had feared when the largely new and unknown New Zealand side arrived in England. On this occasion (and it would be seen later in the tour) there was a danger of underestimating them.

Whatever the strength of the opposition, the feature of the Tourist matches is always the sense of the Arundel cricketing reunion. The match for many is the first cricket of quality they will see at the start of each new season. Duke Miles was one of the early arrivals and it was good to hear him enthuse about "this marvellous traditional fixture" and to share his appreciation, when joined by his son and his glamorous daughter-in-law, of the new working relationships entrusted to Lord Arundel, with the Foundation and the Club.

LAVINIA, DUCHESS OF NORFOLK'S XI v NEW ZEALAND
1ST MAY 1994

NEW ZEALAND

B. R. Hartland	c. Moores b. Law	46
B. A. Pocock	c. Moores b. Headley	0
M. J. Greatbatch	c. Ward b. Hughes	18
S. P. Fleming	not out	86
S. A. Thomson	lbw. Law	0
G. R. Larsen	ct. Speight b. Hughes	48
A. C. Parore	not out	10
M. N. Hart	did not bat	
D. J. Nash		
H. T. Davis		
C. Pringle		
	Extras	21
	Total (for 5 wkts.)	229

Bowling

	O	M	R	W
Headley	10	2	32	1
Law	10	1	43	2
Hughes	10	0	43	2
Fleming	10	0	64	0
Patel	10	1	42	0

LAVINIA, DUCHESS OF NORFOLK'S XI

T. R. Ward	c. Fleming b. Davies	29
P. W. G. Parker	c. Parore b. Pringle	46
M. P. Speight	b. Larsen	0
A. Wells	b. Nash	20
D. W. Randall	lbw. Larsen	0
M. V. Fleming	b. Larsen	0
P. Moores	c. Parore b. Larsen	3
D. R. C. Law	st. Parore b. Hart	14
M. M. Patel	st. Parore b. Hart	2
D. W. Headley	c. Larsen b. Pringle	11
S. P. Hughes	not out	0
	Extras	35
	Total	160

Bowling

	O	M	R	W
Pringle	7.5	0	26	2
Davis	7	0	42	1
Nash	8	0	29	1
Larsen	10	1	17	4
Hart	10	0	33	2

NEW ZEALAND WON BY 69 RUNS – 50 OVER MATCH

Later in the day there was the added pleasure of the company of the Arundel veterans Richard Burton, Geoff Wills and the recently retired Chairman Ronnie Ford.

Richard Burton was in a reminiscent mood and recalled a number of stories about Duke Bernard which appear elsewhere in the book. The conversation turned to who had made the earliest appearance for the Duke. Having the playing records to hand, it was possible to confirm that Richard's invitation to turn out for the Duke came a week after he had first appeared on the ground for the Martlets in 1956.

Geoff Wills recalled that he, too, had been spotted playing for the Martlets in the late fifties and had first turned out for the Duke in 1961. He went on to enthuse about the debut of his son Jonathan (who is on duty at the Match in his role as a Cricket Commentator for BBC Southern Counties Radio) in 1979 adding:

"I must say that I thought Jonathan had blotted his copy book some years earlier. I brought him with me to a number of the games in which I played when he was still quite small. In those days, Jonathan was a small blond-haired boy with an angelic face and an engaging smile which endeared him to Duchess Lavinia. On one occasion, he dropped a glass of lemonade but the glass did not break.

'Pick it up', said the Duchess. 'No', said Jonathan, 'You pick it up'. The scene was like something out of Alice in Wonderland with sharp intakes of breath and embarrassed coughs in a crowded pavilion. 'Do you know who I am', said the Duchess. 'Yes', said Jonathan, 'You are my friend'.

"This seemed to do him no harm and, as a matter of fact, it was then that I realised that the Duchess always respected people who stood up to her and could not bear too much obsequiousness."

At this point, Geoff Wills resumed his earlier recollections of matches in which he had played for Duke Bernard, and Ronnie Ford seized the opportunity of reminding us of his more recent experiences by saying, 'Let me know when you reach my period, will you?'.

While this conversation was in full swing, the New Zealanders were making good progress mainly through a graceful innings by Stephen Fleming. At the lunch interval, they proved to be as charming a side as any of their predecessors. The family atmosphere and sense of reunion was reinforced when talking to the New Zealand High Commissioner, John Collinge, of his days playing for Oxford thirty years earlier. The team coach, Geoff Howarth, also recalled his earlier cricketing days in England and, in particular, his ordeal by hail at Arundel when captaining the New Zealand side in 1983.

When it came to the Duchess' team effort to score 130 to win, the mainly Sussex and Kent side were given a good start by Trevor Ward of Kent and Paul Parker who had just given up first-class cricket to become a schoolmaster at Tonbridge. When they were separated, there was a big disappointment for the crowd as Martin Speight was out for a duck. The fair haired Sussex batsman is always regarded as one of Arundel's own. He played most of his first junior and serious cricket on the Castle ground and, with his skill both as a painter and a musician, has a large following in the crowd which looks forward to his dashing style of batting.

The crowd's disappointment was, if anything, just as great when Derek Randall also fell to Larsen without scoring. The former Nottinghamshire and England batsman returned to the Pavilion and sought out Johnny Barclay to say, as only he might, "I am so sorry to have let you down. I know the crowd were expecting something special from me". There was more disappointment especially for Sir Roger Gibbs when his nephew, the hard hitting Matthew Fleming of Kent, became Larsen's third duck. The New Zealand all-rounder would have been a strong contender for Man of the Match if such an award had been available as he followed his 48 runs with 4 for 17 from 10 overs to play the key role in the New Zealanders' victory.

Sunday 8 May,. Quidnuncs v Harlequins: Part of the fun of cricket at Arundel these days is the opportunity of getting the match booklet which Debbie Osborne and Suzanne Weaver produce before the start of play. This can sometimes be a challenge when some captains are rather uncertain who is playing for them and in what batting order. However, there is no such difficulty when Stephen Henderson for the Cambridge side (who is shown on the scorecard as Worcester and Glamorgan) and R.A.F Luddington, who appears for the Oxford side as both captain and wicket-keeper, give early information to the office. So, before play begins at 11.30, we learn that this is likely to be a typical declaration match with 20 overs bowled from 5.30 onwards. The umpires, we are told, will be R Crisford and J. Smith and the match is sponsored by the insurance brokers Green Denman. Turning over the page, we read, "The Quidnuncs were formed by a group of Cambridge undergraduates from Trinity College in 1851 and were originally conceived to provide Blues and near-Blues, after they had gone down, with continuity of association both on and off the cricket field".

"The Harlequins", we read, "a club of Oxford cricketers, was founded in 1852 at a dinner in the rooms of C. S. Currer, a Fellow of Merton College. The colours of Oxford blue, maroon and buff coincide with the name and, in the early matches, the players wore a complete uniform of these colours".

As the Harlequins took the field at Arundel wearing, in most cases, their famous caps, one's mind turns to the unlikely but fascinating effect there might have been on the crowd on the Hill at Sydney, for example, if the stubborn Jardine had decided to try the effect in those pre-pyjama days of wearing the full Harlequin uniform instead of simply the cap which enraged Australian crowds in the Twenties and Thirties. However, this particular Harlequin side showed themselves friendly enough in allowing quick scoring by the Quidnuncs mainly through their Captain, J. P. C. Mills of Northants and the ever-consistent Paul Parker. As a result, the Harlequins never quite managed to get into the match and despite good innings by Horne and Ellison they finished with the worse of the draw.

J.R.T.B.: "There is a marvellous atmosphere at these games as old competitors and friends meet year after year. We have certainly used them in expanding our list of match managers and it was through this game that we were able to arrange our first fixture against the current Cambridge side in 1993. In 1995 we will follow this with our first match against that year's Oxford side. Of course, it is easy for Hubert to say, 'Come on Johnny you run it'. I am happy to do so but, inevitably, I tend to rely on my regulars. On the other hand, if we get a different match manager, we will no doubt draw in some new faces and that is why it makes obvious good sense to work on one of the Harlequin side to help us get the Oxford game going next year".

Sunday 15 May. v Minor Counties. J.R.T.B.: "This was one of those matches in which I got myself into a bit of a state about whether we had produced a strong enough side. The Minor Counties is a strong combination and I said to Debbie Osborne, "We aren't good enough". For some reason, I thought we might be bowled out for a low score which would lead to a miserable day with an early finish. Of course, you can have a bad day but, for our type of cricket, it is essential to have a good contest. Well, what happened? John Rice was captaining our side and brought with him his former team mate Julian Wood who had just given up playing for Hampshire at the end of the previous season. There was great disappointment when he gave up County cricket and he produced a superb hard hitting century for us. He was well supported by Jonathan Hardy - another former Hampshire player-in a slightly slower 100 and our declaration was perhaps a little bit later than one might have wished. But we did magnificently and the Minor Counties lost wickets in the run chase so I laughed at myself afterwards for creating unnecessary alarm".

A conversation with David Armstrong, Secretary of the

LAVINIA, DUCHESS OF NORFOLK'S XI v MINOR COUNTIES
15TH MAY 1994

LAVINIA, DUCHESS OF NORFOLK'S XI

J. Hardy	not out	133
J. Rice	lbw. Graham	14
J. Wood	not out	103
R. D. V. Knight	did not bat	
G. V. Palmer		
J. While		
R. J. Parks		
J. R. T. Barclay		
D. Goldstraw		
D. Flint		
S. Malone		
	Extras	11
	Total (for 1 wkt. dec.)	261

Bowling

	O	M	R	W
Arnold	12	1	61	0
Graham	10.3	2	30	1
Thomas	6	1	33	0
Evans	9	0	36	0
Smith	10	1	62	0
Hignett	3	0	32	0

MINOR COUNTIES

S. J. Dean	c. Rice b. Flint	22
R. J. Evans	c. Flint b. Palmer	43
M. J. Roberts	c. Parks b. Palmer	17
I. Cockbain	c. Goldstraw b. Malone	32
R. G. Hignett	c. Palmer b. Barclay	25
M. I. Humphries	c. Flint b. Barclay	13
D. R. Thomas	c. Parks b. Barclay	10
R. A. Evans	not out	12
A. Smith	lbw. Flint	0
P. C. Graham	not out	0
K. A. Arnold	did not bat	
	Extras	15
	Total (for 8 wkts.)	189

Bowling

	O	M	R	W
Goldstraw	9	1	42	0
Malone	9	0	47	1
Flint	13	4	41	2
Palmer	9	1	37	2
Barclay	5	2	20	3

MATCH DRAWN

Minor Counties Cricket Association, gave some interesting insights into the composition of his team:

"This fixture started when Geoffrey Howard became our Treasurer after he had retired as the Surrey Secretary. As Johnny Barclay has implied, we have always been able to draw on a number of players with recent first-class experience. For example, in the side today, we have Russell Evans, who played for Nottinghamshire and Ian Cockbain, who turned out for Lancashire. But the real feature of our side is that they are all true amateurs. We have brought along representatives from seven English Minor Counties and one from Wales. They do not receive any match fees and you don't make much out of expenses at 18 pence a mile.

"We are lucky that some of our regulars have jobs which still allow them to play a fair amount of cricket. For example, Russell Evans of Lincolnshire works for Gunn and Moore; Malcolm Roberts of Buckinghamshire is a policeman; David Thomas from Norfolk has a family garage business and Peter Graham who has travelled the furthest distance today has a sports shop in Leeds. But they all love coming here and we never have any difficulty in raising a side."

Sunday 29 May v M.C.C. Young Cricketers: One of the attractions of this match was the representation on each side of the Arundel cricket scholars, Philip Hudson for the Duchess and Mark Newell for the M.C.C. Young Cricketers. Both had been sponsored to play cricket and to help with coaching at Arundel by the Worshipful Company of Pipemakers and Tobacco Blenders. One of their representatives, Nick Freeman, a leading importer of Havana cigars said before the start of play: "Like many Livery Companies we have bequests which allow us to make certain donations. Historically, most of our money has gone to Sevenoaks School but we had a little bit to spare and we were looking for a suitable charity. We invited applications and as a member of the Arundel Castle Cricket Club I put in one on its behalf. This received a prompt response in the shape of an offer to supply nets but the Club persuaded us to cover sponsorship of scholars a year or two ago. The idea was that we might help a good young cricketer who would go on to great things rather along the lines of the Australian Cricket Academy".

In this match the crowd had an early opportunity of seeing their 1994 scholar in action after the Duchess' captain Charles Rowe won the toss and decided to bat. Unfortunately, Philip Hudson was run out when going well and, despite his Captain's half century, a total of 181 for 6 declared seemed inadequate. However, the Captain in his all-rounder role, took off the very old sweater which gives him the look of the first-class amateur of earlier years and, for some time, kept the youngsters quiet by skilful off-spinners and by testing the batsman with the occasional quicker ball. He was well supported by Beagles with off-spinners of the slow medium variety in a manner not unlike that of Bob Appleyard. This attack, supported by keen fielding in which the Poulter broth-

LAVINIA, DUCHESS OF NORFOLK'S XI v M.C.C. YOUNG CRICKETERS
29TH MAY 1994

LAVINIA, DUCHESS OF NORFOLK'S XI

J. S. Kinner	lbw. b. Cole	8
P. Hudson	run out	9
T. Brennan	c. Lynch b. Pratt	16
G. Poulter	run out	1
C. Rowe	b. Pratt	58
N. Pagden	lbw. b. Segdbeer	24
A. Davies	not out	28
S. Poulter	not out	21
B. Head	did not bat	
G. Jonas		
C. Beagles		
	Extras	16
	Total (for 6 wkts. dec.)	181

Bowling

	O	M	R	W
Cole	7	1	14	1
Williamson	8	1	21	0
Pratt	15	4	34	2
Malao	26	9	63	0
Segdbeer	12	1	40	1

MCC YOUNG CRICKETERS

D. Wyrill	c. Poulter b. Beagles	44
K. Segdbeer	lbw. Jonas	19
S. Lynch	c. Poulter b. Beagles	32
K. Forbes	not out	45
D. Williamson	not out	29
M. Newell	did not bat	
N. Pratt		
S. Welch		
A. Pratt		
J. Malao		
A. Cole		
	Extras	13
	Total (for 3 wkts.)	182

Bowling

	O	M	R	W
Jonas	11	1	54	1
Poulter	5	1	21	0
Beagles	13	1	51	2
Rowe	7	0	26	0
Head	3.2	0	22	0

MCC YOUNG CRICKETERS WON BY 7 WICKETS

ers from Arundel were prominent, kept the M.C.C. Young Cricketers under control for sometime. Because of his regular previous appearances on the ground, the Arundel 1993 Cricket Scholar, Mark Newell, was held back in the batting order and he was not required when Wyrill and Lynch made steady progress. When they were dismissed and despite spitting rain, the big hitting of Forbes and Williamson took the young cricketers to a seven wickets victory.

J.R.T.B.: "This game was not just important because of the involvement of our young cricket scholars. It has become part of the regular connection with the M.C.C. and also an opportunity to do some recruiting. I was particularly taken with Jacob Malao playing for the M.C.C. as a quick bowler. He is a young black South African typical of the small quota of overseas players whom the M.C.C. involve in their squad every year. I thought I would like to get him lined up to play for us in one or two of the big games later in the year.

"I am a great supporter of the whole concept of the M.C.C. Young Cricketers. Mark Newell joined them when he finished his time as a scholar with us and he must be about twenty. The rest of the side would be about the same age and the great thing is that they have the benefit of a year-long contract. It means that while they are playing cricket they will be tested to the best of their ability and given winter employment. They live in a big hostel near Lords and they can be registered but not contracted to County cricket clubs. This allows them the odd opportunity to play for one of the Counties but they do not have to make the basic decision which is so difficult for many young cricketers as to whether or not to throw in their lot with a County which may or may not lead to a cap and reasonable long term employment".

Sunday 5 June v The Combined Services: The match booklet reminded us that the first Services team had appeared in the twenties when among their most memorable performances was a strong showing against both Warwick Armstrong's 1921 Australians and the 1924 South African side. The programme concluded, "It is a particular pleasure that the Combined Services are our guests the weekend of the D-Day commemorations and that the South African National Defence forces will be playing them in the United Kingdom in August".

J.R.T.B.: "This has become a very pleasant fixture because our match manager and captain Edward Gordon-Lennox really makes it work. He is one of the Richmond relations who is a very good player. He was at Harrow and later a Captain in the Army who played for the Combined Services. When he left the military, he took on this match for us and he has a real feel for the place and a sense of the occasion.

"Our early batsmen did a pretty useful job and I had plenty of time to wait before I went into bat. As a result I

Guardians of the future – The Friends of Arundel Castle C.C. Committee, 1994
Back row (L to R): Alan Wadey, Ron Gray, Wing Cmmdr. Ronald Ellen OBE, Lt. Col. David Lloyd, Tim Coghlan, John Poland,
Lt. Col. John Stephenson CBE, Major Noel Ormorod, Bill Rice, Bernard Denyer.
Front row (L to R): John Barclay, The Earl of Arundel, Sir Colin Cowdrey CBE, Hubert Doggart OBE, Sir Roger Gibbs,
Richard Burton, John Knight, Peter Robson.

had one of those marvellous experiences which you have in cricket at Arundel which brings together so many old friends. I found myself sitting next to Indy Coomeraswamy. He comes from Sri Lanka and actually works as a senior figure in their High Commission in London. I first met him when he was captain of the Harrow team which we played against in my very first match at Lord's for Eton in 1958. He was a slow left arm spinner and amused me when he told me that he had then been at his peak and it had been 'downhill all the way ever since'. Certainly, I can well remember being bowled by his second ball at Lord's and I hadn't seen him since. We talked for a very long time and it was splendid to find someone like that whose love for cricket has been fostered so much in this country. He told me of his enjoyment of life in London, of his house near Lords and taking his boys to see the cricket there.

"I also had the pleasure of bowling in tandem with him against the Combined Services but we were unable to make any impression on their captain, Richard Greatorex, who scored a splendid century which suggested that he could walk into any Minor Counties side. Overall, I believe that the Services' cricketers have a wonderful time playing high standard cricket without the pressure of the first-class game".

Thursday 9 June v Cambridge University. J.R.T.B.: "I played quite a lot this year, and, despite what I indicated earlier about spreading the load, I often found myself undertaking the manager's job as well as captaining the side. That was my dual role in this match which didn't have anything quite as dramatic as John Crawley's 100 in the previous year when we could all see why he was an England hopeful. But we did produce a very exciting match with a dynamic century for us by Chris Bullen (which showed why, until recently, he had been seen as one of Surrey's specialist one-day players) and an equally enterprising century by Ratledge for them. However, what was especially satisfying for me was to find my young M.C.C. cricket discovery Jacob Malao doing an excellent job for us. He did most of the bowling and kept things tight when we needed to check their run-making challenge and he got rid of Ratledge just when it looked as if he might be set to get the winning runs."

Sunday 3 July v M.C.C.: One of the benefits of the family and cricketing connections in the Arundel Castle Cricket Club was evident when Adrian Ford arranged for the B. R. L. Hardy Wine Company of Australia to sponsor this match. Not surprisingly, liquid refreshment was plentiful and the Arundel taxis did record business later in the day.

There was an intriguing preamble to the game when Andy Lloyd, formerly of Warwickshire and England, and captain of the M.C.C. side went out to inspect the wicket with our newly installed committee member, Colonel John Stephenson, who had volunteered to oversee this particular match. After doing so, the visiting captain was heard to remark, "We have several spinners in our side, I think we might well put them in to bat if I win the toss". When it was pointed out that this would go against the Duke's traditional preference to bat last. he quickly agreed that he would be willing to meet such local customs. However, the matter was taken out of his hands when Peter Mills the home team's captain won the toss and elected to bat.

An amiable and relaxed cricketer, Peter Mills will go through life known as the captain of the Cambridge side who took over the team when Derek Pringle preferred to play for England rather than in the University match. On this occasion, Mills illustrated the effectiveness of the Barclay strategy in his role as a new match manager. Apart from Andrew Davis, a fellow Cambridge Blue and David Holliday, almost all the home team were making their debut at Arundel. Two of them, Simon Lynch of New Zealand and C. Rika, did so to such good effect that they put on 179 and Lynch's eventual 154 not out represented the second highest score ever made for the Duchess.

The M.C.C. responded with equal vigour when Goldsmith and Greenfield put on 100 for the first wicket in 22 overs. With Greenfield going on to his century and with support down the batting order the match built up to a classic Arundel finish with only 2 runs dividing the sides in a drawn match.

While all this was going on, there was an opportunity to talk to the M.C.C.'s twelfth man. The name Knott prompted an obvious question and it was confirmed that he was indeed the son of the England wicket-keeper. "It seems to be my lot to be on the edge of things", he said, going on to explain that he was playing regularly for Kent's second team where, mainly batting in the middle order, he found that there was only time to make a quick 30 or so. This, notwithstanding, he showed all his father's sparkle and a willingness to help with the drinks which on this occasion, were available to the teams in almost embarrassing quantities.

Wednesday 6 July, v I Zingari Australia and Wednesday 20 July v the Grasshoppers of South Africa; J.R.T.B.:

"I particularly enjoyed these mid-week games against overseas Club sides. The Australian IZ. match was especially

SUSSEX v MIDDLESEX (COUNTY CHAMPIONSHIP)
14TH, 15TH AND 16TH JULY 1994

SUSSEX — 1st Innings

N. J. Lenham	c. Tufnell b. Emburey	45
C. W. J. Athey	c. Johnson b. Tufnell	70
J. W. Hall	c. Gatting b. Fraser	18
A. P. Wells	c. Roseberry b. Tufnell	7
M. P. Speight	c. Feltham b. Johnson	30
P. Moores	c. Ramprakash b. Fraser	16
F. D. Stephenson	c. Haynes b. Johnson	13
I. D. K. Salisbury	c. Brown b. Johnson	1
E. E. Hemmings	c. Carr b. Emburey	2
J. Lewry	not out	4
E. S. H. Giddins	c. Brown b. Johnson	5
	Extras	17
	Total (for 94 overs)	228

Bowling

	O	M	R	W
Fraser	17	4	39	2
Johnson	15	1	40	4
Feltham	6	0	28	0
Tufnell	33	7	78	2
Emburey	23	9	32	2

SUSSEX — 2nd Innings

N. J. Lenham	b. Emburey	26
C. W. J. Athey	lbw. b. Fraser	0
J. W. Hall	c. Carr b. Feltham	45
A. P. Wells	c. Gatting b. Fraser	17
M. P. Speight	c. Gatting b. Fraser	97
P. Moores	b. Emburey	7
F. D. Stephenson	c. Brown b. Tufnell	28
E. E. Hemmings	c. Roseberry b. Tufnell	2
I. D. K. Salisbury	c. Emburey b. Tufnell	0
J. Lewry	c. Carr b. Tufnell	4
E. S. H. Giddins	not out	0
	Extras	12
	Total	238

Bowling

	O	M	R	W
Fraser	23.1	4	78	3
Johnson	10	5	16	0
Feltham	13	3	28	1
Emburey	16	1	43	2
Tufnell	24	5	61	4

MIDDLESEX — 1st Innings

D. L. Haynes	run out	13
M. A. Roseberry	lbw. b. Stephenson	0
M. W. Gatting	c. Moores b. Lewry	0
M. R. Ramprakash	c. Moores b. Stephenson	8
J. D. Carr	lbw. b. Lewry	1
K. R. Brown	lbw. b. Lewry	15
M. A. Feltham	b. Stephenson	2
R. L. Johnson	b. Lewry	3
J. E. Emburey	b. Stephenson	22
A. R. C. Fraser	c. Athey b. Stephenson	16
P. C. R. Tufnell	not out	0
	Extras	7
	Total (46.1 overs)	87

Bowling

	O	M	R	W
Stephenson	16.1	4	25	5
Lewry	21	7	40	4
Giddins	7	4	12	0
Salisbury	2	0	4	0

MIDDLESEX — 2nd Innings

D. L. Haynes	lbw. b. Stephenson	2
M. A. Roseberry	c. Moores b. Salisbury	76
M. W. Gatting	c. Moores b. Stephenson	3
M. R. Ramprakash	c. Athey b. Hemmings	37
J. D. Carr	c. Moores b. Salisbury	9
K. R. Brown	not out	45
M. A. Feltham	c. Hall b. Salisbury	25
J. E. Emburey	c. Athey b. Hemmings	1
R. L. Johnson	b. Salisbury	20
A. R. C. Fraser	b. Salisbury	8
P. C. R. Tufnell	c. Athey b. Salisbury	4
	Extras	1
	Total	231

Bowling

	O	M	R	W
Stephenson	8	1	23	2
Lewry	5	0	19	0
Giddins	14	3	34	0
Hemmings	29	7	99	2
Salisbury	17.5	2	55	6

SUSSEX WON BY 148 RUNS

pleasant. It was six years since their last visit and they were a splendid bunch. Then, for us, Philip Hudson, our 1994 cricket scholar, got his first century and J. Chaplin, making his debut as our first change bowler, performed superbly to take 6 for 60 which meant we had the better of a drawn match.

"The match against the South Africans two weeks later was an even rarer event as the political situation had ruled out a return visit for 16 years. It was also said that the Grasshoppers match in 1978 was one in which the atmosphere had been somewhat less than friendly when we actually heard 'sledging' for the first time on this ground. Well, all I can say is that this game could not have been more pleasant and it was a real run-getting feast. They had three big scores, including Mitchell's 122 not out, and 289 to win would mean equalling our second highest ever score on the ground. But 1994 seemed to be the year of success for those making their debut for the Duchess and P Wellings got 139

SUSSEX V MIDDLESEX (AXA EQUITY AND LAW LEAGUE)
17TH JULY 1994

SUSSEX

J. W. Hall	c. Weekes b. Johnson	14
M. P. Speight	b. Fraser	18
F. D. Stephenson	c. Feltham b. Weekes	36
A. P. Wells	st. Brown b Weekes	103
C. W. J. Athey	b. Tufnell	4
K Greenfield	not out	42
P. Moores	not out	1
I. D. K. Salisbury	did not bat	
C. C. Remy		
J. Lewry		
E. S. H. Giddins		
	Extras	7
	Total (for 5 wkts, 40 overs)	225

Bowling

	O	M	R	W
Fraser	8	1	36	1
Johnson	8	0	36	1
Feltham	8	0	62	0
Tufnell	8	0	30	1
Weekes	8	0	57	2

MIDDLESEX

D. L. Haynes	c. and b. Salisbury	42
J. C. Pooley	lbw. b. Stephenson	0
M. R. Ramprakash	b. Athey	33
M. W. Gatting	run out	29
K. R. Brown	c. Hall b. Lewry	28
J. D. Carr	c. Wells b. Lewry	18
P. N. Weekes	b. Stephenson	22
M. A. Feltham	b. Stephenson	9
R. L. Johnson	not out	14
A. R. C. Fraser	b. Stephenson	0
P. C. R. Tufnell	b. Giddins	1
	Extras	11
	Total (39.5 overs)	207

Bowling

	O	M	R	W
Stephenson	8	0	24	4
Giddins	7.5	0	41	1
Remy	6	0	43	0
Lewry	7	0	43	2
Salisbury	8	0	38	1
Athey	3	0	12	1

SUSSEX WON BY 18 RUNS

not out for us as we came within 2 runs of victory.

"Apart from welcoming the new faces, it was especially pleasant to find touring matches also brought back old friends. Before the start of the match against the Grasshoppers, I thought I saw someone I recognised and sure enough it was Willie Strydom. We had played a lot of cricket together for Orange Free State where he was an excellent bowler. We hadn't met since 1978 and it was fun to find myself bowling in partnership with him once again".

Thursday 14 July to Sunday 17 July, Sussex v Middlesex: the County's appearance at Arundel is now well established and has begun to feature in the record books. For example, in the 1993 match against Hampshire, Malcolm Marshall took his 1500th wicket in first-class cricket. 1994 brought an unusual and highly satisfactory double for Sussex over the 1993 County Champions with victory in both the Sunday League and Championship matches.

Support for these matches is growing steadily from year to year and it was good to see some of the old Sussex cricketers here to cheer on their successors. For Les Lenham, this was a highly personal business as he and his wife had come to watch their son Neil playing for the County. He had first come to Arundel as a very young schoolboy and there was an obvious touch of pride in his father's voice when he described his pleasure in following the Sussex County family tradition evidenced in the Parks, Langridge, Cox and Griffith families. He also recalled with a grin the day when, as the National Cricket Coach, he was able to round up so many old Sussex players to represent the Taverners when Billy Griffith had been worried about "whether we would play serious cricket or not".

Sitting next to the Lenhams was 'Tiger' Pataudi. The Nawab said how sad he was that he never had the opportunity to play at Arundel when he was captain of Sussex. "Now", he added "when they asked me if I would come down and play a match this year against I Zingari, I had to say that I can't see and I can't run".

Of the current generation of Sussex players taking part in the match, one of the most engaging is Martin Speight. After a brilliant innings in which he narrowly missed his century and was last man out, he took time during the tea interval to sit and reminisce with some of his predecessors. A true man of Sussex - from Henfield - he recalled how much Arundel meant to him in his early cricketing days.

"I played quite a lot for Sussex Juniors and I remember how keen our cricket was when playing Kent Juniors. I got my first century on the ground here playing for the Martlets against the Duchess' team and my first big time appearance was against the Australians in 1989 when I was at Durham University and I had to drive all the way down for the day".

Later that afternoon, there was time for an enjoyable stop at the Martlets' tent. This venue is one which has a lot of support as a convenient annual meeting place. My hosts were John Newton and Sandy Ross. John had earlier run the match for the Martlets against the Yorkshire Gentlemen at Arundel and had increasingly assumed the role of both keeper of records as well as master of ceremonies at the Club's annual dinner. Sandy Ross was a late cricket developer at Haileybury where he was coached by the former Sussex player Bert Wensley. Now, as a regular performer and captain for the Duchess, he has strong views:

"There is no doubt about it, some captains of what we think of as traditional sporting club sides play in a much more defensive mode these days. Not so long ago, I was captain of the Duchess' team against a side which shall be nameless. Their captain had just hit our slow bowler for a six and two fours when he appealed against the light. Avoiding the obvious remarks about what Duke Bernard would have said, I put it to him bluntly that we were all guests of the Duchess and that everyone would expect us to provide a finish. Well we did, but there wasn't much co-operation coming from the other side.

"I couldn't help thinking of some of the characters I had played with in earlier days to whom results were secondary to a day's cricketing enjoyment. I think particularly of people like A. A. H. White who came from Bracklesham Bay. He was one of the best of those cricketers who play in a totally carefree manner and he had a natural Ted Dexter kind of approach. But he had lots of other interests and we saw all too little of him.

"Then there was somehow always time for a laugh. I can recall Nicco Collin splitting his trousers and carrying on by wearing Cosmo Crawley's cardigan. He put his legs into the arms of the sweater and I imagine that it finished up several sizes too big for Cosmo".

Having talked to several of the senior Martlets, it was refreshing to find in a later conversation that, at the other end of the scale, the tradition of the junior Martlets was maintained by people like Derek Semmence's son, Mark. A student at Durham University, he has much of the look of his father including a similar bowling action when delivering medium-paced in-swingers. His father is still, in his 57th year, playing regularly and, on several occasions, has had the opportunity of taking part in partnerships with his 21 year old son. As Mark said: "I have been coming to this ground as long as I can remember. Indeed, when I was still very young, I would always make sure that I had my cricket gear in the back of the family car. I always hoped that my father's team would be one short and sure enough this happened to me when I was about thirteen, so I found myself playing in a

match against the Arundel Cricket Club. I went into bat at number 10 when I finished with all of 2 not out".

"Somehow I always seem to be lucky here and it was certainly where I made my first appearance of any importance. It is great that I can play with my father and he seems to go on just the same as ever".

J.R.T.B.: I am really delighted that my fellow Martlets seem to be so happy at Arundel and, so far as the wider public is concerned, we have established a firm place on the County cricket circuit. In this match, Middlesex were shot out for a low score and the championship match finished a day early but Mike Gatting made no complaint about the wicket. He just said, in that typical bustling way of his, 'Come on lads, lets get on out there and get after them'. Happily we kept up the pressure and I was delighted to see Franklyn Stephenson bowling with such hostility so long after his first appearance at Arundel with the West Indian Youth Clubs side in 1970. It was good, too, to see a new Sussex medium-paced bowler in Lewry going well. He made his debut here last year playing for the Martlets. And then there was Ian Salisbury's six for 55 in the Championship game which did his Test prospects no harm at all. Last but by no means least it was nice to see the Sussex Captain - in a rather lean season - playing his part, and his century in the one day game was one of his best.

"So far as the future is concerned, with the good crowds and sponsorship in our marquees, it seems that Sussex want to build on the present arrangements. One hopes we can continue to work with them in developing something approaching the Canterbury week here at Arundel".

Sunday 24 July v I Zingari: The score sheet told us that "IZ. was founded in 1845 when W. P. Bolland, who is still, although he has been dead for 100 years, Perpetual President, took a side to play Harrow. It was decided to form a Club which, unlike others at that time, had been wholly amateur. It is by some years the oldest of the many wandering Clubs. One of the original rules, which remains unaltered, reads: 'That the entrance be nothing and that the Annual Subscription do not exceed the entrance' ".

We were further advised that I Zingari is Italian for "the Wanderers" and the Club colours of black, red and gold symbolise an ascent "out of darkness, through the fire, into light".

Simon Doggart continues in his regular role as Captain for the IZ. at Arundel but the match managership and captaincy of the home side has passed from Nigel Draffan to J. F.

LAVINIA, DUCHESS OF NORFOLK'S XI v I ZINGARI
24TH JULY 1994

LAVINIA, DUCHESS OF NORFOLK'S XI

A. J. L. Barr	c. Bruce b. Gubbins	23
A. W. Sexton	c. Durserly b. Gubbins	20
D. Carroll	c. Gubbins b. Lloyd-Jones	99
J. S. Waters	b. Bruce	35
J. C. S. Ball	b. Dean	12
P. J. Istead	not out	21
W. Raja	not out	8
D. J. Anderson	did not bat	
M. Woolridge		
B. A. W. Bellamy		
C. A. Stevens		
	Extras	23
	Total (for 5 wkts. dec.)	241

Bowling

	O	M	R	W
Gubbins	11	1	51	2
Bruce	13	0	60	1
Dean	13	0	63	1
Doggart	12	2	47	0
Lloyd-Jones	3	0	11	1

I ZINGARI

W. Holland	lbw. b. Stevens	12
R. C. W. Mason	b. Anderson	36
R. C. Doggart	c. Carroll b. Bellamy	18
J. Lloyd-Jones	b. Barr	63
H. Durserly	b. Barr	10
W. Featherston	b. Barr	11
C. Anderson	b. Raja	18
R. Gubbins	not out	10
S.J. G. Doggart	not out	8
R. Bruce	did not bat	
G. Dean		
	Extras	14
	Total (for 7 wkts.)	200

Bowling

	O	M	R	W
Stevens	6	2	27	1
Bellamy	6	3	20	1
Raja	14	3	53	1
Anderson	11	5	22	1
Barr	8	1	29	3
Carroll	4	0	38	0

MATCH DRAWN

Walters.

J.R.T.B.: "The match against IZ. was always one of Duke Bernard's favourites because he was one of their members for so many years. They are always a hard side to beat and the Duchess's team has only had two victories against them in almost 20 years. We were in with a chance this year when D. Carroll from the University of New South Wales who is a nephew of Doctor Peter Carroll who played for us in earlier years came within one run of his century. Jeremy Lloyd-Jones after failing to trouble the scorers when playing for the Duchess in two previous appearances at Arundel this time got runs for IZ. But the feature of the game for me was to see Wasim Raja of Pakistan playing for the Duchess. He played a lot of cricket at Arundel after he finished his Test career but he had a bad car accident and it was good to see him back in action. He is still a very useful middle order left-hand batsman and leg-break bowler but somehow, perhaps unfairly, he always makes me think of Tony Greig. On the one occasion I saw Wasim playing in a Test Match at Lords for Pakistan, he whacked Underwood straight down the ground and Tony Greig took off right in front of the sight screen at the Nursery End to take a catch about 10ft in the air which only someone of his height could achieve.

"Nowadays Wasim plays Club cricket as a veteran, and he didn't attempt anything too ambitious at Arundel but he certainly remembered the great catch when I mentioned it."

Another close observer of the match was Colonel Malcolm Havergill who had recently succeeded Sir William Beecher as the IZ. Secretary. He gave a thumbnail sketch of his team:

"Bill Holland is captain of the Old Wykhemist side in the Cricketers' Cup. He is one of our most prolific scorers and it is unusual, as on this occasion, to see him get out early on. R. C. W. Mason who got his head down for us is one of our more distinguished performers as an ex-Hampshire player. Dickie Doggart is one of Hubert's nephews and Jeremy Lloyd-Jones who used to be one of our quicker bowlers now concentrates on his batting and is one of the most faithful supporters of IZ. Our regular captain, Hubert's son Simon Doggart, has taken advantage of his role as a master at Eton to co-opt two of the current college eleven in Harry Durserley and Bob Bruce. Bruce has shown himself to be quite a quick bowler and he still has two years to go at Eton. Charlie Anderson is one of the regular IZ. wicket-keepers and Richard Gubbins will always be remembered as the man who took all ten for us on this ground. He is another faithful performer for IZ. and serves on our committee while Geoffrey Dean can only play for us occasionally these days because of his writing for the *Daily Telegraph*".

Sunday 7 August v Uganda: The visit by the first ever touring side from Uganda was a tribute to the organisational skills and perseverance of Michael Wingfield-Digby. An active Martlet and occasional player for the Duchess' side, he had made many friends while on cricketing tours of Africa. Impressed by Uganda's cricketing potential, he succeeded in raising funds from private backers and sponsorship for this particular game through the financial advisers, Neilson Cobbold. His efforts had been rewarded when Uganda came to Arundel after an undefeated tour with victories over a number of strong sides including the Combined Services.

After the openers had got the Duchess's side off to a good start, there was considerable interest in the form of Mark Semmence playing in only his second match for the Duchess. Remembering the many appearances at Arundel of his father and of his own previous success in playing for the Martlets on this ground, his innings was watched with more than usual expectation. However, the great uncertainty of cricket was evident once again when he was out first ball to the Uganda Captain Walusimbi, who proceeded to exert such a tight grip on the game that he finished with bowling figures of 17-9-23-3.

Johnny Barclay, in turn, kept the match nicely poised as Uganda went for the runs and wickets fell on a regular basis. As the evening shadows lengthened, so his enthusiasm sustained his side and gave the match a sense of real purpose. When, despite a few late alarms, Uganda won the match off the last ball of the game to complete an undefeated tour, it was clear that he enjoyed the outcome almost as much as the visiting side. Afterwards, the visitors who had impressed everyone with their neat turnout in blazers and flannels and their obvious enthusiasm, stayed on for a barbecue which turned into one of the season's liveliest parties.

Sunday 14 August v Arundel Cricket club. The home team for this local Derby was organised by Mark Lawrence another of the Oxford Blues recruited by Johnny Barclay through the Quidnunc/Harlequin gatherings. His side looked in trouble early on but Charlie Hartridge, the Secretary of the Martlets who is a remarkably consistent left-hand batsman these days, played a sheet anchor role in scoring his century to which C. Sweet added another hundred at better than a run a minute. The local rivals were never quite in with a chance of victory and eventually, had to hang on for a draw. This was made possible by a typically gritty and yet attacking innings from Bob Dillon their young Australian Club cricketer. Wearing the traditional Australian floppy hat, he did his team proud in what was thought to be his last appearance for his Club.

Tuesday 16 August v Scotland: Given the increasing activity of Scotland in representative cricket (including the Benson and Hedges Cup and the Nat. West Trophy), and recognising its position as an Associate Member of the

LAVINIA, DUCHESS OF NORFOLK'S XI v ARUNDEL C.C.
14TH AUGUST 1994

LAVINIA, DUCHESS OF NORFOLK'S XI

C. Gates	ct. Dillon b. Mustard	7
I. Gray	b. Mustard	29
J. Appleton	ct. Bishop b. Rhoades	13
C. Hartridge	not out	101
P. Baldwin	ct. Bishop b. Mullen	4
C. Sweet	not out	100
C. Long	did not bat	
E. Gray	did not bat	
S. Dunkley	did not bat	
J. A. Ross	did not bat	
M. P. Lawrence	did not bat	
	Extras	12
	Total (for 4 wkts. dec.)	266

Bowling

	O	M	R	W
Mustard	15.3	1	53	2
Rhoades	9	3	34	1
Mullen	7	2	27	1
Thomas	7	1	40	0
Piggott	7	1	32	0
Chitty	10	1	71	0

ARUNDEL C.C.

A. Wadey	ct. Gates b. Sweet	33
A. Mullen	ct. Gray b. Dunkley	12
R. Dillon	b. Long	104
S. Rowlandson	lbw. b. Long	4
M. Springer	b. Long	1
M. Bishop	b. Lawrence	3
N. Chitty	ct. Hartridge b. Long	20
A. Thomas	ct. Gray b. Gates	1
J. Rhoades	not out	14
N. Mustard	not out	2
I. Piggott	did not bat	
	Extras	22
	Total (for 8 wkts.)	216

Bowling

	O	M	R	W
Ross	13	4	21	0
Gates	9	1	37	1
Sweet	7	1	43	1
Dunkley	12	6	19	1
Long	18	3	55	4
Lawrence	4	0	28	1

MATCH DRAWN

International Cricket Council this year, the Club put out one of its strongest sides of mainly County cricketers including six Surrey players. Of these, it was Adam Holloake who took the eye. Described by Hubert Doggart as "Surrey's most promising young attacking batsman" he fully lived up to his billing in scoring a century in 74 minutes and followed this by taking 4 for 47 so leaving Scotland with little option but to play for a draw.

Sunday 21 August v Sussex Martlets. This match provided a good opportunity to share recollections with **Neil** Trestrail who, with an average of over 65, has been one of the Duchess's most consistent batsmen over the last fifteen years. Born in Kenya, he is one of several Arundel cricketers, like the Rudd brothers and Dudley Owen-Thomas, with roots both in Africa and in the Home Counties. When his family returned to live in Sussex, he played for Horsham and Sussex 2nd XI before moving to Hampshire and becoming captain of the Lymington Cricket Club during the last six years.

At Felstead he had opened the bowling with Derek Pringle and, as he said, "He was quite fast and I was medium. He frightened them and I got wickets at the other end. We got 109 wickets between us in one School season which is still a record. I still bowl medium-slow but the arm is getting rather low."

Having played a good deal of cricket both for the Duchess and the Martlets, he was able to give a full picture of his own involvement in these matches:

"One of the reasons why I was asked to be captain and match manager for the Duchess in these games was because I could draw on a slightly different group coming from Hampshire. I always try to invite three or four who have never played at Arundel before and, on this occasion, I got hold of three South Africans who are numbers one, two and three in the batting order. Most of the rest of the side are drawn from my friends in the Hampshire cricketing club world.

"Running down the order, James Lowe is from Cape Town and his partner Matt Brink is a wicket-keeper batsman who played for the South African Under 19 side. He provided the solid base after we lost a couple of early wickets one of whom was Grant Van Heerden who is a very hard hitting batsman from Border where he has appeared in the Province's Under 25 side. The Martlets were perhaps rather lucky to get him out early on. Paul Gover who got top score for us plays for Havant and has turned out for the Hampshire 2nd XI. Our other half-century came from Paul Hillier who is Captain of the Chichester side. Then we had two Hampshire imports as Colin Coxon comes from Essex but plays for New Forest and Tony Oxley is a Welshman who plays with me for Lymington. Looking down the rest of the list, Eddie Cutler has just finished school at Canford and is playing for us as our off-spinner. That leaves our two opening bowlers, Neil Taylor, who was spotted by Mike Gatting

LAVINIA, DUCHESS OF NORFOLK'S XI v SUSSEX MARTLETS
21ST AUGUST 1994

LAVINIA, DUCHESS OF NORFOLK'S XI

J. Lowe	c Davy b. Spink	9
M. Brink	c. Hartridge b. Spink	56
G. Van Heerden	c. Stevens b. Spink	9
P. Gover	lbw. b. Newton	68
P. Hillier	not out	57
C. Coxon	b. Semmence	5
A. Oxley	not out	7
N. J. L. Trestrail	did not bat	
T. Cutler		
N. Taylor		
J. Whiting		
	Extras	25
	Total	236

Bowling

	O	M	R	W
Spink	13	0	52	3
Ross	11	1	34	0
Semmence	13	0	6	1
Newton	10	0	60	1
Gutteridge	5	1	11	0

SUSSEX MARTLETS

P. Davy	c. Brink b. Whiting	0
D. Gutteridge	b. Taylor	1
C. Hartridge	run out	63
M. Semmence	b. Taylor	55
R. Gutteridge	c. Hillier b. Whiting	43
P. Stevens	c. Taylor b. Whiting	32
R. Seager	b. Whiting	2
J. Carr	c. Brink b. Whiting	7
R. Spink	not out	5
B. Newton	c. Whiting b. Coxon	10
S. Ross	run out	0
	Extras	15
	Total	218

Bowling

	O	M	R	W
Whiting	10.4	2	28	5
Taylor	10	2	36	2
Cutler	8	1	32	0
Trestrail	5	0	42	0
Van Heerden	8	1	44	0
Coxon	6	0	36	1

LAVINIA, DUCHESS OF NORFOLK'S XI WON BY 3 RUNS

playing for Minor Counties and had a season with Middlesex, and John Whiting who opens the bowling with him for New Milton in the Hampshire Cricket League.

"As a matter of fact, I also probably know most of the Martlets as well as anyone having played for and against them so many times. Looking at their batting order, I see several old friends. Philip Davy is like me of Kenyan origin. Then there is the smiling, fair-haired, fresh-faced Mark

Semmence. He bowls in-swingers like his father. Charlie Hartridge, the Martlets' secretary was originally a bowler who batted but now takes his batting seriously. Ben Newton is another of those carrying on the Martlet tradition as the Club record keeper's son. He is a useful spin bowler and I like the way he opened his account with a six today. I was greatly relieved when he was out and that we then ran out Sandy Ross to win the match. Sandy is still a very fine bowler even if he does look a bit more prosperous since the days when he opened the bowling for Horsham.

"As for the match, with a three run victory, this was certainly one of the most exciting games I've played in at Arundel. We had two crucial run outs but it was really our opening attack of Neil Taylor and John Whiting who did the trick for us."

Sunday 28 August v The Lord's Taverners: Despite the all-star cast, this year's Taverners match had about it some of the informality of earlier years. This happened because the main sponsor withdrew, and thanks to the Taverners' amiable Director, Patrick Shervington, it was agreed that the

Sir David Frost batting for The Lord's Taverners against Lavinia, Duchess of Norfolk's XI, 1994.

game would go ahead as a special 35 over fixture in the run-up to the Arundel Centenary.

The Taverners were led by John Edrich who, despite his 57 years, looked and batted much the same as in his prime. He opened the batting with the former Middlesex and Northamptonshire cricketer Tim Lamb, who, as the current T.C.C.B. Cricket Secretary, has done so much to sustain the Tourists' fixtures at Arundel. The rest of the side was made up of the usual collection of veteran cricketers and media and entertainment performers. Of the latter, Tom Adams, who had played in some of the early games in the series at Arundel with his then TV credit 'Enigma Files' against his name, now spoke of the joys of returning to this match:

"I gave up playing about four years ago to concentrate on golf but I suddenly realised that you have a long time out of active sport. So I started playing 3rd XI games and enjoyed it so much that here I am back with my old chums. It has made me wonder whether some of the modern top players who retire so early won't miss it. I bet if you talk to them in fifteen years you will find them full of regret and I've decided to go on until I drop".

The Taverners' former President, Sir David Frost, took up the same theme:

"Apart from Edrich and Lamb we have got Mike Denness, John Snow and John Lever in our side and I have often asked these old professionals what brings them back to play in these games. It can't always be much fun for the bowlers in particular to keep feeding sometimes modest opposition. But you know, they always give the same reply - that they clearly enjoy the atmosphere. In our own way we have really recreated a mix of the gentlemen and players, the amateurs and professionals, all pulling together for a good cause".

His fellow former President of the Taveners, Tim Rice, who was playing this year for the Duchess, summed up some of the traditional rivalries:

"For me it is always great fun to have a bowl at David Frost. I can remember bowling him out on this ground about 10 years ago but he has got a lot of runs against me since. Today I thought I bowled a tolerably good over to him and in fact it was one of those rare events for me - a maiden over. Then, when I was all set to have another go at him, Will Carling bowls him with a full toss and so the great battle will have to wait for another year".

The Taverners 35 overs produced 165 for 9 thanks to support for Edrich by the actor Tim Marriott. During his innings the author, who had been asked by the Taverners'

Sir Tim Rice, for the Duchess' XI, bowls to Robert Powell of the Lord's Taverners watched by his captain, Will Carling, at mid-off. (Photo: K. R. Charlton)

Director to resume his old ground match commentating habits, was told to make an announcement which would persuade the batsman - who was proceeding rather slowly for a limited overs match - to throw his wicket away. However, Tim Marriott ignored the more subtle invitations to retire and it took a false message that his agent was on the telephone anxious to discuss a new contract to ensure his dismissal.

Between the innings, there was an opportunity to chat with Richard Stilgoe who had taken his wicket. He and his attractive wife proved themselves as experts in assessing Arundel ground match commentators. Frazer Hines was voted the best comic and there was general agreement that Rory Bremner took the prize for the best impression when using his Geoffrey Boycott voice to urge caution on a Taverners' batsman who had just hit a six ("There's no need for that. You get your ones and your twos and before you know where you are, you are not out twelve and you have got a draw".)

There was no such defensive approach in the mind of the Duchess' captain, Will Carling. The England Rugger captain had brought one of his fellow Internationals, Bud Rogers with him and both bowled with some success. Despite his disavowal of cricketing ability, the captain proceeded to score runs quickly - including a six - in a brisk partnership with the former Lancashire one day specialist and captain, David Hughes. The latter went on to make top score in the match and, together with his Middlesex namesake Simon Hughes, ensured victory for the Duchess' team off the last ball of the match.

LAVINIA, DUCHESS OF NORFOLK'S SPORTSMEN XII v THE LORD'S TAVERNERS XII
28TH AUGUST 1994

THE LORD'S TAVERNERS XII

J. Edrich	c. Campbell b. Hughes	49
T. Lamb	b. Wingfield Digby	2
A. Mills	b. Hughes	1
Sir D. Frost	b. Carling	12
T. Marriott	b. Stilgoe	38
R. Powell	b. Carling	9
J. Wilson	run out	13
M. Denness	c. Rogers b. Stilgoe	17
N. Cleobury	b. Rogers	0
J. Snow	not out	0
T. Adams	not out	1
J. Lever	did not bat	
	Extras	23
	Total (for 9 wkts. dec.)	165

Bowling

	O	M	R	W
Hughes	5	0	18	1
Wingfield Digby	5	0	27	1
Campbell	5	1	22	0
Hughes	3	1	7	1
Rice	5	1	24	0
Carling	6	0	20	2
Stilgoe	4	0	26	2
Rogers	2	0	10	1

LAVINIA, DUCHESS OF NORFOLK'S SPORTSMEN XII

G. Johnson	b. Lever	11
J. Gifford	b. Snow	6
J. Barclay	c. Lamb b. Powell	21
G. Campbell	b. Wilson	27
W. Carling	c. Edrich b. Cleobury	17
D. Hughes	st. Frost b. Mills	51
B. Rogers	c. Snow b. Mills	1
T. Rice	c. Cleobury b. Mills	0
R. Stilgoe	run out	6
S. Hughes	not out	16
A. Wingfield Digby		1
J. Price	did not bat	
	Extras	11
	Total (for 9 wkts.)	168

Bowling

	O	M	R	W
Snow	4	0	14	1
Lever	4	0	10	1
Powell	4	0	32	1
Wilson	6	1	26	1
Marriott	3	0	9	0
Cleobury	3	0	22	1
Adams	3	0	26	0
Mills	3	0	17	3
Edrich	1	0	7	0

LAVINIA, DUCHESS OF NORFOLK'S SPORTSMEN XI
WON BY 2 WICKETS

So ended what was generally agreed to be one of the most pleasant Taverners' fixtures. What set it apart was undoubtedly the lack of commercial pressure normally required by a sponsor and for major fund raising attractions. These elements will no doubt be necessary in the future if the series is to be sustained but, as a break in routine and as a joyous 99th year exercise, it ended the Club's season on a high note.

With so many performers present, one could not help but reflect on the literary and artistic images of Arundel Castle. Earlier reference has been made to the Duchess's Three Musketeers in founding the Club. Now, looking at the Knights at the long table afterwards, Sir David Frost, Sir Tim Rice and Sir Colin Cowdrey, as an early evening haze descended over the Castle, Camelot came to mind and, with apologies to Alan Jay Lerner's lyrics:

> *"The rain must never fall until after sundown*
> *In August the weather must not be too hot*
> *In short there is simply not*
> *A more congenial spot*
> *For cricket in a dell*
> *Than here in Arundel."*

Saturday and Sunday September 10 & 11: There was a double footnote at the end of the 99th year's cricket at Arundel when two of the country's leading sports journalists paid their own special tribute to the Club. On 11 September, the traditional stable lads competition was given special charitable support when Julian Wilson, racing correspondent for B.B.C. Television, brought a number of his friends including Derek Pringle to support the day's activities. These followed the traditional pattern of two separate games of cricket taking part on each half of the ground and the funds raised were donated to the special fund for Injured Jockeys.

The match on September 10 was organised by E. W. Swanton. The involvement of his team meant that he was responsible for providing sides both at the start and the end of the season but, on this occasion, the opposition came not from the home team but the visiting Holder's Hill village side from Barbados.

Their visit marked both his own and M.C.C. interest in strengthening links with Barbados. The British and Caribbean based businessman John Kidd had done much to attract sponsorship for the visitors tour which included a

E. W. SWANTON'S XI V HOLDER'S HILL VILLAGE, BARBADOS 10TH SEPTEMBER 1994

E. W. SWANTON'S XI

R. R. Montgomerie	run out	21
N. Lenham	c. Griffith b. Hewitt	21
J. D. Robinson	b. Hewitt	66
S. P. Henderson	c. C. Sandiford b. J. Sandiford	9
W. E. J. Holland	not out	40
C. W. C. Rowe	not out	3
I. D. K. Salisbury	did not bat	
J. P. Arscott		
J. R. T. Barclay		
D. R. Law		
H. J. Watkinson		
	Extras	13
	Total (for 4 wkts. dec.)	173

Bowling

	O	M	R	W
Hewitt	13	1	50	2
Phillips	7	0	27	0
Rogers	10	2	39	0
Sandiford	6	0	34	1
Stephenson	5	0	15	0
Griffith	1	0	3	0

HOLDER'S HILL VILLAGE

A. F. G. Griffith	b. Rowe	42
C. A. Brown	st. Arscott b. Rowe	37
N. Phillip	lbw. b. Salisbury	23
F. D. Stephenson	b. Salisbury	21
P. Skeete	b. Salisbury	0
R. Skeete	st. Arscott b. Rowe	5
C. Sandiford	lbw. b. Rowe	2
A. Rogers	c. Montgomerie b. Salisbury	0
J. Bovell	not out	0
S. Hewitt	not out	1
J. Sandiford	did not bat	
	Extras	18
	Total (for 8 wkts.)	149

Bowling

	O	M	R	W
Law	6	1	28	0
Watkinson	3	0	19	0
Rowe	14	1	43	4
Salisbury	12	0	42	4

MATCH DRAWN

match against the M.C.C. as well as that at Arundel. There was also a local response to the sponsorship appeal when the nearby resident, the former Cabinet Minister - Lord Young of Graffham - Chairman of Cable & Wireless, widened his Company's recognition as sponsors of West Indian Test cricket to support the Barbados Club side.

J.R.T.B.: "I was delighted to be involved in this particular match. Jim Swanton struck a nice balance between his regulars from the Arabs and some of our most active Arundel cricketers. Thus, we got off to a good start thanks to Neil Lenham and Mrs Swanton's great nephew R. R. Montgomerie. They were followed by some quick scoring from Jonathan Robinson and Bill Holland and we made the usual declaration.

"They, in turn, went after the runs and it was good to see old friends like Norbert Phillip of Essex as well as the West Indian and our own Sussex Bajan, Franklyn Stephenson, hitting out. However, the real feature of the match was the opportunity it gave us to use our spinners Charlie Rowe and Ian Salisbury. So far as making the match a close contest was concerned it was Ian who did the real damage. We all felt that Franklyn Stephenson needed to stay in another two or three overs and when I said this to Ian Salisbury after he got him out, he typically said, 'Oh I am so sorry'".

After the match, John Kidd gave a picture of Holder's Hill Cricket Club to the Arundel Castle Cricket Club and Jim Swanton gave the Barbados side the flag he had flown in his West Indies tours in 1956 and 1961. Recognising the presence of several of the Arabs' team, he took the opportunity of telling a story which reflected on his feelings when learning that his history of the Club, "Arabs in Aspic", was in heavy demand at the main public libraries in Kent. "I would have preferred", he said "to hear news of purchases in the bookshops and, to rub salt in the wound, they tell me that when they had received an enquiry for the book in the Maidstone library, the attendant said, 'I've vaguely heard of it - why don't you try the Cookery Section?'". Jim Swanton concluded his remarks by saying that this match at the end of the 99th Year of Cricket at Arundel was very much cricket in the spirit which Duke Bernard would so much have enjoyed.

Writing at the start of the Centenary year of 1995, one's thoughts inevitably turn to the future. Will there be another century of Arundel cricket? The answer to this question inevitably depends upon the Club's activities and those upon whom the Club depends for its present and future direction.

Looking to the Chairman, Hubert Doggart, one can see that he has already assumed the mantle of his predecessors as Keeper of the Duke's Conscience. In the Quidnuncs and Harlequins match this year, he was heard to say to both slightly dilatory captains, "I really think we must try to respect the Duke's memory with a prompt start". Later in the season, when he felt that a declaration was becoming overdue, he would mutter to both visiting and home captains alike, "The Duke would be getting restless".

His Vice-Chairman, Colin Cowdrey, retains his role as the Club's visionary and a crucial link with the Norfolk family. He also adds practical common sense on money matters affecting both the Club and coaching through the Foundation. In this he draws added strength from his close links with Sir Roger Gibbs and J. Paul Getty.

There had been speculation about the possible rivalry between Mr Getty's recently constructed ground at Wormsley and the Arundel Castle Cricket Club. Inevitably, there were comparisons made between the two grounds when both were seen as venues for the Touring Teams. However, talking to the Author early in 1995 J. Paul Getty was in no doubt about their relationship:

"For me, Arundel Castle will always be the supreme home of country house cricket and any help I have been able to give to the foundation recognises its unique role in developing new talent for English Cricket. What I would like to see is a possible match between our teams. This might help restore the old idea of a rivalry such as that which applied in Duke Bernard's time between his side and Lord Eldon's. I am in close touch with Hubert Doggart on this idea and even if we cannot manage something for the Centenary Year, I think we will find a way for the future. Meanwhile, I am only too glad to help Arundel Cricket Foundation in any way I can. Colin Cowdrey is a splendid salesman for their cause".

Sir Colin's own view of the future at Arundel is one in which the Club. and the Foundation are mutually supportive:

"We have all the ingredients for continued success. It is splendid to have leading Sussex cricket figures in charge of our affairs in both the Chairman and Director of Cricket. If I have a worry, it is in our ageing membership but I believe we have every chance of retaining the interest of those who will think ,'This is where I got my start in cricket'.

"So far as the Foundation is concerned, thanks to Paul Getty and national institutions like the Foundation for Sport and the Arts, we have completed our capital programme. However, money to cover our operating costs remains a problem but we are fortunate with our regular sponsors and there seems to be a real prospect for greater support from the Local Education Authority, West Sussex County Council. They have begun to discuss our basic costs and how we cover them and they especially seem to recognise the work which Johnny Barclay and his team do in generating interest in their schools, in coaching their pupils here at the ground and, just as important, in training their teachers so that they can coach and encourage in their own schools.

"Putting all this into a national perspective, the cricket project at Arundel is unique and has no counterpart anywhere in the world. This outstanding cricket ground in the historical setting of Arundel Park has become a coaching centre for a host of young people, most of whom would never have had the opportunity of playing cricket at all. In establishing the Arundel Castle Cricket Foundation we have set out to serve youth and education and to take a lead on national concerns over the sale of school sports grounds, the reduced interest in team games and competitive sport and the lack of teachers and coaching facilities within schools.

"We pay regular visits to more than one hundred State schools and we have built up a close relationship with London Boroughs, the London Boys Clubs and London Cricket in the Community which concentrates on ethnic minorities. In addition, a steady flow of inner city youngsters comes not only from London but also from the Midlands and further afield. So we are not without hope that national funding to help with our operating costs may yet come our way."

John Barclay takes up several of the Cowdrey themes in a broader context: "For me, cricket at Arundel is now part of the game in its widest sense. First-class cricket can be very narrow. Whenever I walk into a County dressing room, I am reminded of this. Nobody can think beyond the next match, the next result, their average and whether they will be retained at the end of the Season. Now I see cricket all the way from school to M.C.C. and Test level with Club cricket in between. What, above all, gives hope for the future both in general and for Arundel is the thought that we have the opportunity of introducing thousands of youngsters to the game. We have yet to see how far we can help revive English cricket fortunes but I feel certain that many of these same youngsters will want to put something back by way of lifetime support and interest in everything that happens here at Arundel.

"Apart from the significance of our coaching, the continued commitment of touring teams is another key ingredient in the future of cricket at Arundel. This seems assured judging by the obvious goodwill and enjoyment which our visitors show year after year and, so far as the Test and County Cricket Board is concerned, Arundel retains a true friend in Tim Lamb at Lord's. He still comes down to play for us and

he has already fixed the visit by the touring West Indian team in May 1995".

There are two other regular attendants at the tourist matches. The first is Paul Parker who captained the Duchess's side against Australia in 1993 and New Zealand in 1994 when he commented: "It says a lot for this ground and this game that over 8,000 people will turn up to see a visiting team which has no great names in it. But that is part of the secret of the success of this fixture because year after year we see some of the stars of the future and the presence of established Test players is in that sense a bonus".

The second observer is one who is there in a professional capacity in the person of Alan Curtis. In addition to undertaking ground match broadcasting at the Test Matches, he has become the regular voice of Arundel at the start of the season with support by his deputy the actor Johnny Dennis. Alan Curtis sees it as a great holiday occasion: "I find that, coming here year after year, I see the same families staying at the Norfolk Arms. Among those who came for the New Zealand match this year are some of the regulars from Northamptonshire, Yorkshire and Newcastle and, in a real sense, Arundel seems to have picked up the old Scarborough festival spirit. So far as the visiting players are concerned, I detect that even the most blasé international cricketer earning big money is still bowled over by the atmosphere at Arundel. In many ways it seems to recapture the spirit that existed when they first came into the game".

Another real hope for the future is the increasing involvement and interest of the Earl of Arundel: "I enjoy my link with the Club's Advisory Committee and I see one of my main roles as playing a part in keeping country house cricket on the agenda. That is why, since the mid-eighties, I have raised a side for an annual match against the Estate Eleven. Neither side has any great pretensions in playing skill and, over the years, I have included members of the family such as my brothers-in-law, Roddy Balfour, David Frost and the actor Patrick Rycart. Then there are special friends like Henry Smith the Hambleden heir and the Earl of Strathmore who is about as big a duffer as I am. We do, from time to time, include some friends who are or have been serious cricketers like Ricky Compton from the I.Z., Charlie Cottenham who toured Jamaica with Duke Bernard, Nick Stewart - 'the Colonel' - who can still bowl at a fair pace and Lord Fairfax who is a recognised batsman. But the main thing is that we have fun".

There remains one person whose influence is still evident as the principal driving force in the Club's activities. This is the President, Lavinia, Duchess of Norfolk. The ill health which has ruled out her attendance at recent matches and committee meetings has in no way diminished her role. During the Club's twenty years existence she has retained the prerogative of making personal appointments to the committee and her record of success in finding the right man at the right time from Aird, Cowdrey, Griffith and Harrison to Barclay, Ford and Doggart speaks for itself. When asked about her skill and good fortune in building up and maintaining her team, the Duchess has always given the same crisp and smiling response: "Nonsense. It's all due to Bernard - he is still directing things from Up There".

1994

April 24th. Arabs 204-4 dec (C. J. C. Rowe 63, C. J. T. Holland 54). Lavinia Duchess of Norfolk's XI 205-7 (J. C. M. Atkinson 50). Lavinia Duchess of Norfolk's XI won by 3 wickets.

May, 8th. Quidnuncs 226-5 dec (S. P. Henderson 59, J. P. C. Mills 55). Harlequins 188-7 (D. A. Thorne 59) Match drawn.

June. 5th. Lavinia Duchess of Norfolk's XI 232-6 dec (J. Fricker 66, J. C. D. Stuart 61). Combined Services 237-5 (R. J. Greatorex 117). Combined Services won by 5 wickets.

June 9th. Cambridge University 196-6 dec (J. Ratledge 114). Lavinia Duchess of Norfolk's XI 200-2 (C. Bullen 104*). Lavinia Duchess of Norfolk's XI won by 8 wickets.

July 3rd. Lavinia Duchess of Norfolk's XI 289-4 dec (S. Lynch 154*, C. Rika 86). MCC 287-6 (K. Greenfield 101, P. Bedford 86*) Match drawn.

July 6th. Lavinia Duchess of Norfolk's XI 234-3 dec (P. Hudson 103*, T. Brennan 84). I Zingari Australia 198-7 (A. Wiles 60, J. Chaplin 6-60). Match drawn.

July 20th. Lavinia Duchess of Norfolk's XI 287-4 dec (P. Wellings 139*, J. While 67*). Grasshoppers 288-4 (K. Mitchell 122*, D. Crookes 63, H. Brown 73). Grasshoppers won by 6 wickets.

August 7th. Lavinia Duchess of Norfolk's XI 173-8 dec. Uganda 174-8 (J. Himanshu 60). Uganda won by 2 wickets.

August 16th. Lavinia Duchess of Norfolk's XI 281-4 dec (A. J. Hollioake 101, M. J. Walker 64). Scotland 186-8. Match drawn.

APPENDICES

A   MATCH RECORDS

B   ANNUAL RESULTS

C   HIGHEST AND LOWEST TEAM INNINGS

D   STATISTICS IN MATCHES AGAINST THE TOURISTS

E   CAREER RECORDS

F   LEADING CAREER SUMMARIES

G   HUNDREDS

H   SIX WICKETS IN AN INNINGS

Each appendix (except in appendix D) shows statistics separately for:

1930-1974 BERNARD, DUKE OF NORFOLK'S XI

1976-1994 LAVINIA, DUCHESS OF NORFOLK'S XI

APPENDIX A

MATCH RECORDS 1930-1974

Opponents	Seasons	P	W	L	D
Army	1930	1	1	0	0
Arundel C.C.	1955-1973	18	8	7	3
Arundel Hospital XI	1932	1	0	0	1
Australian Old Collegians	1964	1	0	1	0
Australians	1956-1972	4	1	2	1
Bluemantles	1962	1	0	1	0
Brighton Brunswick	1970	1	0	0	1
British Legion, Arundel Branch	1935-1954	6	1	4	1
Canadian Touring XI	1954	1	0	0	1
C.S.Crawley's XI	1952-1954	3	1	2	0
De Flamingo's (Holland)	1959	1	0	1	0
H.R.H. The Duke of Edinburgh's XI	1953-1957	2	1	0	1
Lord Eldon's XI	1930-1936	8	4	2	2
Emeriti	1954-1965	12	6	5	1
Eton Ramblers	1952-1974	20	6	7	7
Grasshoppers (South Africa)	1968	1	0	1	0
Grenadier Guards, 3rd. Battalion	1939	1	1	0	0
H.M.S.Norfolk	1972	1	1	0	0
Captain The Hon. A.O.J.Hope's XI	1933-1939	7	4	3	0
Lady Mary Fitzalan Howard's XI	1964-1974	11	4	2	5
Indians	1959	1	0	0	1
I Zingari	1956-1974	15	7	5	3
Mayor of Arundel's XI	1931	1	0	1	0
New Zealanders	1958-1965	2	0	0	2
Oxford University OTC	1930	1	1	0	0
Pakistanis	1962	1	0	0	1
Royal Sussex Regiment	1951-1974	18	4	9	5
South Africans	1960	1	0	1	0
Staggerers (Johannesburg)	1963-1967	2	1	0	1
Sussex	1951-1971	11	5	6	0
Sussex Martlets	1934-1974	25	10	7	8
United States Cricket Association	1968	1	0	0	1
West Indians	1963-1969	3	0	3	0
TOTAL	**1930-1974**	**183**	**67**	**70**	**46**

MATCH RECORDS 1976-1994

Opponents	Seasons	P	W	L	D
Arabs	1979-1994	13	3	1	9
Arundel C.C.	1976-1994	17	4	3	10
Australian Combined Services	1993	1	0	0	1
Australian Old Collegians	1989	1	0	0	1
Australians	1977-1993	5	1	3	1
Barbados Wanderers	1979-1985	3	1	0	2
Cambridge University	1993-1994	2	1	1	0
Canada/UK "40" C.C.	1979	1	1	0	0
Cluttons	1989	1	0	0	1
Combined Services	1980-1994	15	3	6	6
Crusaders	1989-1993	3	0	1	2
Crusaders (Australia)	1987	1	0	0	1
De Flamingo's (Holland)	1986	1	0	0	1
England Young Cricketers	1976	1	0	1	0
Eton Ramblers	1976-1994	19	10	2	7
Grasshoppers (South Africa)	1978-1994	2	0	1	1
High Sheriff's Young Sussex XI	1977	1	0	1	0
Indians	1982-1986	2	2	0	0
Ireland	1981-1993	6	1	1	4
I Zingari	1976-1994	19	2	9	8
I Zingari (Australia)	1988-1994	2	0	1	1
Lady Mary & Lady Sarah's XI	1976	1	1	0	0
Lady Mary Fitzalan Howard's XI	1977-1982	6	2	1	3
Lloyd's C.C.	1981-1992	11	2	3	6
Lord's Taverners	1977-1994	12	2	7	3
MCC	1980-1994	15	5	7	3
MCC Young Cricketers	1981-1994	13	2	6	5
Minor Counties	1981-1993	12	2	3	7
New Zealanders	1978-1994	4	1	2	1
Pakistanis	1992	1	0	1	0
President of MCC's XI	1980	1	1	0	0
Rest of the World	1987	1	1	0	0
Royal Sussex Regiment	1976-1987	11	3	2	6
Scotland	1982-1994	2	0	0	2
Sri Lankans	1984-1988	2	0	1	1
Staggerers	1984-1989	2	0	1	1
Sussex XI	1977-1988	2	1	0	1
Sussex Martlets	1976-1994	18	6	3	9
Transvaal	1992	1	0	1	0
Uganda	1994	1	0	1	0
Watney's Invitation XI	1978-1979	2	1	0	1
West Indians	1976-1991	5	1	4	0
Sam Whitbread XI	1989	1	0	0	1
Willows	1985	1	1	0	0
Zimbabwe	1985	1	0	1	0
TOTAL	1976-1994	242	61	75	106

APPENDIX B

ANNUAL RESULTS 1930-1974				
	P	**W**	**L**	**D**
1930	3	3	0	0
1931	2	0	2	0
1932	3	1	0	2
1933	2	1	1	0
1934	3	1	1	1
1935	4	1	2	1
1936	3	2	0	1
1937	2	1	1	0
1938	2	1	1	0
1939	2	1	1	0
1951	2	1	1	0
1952	6	1	4	1
1953	6	2	4	0
1954	7	1	4	2
1955	5	1	2	2
1956	8	4	4	0
1957	7	3	0	4
1958	7	1	4	2
1959	9	5	2	2
1960	7	1	5	1
1961	7	5	2	0
1962	8	5	2	1
1963	8	5	2	1
1964	7	0	6	1
1965	7	2	3	2
1966	7	3	4	0
1967	5	1	3	1
1968	7	2	2	3
1969	5	1	2	2
1970	7	1	2	4
1971	6	1	2	3
1972	8	3	0	5
1973	6	4	1	1
1974	5	2	0	3
TOTAL	183	67	70	46

Notes:

1. *All matches are single innings except v Lord Eldon's XI 1930 & 1932-36 and v Capt. Hope's XI 1933-39, all of which were two innings matches.*

2. *The match v the Indians in 1959 was abandoned without a ball bowled.*

ANNUAL RESULTS 1976-1994				
	P	**W**	**L**	**D**
1976	8	2	5	1
1977	10	4	2	4
1978	10	4	3	3
1979	10	4	1	5
1980	10	3	4	3
1981	13	6	3	4
1982	14	3	5	6
1983	10	1	2	7
1984	12	2	6	4
1985	17	3	4	10
1987	15	4	3	8
1988	13	2	4	7
1989	18	4	8	6
1990	11	1	3	7
1991	14	2	5	7
1992	12	3	5	4
1993	15	5	2	8
1994	15	4	5	6
TOTAL	**242**	**61**	**75**	**106**

Notes:

1. *All matches over one innings.*

2. *On four occasions matches were drawn with the scores tied with the team batting second having wickets in hand:*

   1978 - Royal Sussex Regiment 154 all out, Duchess of Norfolk's XI 154-4.

   1978 - Duchess of Norfolk's XI 138 all out, Grasshoppers 138-8.

   1981 - Minor Counties 225-5d, Duchess of Norfolk's XI 225-5.

   1982 - Lady Mary Fitzalan Howard's XI 226-9, Duchess of Norfolk's XI 226-6.

Appendix C

HIGHEST INNINGS TOTAL
1930 - 1974

For

317	v	Lord Eldon's XI	1933
298	v	Sussex	1959
297-6	v	Lady Mary Fitzalan Howard's XI	1967
294-6 dec.	v	Sussex	1958
293-9 dec.	v	Sussex	1961
290-7 dec.	v	Lord Eldon's XI	1932
285	v	Lord Eldon's XI	1934

Against

320	by	Lord Eldon's XI	1931
299-5	by	Sussex	1958
295-8	by	Sussex	1961
295	by	Sussex	1959
294-9 dec.	by	Lady Mary Fitzalan Howard's XI	1967
282-7 dec.	by	Eton Ramblers	1965
279	by	Captain The Hon. A.O.J. Hope's XI	1934
277-8	by	Lord Eldon's XI	1934

HIGHEST INNINGS TOTAL
1976-1994

For

298-2	v	Eton Ramblers	1989
289-4 dec.	v	MCC	1994
287-4 dec.	v	Grasshoppers (South Africa)	1994
281-4 dec.	v	Scotland	1994
281-5 dec.	v	MCC Young Cricketers	1983
279-6	v	I Zingari	1986
277-6	v	New Zealanders	1990
276-l dec.	v	I Zingari	1992
276-6 dec.	v	I Zingari	1983

Against

314-6 dec.	by	Australians	1989
302-l dec.	by	Minor Counties	1990
299-3 dec.	by	I Zingari	1986
296-4 dec.	by	Eton Ramblers	1989
288-4	by	Grasshoppers (South Africa)	1994
287-2 dec.	by	MCC	1983

LOWEST INNINGS TOTAL
1930 - 1974

For

30	v	Eton Ramblers	1953
32	v	British Legion, Arundel Branch	1953
37	v	Emeriti	1964
38	v	British Legion, Arundel Branch	1938
42	v	Royal Sussex Regiment	1954
50	v	Emeriti	1958
55	v	Captain The Hon. A.O.J. Hope's XI	1939
71	v	Emeriti	1960
72	v	Lord Eldon's XI	1933
73	v	I Zingari	1964

Against

47	by	Oxford University OTC	1930
76	by	Sussex Martlets	1953
80	by	Captain The Hon. A.O.J. Hope's XI	1939
84	by	British Legion, Arundel Branch	1953
90	by	Captain The Hon. A.O.J. Hope's XI	1934
92	by	Captain The Hon. A.O.J. Hope's XI	1937

LOWEST INNINGS TOTALS
1976 - 1994

For

76	v	West Indians	1984
87	v	Royal Sussex Regiment	1986

Against

64	by	Arundel C.C.	1981
81	by	Lady Mary Fitzalan Howard's XI	1979
94	by	by Arundel C.C.	1987

APPENDIX D

DUKE AND DUCHESS OF NORFOLK'S XI v THE TOURISTS

This section gives the records of matches played by the Duke or Duchess of Norfolk's XI at Arundel versus national touring teams playing first-class cricket.

COMBINED MATCH RECORD 1954-1994

Opponents	Seasons	P	W	L	D
Australia	1956-1993	9	2	5	2
Canada	1954	1	0	0	1
India	1959-1986	3	2	0	1
New Zealand	1958-1994	6	1	2	3
Pakistan	1962-1992	2	0	1	1
South Africa	1960	1	0	1	0
Sri Lanka	1984-1988	2	0	1	1
West Indies	1963-1991	8	1	7	0
Zimbabwe	1985	1	0	1	0
TOTAL	**1954-1994**	**33**	**6**	**18**	**9**

HIGHEST INNINGS TOTALS FOR & AGAINST

Opponents	For		Against	
Australia	241	1972	314-6	1989
Canada	163-8 dec.	1954	133-7	1954
India	202-0	1982	217-9	1986
New Zealand	277-6	1990	278-3	1990
Pakistan	240-4	1992	253-3	1992
South Africa	220-8 dec.	1960	224-5	1960
Sri Lanka	214-3 dec.	1988	216-9	1984
West Indies	221-7 dec.	1966	243-4 dec.	1980
Zimbabwe	217-8 dec.	1985	220-3	1985

HIGHEST INDIVIDUAL INNINGS FOR & AGAINST

Opponents	For				Against		
Australia	96	A.W. Greig	1972		114*	D.C. Boon	1989
Canada	44	J.H. Parks	1954		44	R.N. Quintrell	1954
India	107*	Sadiq Mohammad	1982		66*	Yashpal Sharma	1982
New Zealand	131	A.I.C.Dodemaide	1990		89*	M.D. Crowe	1990
Pakistan	82	P.D. Bowler	1992		104	Aamir Sohail	1992
South Africa	56*	F.J. Titmus	1960		72	D.J. McGlew	1960
Sri Lanka	107	G.S. Clinton	1988		58	D.S.B.P.Kuruppu	1984
West Indies	98	J.E. Morris	1991		84	C.G. Greenidge	1976
Zimbabwe	74	N.J. Lenham	1985		88	G.A. Paterson	1985

BEST BOWLING FIGURES IN AN INNINGS FOR & AGAINST

Opponents	For				Against		
Australia	5-51	D.W. Headley	1993		6-35	R.Benaud	1956
Canada	3-27	R.G. Marlar	1954		4-43	B.Christen	1954
India	3-57	G. Monkhouse	1986		2-21	Maninder Singh	1986
New Zealand	4-21	N.Gifford	1965		4-17	G.R.Larsen	1994
Pakistan	1-16	J.R. Gray	1962		4-42	Mohammad Farooq	1962
South Africa	2-39	F.J.Titmus	1960		5-102	H.J. Tayfield	1960
Sri Lanka	3-21	C.M. Wells	1984		4-31	D.S. De Silva	1984
West Indies	3-15	R.M. Ellison	1984		8-65	J.S. Solomon	1963
Zimbabwe	2-75	M.W.W. Selvey	1985		4-43	A.H.Omarshah	1985

APPENDIX E

CAREER RECORDS 1930-1974

(Qualification: at least two matches and a batting or bowling contribution)
* First-class cricketer.   † Test match cricketer.

	Years	I	NO	HS	Runs	Avge	Runs	Wkts	Avge
M.L.Y.Ainsworth *	69-74	9	2	58*	246	35.14	390	8	48.75
R.Aird *	58	2	0	5	9	4.50	-	-	-
D.A.Allen †	63-69	4	3	8	22	22.00	244	4	61.00
E.W.Allen	56-59	9	1	48	146	18.25	-	-	-
G.O.B.Allen †	35-51	3	1	133	164	82.00	-	-	-
H.Allsop	52-55	8	1	41	97	13.86	-	-	-
H.E.Avery	56-58	5	2	87*	247	82.33	11	0	-
H.C.Bagot	34	3	1	10*	14	7.00	-	-	-
I.A.Balding	68-72	3	0	16	17	5.67	-	-	-
J.Balding	66-68	4	0	42	50	12.50	-	-	-
R.W.Barber †	68-69	2	0	30	35	17.50	21	1	21.00
H.M.Barnard *	59-62	2	0	21	21	10.50	-	-	-
D.W.Barrick *	57	2	0	19	32	16.00	95	2	47.50
K.F.Barrington †	60-71	4	0	73	194	48.50	60	0	-
J.A.P.Bartlett	52-55	6	0	8	24	4.00	160	9	17.78
A.V.Bedser †	56-71	5	1	11	25	6.25	185	11	16.82
E.A.Bedser *	63-71	13	3	105*	399	39.90	646	24	26.92
Lord Belper	37-58	26	1	53	255	10.20	6	1	6.00
R.Wheeler Bennett	52	2	1	18*	18	18.00	44	1	44.00
C.J.S.Bidwell	64-72	5	0	42	115	23.00	65	4	16.25
W.S.Blackshaw	72-73	-	-	-	-	-	65	2	32.50
D.E.Blake *	57	2	0	54	79	39.50	-	-	-
J.R.Blanchard	64-74	4	2	7*	19	9.50	315	9	35.00
C.H.Blount	55-64	7	1	76*	153	25.50	-	-	-
A.B.Bowles	64-68	3	1	19	37	18.50	19	2	9.50
D.Parker Bowles	39	2	0	4	6	3.00	-	-	-
E.H.Bowley †	31-32	2	0	34	38	19.00	49	4	12.25
G.Bowser	38-39	2	0	18	20	10.00	36	2	18.00
N.H.Broomfield	55-57	6	2	56*	169	42.25	175	7	25.00
F.R.Brown †	54-58	3	0	28	45	15.00	56	0	-
D.B.Buik	69-71	2	0	6	7	3.50	-	-	-
R.M.Burdon	64	2	0	41	81	40.50	25	0	-
A.G.Burke	64	2	1	4*	7	7.00	40	0	-
M.Burr	70-73	6	1	22	70	14.00	-	-	-
R.H.Burton	56-74	39	1	53	590	15.53	267	22	12.14
C.E.P.Carter *	73-74	1	0	4	4	4.00	-	-	-
B.Carver	38-39	3	1	25*	31	15.50	108	10	10.80
L.Cecil	36	2	1	4*	6	6.00	40	2	20.00
R.C.J.Chichester Constable *	34	3	0	17	34	11.33	82	3	27.33
R.J.Clover-Brown	68-74	13	1	91	383	31.92	85	4	21.25
P.C.R.Coates	62-64	4	1	41	80	26.67	40	1	40.00
R.H.Cobbold *	33-38	10	1	70	228	25.33	489	35	13.97
Viscount Cobham *	56-63	3	0	27	56	18.67	67	3	22.33
T.B.L.Coghlan *	58-73	5	1	51	108	27.00	242	5	48.40
N.S.Collin	52-66	30	3	12	68	2.52	28	1	28.00
A.J.R.Collins	39-67	27	0	42	239	8.85	-	-	-
G.A.K.Collins *	31-32	2	0	41	61	30.50	14	0	-
D.C.S.Compton †	54-58	2	0	4	6	3.00	35	2	17.50
Maharajaha of Cooch Behar	37	4	0	29	30	7.50	71	7	10.14
G.Cook	71-73	4	2	33*	67	33.50	152	6	25.33
W.L.Cornford †	31-32	2	0	10	13	6.50	24	2	12.00
M.C.Cowdrey †	51-72	8	0	70	207	25.88	103	1	103.00
G.Cox,Jnr *	32-74	10	4	119*	394	65.67	364	6	60.67

	Years	I	NO	HS	Runs	Avge	Runs	Wkts	Avge
A.M.Crawley *	30-69	14	0	164	643	45.93	323	22	14.68
C.S.Crawley *	32-66	62	4	144	1220	21.03	124	7	17.71
K.A.G.Crawley	33-35	3	0	54	56	18.67	7	0	-
M.Creswell-Wall	67	2	1	31*	36	36.00	44	1	44.00
M.J.Daly	59	2	0	44	77	38.50	-	-	-
J.Davies	73-74	2	1	32*	42	42.00	75	8	9.38
T.M.E.Dawson	60-65	3	0	23	35	11.67	-	-	-
J.A.Dew *	51-52	2	1	15	15	15.00	-	-	-
E.R.Dexter †	58-72	5	0	52	128	25.60	105	2	52.50
G.H.G.Doggart †	51-58	8	0	100	381	47.63	179	5	35.80
D.Drummond	32-36	6	2	45	72	18.00	13	4	3.25
Lord Dundas	58-63	2	0	23	33	16.50	-	-	-
Lord Dunglass *	32-36	12	1	100*	450	40.91	493	30	16.43
A.H.Duveen	53-57	5	0	42	67	13.40	115	4	28.75
E.D.R.Eagar *	51-57	4	1	35	69	23.00	27	1	27.00
V.J.Eaton *	35	2	1	92*	106	106.00	-	-	-
Earl of Eldon	33-36	6	0	18	64	10.67	51	4	12.75
Earl of Erne	30	2	1	0*	0	0.00	-	-	-
I.Erskine	37-38	5	0	50	119	23.80	113	9	12.56
P.Evans	52-59	1	1	4*	4	-	16	0	-
T.G.Evans †	52-60	13	3	25	46	4.60	25	0	-
J.J.S.Farmer *	63-65	2	0	21	41	20.50	-	-	-
J.H.Fingleton †	56-61	2	0	41	46	23.00	-	-	-
W.E.Forbes	37	2	0	87	87	43.50	55	7	7.86
A.R.Ford	74	2	0	34	52	26.00	-	-	-
E.W.S.Ford	51-63	8	1	18	26	3.71	182	17	10.71
R.A.Gale *	60-61	2	0	29	52	26.00	17	0	-
I.Gardner	71-73	3	1	50	69	34.50	-	-	-
C.R.Gerrard	56	2	1	2*	2	2.00	69	1	69.00
R Gibbs	63-70	5	0	22	32	6.40	-	-	-
A.H.Gooda	59-66	17	2	91	297	19.80	804	29	27.72
J.Graham	31-32	2	0	13	13	6.50	-	-	-
T.W.Graveney †	57-66	4	0	58	132	33.00	26	2	13.00
J.R.Gray *	55-62	2	0	7	13	6.50	58	2	29.00
R.H.Green	70-74	9	0	54	154	17.11	-	-	-
A.W.Greig †	68-72	2	1	96	129	129.00	48	3	16.00
M.G.Griffith *	69-72	2	1	23*	37	37.00	-	-	-
S.C.Griffith †	52-59	9	1	60	125	15.63	-	-	-
E.E.Harrison *	35-74	79	16	58*	987	15.67	3679	172	21.39
P.Hastings (-Bass)	52-58	8	3	27	98	19.60	8	0	-
A.M.Hedley	51-65	5	0	41	69	13.80	46	3	15.33
D.Henderson *	56-59	3	0	25	29	9.67	9	4	2.25
A.Hoare	53-55	3	0	12	15	5.00	23	4	5.75
M.D.Hoare	54-57	3	0	14	32	10.67	96	2	48.00
R.N.S.Hobbs †	65-72	1	0	0	0	0.00	140	5	28.00
C.L.Hodgetts	61-65	5	3	5*	11	5.50	130	8	16.25
Hon.H.Douglas-Home	33-39	15	2	57*	158	12.15	-	-	-
Hon.W.Douglas-Home	33-34	3	0	28	46	15.33	17	1	17.00
Hon A.O.J.Hope *	35-38	16	1	56	361	24.07	435	21	20.71
J.Hope	68-74	2	0	16	18	9.00	-	-	-
Lord J.Hope	51-52	2	0	10	17	8.50	-	-	-
Lord Hopetoun	34-54	7	1	33	47	7.83	164	1	164.00
N.C.H.Hordern	54-60	2	0	6	6	3.00	26	0	-
H.P.Hunloke	31-39	30	3	84	727	26.93	336	7	48.00
K.S.M.J.Indrajitsinhji †	60	3	1	34	77	38.50	-	-	-
A.C.D.Ingleby-Mackenzie *	53-62	8	0	56	217	27.13	-	-	-
D.J.Insole †	56-59	3	0	24	28	9.33	73	2	36.50
D.E.Ironside	59-61	1	0	16	16	16.00	46	4	11.50
J.Jackson (F.Lane-Fox)	32-36	3	1	6*	10	5.00	-	-	-
J.Jeffries	61-62	2	0	10	11	5.50	-	-	-
K.R.Jenkin	58-59	1	0	31	31	31.00	68	3	22.67
T.Joynson	65-66	3	0	18	33	11.00	28	0	-

	Years	I	NO	HS	Runs	Avge	Runs	Wkts	Avge
W.R.H.Joynson *	54-64	27	2	49	559	22.36	350	8	43.75
C.Keswick	64-65	3	0	38	46	15.33	-	-	-
A.Kimmins	66-72	6	0	67	170	28.33	312	14	22.29
S.E.A.Kimmins *	67-74	8	3	104*	281	56.20	500	15	33.33
R.Kingsford	61-71	38	4	93*	860	25.29	766	22	34.82
B.R.Knight †	63-66	2	1	74	82	82.00	24	2	12.00
C.G.Lancaster	30-35	1	0	32	32	32.00	-	-	-
James Langridge †	53-55	3	1	64*	123	61.50	106	4	26.50
John Langridge *	32-53	3	0	64	116	38.67	21	0	-
R.E.Laycock	30	2	1	8	9	9.00	-	-	-
S.D.Leathes	69-70	3	3	2*	3	-	144	4	36.00
L.J.Lenham *	70-71	2	1	53*	53	53.00	46	3	15.33
J.O.Lintott	70-73	2	1	31	38	38.00	56	7	8.00
A.J.Lush	67-70	4	1	110*	218	72.67	157	5	31.40
I.H.McCausland	71-72	2	0	35	60	30.00	59	5	11.80
J.MacRae	33	2	0	4	4	2.00	97	6	16.17
M.Mance	71-74	6	2	16	38	9.50	209	10	20.90
F.G.Mann †	54-66	7	1	68	146	24.33	23	1	23.00
R.G.Marlar *	53-72	22	5	49	305	17.94	1386	86	16.12
R.E.Marshall †	55-71	3	0	50	119	39.67	148	4	37.00
G.D.Massy	61-63	1	1	106*	106	-	26	1	26.00
A.C.Maxwell	30-35	3	0	3	3	1.00	-	-	-
S.Maxwell-Scott	65	5	1	21	39	9.75	-	-	-
P.B.H.May †	64-68	3	0	38	52	17.33	32	0	-
M.E.L.Melluish *	56-58	1	0	23	23	23.00	-	-	-
D.J.Mordaunt *	60	2	0	45	55	27.50	56	7	8.00
A.E.Moss †	57-61	1	0	4	4	4.00	85	2	42.50
E.Mostyn	31-33	3	1	8	15	7.50	-	-	-
J.T.Murray †	58-71	2	2	19*	31	-	-	-	-
D.Nicholson	72-74	2	1	40*	51	51.00	-	-	-
Duke of Norfolk	30-69	99	11	38*	596	6.77	385	14	27.50
T.E.G.Nugent	32-35	3	0	56	134	44.67	59	1	59.00
L.V.O'Callaghan	66-74	2	1	6	6	6.00	226	8	28.25
B.C.O'Donnell	36-37	4	0	12	23	5.75	65	2	32.50
B.O'Gorman	59-68	3	1	79*	170	85.00	165	6	27.50
J.H.Parks *	32-55	3	0	44	93	31.00	70	3	23.33
J.M.Parks *	54-68	4	1	12*	41	13.67	-	-	-
A.G.Pelham *	51-54	5	1	18*	49	12.25	-	-	-
P.Perfect	68-74	2	1	52	53	53.00	-	-	-
J.V.Pollard	55-60	3	0	5	8	2.67	116	2	58.00
R.Poulter	33-35	6	2	14	20	5.00	304	15	20.27
J.S.E.Price †	64-69	-	-	-	-	-	21	1	21.00
J.F.Priestley	52	3	1	42	96	48.00	165	10	16.50
P.Pyemont	71-74	7	2	73*	203	40.60	-	-	-
R.S.O.Rees	70	3	2	2*	3	3.00	162	8	20.25
B.Reid	61-63	4	1	68*	110	36.67	20	0	-
D.Rice *	53-73	35	8	52	296	10.96	1714	83	20.65
W.Rice	65-70	14	5	36	127	14.11	-	-	-
J.Rich	33	2	0	15	17	8.50	88	1	88.00
I.W.Robertson	64-73	2	0	1	1	0.50	-	-	-
R.W.V.Robins †	52-53	2	0	33	35	17.50	91	4	22.75
P.M.H.Robinson *	55-74	43	4	95	1354	34.72	1428	67	21.31
J.A.Ross	68-72	1	1	5*	5	-	91	6	15.17
P.C.Rushton	64-69	2	0	24	38	19.00	29	1	29.00
W.E.Russell †	69-71	2	0	77	79	39.50	54	1	54.00
C.J.Sage	55-57	1	0	33	33	33.00	98	1	98.00
A.Saul	72	2	0	89	155	77.50	-	-	-
C.J.Saunders *	69-74	4	2	19	38	19.00	-	-	-
J.G.Saunders *	71-74	6	0	30	119	19.83	115	2	57.50
Lord G.Scott	30-32	5	0	5	16	3.20	50	0	-
Lord W.Scott	31-35	6	0	32	81	13.50	-	-	-
A.J.Scratchley	54-61	9	1	23	68	8.50	67	5	13.40

	Years	I	NO	HS	Runs	Avge	Runs	Wkts	Avge
G.S.Seaton *	63-70	4	1	14	21	7.00	-	-	-
D.Shackleton †	51-71	3	0	25	41	13.67	139	2	69.50
C.P.Sharman	62-64	3	0	22	37	12.33	-	-	-
M.K.S.Shatrushalyasinhji	59-62	4	0	14	34	8.50	46	2	23.00
K.A.Shearwood *	56-62	2	0	45	71	35.50	-	-	-
D.S.Sheppard †	56-68	5	0	51	193	38.60	21	1	21.00
S.P.Sherrard	68-71	7	0	100	176	25.14	-	-	-
A.C.Smith †	59-63	2	0	5	9	4.50	59	2	29.50
D.V.Smith †	54-58	4	0	85	224	56.00	38	2	19.00
F.E.V.Smith	30	2	0	5	9	4.50	147	11	13.36
M.M.Smith	64-71	6	0	43	88	14.67	33	2	16.50
G.R.Smyth	51-63	19	5	48	220	15.71	-	-	-
C.E.M.Snell	70-71	2	0	31	35	17.50	-	-	-
J. Stallibrass	73-74	3	1	64	122	61.00	-	-	-
R.T.Stanyforth †	31-35	3	0	56	63	21.00	74	0	-
T. Street	69-74	2	0	0	0	0.00	8	1	8.00
P.L.Sugden	62-64	2	1	12*	16	16.00	27	3	9.00
K.G.Suttle *	54	2	0	25	48	24.00	-	-	-
Hon.M.Tennyson	59	2	0	5	5	2.50	-	-	-
A.L.S.S.Thackara *	59-74	54	4	117*	1728	34.56	290	7	41.43
R.A.Thomas	62-68	6	0	36	120	20.00	5	0	-
I.G.Thwaites *	73-74	3	1	40	75	37.50	65	0	-
F.J.Titmus †	60-64	3	1	56*	87	43.50	124	7	17.71
L.L.F.Toynbee	56-69	14	7	7	26	3.71	1455	50	29.10
M.F.Tremlett †	59-61	2	0	79	119	59.50	45	1	45.00
G.E.Tribe †	57-58	3	1	16*	21	10.50	-	-	-
C.E.Underdown	51-62	32	1	71	548	17.68	-	-	-
A.N.C.Wadey *	69-74	6	4	12	31	15.50	507	23	22.04
D.R.Walsh	72-74	4	1	106	223	74.33	27	3	9.00
J.J.Warr †	54-61	4	1	5	7	2.33	177	7	25.29
R.H.C.Waters *	59-63	3	0	49	112	37.33	-	-	-
W.Watson †	60	2	0	19	26	13.00	-	-	-
J.Watt *	60-70	9	0	97	340	37.78	172	6	28.67
R.H.Wethered	30-39	18	4	48	310	22.14	311	11	28.27
P.J.Whitcombe *	60-63	2	0	25	25	12.50	19	3	6.33
A.A.H.White	61-74	13	0	84	274	21.08	232	13	17.85
C.D.White *	61-62	2	0	18	33	16.50	-	-	-
G.A.Wills	61-74	22	1	100	661	31.48	-	-	-
H.L.Wilson *	31	2	0	51	93	46.50	57	2	28.50
V.Wilson	39-54	3	1	42	44	22.00	43	1	43.00
J.Windwood	38	2	1	38*	41	41.00	-	-	-
C.E.Winn *	52-54	3	1	9*	14	7.00	20	0	-
Hon.R.H.Winn	34-39	9	2	15	55	7.86	66	2	33.00
Hon.P.Wood	36-37	6	2	62*	162	40.50	-	-	-
J.C.Woodcock	63-66	3	0	35	78	26.00	-	-	-
B.J.P.Woods *	56-73	6	1	17	55	11.00	362	14	25.86
D.V.P.Wright †	55-56	2	1	5	7	7.00	100	3	33.33

Note: Some assumptions have been made in particular where early score cards are incomplete

The Following also played:-

A.Allen
W.E.Alley *
C.W.Alsford
Lord Althrop
G.G.Arnold †
J.Arthur
A.Barclay
J.R.T.Barclay *
M.T.Barford *
G.Barker *
H.T.Bartlett *
J.N.Bartlett *
R.Bathurst
D.H.H.Beams
J.Beckwith
P.I.Bedford *
V.Biggs
P.Bisset
E.Blackall
A.Blackman
A.Blanchard
A.Borgnis
D.Bowes-Lyon
T.Broadfoot
I.Bryns
M.D.Burden *
P.M.Burgess
F.C.Burroughs
J.A.Bushell
A.Buss *
C.Butler
Capt.Butler
D.B.Carr †
R.Carr-Gomm
J.M.Chaffer
N.P.H.R.Chamberlin
H.P.Chaplin *
J.Charlton
G.C.Clark
A.Clarke
P.Clarke
P.Clift
L.J.Coldwell †
W.A.R.Collins
P.C.Collymore
L.N.Constantine †
C.Coppinger
R.M.H.Cottam †
J.F.Crapp †
J.M.Crawford
R.S.Crawley
H.J.Davy
A.C.Dawnay

A DeGrey
M.H.Denness †
A.Dickenson
J.H.V.Dicks
F.J.Drake
E.Drummond
A.R.Duff *
J.Dundas
A.Dunn
P.Dunn
W.Earp
J.H.Edrich †
W.J.Edrich †
R.F.Eliot *
M.Ellewood
R.A.G.Evans
A.K.Falcon
I.Faulkner
J.P.Fellows-Smith †
W.Fielding
E.H.Firth
L.B.Fishlock †
N.M.Ford *
C.Fowler
M.Fox
C.A.Fry *
J.Fyvie
J.R.Gardiner
P.F.Gardiner-Hill *
D.W.M.Gay *
P.A.Gibb †
R.G.Gibbs
N.Gifford †
S.Gilbert
R.M.C.Gilliat *
A.H.H.Gilligan †
C.Gladwin
G.Goonesena *
A.R.Gover †
A.Grace
C.J.H.Green
D.M.Green *
W.T.Greensmith *
C.F.Greenwood
J.A.H.Greville
C.Griffiths *
J.Guess
D.G.Guilford
P.M.Hall
J.J.Hall-Smith
K.Hamilton
H.E.Hammond *
A.Hardman

Sgt.Maj.Harris
J.Harris
L.Harrison *
R.Harvey
A.Head
A.A.Henderson *
E.W.Herbert
R.S.Hickman
N.W.Hill *
J.A.D.Hobbs *
M.Hobley
E.R.T.Holmes †
H.Horton *
M.J.Horton †
M.F.Howard
T.Howard
A.Howell
R.A.Hubbard
D.J.Hulbert
V.Humphries
N.J.I.Hunter
A.Hurd *
R.J.Hurst
L.Hutton †
T.R.Jakobson *
A.E.James *
J.A.Jameson †
R.I.Jefferson *
J.Jenkinson
S.Jennings
I.J.Jones †
W.E.Jones *
M.Keith
M.Kimmins
A.P.E.Knott †
J.D.F.Larter †
A.H.C.Latchman *
K.S.Lawton
P.Lever †
A.R.Lewis †
A.O.L.Lithgow
D.A.Livingstone *
C.M.D.V.Llewellyn
D.R.Lock
G.A.R.Lock †
P.G.Lowndes
D.R.Lysons
C.L.McCool †
I.M.McLachlan *
R.Makins
A.Mance
B.W.Marshall
J.C.Masterman *

M.C.Maxwell
S.K.Maxwell
K.R.Miller †
O.Miller
A.P.Mitchell
D.Montague
J.M.Murray-Willis
D.Naylor-Leyland
D.M.G.Neligan
R.G.Newman *
S.J.B.Newsom
C.D.Nichols
C.Oakes *
W.F.T.O'Byrne *
R.Moore O'Farrell
Lord O'Neill
N.Ormerod
C.H.Palmer †
K.E.Palmer †
P.H.Parfitt †
W.G.A.Parkhouse †
A.C.Parsons
N.A.Paul *
G.S.Pearce *
G.F.Pearson
D.S.Perrett
B.Pfaff
D.Pickering
A.N.Player
P.I.Pocock †
J.M.Poland
R.G.Pollock †
C.Ponsonby-Fane
Lord Porchester
J.S.Porter
G.Potter *
D.P.Priddy
G.Puttock
A.C.Rawlings
T.H.Reed
A.C.Revill *
E.Rice
B.A.Richards †
P.E.Richardson †
H.M.Rimmer
A.Roberts
J.S.Roberts
E.Rowcroft
Lord Royston
Lt.Commander Ruck
Keen
P.J.Sainsbury *
T.Scott

G.N.Scott-Chad *
D.Shelley
R.Sheppard
A.N.Sims
J.M.Sims *
J.Smart
A.Smith
C.S.Smith *
G.J.Smith *
M.J.Smith *
M.J.K.Smith †
R.Smith *
M.R.Soames
A.Soutry
J.B.Statham †
Lord Stavordale
M.J.Stewart †
N.Stratford
M.W.Tate †
B.Taylor *
A.Thomas
N.Thorneycroft
C.W.Thring
O.Thynne
P.B.Trappes-Lomax
C.Treverton-Jones
A.Trubshaw
C.Tufton
J.D.C.Vargas
W.Voce †
P.M.Walker †
J.E.Walsh *
A.Walters
W.A.Walton
A.Ward
A.R.Wassell *
H.Waterhouse
A.J.Watkins †
M.J.H.Weedon *
J. Westing
D.W.White †
R.J.White
G.L.Willatt *
P.F.Williams
D.Wilson †
J.R.Windle
J.Wood
P.R.Woods
W.Wooller *
J.Young

CAREER RECORDS 1976-1994

	Years	I	NO	HS	Runs	Avge	Runs	Wkts	Avge
A.M.A.Aduhene	90-93	5	0	14	17	3.40	196	5	39.20
J.P.Agnew †	84-89	1	0	13	13	13.00	70	3	23.33
M.E.Allbrook *	83-91	4	0	10	20	5.00	432	11	39.27
C.Allen	85-86	1	0	6	6	6.00	131	1	131.00
P.B.Allen	84-89	5	0	26	101	20.20	-	-	-
R.Allpress	80-86	2	1	38	47	47.00	6	0	-
J.Appleton	84-94	7	2	62	197	39.40	59	1	59.00
J.P.Arscott *	90-94	2	0	40	55	27.50	-	-	-
S.Ashfield	86-87	2	0	0	0	0.00	39	0	-
J.R.N.Ashworth	92-94	2	0	20	20	10.00	195	7	27.86
D.G.Aslett	82-86	2	1	47*	92	92.00	94	2	47.00
P.Bainbridge *	88-91	2	0	58	66	33.00	59	4	14.75
A.Baker	77-81	2	0	5	8	4.00	-	-	-
I.A.Balding	83-84	2	0	34	36	18.00	7	0	-
R.F.A.Balfour	86-89	1	0	1	1	1.00	33	0	-
J.R.T.Barclay *	77-94	30	13	83	364	21.41	1123	42	26.74
M.T.Barford *	82-92	5	1	33	45	11.25	34	1	34.00
A.H.Barker *	77-89	7	2	16	58	11.60	389	12	32.42
K.J.Barnett †	84-91	2	0	12	12	6.00	32	1	32.00
S.Battersby	85-88	3	1	3	5	2.50	13	0	-
C.Beagles	93-94	-	-	-	-	-	146	2	73.00
A.P.Beagley	89-90	-	-	-	-	-	117	2	58.50
J.M.Bebb	88	2	0	7	14	7.00	-	-	-
F.C.Bennett	86-87	-	-	-	-	-	40	3	13.33
D.J.Bicknell *	87-88	2	0	39	58	29.00	-	-	-
M.P.Bicknell †	87-88	-	-	-	-	-	61	2	30.50
G.H.L.Bird	80-87	1	1	9*	9	-	10	0	-
H.Bishop	87-89	-	-	-	-	-	58	1	58.00
T.E.Blain †	86	2	0	2	2	1.00	-	-	-
G.I.Bowman	77-82	9	0	34	144	16.00	1	0	-
J.A.L.Boyd	89-93	3	0	18	23	7.67	8	1	8.00
R.Boys-Stones	85-86	1	0	5	5	5.00	17	0	-
M.Bozman	82-90	2	2	6*	8	-	24	1	24.00
G.E.Bradburn	85	2	0	5	8	4.00	21	0	-
A.M.Bredin *	85-93	-	-	-	-	-	159	6	26.50
T. Brennan	94	2	0	84	100	50.00	-	-	-
D.Brewer	84-85	1	0	11	11	11.00	107	2	53.50
D.Briance	82-94	5	0	39	123	24.60	15	3	5.00
R.Briance	81-86	3	0	16	32	10.67	-	-	-
W.R.Bristowe *	82-86	2	0	36	67	33.50	-	-	-
R.A.Brooks *	78-80	3	1	34	74	37.00	-	-	-
A.L.Browne	80-81	2	1	94*	148	148.00	-	-	-
D.Buck	83-91	5	0	20	50	10.00	119	5	23.80
D.B.Buik	81-82	2	0	0	0	0.00	-	-	-
C.K.Bullen *	93-94	2	1	104*	113	113.00	19	0	-
G.P.Burnett *	90-93	2	0	45	49	24.50	-	-	-
A.J.Burridge *	81-94	15	3	119	655	54.58	100	0	-
R.O.Butcher †	91-92	2	1	5*	5	5.00	-	-	-
N.A.Butler	77-78	1	1	6*	6	-	67	0	-
D.J.Callaghan *	84-92	4	0	86	206	51.50	30	2	15.00
P.R.Carroll *	77-87	4	0	44	75	18.75	-	-	-
G.R.Cass *	89-90	2	0	32	44	22.00	-	-	-
P.J.Cattrall	79-84	-	-	-	-	-	19	4	4.75
R.G.L.Cheatle *	82-83	1	0	1	1	1.00	195	7	27.86
J.Clare	87-91	3	1	14	23	11.50	103	2	51.50
E.A.Clark *	77-82	7	2	65	253	50.60	101	3	33.67
J.A.Claughton *	87-93	8	0	56	211	26.38	-	-	-
A.B.Cleaver	86-91	6	0	53	83	13.83	88	7	12.57
G.S.Clinton *	84-91	3	0	107	271	90.33	62	2	31.00
J.S.Coad	86-88	2	0	20	30	15.00	-	-	-

	Years	I	NO	HS	Runs	Avge	Runs	Wkts	Avge
P.Coggan	92-93	2	0	20	32	16.00	28	0	-
T.B.L.Coghlan *	78-86	2	0	12	18	9.00	-	-	-
D.Cornthwaite	89-92	1	0	0	0	0.00	80	1	80.00
T.Cotton	77-78	1	1	10*	10	-	81	1	81.00
N.G.Cowans †	81-92	2	0	4	6	3.00	25	0	-
M.C.Cowdrey †	76-86	29	10	96*	579	30.47	862	32	26.94
A.Cunningham	81-85	3	0	24	46	15.33	77	6	12.83
S.A.B.Daniels *	88-93	2	1	6*	8	8.00	156	1	156.00
A.G.Davies *	86-94	6	2	56	166	41.50	15	0	-
J.Davies	76-81	7	2	89*	255	51.00	171	16	10.69
B.F.Davison *	80-81	2	0	6	6	3.00	-	-	-
P.M.Davy	84-93	4	0	32	90	23.75	-	-	-
J.W.Dean	89-93	4	1	102	110	36.67	189	11	17.18
M.H.Denness †	81-94	9	1	62	285	35.63	-	-	-
B.Dennis	81-82	2	0	2	2	1.00	-	-	-
A.R.Dewes *	89-92	2	0	19	30	15.00	12	0	-
J.H.Dixon *	86-92	3	1	25*	52	26.00	39	0	-
A.I.C.Dodemaide †	85-92	3	0	131	173	57.67	37	0	-
G.H.G.Doggart †	76-77	1	1	22*	22	-	-	-	-
S.J.G.Doggart *	86-94	1	0	18	18	18.00	42	1	42.00
W.A.Donald *	91-93	2	0	36	40	20.00	-	-	-
B.T.P.Donelan *	89-92	4	1	4*	8	2.67	275	6	45.83
N.G.H.Draffan *	84-93	8	1	55	132	18.86	84	1	84.00
P.Dunn	77-85	3	2	2*	2	2.00	168	6	28.00
M.Durden-Smith	92-93	2	1	18*	36	36.00	62	0	-
C.Duval	77	2	1	8	8	8.00	140	7	20.00
S.Dyson	79-80	-	-	-	-	-	74	5	14.80
R.Q.East	85-87	2	0	24	44	22.00	74	2	37.00
B.A.Edgar †	78-86	2	0	34	41	20.50	-	-	-
R.Edgar	78-80	4	2	28*	57	28.50	-	-	-
P.H.Edmonds †	77-93	3	0	90	142	47.33	75	4	18.75
J.H.Edrich †	79-93	1	0	15	15	15.00	-	-	-
S.Edwards	83-86	-	-	-	-	-	98	3	32.67
R.F.Eliot *	76-77	1	0	4	4	4.00	86	2	43.00
R.G.P.Ellis *	83-91	3	0	61	95	31.67	-	-	-
N.J.Falkner *	92-93	3	0	63	110	36.67	-	-	-
A.Ferrier	84-85	2	1	32*	45	45.00	-	-	-
A.L.R.Fincham *	79-84	1	1	0*	0	-	57	2	28.50
I.Fisher	80-81	1	1	6*	6	-	76	3	25.33
R.I.B.Fisher	77-82	1	0	67	67	67.00	41	5	8.20
M.V.Fleming *	83-94	12	1	95	281	25.55	331	6	55.17
A.Ford	85-87	2	1	11	17	17.00	-	-	-
A.R.Ford	76-91	34	2	117	893	27.91	93	1	93.00
S.C.C.Ford	78-86	6	1	17	39	7.80	-	-	-
D.J.Foreman *	77-85	3	0	35	56	18.67	82	4	20.50
D.R.J.Foster	81-87	3	1	44	65	32.50	-	-	-
D.B.M.Fox	89-90	-	-	-	-	-	41	0	-
A.G.J.Fraser *	84-94	2	0	76	118	59.00	90	3	30.00
J.Fricker	93-94	2	1	66	77	77.00	-	-	-
N.J.Froome	78-82	-	-	-	-	-	90	7	12.86
D.R.C.Gale	80-94	3	1	12*	20	10.00	102	3	34.00
R.A.Gale *	77-82	7	1	76	146	24.33	127	5	25.40
R.Gartrell	84	2	0	99	113	56.50	19	0	-
C.N.Gates	86-94	7	0	52	152	21.71	55	1	55.00
N.Gaynor	88-89	1	1	8*	8	-	83	0	-
M.E.Gear	83-89	4	0	103	128	32.00	-	-	-
J.T.Gifford	79-94	4	0	22	33	8.25	-	-	-
N.Gilbert	91-94	2	0	4	4	2.00	-	-	-
C.F.E.Goldie *	79-89	2	0	36	46	23.00	-	-	-
G.Goldie	88-92	2	0	1	1	0.50	212	4	53.00
D.J.Goldsmith	91-94	1	1	2*	2	-	-	-	-
S.C.Goldsmith *	84-86	2	0	28	28	14.00	-	-	-

	Years	I	NO	HS	Runs	Avge	Runs	Wkts	Avge
J.Goodacre	89-90	1	0	72	72	72.00	-	-	-
E.C.Gordon-Lennox	92-94	2	0	63	75	37.50	16	1	16.00
I.J.Gould *	88-93	6	4	82*	201	100.50	23	0	-
P.Gover	93-94	2	0	68	69	34.50	3	0	-
D.I.Gower †	80-89	2	0	13	22	11.00	-	-	-
R.M.K.Gracey	83-87	4	0	46	86	21.50	222	9	24.67
R.M.Graham	85-91	5	0	37	65	13.00	231	7	33.00
V.Grant	89-91	3	1	17*	32	16.00	29	0	-
O.Gravell	85-86	-	-	-	-	-	47	1	47.00
P.J.Graves *	81-94	25	3	61	363	16.50	41	3	13.67
J.R.Gray *	81-88	3	0	65	75	25.00	-	-	-
A.K.C.Green	89-93	1	0	0	0	0.00	-	-	-
A.M.Green *	81-92	2	1	47	75	75.00	3	2	1.50
K.W.Green	81-83	4	3	7*	11	11.00	-	-	-
K.Greenfield *	88-89	2	0	2	2	1.00	-	-	-
I.A.Greig †	88-93	2	0	12	18	9.00	75	1	75.00
M.G.Griffith *	76-88	28	5	66*	723	31.43	20	0	-
R.Groom	86-91	3	1	5	6	3.00	67	5	13.40
R.Gubbins	85-87	1	1	11*	11	-	20	1	20.00
D.Gutteridge	90-92	2	0	39	56	28.00	-	-	-
R.G.Gutteridge	92-94	3	1	57	88	44.00	41	1	41.00
S.E.Haggas	84-94	1	0	32	32	32.00	121	7	17.29
P.M.Hall	76-86	9	2	78*	152	21.71	121	1	121.00
C.F.T.Halliday	78-80	2	0	11	15	7.50	6	0	-
C.B.Hamblin *	77-80	3	0	20	40	13.33	66	3	22.00
R.Hanley *	90-91	2	0	12	20	10.00	-	-	-
A.R.Hansford *	90-91	1	0	0	0	0.00	110	1	110.00
D.Hanson	85-87	1	0	3	3	3.00	-	-	-
J.Harris	87-91	3	1	30	63	31.50	-	-	-
R.T.Hart *	83	2	0	54	54	27.00	-	-	-
C.Hartridge	88-94	6	2	101*	214	53.50	212	8	26.50
M.J.Hastwell	90-92	3	1	60*	98	49.00	74	1	74.00
D.L.Hays *	78	2	0	102	102	51.00	-	-	-
J.Hayward	79	2	0	13	19	9.50	57	6	9.50
T.J.Head *	77-91	4	1	12	16	5.33	-	-	-
D.W.Headley *	93-94	2	0	16	27	13.50	83	6	13.83
S.P.Henderson *	86-91	2	0	10	17	8.50	4	0	-
A.J.Herbert	84-89	3	0	22	39	13.00	93	0	-
R.S.Herman *	85-86	2	0	6	6	3.00	28	1	28.00
T.Heslop	77-79	2	0	0	0	0.00	-	-	-
S.R.Hicks	85-89	3	1	2	2	1.00	2	0	-
M.P.Hickson	81-86	1	0	0	0	0.00	57	4	14.25
P.Hillier	92-94	4	2	57*	126	63.00	-	-	-
L.Hirst	87-91	1	1	1*	1	-	97	4	24.25
R.N.S.Hobbs †	76-82	-	-	-	-	-	312	7	44.57
K.I.Hodgson *	85-90	3	1	62*	130	65.00	30	0	-
D.Hole	77-83	3	0	48	58	19.33	-	-	-
D.C.Holliday *	93-94	2	0	30	34	17.00	49	0	-
R.W.Hooker *	81-83	2	2	43*	44	-	84	2	42.00
J.M.M.Hooper *	78-87	14	3	95	605	55.00	16	0	-
G.P.Howarth †	85-91	2	0	21	29	14.50	-	-	-
A.C.Howeson	77-80	-	-	-	-	-	97	8	12.13
P.G.Hudson	93-94	6	1	103*	146	29.20	60	3	20.00
S.P.Hughes *	88-94	2	2	16*	16	-	67	3	22.33
S.Humphries *	91-92	1	0	28	28	28.00	-	-	-
I.J.F.Hutchinson *	90-93	2	0	73	92	46.00	-	-	-
R.A.Hutton †	82-83	3	0	49	99	33.00	54	1	54.00
D.Hylton	88-90	3	0	51	109	36.33	-	-	-
Imran Khan †	81-88	3	2	56*	86	86.00	28	1	28.00
Intikhab Alam †	79-81	1	0	48	48	48.00	16	2	8.00
R.J.Inverarity †	76-77	3	0	104	124	41.33	67	3	22.33
K.D.James *	80-86	4	1	50*	85	28.33	141	10	14.10

	Years	I	NO	HS	Runs	Avge	Runs	Wkts	Avge
T.M.H.James	92-94	2	0	31	32	16.00	40	0	-
G.Jenkinson	88-90	1	1	0*	0	-	46	0	-
A.Jenner	92-94	-	-	-	-	-	23	0	-
H.Jenner	83-89	5	0	33	66	13.20	-	-	-
T.E.Jesty *	78-86	3	1	74	159	79.50	43	2	21.50
G.W.Johnson *	79-64	3	0	51	90	30.00	70	2	35.00
R.N.Johnson	80-90	8	1	37	154	22.00	-	-	-
D.Jones	93-93	1	0	1	1	1.00	17	0	-
J.Kelly	87-89	4	0	23	44	11.00	131	6	21.83
N.J.Kemp *	83-91	3	0	67	147	49.00	98	1	98.00
J.R.Kilbee *	87-89	2	1	127*	186	186.00	35	0	-
R.C.Kinkead-Weekes	77	2	0	18	21	10.50	-	-	-
J.M.Knight *	82-91	5	1	62	101	25.25	127	3	42.33
R.D.V.Knight *	78-92	17	9	101*	479	59.88	299	13	23.00
P.Z.M.Krazinski	93-94	-	-	-	-	-	63	2	31.50
T.M.Lamb *	85-90	1	1	9	9*	-	29	0	-
D.R.C.Law *	93-94	2	0	14	17	8.50	116	5	23.20
G.A.Law	83-84	2	0	63	112	56.00	-	-	-
M.P.Lawrence *	85-94	3	2	5*	10	10.00	328	20	16.40
S.D.Ledlie	77-87	6	1	24	70	14.00	108	2	54.00
L.J.Lenham *	77-89	2	0	20	39	19.50	87	4	21.75
N.J.Lenham *	84-92	9	0	75	328	36.44	53	0	-
J.K.Lever †	76-94	1	1	0*	0	-	157	3	52.33
P.J.Lewington *	85-86	1	1	23*	23	-	96	6	16.00
R.V.Lewis *	80-90	12	3	82	370	41.11	-	-	-
C.Light	93	2	0	61	103	51.50	95	6	15.83
J.F.P.Lloyd-Jones	91-94	2	1	0	0	0.00	48	1	48.00
M.Lodder	89	5	0	33	88	17.60	-	-	-
A.Long *	83-84	1	1	0	0*	-	44	2	22.00
C.M.Long	86-94	4	2	58*	61	30.50	230	11	20.91
J.I.Longley *	86-90	2	0	22	32	16.00	-	-	-
R.E.A.Lowe	80-91	1	1	2*	2	-	55	0	-
B.W.Luckhurst †	78-85	2	0	33	57	28.50	-	-	-
M.A.Lynch *	86-94	2	0	24	42	21.00	-	-	-
S.C.Lyon	81-85	1	1	0*	0	-	39	1	39.00
A.McCrone	92-93	1	1	1*	1	-	26	0	-
T.McGhie	92-93	2	0	0	0	0.00	18	0	-
R.D.O.MacLeay	87-93	3	1	46	82	41.00	-	-	-
G.I.MacMillan *	89-90	3	0	28	67	22.33	8	0	-
B.E.McNamara *	84-88	5	1	126	305	75.50	92	6	15.33
S.J.Malone *	87-93	-	-	-	-	-	156	6	26.00
A.W.Mansell *	82-86	3	2	21*	42	42.00	-	-	-
V.J.Marks †	76-90	2	0	33	38	19.00	101	3	33.67
S.A.Marsh *	82-85	4	0	32	63	15.75	-	-	-
R.P.T.Marshall *	79-89	3	1	18	20	10.00	171	4	42.75
B.R.Martin *	77-79	3	1	9	15	7.50	55	1	55.00
J.Martin	91	2	1	33*	42	42.00	-	-	-
R.J.Maru *	80-84	-	-	-	-	-	88	5	17.60
R.C.W.Mason	90-94	5	0	74	180	36.00	62	2	31.00
S.Massey	81-84	2	0	9	10	5.00	104	2	52.00
A.Meads	77-89	4	0	30	43	10.75	5	1	5.00
R.P.Merriman	92-93	2	0	14	16	8.00	34	1	34.00
C.Metcalf	82-83	2	0	93	101	50.50	26	1	26.00
M.Mildred	72-85	1	0	0	0	0.00	145	3	48.33
R.J.Miles	81-85	3	1	7	7	3.50	168	8	21.00
A.J.T.Miller *	83-90	2	0	53	96	48.00	-	-	-
D.Mills	78-80	1	0	1	1	1.00	75	4	18.75
P.Mills	93-94	1	0	40	40	40.00	-	-	-
M.E.Milton	79-91	5	1	69	244	61.00	109	1	109.00
G.Monkhouse *	81-86	3	1	78	123	61.50	104	6	17.33
M.H.Moore	77-82	2	0	11	11	5.50	117	2	58.50
P.Moores*	89-94	2	1	3	4	4.00	49	3	16.33

	Years	I	NO	HS	Runs	Avge	Runs	Wkts	Avge
G.Morgan	79-89	3	0	59	68	22.67	-	-	-
J.D.Morley*	85-89	2	0	30	48	24.00	16	1	16.00
A.J.Murley	89-90	2	0	8	9	4.50	-	-	-
I.A.Murray	90-91	2	0	16	21	10.50	52	4	13.00
J.T.Murray †	76-80	4	1	29*	54	18.00	-	-	-
T.Mynott	88-92	4	0	53	87	21.75	60	0	-
S.M.Nasir Zaidi *	85-87	2	0	25	26	13.00	127	5	25.40
K.Newell	93	2	0	56	56	28.00	-	-	-
M.Newell	93	5	1	69	292	73.00	-	-	-
J.Newton	87-89	3	0	13	23	7.67	42	0	-
M.C.J.Nicholas *	84	2	0	36	43	21.50	5	0	-
J.D.Nicholson	77-83	4	1	13	39	13.00	-	-	-
T.Nicholson	87-94	2	0	47	74	37.00	-	-	-
J.A.North *	89-91	2	0	66	79	39.50	52	1	52.00
L.V.O'Callaghan	77-82	-	-	-	-	-	67	4	16.75
T.J.G.O'Gorman *	91-92	2	0	69	82	41.00	-	-	-
D.A.Oldridge	81-89	2	0	51	51	25.50	1	0	-
C.R.Oliver-Redgate	76-78	5	2	29	51	17.00	163	4	40.75
C.Olver	88-89	1	1	1*	1	-	-	-	-
J.O.D.Orders *	87-89	4	1	106*	236	78.67	8	0	-
D.Orton	85-86	1	0	2	2	2.00	16	0	-
P.Osborne	86-92	2	1	5*	5	5.00	113	3	37.67
D.R.Owen-Thomas *	77-91	14	4	100	363	36.30	36	2	18.00
N.Pagden	92-94	2	0	24	45	22.50	11	2	5.50
R.W.M.Palmer *	88-91	4	2	9*	13	6.50	167	5	33.40
P.W.G.Parker †	79-94	8	0	90	400	50.00	1	0	-
R.Parkin	77-79	3	0	12	12	4.00	-	-	-
R.J.Parks	84-93	2	1	5*	6	6.00	-	-	-
A.C.Parsons	85-90	6	1	104	161	32.20	80	3	26.67
G.J.Parsons *	85-89	-	-	-	-	-	76	2	38.00
N.A.Paul *	77-85	5	2	116*	147	49.00	19	0	-
J.Pelly	77-78	2	0	14	23	11.50	-	-	-
C.Penn *	82-94	-	-	-	-	-	39	1	39.00
D.J.Pepperell	92-93	2	1	130*	245	245.00	-	-	-
W.B.Phillips †	81	2	1	86	152	152.00	96	2	48.00
N.C.Philpot	80-92	6	1	37	55	11.00	483	13	37.15
A.C.S.Pigott †	81-89	3	0	104	133	44.33	21	0	-
P.I.Pocock †	78-88	-	-	-	-	-	171	7	24.43
M.Poland	81-82	2	1	101*	101	101.00	-	-	-
L.Potter *	82-84	2	0	103	147	73.50	6	1	6.00
G.Poulter	88-94	3	0	9	18	6.00	-	-	-
S.J.Poulter *	91-94	1	1	21*	21	-	59	0	-
N.W.Pretorius *	89-92	3	2	2*	3	3.00	177	7	25.29
J.S.E. Price †	78-94	-	-	-	-	-	51	1	51.00
R.J.Priestley	77-83	2	0	34	52	26.00	61	0	-
M.W.Pringle †	88-90	9	2	79*	263	37.57	211	7	30.14
P.Pyemont	76-82	2	0	34	66	33.00	-	-	-
C.T.Radley †	78-89	3	1	37	51	25.50	31	2	15.50
D.W.Randall †	77-94	3	0	41	54	18.00	32	0	-
A.Ratnayake	87-89	2	1	7*	7	7.00	8	0	-
C.M.G.Redmayne	88-94	1	1	20*	20	-	62	0	-
S.Reed	80-88	4	4	9*	9	-	342	7	48.86
D.A.Reeve †	85-86	2	0	82	102	51.00	-	-	-
J.M.Rice *	85-93	24	3	134	1094	52.10	130	1	130.00
B.A.Richardson *	81-87	6	0	32	78	13.00	1	0	-
P.D.Richardson	88-92	1	0	18	18	18.00	75	0	-
M.C.Robertson	77-79	1	0	23	23	23.00	-	-	-
R.V.C.Robins *	77-78	-	-	-	-	-	25	0	-
W.Robins	84-91	3	0	64	76	25.33	59	1	59.00
J.D.Robinson *	82-93	6	1	83	194	38.80	47	1	47.00
P.M.H.Robinson *	77-88	7	1	59*	178	29.67	187	7	26.71
A.G.Robson *	90-92	-	-	-	-	-	95	0	-

	Years	I	NO	HS	Runs	Avge	Runs	Wkts	Avge
G.R.J.Roope †	78-87	1	0	7	7	7.00	8	5	1.60
J.A.Ross	81-94	4	1	18	33	11.00	386	16	24.13
N.P.D.Ross *	80-88	7	0	81	148	21.14	113	5	22.60
C.J.C.Rowe *	81-94	12	2	149*	696	69.60	522	12	43.50
F.Russell	88-91	3	0	32	51	17.00	-	-	-
Sadiq Mohammad *	82-86	1	1	107*	107	-	-	-	-
P.J.Sainsbury †	79-81	-	-	-	-	-	47	3	15.67
G.Sandes	86-87	-	-	-	-	-	19	1	19.00
R.R.Savage	89-93	3	1	87	173	86.50	-	-	-
S.Savant	91-94	5	1	38*	114	28.50	196	7	28.00
A.M.G.Scott *	89-94	-	-	-	-	-	95	0	-
R.Scott	79-85	4	0	62	117	29.25	163	4	40.75
R.J.Scott *	85-86	3	0	79	99	33.00	19	0	-
D.J.Scrivens	80-91	4	1	26	83	27.67	-	-	-
M.W.W.Selvey †	78-85	1	1	3*	3	-	153	5	30.60
D.J.Semmence *	77-92	13	3	90	447	44.70	203	8	25.38
M.J.Semmence	90-94	2	1	1*	1	1.00	60	2	30.00
A.P.Sheahan †	78	2	1	49*	49	49.00	27	2	13.50
Shoaib Mohammad †	85-86	2	1	44*	56	56.00	-	-	-
P.D.B.Short	80-82	2	0	24	30	15.00	-	-	-
J.E.Skinner	91-94	3	0	107	132	44.00	-	-	-
A.Smales	84-85	1	1	11*	11	-	2	0	-
A.Smith	81-87	1	1	64*	64	-	-	-	-
C.L.Smith †	82-84	3	0	33	43	14.33	-	-	-
K.B.Smith *	82-86	5	0	77	171	34.20	28	0	-
M.J.Smith *	80-87	4	0	14	26	6.50	23	2	11.50
M.J.K.Smith †	76-78	4	0	31	55	13.75	36	0	-
P.Smith	81-87	3	1	7*	11	5.50	56	2	28.00
R.A.Smith †	81-83	4	2	115*	235	117.50	-	-	-
M.P.Speight *	88-94	4	0	55	94	23.50	-	-	-
J.Spencer *	79-93	17	7	36	165	16.50	851	23	37.00
J.Stallibrass	77-86	3	2	19*	26	26.00	60	6	10.00
D.K.Standing *	83-89	5	2	59*	108	36.00	37	1	37.00
T.R.Stephens	80-82	1	0	1	1	1.00	25	2	12.50
J.R.G.Stephenson	76-86	4	1	52	62	20.67	162	5	32.40
C.A.Stevens	91-94	1	0	8	8	8.00	95	2	47.50
A.J.Stewart †	85-88	4	1	87	134	44.67	-	-	-
D.A.Stewart	80-87	2	0	113	144	72.00	-	-	-
N.J.W.Stewart	78-89	13	1	40*	150	12.50	796	32	24.88
C.Stone	89-92	2	1	1	1	1.00	151	4	37.75
I.C.D.Stuart	87-94	4	0	61	134	33.50	109	5	21.80
S.Surridge *	81-91	1	1	17*	17	-	-	-	-
K.G.Suttle *	78-89	6	1	66*	93	18.60	198	5	39.60
C.P.Sweet	87-94	5	1	100*	160	40.00	91	3	30.33
A.Sykes	87-93	5	0	25	81	16.20	-	-	-
J.F.Sykes *	84-88	2	1	41	70	70.00	82	0	-
R.Syrett	81-94	3	1	40	70	35.00	60	0	-
P.Tapper	92-93	1	1	0*	0	-	80	1	80.00
C.W.Taylor *	90-94	3	1	4	6	3.00	60	1	60.00
L.B.Taylor †	81-89	-	-	-	-	-	67	4	16.75
R.W.Taylor †	78-86	-	-	-	-	-	8	0	-
A.L.S.S.Thackara *	76	3	0	10	17	5.67	-	-	-
D.J.Thomas *	82-85	-	-	-	-	-	49	1	49.00
R.W.Tolchard †	81-87	1	1	0*	0	-	-	-	-
K.P.Tomlins *	79-85	2	1	41*	62	62.00	0	1	0.00
J.Tomlinson	83	2	1	5*	5	5.00	68	0	-
R.Tomlinson	77-78	1	0	0	0	0.00	46	1	46.00
G.J.Toogood *	86-91	3	1	67*	78	39.00	93	5	18.60
T.D.Topley *	83-84	-	-	-	-	-	42	1	42.00
J.R.A.Townsend *	80-85	4	1	97	223	74.33	-	-	-
N.J.L.Trestrail	80-94	10	4	116*	393	65.50	221	8	27.63
A.E.Tucker *	91-92	3	0	22	33	11.00	157	3	52.33

	Years	I	NO	HS	Runs	Avge	Runs	Wkts	Avge
S.Turner *	84-88	2	2	109*	141	-	107	1	107.00
J.Tutt	88-90	2	0	12	18	9.00	-	-	-
D.L.Underwood †	79-88	-	-	-	-	-	49	0	-
C.J.Van Heerden *	88	2	0	25	45	22.50	16	0	-
G.G.M.Van Heerden	93-94	2	0	9	9	4.50	44	0	-
R.W.Venables	77-78	2	0	32	43	21.50	-	-	-
M.S.Venter *	82	2	0	59	76	38.00			
M.J.Vernon *	78-79	-	-	-	-	-	35	1	35.00
L.P.Vorster *	86-88	3	1	132	251	125.50	-	-	-
R.Vyvyan	85-90	4	0	56	130	32.50	12	1	12.00
A.N.C.Wadey *	76-83	12	8	41	89	22.25	1262	62	20.35
M.C.Wagstaffe *	79-85	1	1	21*	21	-	29	4	7.25
C.E.Waller *	88-92	2	1	11	14	14.00	256	12	21.33
D.R.Walsh *	79-86	2	2	120*	124	-	-	-	-
T.R.Ward *	86-94	3	0	145	207	69.00	-	-	-
I.C.Waring *	84-86	1	0	28	28	28.00	44	1	44.00
C.Warner	87-88	2	0	37	39	19.50	-	-	-
R.Warriner	85-86	1	0	5	5	5.00	-	-	-
A.Waters	93-94	-	-	-	-	-	79	0	-
J.S.Waters	92-94	2035	36	18.00	43	2	21.50		
S.N.V.Waterton *	84-90	2	0	45	46	23.00	-	-	-
J.Watt *	76-78	5	0	124	199	39.80	134	3	44.67
M.Weaver	79-81	2	0	23	26	13.00	27	1	27.00
A.P.Wells *	90-94	3	0	30	66	22.00	-	-	-
C.M.Wells *	81-90	3	0	21	23	7.67	71	4	17.75
R.R.C.Wells *	85-88	2	1	39*	39	39.00	-	-	-
J.While	86-94	14	3	109*	455	41.36	242	5	48.40
P.D.Whitby	79-80	1	0	3	3	3.00	-	-	-
D.W.White †	78-80	1	0	43	43	43.00	171	7	24.43
J.Whittaker	85-87	3	0	54	57	19.00	-	-	-
H.M.Whitty	85-87	1	0	1	1	1.00	-	-	-
I.Wilks	88-91	4	2	64	101	50.50	78	2	39.00
P.Willey †	77-89	4	0	105	234	58.50	70	0	-
M.V.C.Williams	90-91	1	1	1*	1	-	-	-	-
D.Willis	84	2	0	39	42	21.00	26	1	26.00
R.G.D.Willis †	83-85	-	-	-	-	-	95	1	95.00
S.L.D.Willis	82-88	1	0	5	5	5.00	109	3	36.33
A.Willows *	81-83	1	0	11	11	11.00	132	3	44.00
G.A.Wills	76-83	23	6	100	651	38.29	-	-	-
J.G.Wills	79-94	30	8	43*	526	23.91	604	15	40.27
R.Wills	90-91	2	0	52	67	33.50	54	1	54.00
D.Wilson †	78-89	5	1	28*	51	12.75	400	20	20.00
D.C.Wilson	83-84	2	0	19	19	9.50	-	-	-
A.R.Wingfield-Digby *	87-94	3	2	8*	15	15.00	100	3	33.33
M.Wingfield-Digby	89-94	5	3	62*	96	48.00	-	-	-
N.Wisdom *	77-87	23	2	67	524	24.95	359	17	21.12
A.Wix	86-90	5	0	30	82	16.40	89	4	22.25
J.M.Woolley	85-87	3	0	63	84	28.00	34	3	11.33
R.A.Woolmer †	76-87	6	1	50	119	23.80	123	6	20.50
C.F.Worlidge	79-92	10	0	65	151	15.10	-	-	-
A.Wreford	79-86	-	-	-	-	-	151	6	25.17
T.Wright	86-89	3	0	21	22	7.33	-	-	-
T.J.Zoehrer †	81	2	1	37*	43	43.00	-	-	-

The following also played:

M.B.Abington *	J.Allison	L.Andrews	M.Asif Din *	M.Atkinson
B.Adler	D.L.Amiss †	S.Annan	Asif Iqbal †	G.Austin
S.Alderson	D.J.Anderson *	J.Appleyard	C.W.J.Athey †	M.Azharuddin †
D.A.Allen †	N.Anderton	P.A.N.Armstrong	W.Atkins	A.M.Babington *
M.Allen	C.R.Andrew *	R.A.Arscott	J.C.M.Atkinson *	N.H.P.Bacon

D.Bailey *
M.Bainbridge
D.L.Bairstow †
J.C.Balderstone †
P.Baldwin
J.C.S.Ball
S.J.Ball
E.A.E.Baptiste †
B.Barker
E.J.Barlow †
G.D.Barlow †
A.J.L.Barr
M.Barratt
B.J.Barrett *
Z.Barthley
R.Bartholomew
A.H.Bartlett
S.J.Base *
K.G.Bauermeister
B.A.W.Bellamy
N.Bennett
M.R.Benson †
T.Bevan-Thomas
G.Bewick
S.Bird
A.V.Birrell *
P.Blackler
D.Blackwood
M.C.Blundell
P.V.Boarer
J.Boiling *
M.Boobbyer
D.C.Boon †
T.J.Boon *
F.Booth
S.C.Booth *
M.Bose
I.T.Botham †
N.Boustead
G.P.J.Bowden
D.Bowes-Lyon
P.D.Bowler *
P.Box-Grainger
J.G.Bracewell †
J.M.Brearley †
S.Brebner
C.Bridge
N.E.Briers *
M.Brink
D.J.Broad *
M.S.B.Broadbent
D.A.Brocklehurst
R.H.A.Brodhurst
K.G.Brooks *
A.Brown
J.Brown
K.R.Brown *
R.P.Brown
S.Brown
N.Browning
S.Buch

J.Bull
R.A.Bunting *
G.Burdon
I.Burns
M.Burr
R.H.Burton
J.Bushell
M.A.Buss *
A.R.Butcher †
M.A.Butcher *
C.L.Cairns †
P.R.C.Came
G.Campbell
W.D.C.Carling
J.D.Carr *
S.M.Carrington *
D.Carroll
T.W.Cartwright †
M.Cass
C.Castleman
P.Cayford
T.K.Chadwick
N.P.H.R.Chamberlin
W.Chambers
L.Champness
V.Chandler
J.Chaplin
H.P.J.Chetwood
I.J.Chivers *
A.Clark
J.E.Clarke
M.Clarke
S.T.Clarke †
T.Cockcroft
J.Coles
P.C.Collymore
B.E.Congdon †
C.R.Cook *
G.W.Cook *
R.M.O.Cooke *
J.Coomeraswamy
M.R.Copping
G.Corcoran
T.M. Cordaroy
A.R.Cornford
N.J.Cosh
M. Costello
R.M.H. Cottam †
T.A. Cotterell *
N. Cousins
R.S. Cowan *
C.S. Cowdrey †
G.R. Cowdrey *
N.G. Cowley *
G. Cox Jnr. *
I. Cox
C. Coxon
D. Crawford
W.J. Cronje †
M.D. Crowe †
D. Culhane

D.J.Cullinan †
J. Cunliffe
B. Curness
T.S. Curtis †
T. Cutler
C.S. Dale
K. Dallimore
R. Dalzell
D. Dandridge
G. Daniels
R.C. Daniels
R. Davey
N. Davies
S.Davis
T.A.J.Dawson
T.M.E.Dawson
R.Day
G.H.Dean
K.Dean
A.De Grey
M.De Jode
D.Devitt
E.R.Dexter
P.Dickinson
T.Dickson
R.Dillon
A.Dindar
J.R.Dinwiddy
M.C.Dobson
M.W.G.Doggart
B.L.D'Oliveira
D.B.D'Oliveira
R.J.Doughty
P.Dowling
T.Downs
P.R.Downton
R.B.H.Du Boulay
S.Dunkley
A.P.H.Dunlop
A.During
R.I.H.B.Dyer
J.Eastcott
M.E.Edmunds
D.Elkins
T.Elliott
R.M.Ellison
J.E.Emburey
D.English
J.Evans
A.Evans-Jones
R.A.B.Ezekowitz
M.J.J.Faber
R.Fawcet
R.Felloines
M.Felton
D.Ferreira
O.F.O.Findlay
J.Fitzgerald
P.B.Fitzherbert
B.J.Flick
D.P.J.Flint

A.Flower
G.Fowler
N.Fox
K.Foyle
M.Frater
M.Freeland
A.Frome
A.Frost
J.Garforth-Bless
J.Garner
P.Garner
M.Gaskell
S.Gatting
L.Germishuys
D.Gibbs
N.Gibbs
B.Gilbert
D.R.Gilbert
C.Gladwin
S.Godfrey
P.J.T.Goggin
R.A.Gordon-Walker *
J.N.Graham *
D.P.Grammer
D.A.Graveney *
T.W.Graveney †
I.Gray
R.J.Greatorex
H.Green
P.Green
R.H.Green
T.Greenidge
A.W.Greig †
D.Gretten-Smith
M.P.Gretton
J.Griffin
J.J.Groome *
J.Grootmeyer
P.Grubb
D.R.Hadlee †
I.Haig
J.E.Hall *
J.W.Hall *
J.J.Hall-Smith
J.H.Hampshire †
I.Hanson
P.D.Hanson
M.Happell
B.R.Hardie *
J.J.E.hardy *
G.A.R.Harris *
E.E.Harrison *
T.Harrison
J.D.Harvey
J.F.Harvey *
J.R.W.Harvey *
K.Harvey
S.B.Hassan *
J.Hawksfield
N.Hay
P.J.Hayes

C.R.Hayles
B.Head
D.Head
T.Heap
R.Heard
J.R.P.Heath *
I.M.Henderson *
M.Hendrick †
W.Hendricks
I.L.M.Henry
D.Herbert
N.Herps
A.Herrington
P.A.W.Heseltine *
A.Hesp
G.A.Hick †
N.D.Hicks
K.Higgs †
S.G.Hinks *
J.Hoare
S.Hobson
B.Hoffman
A.J.Hollioake *
M.Hooker
A.M.Hooper
N.C.H.Hordern
F.Horn
D.P.Hughes *
D.Hunt
C.C.Hunte †
R.Hunter
J.Hurley
M.Hussain
A.P.Igglesden †
J.Illingworth
R.K.Illingworth †
J.D.Inchmore *
A.C.D.Ingleby-
Mackenzie *
M.Islam
P.J.Istead
R.D.Jackman †
J.A.Jameson †
Javed Kureishi
M.Jean-Jacques *
M.Jeffrey
M.Jeffries
A.Jeremiah
A.Jermaine
G.R.Jonas *
A.A.Jones *
A.N.Jones *
G.W.Jones *
A.Juster
J.Keenan
C.L.Keey *
D.J.M.Kelleher *
G.Kelly
C.M.Kemp
P.Kemp
N.M.Kendrick *

I.Kennedy
J.Kennedy
B.L.G.Kenny
M.F.Kent †
G.J.Kersey *
S.J.S.Kimber *
S.E.A.Kimmins *
M.M.King
T.King
R.J.Kirtley
P.Knowles *
S.Koch
K.M.Krikken *
C.Lane
M.Lane
J.S.Laney
C.Langdon
P.Last
T.N.Lazard *
T.A.Lester *
J.D.Lewry *
A.Licudi
P.Liddington
J.Lindsay
G.Lineker
N.J.Llong *
R.Lloyd
G.H.Lock
I.Lock
J.Lofting
G.Longfield
A.N.M.Longmore *
G.B.T.Lovell *
J.Lowe
C.Loyd
C.J.Lush
P.M.Lush
S.Lynch
I.McEwan
K.S.McEwan *
D.N.MacFarlane
D.McGovern
J.H.M.MacKinnon
G.C.MacKintosh
N.R.C.MacLaurin
K.H.MacLeay *
T.MacMillan
Majid Jahangir †
D.Malan
J.Malao
R.G.Marlar *
T.Marriott
Sir Michael Marshall
M.D.Marshall †
R.Marshall
G.C.Martin
K.Martin

C.D.A.Martin-Jenkins
C.W.H.May
R.Mee
W.G.Merry *
I.Merryweather
J.Middleton
G.Miller †
F.W.Millett *
H.Milner
T.Mohammed *
A.H.V.Montehuis
L.J.Moody
J.Moore
R.Moore
D.J.Mordaunt *
N.D.Morrill
J.E.Morris †
O.H.Mortensen
J.M.Morton
A.Mosedale
G.Moss
P.Moyer
Mushtaq Mohammad †
H.Mutton
P.A.Neale *
A.Needham *
P.J.E.Needham *
I.Newman
P.J.Newport †
B.Newton
F.J.Newton
M.Newton
R.Nicholls
A.O.Norman
M.O'Dwyer
B.O'Gorman
C.M.Old †
M.O'Neill
M.Orton
A.Oxley
G.V.Palmer *
D.Panto
B.G.Parkinson
D.Parry
P.Parvin
A.S.Patel *
D.N.Patel †
M.M.Patel *
B.Patterson
R.Patterson-Knight
D.B.Pauline *
D.Peacock
N.H.Peters *
C.P.Phillipson *
A.R.K.Pierson *
B.Piper
R.Plank

N.E.J.Pocock
J.R.Polk
A.Pope
D.C.Popplewell
E.J.Popplewell
V.A.L.Powell
C.N.R.Prentice *
D.Prentice
J.R.Prentis
K.Price
N.J.Pringle *
S.Priscott
J.Pugh
A.Purbrick
I.Purser
C.P.Pyemont *
P.D.Pyemont
D.Ralfs
K.Ranansinge
N.Ratcliff
R.J.Ratnayake †
A.Rawlinson
J.L.Rawlinson *
M.V.Rawlinson
P.Ray
B.L.Reed *
O.Reed
M.Reeve
C.C.Remy *
C.Rendall
C.E.B.Rice *
T.Rice
T.R.F.Rice
M.H.Richarson
C.Rika
D.Roberts
J.Roberts *
T.Roberts
G.R.V.Robins
L.Robinson
M.H.B.Robinson
H.Roebuck
P.M.Roebuck *
R.Roebuck
B.Rogers
M.A.Roseberry *
P.G.Roshier
S.Ross
M.Rowland
M.J.B.Rudd
P.S.B.Rudd *
T.Rudd
A.J.Russell
N.Russell
R.C.Russell *
P.N.B.Sabine *
P.Sadler

I.D.K.Salisbury *
J.F.W.Sanderson *
A.Saul
J.G.Saunders *
R.M.Sawney
M.S.Scott *
R.A.Scott
J.Sellers
A.W.Sexton
D.Shackleton *
J.H.Shackleton *
T.Shaw
N.Shepherd
L.Sherrell
W.Short
A.Shuckburgh
M.Sibley
P.Silicich
G.Simpson
T.Simpson
L.Sivaramakrishnan
P.A.Slocombe *
A.W.Smith *
D.Smith
S.J.H.Smith
L.Smithers
J.A.Snow †
P.Somerville
J.Stafford
J.Staniforth
C.Stansfield-Smith
D.S.Steele †
J.F.Steele *
P.Stenning
P.J.Stevens
R.Stilgoe
D.A.Stirling †
B.Stoodley
S.J.Storey
R.D.Stormonth-
  Darling
M.Stoute
A.W.Stovold *
H.D.A.Stuart
E.Sutton
J.Sutton
A.Symondson
D.Talbot
G.Taylor
J.Taylor
M.N.S.Taylor *
N.R.Taylor *
G.H.Tedstone *
R.Thelwell
J.D.Thicknesse
C.Thomas
D.R.Thomas *

C.Thompson
I.Thompson
K.Thompson
G.P.Thorpe †
I.G.Thwaites *
R.M.Tindall *
F.J.Titmus †
H.F.Torkington
A.Townsend
A.D.Towse *
C.R.Trembath *
D.Turnbull
D.G.Ufton *
V.A.P.Van der Bijl *
M.Van der Walt
N.Van-Leuven
M.R.J.Veletta †
N.Venny
I.P.Wadey
A.Wagner
M.J.Walker *
H.Walton
J.Warburton
D.M.Ward *
Wasim Hasan Raja †
D.Waterfield
P.A.Waterman *
M.E.Waugh †
S.R.Waugh †
S.D.Weale *
G.Weaver
D.M.Wellham †
P.Wellings
V.J.Wells *
M.Welsh
A.Wessels *
J.White †
B.Whitfield
J.Whiting
J.H.Whittaker
P.Whitticase *
J.M.S.Whittington *
D.Whyte
D.Wighton
C.W.Wilkinson
M.D.Willett *
N.F.Williams †
M.Wilmore
P.H.L.Wilson *
A.S.P.deW.WinlawW.N.
J.Withall
L.J.Wood *
B.H.Woodbridge
J.Woodhouse
G.Wright

APPENDIX F

LEADING CAREER SUMMARIES

Most Runs 1930-1974

1728	A. L. S. S. Thackara	1959-1974
1354	P. M. H. Robinson	1955-1974
1220	C. S. Crawley	1932-1966
987	E. E. Harrison	1935-1974
860	R. Kingsford	1961-1971
727	H. P. Hunloke	1931-1939
661	G. A. Wills	1961-1974
643	A. M. Crawley	1930-1969
596	Duke of Norfolk	1930-1969
590	R. H. Burton	1956-1974
559	W. R. H. Joynson	1954-1964
548	C. E. Underdown	1951-1962

Most Wickets 1930-1974

172	E. E. Harrison	1935-1974
86	R. G. Marlar	1953-1972
83	D. Rice	1953-1973
67	P. M. H. Robinson	1955-1974
50	L. L. F. Toynbee	1956-1969
35	R. H. Cobbold	1933-1938
30	Lord Dunglass	1932-1936

Most Runs 1976-1994

1094	J. M. Rice	1985-1993
893	A. R. Ford	1976-1991
723	M. G. Griffith	1976-1988
696	C. J. C. Rowe	1981-1994
655	A. J. Burridge	1981-1994
651	G. A. Wills	1976-1983
605	J. M. M. Hooper	1978-1987
579	M. C. Cowdrey	1976-1986
526	J. G. Wills	1979-1994
524	N. Wisdom	1977-1987
479	R. D. V. Knight	1978-1992
455	J. While	1986-1994

Most Wickets 1976-1994

62	A. N. C. Wadey	1976-1983
42	J. R. T. Barclay	1977-1994
32	M. C. Cowdrey	1976-1986
32	N. J. W. Stewart	1978-1989
23	J. Spencer	1979-1993
20	M. P. Lawrence	1985-1994
20	D. Wilson	1978-1989
17	N. Wisdom	1977-1987
16	J. Davies	1976-1981
16	J. A. Ross	1981-1994
15	J. G. Wills	1979-1994

APPENDIX G

HUNDREDS 1930-1974

For (20)

A. M. Crawley (3)

147	Lord Eldons's XI	1930
164	Lord Eldons's XI	1930
155	Lord Eldons's XI	1932

C. S. Crawley (2)

144	Lord Eldons's XI	1933
136	Lord Eldons's XI	1934

Lord Dunglass (2)

100*	Lord Eldons's XI	1935
100	Lord Eldons's XI	1936

G. O. B. Allen

133	Capt A. O. J Hope's XI	1935

G. H. G. Doggart

100	Sussex	1951

G. Cox, jnr.

119*	Sussex	1956

I. M. McLachlan

123	Sussex	1958

A. L. S. S. Thackara

117*	Royal Sussex Regiment	1962

E. A. Bedser

105*	Sussex Martlets	1963

G. D. Massy

106*	Staggerers	1963

S. E. A. Kimmins

104*	Eton Ramblers	1968

A. J. Lush

110*	Sussex Martlets	1969

S. P. Sherrard

100	Eton Ramblers	1970

A. C. Parsons

111*	Eton Ramblers	1974

D. R. Walsh

106	Lady Mary Fitzalan Howard's XI	1974

G. A. Wills

100	I Zingari	1974

Against (22)

C. M. D. V. Llewellyn (2)

115	Lord Eldons's XI	1931
102	Lord Eldons's XI	1935

G. Cox, jnr.

110	Sussex	1954

K. G. Suttle

122	Sussex	1955

D. N. Mantell

103*	Royal Sussex Regiment	1956

N. C. H. Hordern

102*	Royal Sussex Regiment	1957

J. M. Parks

105	Sussex	1958

A. H. Chignell

100*	Emeriti	1959

D. J. Mordaunt

144	I Zingari	1959

G. M. Aim

130	De Flamingo's	1959

J. T. Bell

128*	Emeriti	1961

G. C. Cooper

107	Sussex	1961

L. Barry

150*	I Zingari	1961

C. H. Gibson

101*	Eton Ramblers	1962

R. O. L. Lithgow

101*	I Zingari	1962

P. J. Workman

114*	I Zingari	1963

M. A. J. Sargent

102*	Australian Old Collegians	1964

P. Perfect

104	Sussex Martlets	1969

C. J. S. Bidwell

103*	Sussex Martlets	1969

B. Lock

100*	Arundel C. C.	1969

T. D. Barber

100	Eton Ramblers	1970

J. J. S. Farmer

100*	Eton Ramblers	1974

HUNDREDS 1976-1994

For (58)

J. M. Rice (4)		
106	Minor Counties	1987
134	Eton Ramblers	1992
105*	Minor Counties	1992
104	Arabs	1993

A. J. Burridge (2)		
105	Combined Services	1983
119	Arundel C. C.	1985

L. P. Vorster (2)		
119*	Minor Counties	1986
132	Combined Services	1988

C. J. C. Rowe (2)		
149*	Sussex Martlets	1988
131	Eton Ramblers	1989

D. J. Pepperell (2)		
130*	I Zingari	1992
115	I Zingari	1993

J Watt		
124	Lady Mary & Lady Sarah's XI	1976

R. J. Inverarity		
104	Sussex Martlets	1977

A. R. Ford		
117	Royal Sussex Regiment	1977

D. R. Owen-Thomas		
100	Sussex Martlets	1978

D. L. Hays		
102	Eton Ramblers	1978

P. Willey		
105	Watney's Invitation XI	1978

C. N. R. Prentice		
105	Lady Mary Fitzalan Howard's XI	1979

N. A. Paul		
116*	Barbados Wanderers	1979

G. A. Wills		
100	Canada/UK "40" C. C.	1979

M. O'Neill		
109*	Combined Services	1980

B Whitfield		
111*	Royal Sussex Regiment	1981

M. Poland		
101*	Lady Mary Fitzalan Howard's XI	1981

A. C. S. Pigott		
104	M.C.C. Young Cricketers	1981

R. A. Smith		
115*	Ireland	1981

Sadiq Mohammed		
107*	Indians	1982

L. Robinson		
118*	M.C.C. Young Cricketers	1982

L. Potter		
103	Arabs	1984

J. Bull		
163*	Combined Services	1984

M. R. Benson		
100	I Zingari	1984

R. D. V. Knight		
101*	Minor Counties	1985

B. E. McNamara		
126	Barbados Wanderers	1985

A. C. Parsons		
104	Lord's Taverners	1985

D. R. Walsh		
120*	I Zingari	1986

T. R. Ward		
145	M.C.C. Young Cricketers	1986

S. Turner		
109*	Ireland	1987

D. A. Stewart		
113	Arundel C. C.	1987

G. S. Clinton		
107	Sri Lankans	1988

J. R. Kilbee		
127*	Eton Ramblers	1989

J. While		
109*	Minor Counties	1989

M. E. Gear		
103	Australian Old Collegians	1989

P. J. T. Goggin		
101*	I Zingari	1989

J. O. D. Orders		
106*	M.C.C.	1989

A. I. C. Dodemaide		
131	New Zealanders	1990

R. I. H. B. Dyer		
111*	Ireland	1991

G. A. Tedstone		
106*	M.C.C.	1992

N. J. L. Trestrail		
116*	I Zingari	1992

P. R. Downton		
111	Lord's Taverners	1992

J. E. Skinner		
107	Australian Combined Services	1993

J. W. Dean		
102	Arundel C. C.	1993

C. K. Bullen		
104*	Cambridge University	1994

S. Lynch		
154*	M.C.C.	1994

P. G. Hudson		
103*	I Zingari (Australia)	1994

P. Wellings		
139*	Grasshoppers (South Africa)	1994

C. Hartridge
    101*   Arundel C. C.   1994

C. P. Sweet
    100*   Arundel C. C.   1994

A. J. Hollioake
    101   Scotland   1994

Against (46) 1976-1994

P. M. Davy (2)
    107*   I Zingari   1987
    102   Sussex Martlets   1992

N. Gilbert (2)
    112   Minor Counties   1989
    172   Minor Counties   1990

R. J. Greatorex (2)
    102   Combined Services   1991
    117   Combined Services   1994

M. F. M. Wright
    142   I Zingari   1976

M. Asif Din
    107   Royal Sussex Regiment   1980

J. O. D. Orders
    110*   Arabs   1982

P. G. Lowndes
    113   Eton Ramblers   1982

P. S. B. Rudd
    101*   I Zingari   1982

F. W. J. Cornwallis
    116*   I Zingari   1983

N. J. L. Trestrail
    103*   M.C.C.   1983

Mushtaq Mohammad
    133   M.C.C.   1983

S. Woodward
    135   Staggerers (South Africa)   1984

P. Pyemont
    104   Royal Sussex Regiment   1985

M. A. Masood
    111   Ireland   1985

T. A. Cotterell
    110   I Zingari   1986

J. J. Sheldon
    100*   I Zingari   1986

M. E. Waugh
    146*   M.C.C. Young Cricketers   1986

J. Harris
    130*   Minor Counties   1986

J. M. Brearley
    110   M.C.C.   1986

P. A. Todd
    153   Minor Counties   1987

E. Shade
    100*   Crusaders (Australia)   1987

D. M. Jones
    143*   Rest of the World   1987

M. P. Speight
    103   Sussex Martlets   1987

J. E. Skinner
    117*   Lloyd's C.C.   1988

J. P. Barrett
    100*   Combined Services   1988

M. V. Fleming
    106   Combined Services   1988

D. C. Boon
    114*   Australians   1989

P. J. T. Goggin
    102*   Sussex Martlets   1989

R. G. Blair
    109*   Minor Counties   1990

R. D. O. Macleay
    100   I Zingari   1990

R. C. Daniels
    107   Eton Ramblers   1991

M. R. Bate
    118*   M.C.C. Young Cricketers   1991

Aamer Sohail
    104   Pakistanis   1992

C. K. Bullen
    132*   M.C.C.   1992

W. E. J. Holland
    123*   I Zingari   1992

R. C. Doggart
    111   I Zingari   1992

J. P. Crawley
    108*   Cambridge University   1993

A. Jones
    100*   Australian Combined Services   1993

D. Bloom
    120*   Australian Combined Services   1993

J. Ratledge
    114   Cambridge University   1994

K. Greenfield
    101   M.C.C.   1994

K. Mitchell
    122*   Grasshoppers   1994

R. Dillon
    104   Arundel C. C.   1994

APPENDIX H

MOST WICKETS IN AN INNINGS 1930-1974

For

6-21	R. Makins	Oxford University O.T.C.	1930
6-41	F. E. V. Smith	Lord Eldon's XI	1930
6-58	A. O. J. Hope	Lord Eldon's XI	1932
6-38	A. O. J. Hope	Lord Eldon's XI	1933
6-30	R. H. Cobbold	Sussex Martlets	1935
6-60	J. C. Masterman	British Legion, Arundel Branch	1935
6-32	Lord Dunglass	Lord Eldon's XI	1936
7-42	R. H. Cobbold	Capt The Hon. A.O.J.Hope's XI	1936
7-40	A. O. J. Hope	British Legion, Arundel Branch	1937
9-47	D. Rice	Eton Ramblers	1953
6-29	E. W. S. Ford	British Legion, Arundel Branch	1953
6-52	R. G. Marlar	I Zingari	1956
6-46	R. G. Marlar	Sussex Martlets	1960
7-43	D. J. Mordaunt	Arundel C.C.	1960
6-9	A. H. Gooda	Arundel C.C.	1962
7-54	P.M.H.Robinson	Arundel C.C.	1970
6-8	M. Mence	Royal Sussex Regiment	1971
6-54	R. G. Marlar	I Zingari	1971
6-36	A. N. C. Wadey	Eton Ramblers	1973
7-31	J. Davies	Arundel C.C.	1973

R. H. Cobbold took 11-89 in two innings match v Captain The Hon. A. O. J. Hope's XI in 1936

Against

6-99	L. Harfield	Lord Eldon's XI	1930
6-121	R. A. C. Foster	Lord Eldon's XI	1933
6-72	J. C. Masterman	Capt The Hon. A.O.J.Hope's XI	1935
6-42	E. W. S. Ford	Lord Eldon's XI	1936
6-46	J. C. Masterman	Capt The Hon. A.O.J.Hope's XI	1936
7-19	B. Carver	British Legion, Arundel Branch	1937
6-46	D. Stephens	Capt The Hon. A.O.J.Hope's XI	1938
7-61	P. Fleming	Royal Sussex Regiment	1952
8-17	A. G. Pelham	Eton Ramblers	1953
6-17	E. Blackall	British Legion, Arundel Branch	1953
6-38	J. Bredin	Emeriti	1954
8-11	B. W. Hardman	Royal Sussex Regiment	1954
6-42	A. E. R. Hill	British Legion, Arundel Branch	1954
8-20	B. W. Hardman	Royal Sussex Regiment	1955
6-35	R. Benaud	Australians	1956
7-57	L. L. F. Toynbee	I Zingari	1956
7-48	M. A. Craft	Sussex Martlets	1956
9-35	P. D. Hill-Wood	Eton Ramblers	1958
6-26	D. Massy	I Zingari	1959
6-49	D. T. Adams	Royal Sussex Regiment	1959
6-23	J. L. Toole	Royal Sussex Regiment	1960
8-65	J. S. Solomon	West Indians	1963
7-79	A. J. G. Pearson	Emeriti	1963
8-10	J. E. Melville	Emeriti	1964
6-33	L. L. F. Toynbee	I Zingari	1964
7-40	P. Spencer	Arundel C.C.	1964
6-49	J. R. Allison	Royal Sussex Regiment	1966
6-54	A. J. N. Dawson	Eton Ramblers	1966

R. A. C. Foster took 10-157 in a two innings match for Lord Eldon's XI in 1933.

MOST WICKETS IN AN INNINGS 1976-1994

For

6-51	J. Davies	I Zingari	1976
6-60	J. Stallibrass	Arundel C.C.	1977
6-51	A. Cunningham	Eton Ramblers	1984
7-37	S. Savant	Combined Services	1993
6-60	J. Chaplin	I Zingari (Australia)	1994

Against

6-54	N. Chitty	Arundel C.C.	1977
6-50	C. H. M. Ridley	I Zingari	1987
7-66	M. Russell-Wick	Lloyd's C.C.	1988
6-62	P. J. Remnant	Eton Ramblers	1988
10-80	R. S. Gubbins	I Zingari	1988
7-62	N. Woodruff	Arundel C.C.	1988
6-25	J. P. Barrett	Combined Services	1989
6-39	T. K. Marriott	M.C.C. Young Cricketers	1990
6-76	G. Wright	Sussex Martlets	1990
6-60	C. Howard	Crusaders	1993

INDEX

A selective index of those active in supporting cricket at The Castle